Stanley Gibbons

CHANNEL ISLANDS

Specialised Catalogue of
Stamps and Postal History

Stanley Gibbons
CHANNEL ISLANDS
Specialised Catalogue of
Stamps and Postal History

FIRST EDITION

Stanley Gibbons Publications Ltd
391 Strand, London WC2R 0LX

**By Appointment to H.M. the Queen
Stanley Gibbons Ltd., London
Philatelists**

© Stanley Gibbons Publications Ltd., 1979

ISSN 0142–5625   ISBN 0 85259 021 0

1st edition—April 1979

Printed in Great Britain by Spottiswoode Ballantyne Ltd.,
Colchester and London

Contents

Preface

Collectors have had a strong interest in the Channel Islands for many years. The postal history has engaged many notable students, offering as it does a most varied field from the pre-adhesive days to such modern events as the wartime Occupation.

Numerous new adherents have been attracted to the Channel Islands since Jersey and Guernsey became postally independent in 1969. In this tenth anniversary year we commend the moderate policies followed by both Authorities in producing stamps of high quality, relevant to their place of origin and full of philatelic interest.

Stanley Gibbons since 1972 have published regular editions of *Collect Channel Islands Stamps* to meet the demand from collectors. That full-colour checklist in popular style will be continuing but we are now presenting the first Stanley Gibbons Specialised Catalogue to treat postal history in depth. It replaces the *Priced Catalogue of Channel Islands Postal Markings* and the *Priced Catalogue of Channel Islands Stamps*, compiled by O. W. Newport, by agreement with the publishers, the Channel Islands Specialists' Society, and those works have now been withdrawn.

The Society and individual members have extended full co-operation in preparing this First Edition. Particularly helpful were extensive contributions to the Sections covering Jersey and Guernsey sub-offices, Airmails and Hovercraft Mail, the Red Cross Message Service, Internee Mail Service and Prisoner of War Mail. The task of creating a completely new work has been undertaken by a number of us in the Catalogue Department of Stanley Gibbons Publications Ltd. in collaboration with colleagues in the Great Britain and Postal History Departments of Stanley Gibbons Ltd.

As for the stamp catalogue, forming the second part of this volume, there is no surer foundation than the long-established and pre-eminent Gibbons Catalogue. We have begun to build further, however, by including in this First Edition booklet panes, postal stationery and reply coupons and by providing prices for cylinder blocks. From the local delivery services the stamps issued by the bus and railway companies as well as earlier issues by the shipping companies have been catalogued, since there is no question of their legitimate status. We defer any more extensive treatment of local carriage labels pending further study and discussion.

As with all Gibbons Catalogues the most careful attention has been given to pricing throughout. A particular endeavour was to price as many items of postal history as possible, since market valuations we believe to be particularly needed here.

Most collectors are aware that the market for fine postage stamps is exceedingly healthy and that good-quality material consistently holds its value. In recent years this has been paralleled by the increasing strength of demand for items of postal history and prices are inevitably reflecting this upsurge of interest.

This new and thorough Catalogue will suggest numerous attractive subjects for specialisation. With such a worthwhile area as the Channel Islands, collections of many different types, formed with intelligence and discrimination, will amply repay their owners.

JAMES NEGUS

Acknowledgements

We acknowledge, with grateful thanks, the help given in drafting and checking the text and with illustration material by: Michael Briggs, John de Havilland, Michael Goodman, T. D. Green, David Gurney, Roger Harris, John Hobbs, Donald McKenzie, David Picton-Phillips, Georges Robbé, John Sussex and J. M. Y. Trotter. John Simpson, in addition, gave valuable advice during a final reading of many sections of typescript, simultaneously providing numerous items for the illustrations. We have also had the helpful assistance of the Channel Islands Specialists' Society and the Postal Administrations of Guernsey and Jersey and wish to thank them.

William Heinemann Ltd., the London publishers, permitted very generous use of the text and illustrations in *Stamps and Postal History of the Channel Islands*, the standard handbook by William Newport published by that company. We are indebted to John St. John for this valuable co-operation.

For Section 19 on the Red Cross Message Service, Picton Publishing of Chippenham, Wiltshire, have provided all nineteen illustrations, permitting their reproduction from *The Red Cross Mail Service for Channel Island Civilians 1940–1945*. For this courtesy we thank the author, Donald McKenzie, and the publisher, David Picton-Phillips.

The illustration for Type **J14** was provided by *Philatelic Magazine* and for Type **J56** by Robson Lowe Ltd. We express our thanks to both.

STANLEY GIBBONS PUBLICATIONS LTD.

Introductory Notes

British Currency. Before February 1971 British currency was:

$£1 = 20s.$ One pound = twenty shillings *and*
$1s. = 12d.$ One shilling = twelve pence.

Upon decimalisation this became:

$£1 = 100p$ One pound = one hundred (new) pence.

Price Columns. In the Catalogue lists our method of indicating prices is:
Numerals for pence, e.g. 20 denotes 20p (20 pence).
Numerals for pounds and pence, e.g. 4·50 denotes £4·50 (4 pounds and 50 pence).
For £100 and above, prices are in whole pounds.

Value Added Tax. Pricing in this and all other current Gibbons catalogues is on a tax-inclusive basis as at the date of going to press. Price changes reflect the international market and, in addition, if there is any change in the rate of V.A.T. this may be reflected in an increase or decrease in the quoted price.

Correspondence. Letters should be addressed to the Catalogue Editor, Stanley Gibbons Publications Ltd., 391 Strand, London WC2R 0LX, and return postage is appreciated when a reply is sought. New information and unlisted items for consideration are welcomed.

Expertisation. We do not give opinions as to the genuineness of stamps. Expert Committees exist for this purpose and enquiry can be made of the Royal Philatelic Society, 41 Devonshire Place, London W1N 1PE, or B.P.A. Expertising Ltd., 1 Whitehall Place, London SW1A 2HE. The Committees charge a fee for their services.

ABBREVIATIONS

c.d.s	circular datestamp
d.c.	double circle
des	designer, designed
eng	engraver, engraved
f.d.c.	first day cover
litho	lithographed

mm	millimetres
MS	miniature sheet
No.	number
perf	perforated
photo	photogravure
recess	recess-printed
s.c.	single circle
typo	typographed
wmk(d)	watermark(ed)
†	Not known to exist
—	(in price column) Exists, but no market price is known.

In columns of type numbers, a blank implies that the number quoted immediately above is repeated.

PART 1: POSTAL HISTORY

Prices

General. Just as with adhesives, the condition of a cover or entire affects the value. Damage, tears or soiling will reduce the market value. The visual appeal is likewise important, a cover of attractive general appearance commanding a higher price than its duller conterpart.

In more detail, categories covered by this Catalogue are as follows; *to find the relevant price-lists refer to the Contents, pages v–vi.*

Agents' Letters. We have listed all the known agents and we price letters bearing their names and endorsements. Not all agents endorsed the letters handled by them with their names and charges and in many cases collectors have to be content with letters simply addressed in the care of a particular agent. Prices are for complete letters or outer wrappers.

Pre-adhesive Markings. Prices for postal markings prior to 1840 are for clear and complete marks on complete letters (entires) or outer wrappers. Poor strikes are worth considerably less and really superb marks on attractive entires are worth substantially more than the Catalogue price.

Mulreadys and Penny Blacks and Reds. Prices for Mulready envelopes and lettersheets and for Penny Blacks and Reds are for those with clear Maltese Cross cancellations and with the Jersey or Guernsey datestamp. Covers with stamps should have four-margined examples. Poor adhesives or indistinct cancellations are worth considerably less.

*Cancellations and Markings from 1844. Prices for these later cancellations are for clear marks on covers or postcards.

*Parcel Post strikes on piece. Parcel post strikes, particularly the large "label" types, are difficult to find whole. Prices are for good and complete examples. For the parcel post labels add to the price of the label itself the value of the markings and the used price of any high-denomination postage stamps.

*Special Handstamps. Prices are for clear examples on covers or postcards franked at normal postal rates.

First Day Covers. In Part 2 of this Catalogue are prices for "first day covers" of each issue of postage stamps. Such covers bear the stamps specified (for commemoratives a full set) and have one of the official cancellations detailed in Section 15. Where it was available, the cover itself is taken to be a Post Office issue or alternatively one commercially marketed (e.g. by a stamp dealer) and suitably inscribed. There is no difference in value between the alternative forms. Covers with full sets prepared privately by individual collectors are valued at three-quarters of these "official" first day covers. Covers bearing odd values or incomplete sets and posted on the first day of issue should be valued according to the notes in Section 15.

*Slogans. Values of slogan cancellations are for examples complete with associated datestamp on whole covers or postcards franked at normal postal rates. Cut-outs are worth one-quarter of Catalogue price.

*Cachets. Prices for cachets are for those clearly struck on covers or post-cards that have passed through the post. Those on unused postcards, which were often applied before the cards were sold, are—unless exceptionally scarce—worth one-half of used examples.

*Mail with France. The prices in Section 17 refer to letters originating in the Channel Islands or sent to the Islands where the marking was also simul-taneously in use on mail from or to the U.K. The P-F and P-D markings will need their value increasing according to other postal markings on the cover. Prices for the French lozenge obliterations are for those on the most commonly used 3d. and 4d. adhesives. Covers bearing other values are worth considerably more.

---

* For the era of adhesives, account must be taken not only of the marking but of the postage stamps on the cover, too. The price-lists show the value of the marking. For categories asterisked above, however, find the prices for postage stamps in used condition from the Stanley Gibbons Catalogue. If the figure exceeds the price of the marking it should be *added* to obtain the total valuation. If it is less, the cover (including its stamps) is valued as shown in our price-lists for the marking.

It often happens that common markings are found used in conjunction with rarer ones. In valuing such covers take the highest priced mark and add half the value of all others listed at £10 or over.

xii *Introductory Notes*

Red Cross Messages. In Section 19 prices are for forms showing the most common types of cachet. Those with scarce cachets should add the figure from the separate price-list of cachets also given.

Internee Mail. In Section 20 postcards in pristine condition and lettersheets in fine condition are worth 20% more than Catalogue. Covers are priced as bearing the cheapest variety of censor mark, where applicable. Covers with additional or more expensive marks are priced at the value of the dearest mark.

Stamps on piece and Loose stamps. We do not normally price stamps on piece or loose stamps with particular cancellations. The exceptions (they are stated in the listings) are for extremely rare marks, such as the Alderney Cross, or for items like parcel post cancellations where "on piece" would be the usual mode of collecting.

PART 2: POSTAGE STAMP CATALOGUE

Catalogue numbers. Basic catalogue numbers are those of the Stanley Gibbons *British Commonwealth* Catalogue, 1979 edition. The extension of the lists into shades, papers, printings, etc., follows the numbering given in the *Elizabethan* Catalogue, 1979 edition, but employs the suffix "S" (for "Specialised") in place of "E" (for "Elizabethan"). Thus:

> Guernsey 13 $\frac{1}{2}$d. deep magenta and black
> V270. Nick in frame
> Sa. Thin paper
> Sa. V270. Nick in frame

The numbering of varieties using prefix "V" is as in the *Elizabethan*. New varieties, not in the *Elizabethan*, have been listed in this Catalogue with "SV" numbers, e.g.

> Guernsey 26 5s. multicoloured
> SV1. Mauve "balloon" flaw

Layout. Stamps are set out chronologically by date of issue. In the lists the first numeral is the Stanley Gibbons catalogue number; the black (boldface) numeral alongside is the type number referring to the respective illustration. The denomination and colour of the stamp are then shown. The left-hand price column is for unused stamps and the right-hand for used.

Prices. Prices quoted in this Catalogue are our selling prices at the time the book went to press. They are for stamps in fine average condition; in issues where condition varies we may ask more for the superb and less for the substandard. With unused stamps prices are for lightly hinged examples in the pre-1948 issues and unmounted mint thereafter (though where not available unmounted, stamps are often supplied at a lower price). Used prices are normally for stamps postally used but may be for stamps cancelled-to-order where this practice exists. All prices are subject to change without prior notice and we give no guarantee to supply all stamps priced, since it is not possible to keep every catalogued item in stock.

Listings

Sheet sizes. The number of stamps across the sheet is given first. For example, "50 (5 × 10)" indicates a sheet of 50 stamps made up of ten horizontal rows of five stamps each.

Papers. Only distinctive types are mentioned. *Granite paper* is easily distinguished by the coloured lines in its texture. *Chalky* or *chalk-surfaced* applies to paper which shows a black line when touched with silver.

Phosphor bands. Though not always easy to see, phosphor bands are usually visible as broad bands when the stamp is held up to the light at eye level. Misplaced bands are not unusual, but such varieties would only be listed where the misplacement affects the number of bands.

Perforations. Perforations are given to the nearest half, with the Stanley Gibbons *Instanta* gauge as standard. We distinguish perforation by *line* (L) or *comb* (C) machine. Perforations are expressed as follows:

Perf 14 Perforated alike on all sides.
Perf 14 × 15 Compound perforation. The first figure refers to top and bottom, the second to left and right sides.

Minimum price. The minimum price quoted is 5p. This represents a handling charge rather than a basis for valuing common stamps.

Stanley Gibbons International Ltd.

Stanley Gibbons Ltd.
391 Strand, London WC2R 0LX. Sales and buying departments for popular stamps, albums, catalogues and accessories; mail order; new issues and approvals; postal history.
RETAIL SHOP: 391 Strand, London WC2R 0LX.
SPECIALIST AND RARE STAMP DEPARTMENTS: Romano House, 399 Strand, London WC2R 0LX. Classic and rare material; Specialist Register; investment advice; the Gibbons Gallery of changing exhibitions.

Stanley Gibbons Publications Ltd.
EDITORIAL OFFICES: Drury House, Russell Street, Drury Lane, London WC2B 5HD. The S.G. range of catalogues, books, albums and accessories; publications mail order service (hotline 01-836 0974).
WHOLESALE AND TRADE: Stangib House, Sarehole Road, Hall Green, Birmingham B28 8EE.

Stanley Gibbons Auctions Ltd.
Stanley Gibbons Magazines Ltd.
Drury House, Russell Street, Drury Lane, London WC2B 5HD.

Stanley Gibbons Currency Ltd.
Stanley Gibbons Antiquarian Books Ltd.
395 Strand, London WC2R 0LX.

Stanley Gibbons Mapsellers Ltd.
37 Southampton Street, London WC2E 7HE.

Stanley Gibbons Products Ltd.
Stangib House, Sarehole Road, Hall Green, Birmingham B28 8EE.

ALL LONDON ADDRESSES: Telephone 01-836 8444; Telex 28883.
BIRMINGHAM OFFICES: Telephone 021-777 7255; Telex 28883.

StanGib Ltd.
601 Franklin Avenue, Garden City, New York, NY 11530, U.S.A. Tel. 0101 516 746-4666 and 4667; Telex 96-7733.

Gibbons (Philatelists) Ltd.
Rockefeller Center, Suite 2906, 1270 Avenue of the Americas, New York, NY 10020, U.S.A. Tel. 0101 212 582-0165 and 0166; Telex 96-7733.

Stanley Gibbons Currency Inc.
P.O. Box 3034, San Bernadino, CA 92413, U.S.A. Tel. 0101 714 883 5849.

Stanley Gibbons Frankfurt G.m.b.H.
D-6000 Frankfurt am Main, Zeil 83, West Germany. Tel 010 49 611-287477; Telex 4189148.

Stanley Gibbons Monaco S.A.M.
2 Avenue Henry Dunant, Monte Carlo, Monaco. Tel. 010 3393 506862.

PART ONE

Postal History

1. Letter Forwarding Agents

Before the establishment of Post Offices in Jersey and Guernsey and the provision of a regular packet service to the Islands in 1794, letters for those places were sent to an agent, usually at Southampton, but occasionally at Portsmouth or another South Coast port. The agent paid the inland postage and then handed the letters to the captain of a ship sailing for the Channel Islands. On arrival at Jersey or Guernsey the captain handed over the letters to another agent, from whom they were collected by the addressee upon payment of the British inland postage plus a fee of 3d.—1d. for the ship's master and 1d. for each agent. Letters from the Channel Islands to England were handed over to the Post Office at Southampton by the ship's captain and therefore cost only 2d. on top of the postage.

The majority of the agents were merchants but some were also ship owners and one or two shopkeepers or bankers. Many of the London coffee houses also acted as agents and bags for particular ship's captains were often to be found in them.

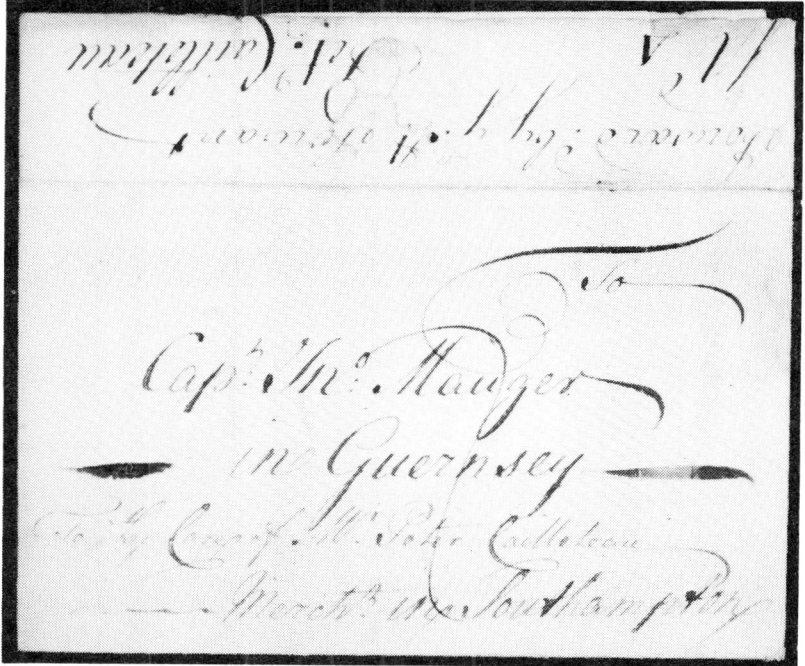

Letter for Guernsey with agent's endorsement on flap

There were also agents in Bristol, Falmouth, Gosport, Plymouth, Poole and Weymouth but most of these started up after the packet service was established, and ran in competition with it.

The Southampton agent doing the largest business in the latter half of the eighteenth century was William Seward who, alone, or with a partner, was an agent from 1756 to 1793. He charged the usual 1d. except in cases where he had paid more than a shilling postage, when the charge was generally 2d.

Brixham was used as a port for Guernsey mails when the wind was south-westerly, which was directly adverse from the Needles. James Ahier was at work in Weymouth from 1798, and was joined by Nicholas Robilliard in 1802. In the following year Robilliard took over altogether and carried on until 1810. A considerable quantity of mail from Britain and overseas went through his hands and it is suspected that he paid members of the packet crews to smuggle letters into the Channel Islands for him.

Most of the agents endorsed their letters"Forwarded by your humble servant (signature)" and one such is illustrated. A number of them also added their charge in manuscript, after deleting the inland postage charge and substituting a higher one; then the Guernsey or Jersey agent would cross out that figure and add his own and the captain's penny, writing the final sum to be collected from the addressee. Letters addressed to local firms were often charged on account rather than individually. One or two of the early Southampton agents worked at such cheap rates as $\frac{1}{4}$d. and $\frac{1}{2}$d., so that one finds letters charged at such curious sums as $3\frac{1}{4}$d. An oval rubber stamp struck in blue by N. M. Priaulx, of Southampton, in 1840 is recorded.

There were also agents in France and many other European countries and their endorsements can be found on letters. The following is a list of agents whose endorsements are known.

LETTER FORWARDING AGENTS

Agent	Dates			Price for entire
Southampton				
Caesar Knapton	1673	..	.. ..	£120
Grevichy	1689	..	.. ..	£180
Aaron Deveule	1703	..	.. ..	80·00
Bandinell & Co.	1718	..	.. ..	60·00
Bandinell & Hilgrove	1718–19		.. ..	50·00
Thomas Bandinell	1719–29		.. ..	60·00
John Grove	1713–41		.. ..	30·00
T. Le Cocq	1726	..	.. ..	£120
Richard Taunton	1711–33		.. ..	40·00
Bonner	1737–45		.. ..	40·00
Peter Cailleteau	1735–58		.. ..	40·00
Esther Cailleteau & Co.	1758	..	.. ..	50·00
Clement Hilgrove	1777–79		.. ..	40·00
Hilgrove & Durell	1779–85		.. ..	30·00
Thomas Durell	1786–93		.. ..	30·00
Seward & Marett	1756–58		.. ..	30·00
William Seward	1758–86		.. ..	25·00
Seward & Le Feuvre	1785–88		.. ..	30·00
Seward & Pipon	1791–93		.. ..	30·00
Seward & Co.	1785–93		.. ..	30·00
P. Le Feuvre	1791–1817	..	..	25·00

Agent	Dates	Price for entire
P. Le Feuvre & Son	1818	40·00
W. I. Le Feuvre	1820–35	30·00
Priaulx & Bienvenu	1796–1829	40·00
Priaulx & Sons	1829	50·00
N. M. Priaulx	1830–40	50·00
Helleur	1839	60·00
Brixham		
John N. Tozer	1738	£120
Samuel Tozer	1790–94	£120
Thomas Parkinson	1781–83	£120
Weymouth		
James Ahier	1798–1804	45·00
Ahier & Robilliard	1802	50·00
Nicholas Robilliard	1803–10	30·00
Thomas Martin	1803–05	50·00
John Sandford Jnr.	1813	60·00
Falmouth		
George C. Fox & Son	1805	£120
Jos. Banfield	1810	£120
Bristol		
Edward Gwatkin	1759	£140
Ball, Davis, Vaughan & Co.	1804	£140
Portsmouth		
James Wilkinson	1741–46	£150
John Carey	1812	£150
Gosport		
William Carver	1798	£150
Lyme		
Henry Chard	1793	£150
Poole		
Thomas Nicholson	1723	£140
Plymouth		
Francis De la Combe	1758	£140
Noel	1794	£120
St. Austell		
Henry Lambes	1783	£120
London		
M. Perchard	1757	80·00
Cazelet & Sons	1783	75·00
Peyerimhoff, De Mierro & Crispen	1784	70·00
P. Perchard	1791	60·00
Perchard & Brock	1792–95	60·00
Le Mesurier & Secretin	1793	50·00
Battier Zornlen	1793–95	45·00
Perchard, Brock & Le Mesurier	1795–98	45·00
Brock & Le Mesurier	1798–1810	45·00
Paul, Havilland & Le Mesurier	1799–1802	60·00
Wombell, Gautier & Co.	1806	50·00
E. Boehm & J. Tayler	1807	50·00
Ed. Rodd	1807	60·00
Boyd, Miller & Co.	1808	60·00
Geo. H. Aylwyn	1810	70·00
Fred De Lisle	1811–12	60·00

Agent	Dates	Price for entire
Andrews & Tariner	1812	50·00
Sandeman, Gooden & Foster	1814–20	60·00
J. Levy, Jnr.	1815	50·00
Jno. McNeill & Co.	1817–18	50·00
Bell & Grant	1833–34	50·00
Samuel Dobrée & Sons	1834–51	40·00
Jersey		
Philip Hamond, appointed Postmaster to States	1787	£120
Pierre Mallet	1792	£150
Madame Anne Ashley	1793	£150
Josué Priaulx	1798	£150
Hemery Bros. & Co.	1810	£100
Winter, Nicolle & Co.	1814	£100
J. Le Bailley	1822	£100
William Fruing	1825–49	£100
Amiraux Le Breton & Co.	1826	80·00
P. & I. Danirin	1830	£100
T. & P. Duhamel	1833–35	80·00
Godefroy Sons & Co.	1842	80·00
Guernsey		
Maugher	1718	£150
Mrs. Ann Watson	1780–94	£100
(Govt. Postmistress	1794–1814) ..	—
Harry Dobrée	1810–16	£100
William Lihou	1812	£120
E. Shale	1812	£130
James & John Cochran	1820	£130
Sinclair	1823	£130
John Le Marchant	1826	£150
Aaron Symes	1828–39	£100
Harris	1828	£100
George S. Syvret & Matthieu Barbet (Foreign P.O.) (also for some years before and after these dates)	1823–41	£100
Francis de Putron	1830–37	80·00
Edward Le Pelley	1837	80·00
Priaulx Langa & Co.	1840	80·00
St. Malo		
Mace Cohue	1676	£100
J. Monie	1678	£100
Jean Hardy	1682–85	£100
Sebire, Laisne & Cie.	1763–83	70·00
Beaugard & De Segray	1772–73	70·00
Jacques La Dure	1777–90	70·00
Barbier, Robbereckts & Cie.	1802	70·00
Monsieur Blaize	1790–93	40·00
Louis Blaize & Cie.	1802–27	30·00
Louis Blaize	1802–32	30·00
Dupuy, Fromy Frs.	1815–16	50·00
J. B. Gaultier	1826–27	35·00
Fontan Frs.	1825–30	35·00
Mme Veuve Fontan Jun.	1827	45·00
Mauger Frères	1827–29	35·00
Matthieu Barbet	1829–32	40·00

Agent	Dates	Price for entire
Calais		
A. Mancel	1815	60·00
C. Sturmer	1823	80·00
Morlaix		
P. Aurrere & Fils.	1815	80·00
H. Dobrée Jnr.	1816	70·00
Le Havre		
Charles Sturmer	1814–15	80·00
Cherbourg		
Captain Poullain	1820–23	40·00
J. Boulabert	1823	60·00
de Bonfils	1827	60·00
Paris		
Thomas De Lisle & Co.	1842	40·00
Bayonne		
Francis Giffard & Son	1815	80·00
Alicante		
John Carey	1812	80·00
Cadiz		
R. W. Meade	1812	80·00
Gordon, Shaw & Co.	1812	80·00
Lisbon		
Sealys & Goodall	1813	60·00
Naples		
Bardon, Maingy & Price	1817–18	60·00
Rome		
Pierre Meraj	1802	60·00
Trieste		
J. Janvrin	1822	30·00
Gibraltar		
Robinson & Lihou	1809	75·00
Matthew G. Price	1810	75·00
Dobrée, Price & Co.	1811–12	70·00
Robert Anderson & Co.	1832	70·00
Malta		
E. C. Puslow	1815	80·00
Bolzano (Botzen)		
G. Giacomo Graff	1803	80·00
Altona		
John Hutchinson	1804	80·00
Hamburg		
J. B. Paschen & Co.	1793	60·00
H. D. Schaffler	1803	60·00
J. A. Schroders	1836	50·00
Elsinore		
Balfour & Rainols	1807	60·00
St. Thomas		
Bergeert & Ulhorn	1813	75·00

2. Establishment of the Postal Service

Between 1778 and 1783 there was an attempt to carry mails to the Channel Islands as a war measure and the cutter *Express*, of 40 tons, sailed from Southampton "as often as practicable". In 1783 she returned to Dover to continue in service on the Dover–Calais run. Letters carried on this service are rare.

(Price from £100.)

In 1791 the Postmaster of Southampton was ordered to make a census of all letters addressed to the Channel Islands over a period of four weeks, and from this it was deduced that the number of letters to be carried annually would be around 30,000. On this basis it was considered that a packet service would not be self-supporting, but that, in view of the importance of the Islands during a war with France, such a service should be established as a matter of state.

On 3 February 1794 (and other dates during the month) a notice regarding a packet service to the Channel Islands was published in the *London Gazette* and the first packet, the 80-ton cutter *Royal Charlotte*, sailed from Weymouth for Guernsey on 13 February. An Act of Parliament establishing the packet service was passed on 28 March 1794: 34 Geo. III, Cap. XVIII (1794). It also fixed rates of postage and authorised the Postmaster General to establish post offices and post roads in the Islands. The Act was registered by the Royal Court of Guernsey on 6 October 1794, but was never registered by the Royal Court of Jersey and so was not law there.

A Post Office Surveyor, Christopher Saverland, went over on the first packet, and appointed Mrs. Ann Watson Postmistress of Guernsey and Charles William Le Geyt Postmaster of Jersey.

Postage Rates

The packet rates between Weymouth and the Channel Islands in 1794 were 2d. per single letter, 4d. per double letter, 6d. per treble letter and 8d. per ounce letter. In November 1805 they were raised to 3d. per single letter and pro rata. The inter-island rates were the same as those above.

The postage from London to Weymouth was 5d., which, with the packet charge, made 7d. for a single letter to the Channel Islands in 1794. It rose to 9d. in 1796, to 10d. in 1801, to 11d. in 1805 and to 1s. 1d. in 1812.

3. Pre-adhesive Markings

JERSEY

Jersey's first postal marking, which came into use in 1794 and remained till 1799, consisted simply of the word JERSEY arranged in a concave curve (Type **J1**). From 1797 a straight-line stamp was used concurrently with the previous mark for a while and continued in use until 1810. During this time two quite different types existed. Type **J2** measures 32 × 5mm, has a full loop to the J and wide letters. Type **J3** is 30 × 5mm; the loop to J gradually almost disappeared and it sometimes has a small dot over it.

The scroll type came into use in 1810 and, again, two distinct types exist. The first (Type **J4**) was used from 1810 to 1830 except for the years 1817–22. It can be distinguished by the lettering, which is large, the shape of the J of JERSEY and finally the full stop. The second type (Type **J5**), which came into use in 1817 and remained until 1830, has smaller lettering, shows a more distinctive J and the full stop after JERSEY is omitted.

With the setting up in Jersey of the Penny Post in the 1830s a new handstamp was introduced (Type **J6**). This mark was used until 1840 in conjunction with village number markings (Types **J7–10**). These latter handstamps, numbered 1 to 4, were used on their own after 1840. The parishes represented were St. Aubin, Gorey, St. Peter's and St. Clement's respectively and of these St. Aubin (No. 1) is the commonest. Numbers 5 and 6 were also allocated, it is believed to St. Saviour's and Trinity.

The year 1830 also saw the introduction of Jersey's first datestamp. This handstamp was applied to the backs of letters and remained in use until 1849. *See* Section 9.

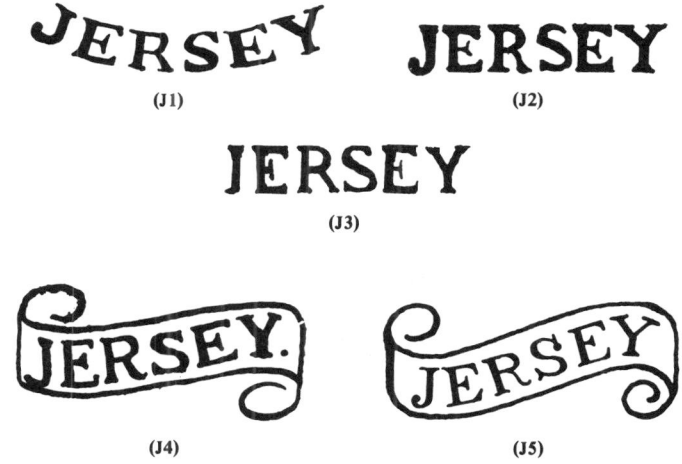

(J1)   (J2)

(J3)

(J4)   (J5)

(J6)

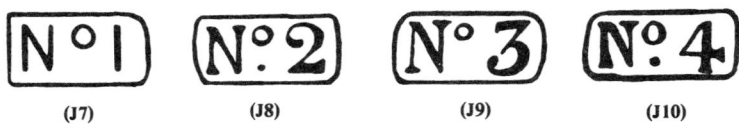

| (J7) | (J8) | (J9) | (J10) |

Cat. No.	Type No.	Dates of use	Colour	Price on cover
JC1	**J1**	1794–99	Black	£275
JC2	**J2**	1797–1806	Black	£200
JC3	**J3**	1807–10	Black	£200
JC4	**J4**	1810–17 and 1822–30	Black	£150
JC5	**J5**	1817–30	Black	£150
JC6	**J6**	1831–40 (used with JC7–10)	Black .. .. *..from*	£300
JC7	**J7**	1840	Black	£150
JC8	**J8**	1840	Black	£200
JC9	**J9**	1840	Black	£200
JC10	**J10**	1840	Black	£200

GUERNSEY

The first handstamp used in Guernsey after the establishment of the Post Office in 1794 was very similar to that of Jersey, taking the form of the word GUERNSEY set out as a concave curve (Type **G1**). Three distinct settings exist, the first, measuring 46mm wide being used from 1794 to 1801, the second, 49mm wide, from 1802 to 1807 and the third, the smallest, being only 37mm wide, from 1807 to 1810. This last type is considerably scarcer than either of the first two types and is always much fainter than the other two.

The next handstamp to be used was the scroll type. Two types of this strike exist. The first (Type **G2**), in use from 1810 to 1817, included a full stop after the word GUERNSEY, though the easiest way of distinguishing it from the later type is by the positioning of the letter G which is very close to the left-hand edge of the frame. The second type (Type **G3**) was used from 1817 to 1830, and here the full stop is omitted and the letter G is much farther from the frame edge.

Though long out of use the Type **G2** scroll evidently survived, as it is known struck on Telegraph forms in 1870–72.

The Guernsey Penny Post was established between January and March 1836 but no handstamps have yet been found. Hendy records that it served La Valle and Torteval.

From 1830 a circular datestamp with serifed letters was used and this marking continued in use after the introduction of Uniform Penny Postage in 1840. *See* Section 9.

(G1)

(G2)   (G3)

Cat. No.	Type No.	Dates of use	Colour					Price on cover
GC1	G1 (46mm wide)	1794–1801	Black	..	..	..	..	£250
GC2	G1 (49mm wide)	1802–07	Black	..	..	..	..	£250
GC3	G1 (37mm wide)	1807–10	Black	..	..	..	..	£325
GC4	G2	1810–17	Black	..	..	..	..	£150
GC5	G3	1817–30	Black	..	..	..	..	£150

4. Ship Letters

The establishment of the Post Office in Jersey in 1794 brought with it the same procedures which were uniform throughout the United Kingdom. In the case of letters which were carried by private ships it meant that these letters would be subject to the standard ship letter charges.

As a result of the setting up in 1799 of the Ship Letter Office in London a new type of handstamp was introduced and around 1802 Jersey received its copy (Type **J11**). It consisted of a double oval and crown bearing the words SHIP-LETTER/JERSEY. This strike is extremely rare and so far only one example has been recorded (it is in the British Museum). This was because there was considerable opposition to the charges imposed upon letters carried by private ships whose owners in the main were themselves islanders. The letters forwarded from overseas were for the most part addressed to islanders and they objected to this "outrageous procedure". Most of the mail was therefore not handed over to the Post Office but was delivered by other means, accounting for the lack of usage of this handstamp.

In 1834 a new handstamp (Type **J12**) was introduced. This is mainly found on mail from Rio de Janeiro and Bahia handed over at Jersey from ships bound for France. Most of this mail was addressed to London, and it was before being forwarded that this strike was applied. This handstamp remained in use until 1843 and is the most frequently found Jersey ship letter mark.

A similar type of handstamp, but with the wording transposed to read SHIP LETTER/JERSEY (Type **J13**), is known used in 1837. This mark in red is believed to have been applied in London as Jersey had no red ink pad at this time though they were in use in London. In addition, it does not seem likely that the island would have used two different types at the same time. It is believed that letters from Brazil for the same addressee were bundled there and forwarded intact to

(J11)

JERSEY
SHIP LETTER

(J12)

SHIP LETTER
JERSEY

(J13)

JERSEY
SHIP LETTER
(J14)

JERSEY
SHIP-LETTER
(J15)

London where they were separated and duly stamped by the Post Office before being delivered. Only two examples of this mark have so far been recorded.

A step-type of marking (Type **J14**) was in use in 1840 and is known in red. It is extremely rare, only one example having so far come to light.

A new handstamp was used from 1843 until 1853 (Type **J15**). This marking is normally found in black although it is known in blue and yellow, only one example being recorded in blue.

It also occurs used as a cancellation on the 1841 1d. red adhesive of Great Britain.

(*Price off cover* £200.)

Cat. No.	Type No.	Dates of use	Colour	Price on cover
JC11	**J11**	1802	Black	—
JC12	**J12**	1834–43	Black	£250
JC13	**J13**	1837	Red	£2750
JC14	**J14**	1840	Red	£4000
JC15	**J15**	1843–53	Black	£350
JC16		1851	Blue	£4000
JC17		1852	Yellow	£2750

GUERNSEY

In Guernsey, as in Jersey, subsequent to the setting up of the Ship Letter Office in London in 1799, letters arriving which had been carried by private ships had to be handed over to the Post Office for onward transmission.

In 1802 the island was supplied with its standard crown-in-double-oval marking inscribed SHIP-LETTER/GUERNSEY (Type **G4**). This type was used from 1802 to 1815 and was brought back into use in 1844 until 1849. Examples of its usage during the earlier period are scarcer than those of the period 1844–49.

The next type to come into use was a box inscribed GUERNSEY/SHIP LETTER (Type **G5**). This was received by Guernsey in 1834 and was used until 1842. As with Jersey, a similar type but with the wording transposed exists, and it is probable that this was used in London for the same purpose as the Jersey mark. This type (Type **G6**) was used from 1836 to 1840 and is only known in red.

In 1842 an unusual step-type of handstamp came into use (Type **G7**), though this marking remained in use for a very short time so that only a handful of examples have been found.

By far the rarest of all the ship letter handstamps used in Guernsey is the INDIA LETTER/GUERNSEY (Type **G8**). Only one example of this strike is known, used on a letter from Singapore to London in 1836.

Packet Stamp

An unusual type of handstamp to be found on mail from both Guernsey and Jersey is the straight line FROM GUERNSEY (Type **G9**). This marking was applied at Weymouth to packet letters from the Islands to enable them to be distinguished from overseas ship letters for which a higher charge was levied. To avoid the trouble of having handstamps for each island the Weymouth authorities settled for this mark, bearing in mind that Guernsey was the last port of call for ships returning to Weymouth. It was used from 1810 to 1837 and has been found on letters from both islands.

GUERNSEY
SHIP LETTER

(G5)

(G4)

SHIP LETTER
GUERNSEY

(G6)

GUERNSEY
SHIP LETTER

(G7)

INDIA LETTER
GUERNSEY

(G8)

FROM GUERNSEY

(G9)

Cat. No.	Type No.	Dates of use	Colour	Price on cover
GC6	**G4**	1802–15	Black	£1600
GC7		1844–49	Black	£1300
GC8	**G5**	1834–42	Black	£300
GC9	**G6**	1836–40	Red	£800
GC10	**G7**	1842	Black	£1300
GC11	**G8**	1836	Black	£4000
GC12	**G9**	1810–37	Black	£600

Wrecks

Many ships have been wrecked on the rocky shores of the Channel Islands but only one handstruck mark has so far been recorded as having been applied to recovered mail.

The Great Western Railways vessel s.s. *Ibex* left Weymouth on 4 January 1900 and struck a rock in the east channel on the Little Russel, near the Platte Fougère, at 6 a.m. on 5 January. One sailor was lost but all the passengers were saved. Forty-four bags of mail went down with the vessel but as she rested on an even keel, with masts, funnels and parts of the superstructure above water at low tide, divers were able to start work on her straight away and two parcel hampers were salvaged on the day of the sinking.

On 9 January the *Star*, a Guernsey newspaper, reported that the mail-bags were found to be floating under the poop deck. Five had been recovered by this date, three for Guernsey and two for Jersey. The letters were in fair condition but the newspapers were reported to be pulp. The Guernsey letters were dried and delivered on the 9th, postmen being instructed to explain that they were from the *Ibex*. Salvage continued and by the 12th, thirty-three mail-bags had been recovered.

By 20 January all the mail-bags except two had been recovered. One was from London to Jersey and one from Dorchester to Guernsey. On 25 January the *Star* reported that a bag of mail from the *Ibex* had been washed ashore at St. Brelade's Bay, Jersey.

Letters for Jersey, Alderney and Sark recovered from the wreck were, after drying, tied up in bundles, or put into envelopes with a manuscript note to say where they had come from.

No handstamps were used at Guernsey to identify these letters. Nevertheless, two slightly different cachets reading MAIL PER S.S. IBEX are known. Both types are 40mm long with letters from printer's type, but one (Type **J16**) has all the letters 3mm high (except the ER of PER which are 2½mm) and full stops after the s.s., while the other (Type **J17**) has the words MAIL and IBEX in letters 3mm high, PER SS in letters of 2½mm and no stops after ss.

About nine covers are known with these cachets and all are addressed to Jersey; it would appear, therefore, that the cachets were applied by the Jersey Post Office after the letters were received from Guernsey, or possibly to letters washed up off Jersey.

A news-wrapper from the magazine *Commerce* addressed to Jersey has in manuscript "Recovered from wreck of G.W. Rly. s.s. Ibex lost off Guernsey about 28/12/99—received 14/1/1900". It bears the *Ibex* cachet Type **J16** with small ER of PER and stops after the s.s., and so do the other entires delivered around this date. One is known with the Jersey datestamp of 12 January 1900. The later covers, however, with Jersey datestamps of 30 July and 1 August 1900, have the cachet Type **J17** with small PER SS and no stops after the SS. A possible explanation of this is that a further bag of letters was found in the *Ibex* after she had been taken into St. Peter Port on 21 July, having in some miraculous way been preserved from the ravages of the sea, and when these letters were delivered in Jersey a new cachet had to be made, the earlier one having been destroyed some months before when it was thought unlikely that any further letters would be recovered.

One of the later covers is a piece of French postal stationery with impressed 5c. green Peace and Commerce stamp cancelled at Le Havre on 31 December 1899. It has an "officially sealed" label bearing the Jersey datestamp of 30 July 1900, and the *Ibex* cachet Type **J17**. Another cover with this cachet is recorded with Jersey arrival stamps of 1 and 2 August 1900.

A number of loose stamps—we have seen Canadian, Belgian and Dutch—have been found with cachet Type **J17** impressed diagonally. It is thought that these were found in the bottom of the mail-bag, cancelled, and handed over with the letters on delivery.

(*Price on loose stamps £75 each.*)

MAIL PER S.S. IBEX
(J16)

MAIL PER S S IBEX
(J17)

Cat. No.	Type No.	Dates of use	Colour			Price on cover
JC18	J16	Jan. 1900	Black	..	..	.. £500
JC19	J17	July–Aug. 1900	Black	..	..	.. £500

5. Uniform Fourpenny Post

The experimental introduction of a uniform postal rate at 4d. commenced on 5 December 1839. It lasted until 9 January 1840, the uniform 1d. rate being introduced on 10 January.

Usually the fourpenny rate was marked in manuscript, but a few towns in Great Britain had a handstruck "4".

In Jersey and Guernsey the "4" was applied in manuscript and such letters are quite scarce.

(Price on entire £85.)

Manuscript 1d. marks were used in both islands prior to the introduction of handstruck numerals carved from wood.

(Price on entire £20.)

6. Handstruck Numerals

JERSEY

The handstruck numerals were introduced in Jersey in the early 1840s. The first type of the 1d. known to have been used (Type **J18**) has been found on covers of 1843 struck in red. The next type (Type **J14**) has been found on a number of covers which prove that it was in use from 1844 to 1848. This handstamp was also struck in red.

The 2d. handstamps date back to 1842 (Type **J20**), this type having been used in that year and in 1843. It was struck in black. The next type to be recorded (Type **J21**) was used between 1849 and 1851 and was generally struck in black, although examples of it have been found in blue on letters of 1851. In 1852 a similar type, although considerably thinner (Type **J22**), was used for a time and was struck in blue. This handstamp was brought back into use in 1866–67, on this occasion being struck in black. In 1853 the authorities used another type (Type **J23**) for a while.

A figure "8" (Type **J24**) was used on mails in 1851 to collect ship letter charges. This type was struck in blue. A further type (Type **J25**) is known to have been applied in 1868 on an unpaid letter to France. It was struck in black.

(J18)   (J19)

(J20)   (J21)   (J22)   (J23)

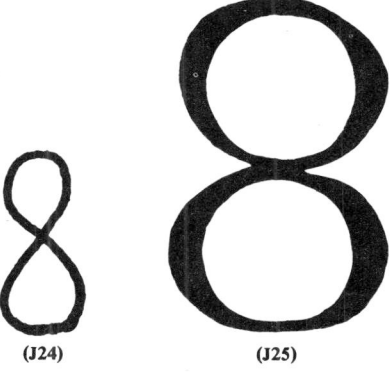

(J24) (J25)

Cat. No.	Type No.	Dates of use	Colour				Price on cover
JC20	**J18**	1843	Red	..	..	..	£200
JC21	**J19**	1844–48	Red	..	..	..	£200
JC22	**J20**	1842–43	Black	..	..	..	£225
JC23	**J21**	1849–51	Black	..	..	..	£225
JC24		1851	Blue	..	..	..	£275
JC25	**J22**	1852	Blue	..	..	..	£275
JC26		1866–67	Black	..	..	..	£180
JC27	**J23**	1853	Black	..	..	..	£150
JC28	**J24**	1851	Blue	..	..	..	£300
JC29	**J25**	1868	Black	..	..	..	£600

GUERNSEY

Guernsey had its own distinctive 1d. paid and 2d. unpaid handstamps. The 1d. (Type **G10**) was struck in red and is known used between 1843 and 1846.

Two different types of 2d. stamps are known. The first (Type **G11**) was used from 1842 to 1843 and was struck in black; the second (Type **G12**) is known used in 1847 and is also in black.

(G10) (G11) (G12)

There is also known a handstruck "8" (Type **G13**), which was used between 1844 and 1846 on mail from France arriving in the island unpaid.

(G13)

Cat. No.	Type No.	Dates of use	Colour			Price on cover
GC13	**G10**	1843–46	Red	..	..	.. £200
GC14	**G11**	1842–43	Black	..	..	.. £225
GC15	**G12**	1847	Black	..	..	.. £275
GC16	**G13**	1844–46	Black	..	..	.. £325

7. Use of First Adhesives and Mulreadys

Handstamps in the form of Maltese Crosses were distributed for use with the first adhesive postage stamps of Great Britain and the Mulready covers in 1840. Though mass-produced their hand manufacture led to small differences in detail in each handstamp and the more unusual ones are much sought by collectors. For further information refer to Stanley Gibbons *Great Britain Specialised Stamp Catalogue*, Volume 1.

At May 1840 a red ink was used with the Maltese Crosses and it was superseded by black in February 1841.

Jersey received Type **J26** and it was struck in red until February 1841. Covers are known, however, dated November 1840 struck in black and this was almost certainly by mistake.

The *Guernsey* Maltese Cross (Type **G14**) is distinctive in that the centre diamond is blunted at one side and the lower left-hand side of the inner cross has a blunted point.

Reference in philatelic literature is often made to a type of Maltese Cross for "the Channel Islands" in general. This should be read as meaning the Alderney Cross (Type **1** of Alderney).

The Mulready envelopes and lettersheets were used in Jersey and Guernsey as were the One Penny Black and Twopence Blue adhesives. All plates of the Penny Black can be found on covers from the Islands except for Plate 11, no example of which has yet been seen. The 1840 Twopence Blue (no lines) has not to date been found on cover from the Islands.

Up to 1844, when numeral obliterators came into use, covers of the period would normally have had the stamps cancelled with the Maltese Cross and a Jersey or Guernsey datestamp would be struck elsewhere on the cover.

(J26)

(G14)

Mulready Envelope or Lettersheet

1d. with Jersey or Guernsey datestamp in addition to Maltese Cross .. ..*from*	£100
1d. with Southampton Ship Letter in addition to Maltese Cross .. .. ..*from*	£150
2d. with Jersey or Guernsey datestamp in addition to Maltese Cross .. ..*from*	£300

1840 1d. Black

Used on cover from Jersey or Guernsey .. ..*from*	£120
Used on cover from Jersey with boxed handstamp No. 1, 2, 3 or 4 (Types **J7–J10**) .. ..*from*	£180

1841 2d. Blue

Used on cover from Jersey or Guernsey .. .. 90·00

1841 1d. Red

Used on cover from Jersey or Guernsey .. .. 20·00

Used on cover from Jersey with boxed handstamp
No. 1, 2, 3 or 4 (Types **J7–J10**) .. .. *..from* £130

*For 1d. red cancelled with Jersey datestamp Type **J33** see Section 9.*

8. Numeral Obliterations

The Maltese Cross cancellation was replaced in 1844 by numeral obliterators. Guernsey and Jersey were given numbers in the series allotted to England and Wales, the former receiving the number 324 and the latter 409.

JERSEY

Several different types were in use in Jersey between 1844 and 1902. The first (Type **J27**) was sent out in April 1844, had the number 409 with two curved bars on each side of it and three bars above and below, the whole making an oval of which the curved bars form the sides. This is No. JC30 in the catalogue listing.

No. JC31 is very similar but the cross bar of the 4 is 2mm from the base, the loop of the 4 is 3mm wide and the height of the figures is 6½mm. The Type **J27** obliterator is 22½mm wide but this is 21½mm. No. JC31 appears to have been used from 1861 to 1864 and is mainly found on letters addressed to the Continent and on French stamps used on the Boîte Mobile Service.

No. JC32 is again somewhat similar to Type **J27** but the cross bar of the 4 is 3mm from the base. It appears to have been used from 1864 to 1870 and is often heavily struck so that the horizontal and vertical bars appear to form an unbroken oval. It is known on a number of letters addressed to France and on French stamps from the Boîte Mobile Service, but was not used exclusively for this purpose.

Type **J27a** was a recut of Type **J27** and came into use in July 1857. It can be distinguished by its figures, which are much smaller (5½mm high against 7mm of the original figures). The loop of the 4 is 4mm wide and the cross bar just under 2mm from the base. There is also a similar type with a blunt point to the 4 (No. JC34).

The next type (Type **J28**) is the first of the duplexes. It was dispatched from the G.P.O. on 22 April 1858 and the earliest date of use recorded is 14 October 1858. It was replaced about 1863 by a very similar one having a datestamp 19mm wide (1mm wider than the one it replaced) and this is No. JC36.

With Type **J29** the numeral part of the duplex changed from horizontal to vertical format. The oval is 20–21mm in diameter and the loop of the 9 is oval. It was sent to Jersey on 15 October 1866 and the earliest recorded date of use is 4 November.

Type **J29a** is the largest of all the duplexes. The oval is 22–23mm in diameter and the loop of the 9 is rounder. It was dispatched from the G.P.O. on 17 January 1870 and the earliest date of use recorded is 25 February. It remained in use until 1874.

The last of the duplex types (**J30**) was taken into use in 1872 and remained in use until 1880. The earliest date seen is 14 November 1872, and the latest 27 August 1880. The datestamp has the name JERSEY around the circumference.

There are two slightly different types of this stamp: No. JC39 is 19mm in diameter and has a sharp point to the 4; No. JC40 is 18mm in diameter and has a blunt point to the 4. The two shapes of the figure 4 are illustrated.

What appears to be a sub-type (**J30a**) is dated 5 February 1881 and is lettered A in the datestamp. The numerals are shorter, the zero is rounder, and the upright of the 4 leans over to the right. The lettering in the datestamp is also larger. This is No. JC41.

Types **J28, 29** and **29a** are lettered A, B or C (an example of Type **J29a** is also known lettered O in 1874), and Type **J30** is lettered B, C or D in the datestamp.

Type **J31** is a single obliterator used mainly on newspapers and on mail arriving from France on the Boîte Mobile Service between 1875 and 1881. It is 19mm wide and has three bars at the top and bottom. There is a full stop after the 9 and the tip of the 4 is 2mm from the upright. A later type, found on the French Peace and Commerce issues, has no stop after the 9, the tip of the 4 is 3mm from the upright, and the 0 and 9 almost touch each other. This is Type **J31a**.

Type **J32** is also a single obliterator 19–20mm in diameter. It was used almost exclusively on registered mail and is known used in conjunction with the oval registered stamp between 1888 and 1902. Type **J32a** has a wider oval (20mm) and the side bars are heavier. The figure 4 is also wider.

There is also a further type that should be mentioned although no examples of it have yet been seen. On 16 November 1881 the G.P.O. dispatched to Jersey a large oval obliterator (No. JC44) and a separate datestamp. It was marked "For Stamping Machine 180504".

There are several single obliterators rather similar to Types **J31** to **J32a** but differing slightly in detail.

(J27)

(J27a)

(J28)

(J29)

(J29a)

(J30)

From JC39   From JC40

(J31)   (J31a)   (J32)   (J32a)

No. JC44

Cat. No.	Type No.		Dates of use				Price on cover from

All struck in black; No. JC30 also occurs in blue.

Barred Ovals

JC30	**J27**	(7mm figures)	1844–56	..	..		20·00
JC31		(6½mm figures)	1861–64	..	..		20·00
JC32		("unbroken" oval)	1864–70	..	..		20·00
JC33	**J27a**	(recut; 5½mm figures)	1857	..	..		22·00
JC34		(blunt point to 4)	..	..	..		22·00

Cat. No.	Type No.		Dates of use		Price on cover from
Duplexes					
JC35	**J28**	(18mm datestamp)	1858–63	.. ..	.. 22·00
JC36		(19mm datestamp)	1863–66	.. ..	.. 25·00
JC37	**J29**		1866–72	.. ..	.. 18·00
JC38	**J29a**	(larger oval)	1870–74	.. ..	.. 20·00
JC39	**J30**	(19mm datestamp)	1872–80	.. ..	.. 18·00
JC40		(18mm datestamp)	.. ..	.. ..	.. 18·00
JC41	**J30a**	(larger lettering)	1881 ..	.. ..	.. 18·00
Single Obliterators					
JC42	**J31**		1875–81	.. ..	.. 16·00
JC43	**J31a**	(no stop after 9)	1878–81	.. ..	.. 16·00
JC44		(G.P.O. recorded)	—	.. ..	.. —
JC45	**J32**		1888–1902	..	.. 16·00
JC46	**J32a**	(wider oval)	1888–1904	..	.. 16·00

GUERNSEY

Various types of numeral obliterator can be recorded for Guernsey between 1844 and the 1890s. The first was sent out in April 1844 and was put into use in May (Type **G15**).

No. GC18 is very similar to Type **G15** but has the serif of the 2 pointing to the point of the 4 instead of being almost vertical. It is known used in 1857. There is also a similar type with the bottom loop of the 3 much flatter. This is No. GC19.

Type **G15a** is described in the Proof Books as a recut of the original and was dispatched from the G.P.O. on 14 October 1853. The earliest date seen is 15 February 1854. It can be distinguished from the original by the figures, which are considerably smaller (5mm high against the 6½mm of Type **G15**).

Type **G16** is the first duplex. It was dispatched from the G.P.O. on 15 June 1858, and can be identified when off cover because it has a much rounder appearance than the single obliterator. The earliest date of use seen is 6 September 1858.

In July 1860 two further examples of a duplex similar to Type **G16**, but having a datestamp closer to the numeral and with the figures of date more widely spaced, were dispatched from the G.P.O. (Type **G16a**). In the numeral part of this obliterator the centre point of the 3 is straight instead of pointing downwards as in the previous type, the serif of the 2 is well clear of the curve of the 2, the foot of the 2 and loop of the 4 are larger and the 4 has a flat top. Types **G16** and **16a** were both in use until the autumn of 1867.

By 14 November 1867 a new type with vertical oval containing the numerals 324 was introduced (Type **G17**). It remained in use until replaced by a similar but heavier type in 1875 (Type **G17a**). These two types are very difficult to distinguish off cover, but **G17** has a larger datestamp with larger letters than **G17a**. The numeral parts differ in the following ways: **G17** has a short foot to the 2 and the serif points to the point of the 4; **G17a** has a longer foot to the 2 and the serif points inside the 4. The bars of **G17a** are heavier than **G17** and there is very little space between the bottom two.

Type **G17b** was put into use in 1880, and the earliest date recorded is 28 February. It is a much lighter type than the previous two, and the figure 4 is much narrower. It is known used up to 1888. An example used in 1887 appears to be much heavier and has the centre point of the 3 horizontal instead of sloping downwards, the serif of the 2 almost vertical, and the top of the 4 more pointed. This is possibly due to wear or else the stamp needed cleaning.

Two vertical 324 single obliterators are known used on newspapers. A type with three bars at the top and bottom was used in the 1870s (Type **G18**) and one with two bars at top and bottom in the 1890s (Type **G19**). There was also a three-bar type with flat-topped 3 used in the 1890s (No. GC27).

(G15) (G15a) No. GC18

(G16) (G16a)

(G17)

(G17a) (G17b)

Cat. No.	Type No.		Dates of use			Price on cover from
		All struck in black.				
Barred Ovals						
GC17	**G15**	(6½mm figs.; vert. serif)	1844–53	..	..	20·00
GC18		(serif pointing right)	1857 ..	..	..	20·00
GC19		(flatter loop to 3)	.. ..	..	..	20·00
GC20	**G15a**	(recut; 5mm figures)	1854–58	..	..	20·00
Duplexes						
GC21	**G16**		1858–67	..	..	18·00
GC22	**G16a**	(datestamp closer)	1860–67	..	..	18·00
GC23	**G17**		1867–75	..	..	18·00
GC24	**G17a**	(heavier bars)	1875–80	..	..	18·00
GC25	**G17b**	(narrower 4)	1880–88	..	..	18·00
Single Obliterators						
GC26	**G18**	(three bars)	1870s ..	..	..	14·00
GC27		(flat top to 3)	1890s ..	..	..	30·00
GC28	**G19**	(two bars)	1890s ..	..	..	12·00

ALDERNEY

The number 965 was allotted to Alderney in May 1848. A type with four bars at top and bottom was in use from 1848 to the mid-1860s when it was replaced by one having three bars at top and bottom and slightly narrower figures. Both types can be found on the 1d. lilac adhesive and were in use up to 1897.

There was no duplex type for Alderney, but the numerals 965 were used in error for 963 at Winchfield, Hampshire in 1896 and 1897.

Prices and further details will be found in Section 13.

9. Datestamps and Other Cancellations

JERSEY

First Type

Jersey's first datestamp was Type **J33** introduced in 1830. Known as "the improved steel datestamp with a double set of figures" it is recorded in the G.P.O. Proof Books as having been dispatched to Jersey on 31 May 1830. It was taken into use in June 1830 and is found struck in black up to 1843 and then in red to 1845. It is interesting to note that it was used occasionally with some figures of the date missing, probably through carelessness. One example, used in 1832, has the date completely missing.

The datestamp having apparently become worn in use, a recut was provided and this was dispatched by the G.P.O. on 7 November 1845. This is Type **J33a**, distinguishable by its sans-serif letters. The datestamp underwent another recut in 1848 and was dispatched to Jersey from the G.P.O. on 17 June 1848. It is known used up to 18 April 1849 but cannot be distinguished from the 1845 recut.

Red ink had continued in use from 1845 so that both recuts are struck in this colour.

Because the first datestamp was not normally used as a cancellation it is highly desirable when found on loose adhesives.

Travelling Types

The so-called "travelling" or "skeleton" handstamps were made up locally from movable letters in a skeleton frame. They were kept as standby for use when the permanent datestamps were unavailable for one reason or another.

Three types are known from Jersey at this period. Type **J34**, recorded struck in black in 1843, resembled the illustrated Type **J34a** with the addition of a cross as ornament below the date. Type **J34a** itself occurs in red in 1848 at the time of the second recutting of the first permanent datestamp.

The first recut, which had produced No. JC49, was covered by another travelling handstamp (Type **J35**). This latter is known struck in red dated between 29 October and 10 November 1845.

Double-arc Type

In 1849 the double-arc type was introduced (Type **J36**). It was dispatched from the G.P.O. in July 1849, and the earliest date of use seen is 4 October 1849. Three slightly different types exist: (*a*) with J and Y of JERSEY level with the top of the date (month); (*b*) with J below top of date and Y level with top; (*c*) with J and Y well above date line. This stamp had a somewhat colourful existence: it started with red in 1849, changed to blue in 1851, then to orange in December 1852, changed to black in 1854, went to a dirty green in 1855 and to grey-black in mid-1855, reverted to blue in 1857, and ended with black in 1858. Below the date appeared the letter A, B or C.

Early Single Circles

In 1858 a small single-circle datestamp 19mm in diameter was brought into use, chiefly as a backstamp (Type **J37**). Two examples were dispatched from the G.P.O. on 22 April 1858. They can be found lettered A, B, C, D, E, F, A2, B2, F2, and without any letters at all, and were in use up to the late 1890s. The letters referred to the time of collection; stamps without letters were used for counter work.

Single-circle datestamps ranging from 19 to 25mm in diameter with the name JERSEY in short or tall letters round the top and the date in two lines across the centre were in use at various times between 1870 and the 1930s (Type **J38**). They are known with the following letters above the date: A, B, C, D, O and P (telegraphic); also without any letters at all, or with letter and figure combinations such as A1, A2, B1, B2, C1, C2, D1, D2, E1, G2, GFXA, 11XA or with an asterisk. From about 1899 the letters were replaced by the time of the collection or the time the mail was made up.

Squared Circles

In 1881 what was officially called the "combined obliterator" (Type **J39**) was introduced to replace the duplex types. It was dispatched from the G.P.O. on 15 March 1881 and the earliest date of use seen is 23 March 1881. It can be found lettered A, B, C, D and E and has four corner lines outside the circle. A similar type but with only three corner lines outside the circle (Type **J39a**) was brought into use round about April 1884 and is known lettered B, C, D and E. On 9 December 1886 a slightly larger type (**J39b**) but with two long thin bars forming almost complete circles (except for four breaks of 5mm), one shorter thin bar and solid corners outside the circle, was dispatched from the G.P.O. The earliest date of use seen is 26 September 1887, and the latest 10 November 1896, lettered A, B (reversed), C, D or F. A fourth type of the obliterator, with one line and a solid corner outside the circle, came into use towards the end of 1892 and appears to have continued until about 1905 (Type **J39c**). It can be found lettered C, D, E, F, G and H, and from about 1899 with the time instead of a letter. Several of these obliterators were in use at the same time and the sizes of the letters of JERSEY vary a lot. This cancellation is commonly known as the "squared circle".

Double Circles

From 1896 a double-circle datestamp with solid bars separated by a cross was put into service (Type **J40**). About ten sub-types exist with different sizes of letters and cross and with bars of different thickness. It was used up to 1929. A similar type (**J41**) with a sans-serif figure 1 at the bottom instead of the cross appears to have been introduced in 1906. This can be found in six sub-types with different sizes of letters and figures and with either thin or thick bars. Both types were used concurrently from 1906. Up to 1914 all the Jersey datestamps had the month preceding the day but from then onwards the day preceded the month. (This change was common throughout Britain.)

About 1930 a double-ring circular datestamp reading JERSEY (ST. HELIERS) CHANNEL ISLANDS was introduced (Type **J42**). In 1938 a similar type (**J43**) was sent in which the words CHANNEL ISLANDS have been abbreviated to CH. IS., although the correct postal name of the town is St. Helier. Type **J42** has been seen as late as 1944.

A double-circle cancellation (Type **J44**) reading JERSEY. CHANNEL ISLANDS/1 (serifed), introduced about 1928, was replaced about 1934 by JERSEY/CHANNEL ISLANDS (Type **J45**). The year 1945 saw the introduction of a new one reading JERSEY C.I./1 (Type **J46**) and this has also been seen with a 2 at the bottom.

The "JERSEY. CHANNEL ISLANDS" type was brought back in 1952 with a 3 at the bottom. During the 1950s, also, a new version with this wording and numbered 1, 2 or 4 had been introduced. This is Type **J44a**, recognisable by the thin arcs on each side of the serial number.

Modern Single Circles

Several types of single circle have been used in recent times: one introduced in 1935 (Type **J47**) reads JERSEY/CHANNEL ISLANDS, the space between the last two words varying.

A type reading JERSEY CHANNEL ISLANDS (**J48**), with numbers between 1 and 16 at the foot, has seen use since 1938. The cancellers show individual differences in sizes of lettering and the presence or absence of a full stop after JERSEY. Above the date there is an asterisk or a code letter, of which A, B, C, D, E, F, G, H, O, R, S and W have been noted. Number 12 has also been seen without a code letter.

A 25mm cancel reading JERSEY. CHANNEL ISLANDS 21 or 22 continuously round the circle is used on letters posted "out of course" (Type **J48a**). It is occasionally found as a normal cancel on stamps which have missed the machine cancel.

Type **J49** is similar but the words are abbreviated to JERSEY. CHANNEL IS. Known in this type are an unnumbered datestamp, one numbered 3 and no code letter, one numbered 9 with code letter Z and one numbered 11 and no code letter.

Large circular datestamps of rubber are met with: these will be found below under the heading "Cancellations for small packets".

Machine Cancellations

The first machine cancellation, a Krag type, was introduced in 1923. Up to 1928 it had the word JERSEY measuring 18–19mm (Type **J50**), but after 1928 this measured only 14–16mm (Type **J50a**). The datestamp occurs on both sides of the wavy lines as it is a continuous impression. At Christmas time each year the time, which normally appeared above the date, was removed. In some dies there was a cross below the date.

The Krag machine was replaced in 1930 by a Universal type having a circular datestamp and continuous wavy lines. It had six bars in 1930–31 (Type **J51**), five in 1931–35 (**J51a**) and seven from 1935 onwards (**J51b**). The continuous wavy lines were in use until 1937 when a type with two breaks between the bars was used (Type **J51c**). The removable centre-piece could be put into the machine either way up.

During 1942 continuous lines again appeared (No. JC83) but the segmented type was again reverted to from 1943 (No. JC86). During the Occupation the zero of "1940" was cut in half for "1941" and from 1942 to 1946 the last two figures of the date had to be made locally and are easy to recognise. Later in 1946 the correct figures were again in use (No. JC85) and in 1948 the continuous-lines Type **J51b** was brought back. Examples used from 1950 show one or two damaged bars.

In 1953 the bars with breaks were again used but with a new datestamp which lacks the curved line at the bottom (Type **J52**). A new datestamp with larger letters was introduced in 1960 (Type **J53**). A further type came into use in the 1960s with small letters and a large curved arc. The time was sometimes replaced by a line (Type **J53a**).

On 1 December 1969 new cancelling bars in the form of a box containing three unevenly spaced horizontal lines was introduced by the Independent Postal Administration (Type **J54**). The box is found either way up in relation to the datestamp.

Slogans

Since 1931 Jersey has made use of machine cancellations to introduce slogans from time to time in place of the wavy lines. The first said "The Best Investment a Telephone" and this was followed in 1932 by one reading "The Telephone Makes Life Easier", which remained in use for about a year. Some of the numerous types employed since then are listed in Section 15.

Crown Registered Marks

The first registration stamp used in Jersey was the Crown and REGISTERED marking. Two types are known. The first (Type **J55**) was used from 1855 to 1859 in black. Type **J56**, which shows a different crown, was used from 1859 to 1870 usually in red, but an example on a cover of 1864 is known in black.

Registration Cancellations

Circular datestamps were usually used for registration purposes on covers and often on parcels, although ovals also exist. The first oval bore only the name of the island (Type **J57**) and is recorded as being dispatched to Jersey on 19 August 1879. It is known lettered from A to E and without any letter at all. By 1936 it was replaced by one having JERSEY CHANNEL ISLANDS at the bottom (Type **J58**). The letters are small and the words "Channel Islands" are in upper and lowercase letters. One used in 1938 has a serrated edge, due to wear. By 1939 another type with the words JERSEY CHANNEL IS. in small capitals had been introduced (Type **J58a**) but since 1947 another one (**J58b**) with larger letters has been in use. Similar stamps in use at present read REGISTERED at the top, JERSEY CHANNEL ISLANDS at the bottom, and have a figure 2, 3 or 4 below the date (**J59**).

Type **J60**, recorded as used on various occasions between 1939 and December 1946, bears no date and has the word REGISTERED across the middle.

Money Order Office Cancellation

The cancellation of the Money Order Office (Type **J61**) is occasionally seen on parcel post labels and is known cancelling stamps between 1900 and 1908.

Parcel Post Cancellations

The first cancellation for parcel post purposes (Type **J62**) was dispatched from the G.P.O. on 24 November 1886 and was made of rubber. Several examples of its use are known, the latest being on a parcel post label of 1911. The cancel consisted of a barred oval with JERSEY across the middle measuring 18mm. A second type (**J62a**), in which JERSEY measures 23mm, is known on a parcel post label used in 1890. The first oval measures 27mm across and the second 30mm, with the J and the Y much nearer to the sides.

More usually found is the double-ring rubber type with the name across the middle (Type **J63**). It was first sent to Jersey on 9 September 1892, others following in 1893, 1894, 1898 and 1904. These replacements differ in details. In one the inner arcs are above and below the first E and in another they come between the J and the E.

The first label type appears to have been used in 1915 (Type **J64**). A replacement in similar design but with the figure 1 incorporated was dispatched in 1917 (Type **J64a**).

A new label type (**J65**), the words PARCEL/POST appearing at the sides and reading upward, came into use in the 1930s. It is noteworthy for having the words CHANNEL ISLAND in the singular.

This appears to have been altered later, the wording CHANNEL ISLANDS (plural) being recorded in 1960 (Type **J65a**).

Also in the 1930s there appeared a further large label type (**J66**), numbered either 1 or 2 at top right. Number 3 in this series followed in 1956.

In use for a short time in the 1950s was Type **J67**, a label type of smaller format and incorporating the name St. Heliers.

A single-circle parcel cancellation of 33mm diameter, with PARCEL POST round the top, CHANNEL ISLANDS round the bottom, and JERSEY and the date in two lines in the centre, was introduced in July 1970 (Type **J68**).

Cancellations for Small Packets

Type **J69** was a single-circle cancellation as **J70** but without ST. HELIERS, dispatched to Jersey on 9 October 1893. Type **J70** itself was sent on 7 March 1898; it was reissued on 23 September 1905 and 24 June 1909 but these latter cancellations have no recognisable differences. The diameter was 30mm, and a larger type (**J70a**), 42mm in diameter, is known cancelling a 1951 King George VI 2d. pale red-brown adhesive (S.G.506) on a newspaper wrapper addressed to Southampton.

A further mute type (**J71**) is recorded in 1952. This single circle reading JERSEY/CHANNEL ISLANDS, has five bars across the centre instead of any date.

A small rectangular cancel, reading JERSEY (ST. HELIERS)/CHANNEL ISLANDS with the date across the centre is known used in 1938 (Type **J72**).

A roller type (**J73**) was used on small packets in 1957 but it wore out in a few weeks. It had the word JERSEY set between double lines above and below and repeated continuously as the roller was applied.

Cancellations in single-circle type and made of rubber are commonly used for small packets. Put into use in 1938 was Type **J74** of 30mm diameter with JERSEY at the top, CHANNEL ISLANDS at the bottom, and the date and time in two lines across the centre. A figure 1 or 2 appears above the date. Type **J74a** is similar but the lettering is larger and it has CH.IS. at the bottom. It is numbered 1.

An unnumbered cancellation (Type **J75**) was introduced in the 1960s reading JERSEY/CHANNEL ISLANDS. It is a single circle, diameter 30mm, with the date in one line.

In December 1969 another single-circle rubber cancellation was put into use. This is Type **J76**. It has JERSEY at the top, CHANNEL ISLANDS at the bottom and the date between two horizontal lines across the centre.

Triangles
Cancellations of triangular shape are used on circulars and printed matter. They bear the figures or telegraphic code letters allotted to the post office by the G.P.O.

A small 409 in a triangle with base 17mm (Type **J77**) is known on King Edward VII $\frac{1}{2}$d. stamps and on the Occupation issue; it was dispatched on 4 August 1909. It appeared in 1934 with the wavy lines as part of a machine cancellation in place of the normal datestamp (Type **J77a**).

In the 1930s a larger version of the triangle, approximately 25mm at the base, was put into use (Type **J78**) and, again, a similar type was used with wavy lines as a machine cancellation, this time dating from 1952 (Type **J78a**).

The letters JE in a triangle (Type **J79**) are known cancelling a wartime cover. It is possible this is still in use.

Triangular cancellations with wavy lines are occasionally employed during a census or count of mail.

"Paid" Handstamps
Various PAID handstamps, applied in red, are to be found, usually on news-wrappers or circulars.

On 26 June 1919 a handstamp Type **J80** (resembling **J81** but without CHANNEL ISLANDS) was sent from the G.P.O. and this had a $\frac{1}{2}$d. fixed value.

On the same day was dispatched the handstamp Type **J81** wherein the value was movable. Its diameter was 29mm.

PAID handstamps had another useful role during the German Occupation. The 2$\frac{1}{2}$d. was put into service when postage stamps were not available, when the franking machine was being repaired, or when supplies of electricity were cut off. Lack of paper in 1942 prevented any stamps being printed for several months and this cancellation had to be put into use then. It can also be found on mail posted after 15 November 1944, when stamp supplies finally ran out.

Some envelopes with this handstamp without date were sold in quantities of a dozen or more to residents of country districts, who posted them in pillar boxes. This avoided a journey into St. Helier for letters to be franked when stamps were unobtainable. The envelopes on arrival at the Head Post Office were given the normal machine cancellation.

A 1d. PAID handstamp was used in 1941 before the first Jersey 1d. stamp was ready and again later on. Another 1d. value (Type **J81a**) appears to have been made by removing the 2 from the $\frac{1}{2}$d., but no examples of the original $\frac{1}{2}$d. used properly are recorded.

The handstamp with movable values was supplemented in the 1950s by one in the larger size of 32mm (Type **J81b**).

Machine "Paid" Stamps
The first type of PAID marking applied by machine (**J82**) is believed to have consisted of the words JERSEY/PAID $\frac{1}{2}$d./date in three lines. It was in use from

about 1926 to 1929 and in the latter year the words GREAT BRITAIN were added, giving Type **J83**. These were used in conjunction with the wavy lines of the Krag cancelling machine.

A boxed type (**J84**) followed in 1932. This had an inner square containing ½D. and the date in two lines above; the outer square read JERSEY/PAID (top and bottom) and GREAT BRITAIN (left and right, both reading upwards).

Type **J85** came into use about 1937. This consists of a circular datestamp inscribed JERSEY/GT. BRITAIN and with date in two lines across the centre. Beside the datestamp is (value)/PAID, on each side of which are seven wavy lines.

The value in 1937 had been ½d. When postage was raised in 1940 a 1D/PAID die was introduced; similarly in 1951 a 1½D. die was brought in for the new printed paper rate. Since then higher values have made their appearance to cope with increasing postal rates (values noted have been 2d., 2½d., 3d., 4d., 4½d., 5d., 6d. and 7d.) and the c.d.s. no longer contains GT. BRITAIN (Type **J85a**). A new cancel used in 1955 had the curved line absent from the c.d.s. (Type **J85b**).

Like the PAID handstamps, the 1D/PAID machine version found an additional use during the Occupation, serving in lieu of adhesives when these ran out from time to time.

When the two-tier service began in 1968 the values in Type **J85** were replaced by 1ST PAID or 2ND PAID (Type **J86**). In its turn this was abandoned in February 1971, giving rise to Type **J87** which reads POSTAGE PAID. Type **J88** has POSTAGE R PAID between the wavy lines, the "R" signifying Rebate (bulk postings of circulars).

The children who each year send letters to Father Christmas have (if they include their address) received a reply in recent times through special arrangements made by the Post Office. Type **J89**, struck in red, is SANTALAND/POSTAGE PAID in a circular datestamp with a boxed slogan showing Father Christmas and MERRY CHRISTMAS. It was used in 1974 and 1975. In 1976 it was replaced by a similar stamp but with Santa in a sleigh.

Postal Administration "Paid" Marking

Since 1969 the Jersey Postal Administration has been using a 31mm single-circle handstamp reading POSTAL ADMINISTRATION/JERSEY CHANNEL ISLANDS (Type **J90**). Across the centre is POSTAGE/date/PAID.

Meter Stamp

Various official and private organisations use meter postage in Jersey but their numerous markings are outside the scope of this Catalogue.

During the German Occupation the Head Post Office at St. Helier commandeered Neopost No. 8 from the Airport and it was used from time to time in lieu of adhesives. The machine is known to have franked covers in the denominations of ½d., 1d., 1½d. and 2½d. It was operated by the P.O. clerks on prepayment of cash by the public.

During its first use as a ½d. stamp the die appears with a vertical crack down the centre, but this seems to have been repaired later.

Philatelic Bureau Cancellations

Jersey has a Philatelic Bureau (address P.O. Box 304, St. Helier) offering many services to collectors.

For its own mail the Bureau uses Type **J90** or Type **J91**. This latter is inscribed PHILATELIC BUREAU with the lettering in various sizes.

A similar type (**J92**), containing the words PHILATELIC SERVICE, has been in use since 1 January 1970 but this is solely for the cancelling-to-order of loose adhesives.

The various "First Day of Issue" markings are dealt with in Section 15.

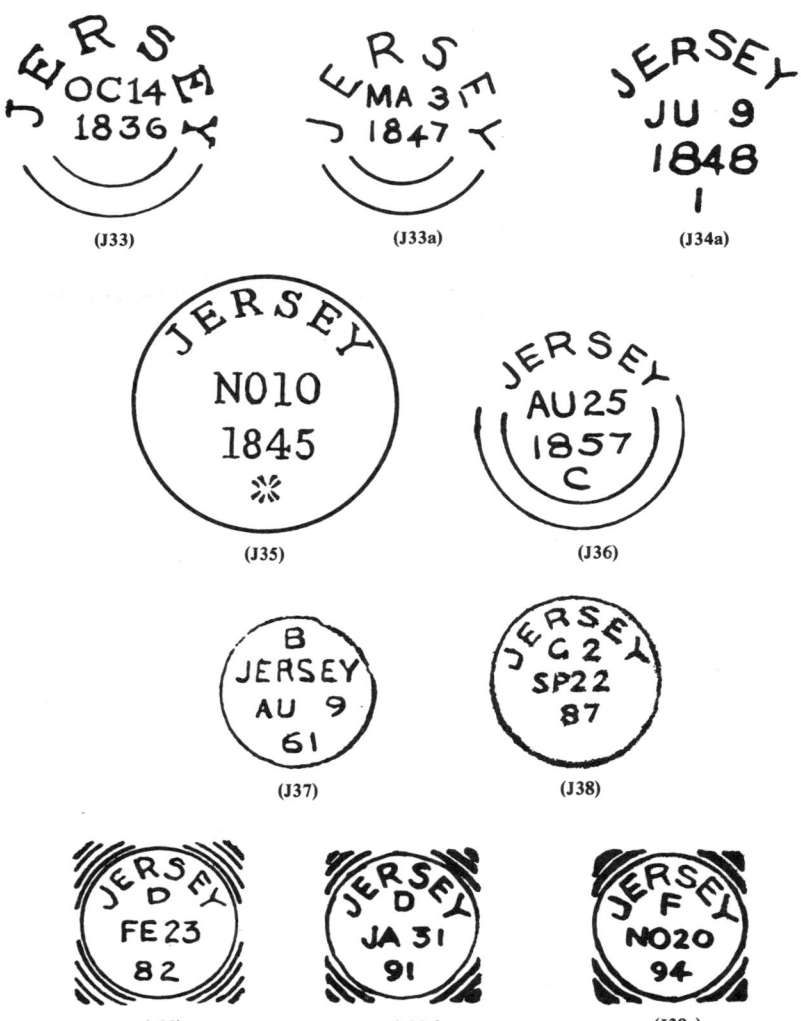

(J33)   (J33a)   (J34a)

(J35)   (J36)

(J37)   (J38)

(J39)   (J39a)   (J39c)

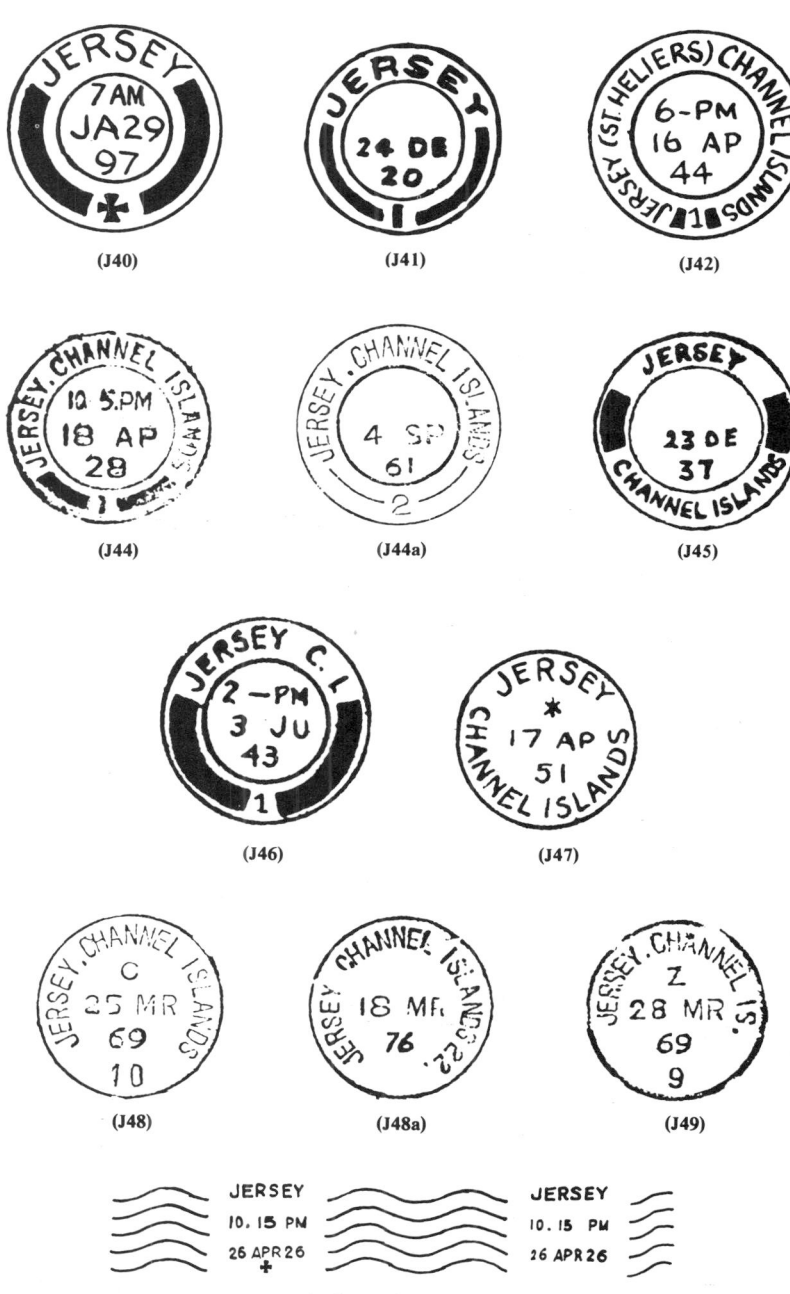

(J40)

(J41)

(J42)

(J44)

(J44a)

(J45)

(J46)

(J47)

(J48)

(J48a)

(J49)

(J50) *Reduced by half*

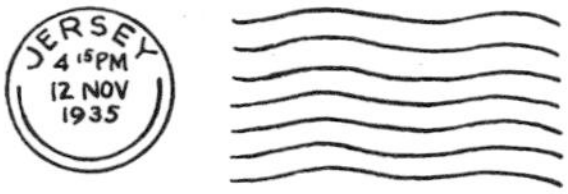

(J51b)

Reduced by half

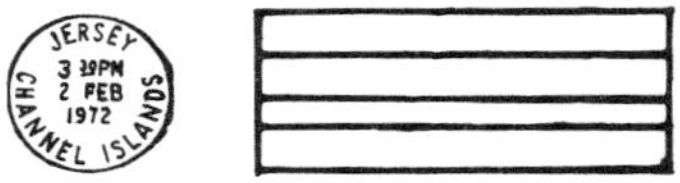

(J54)

(J55)

(J56)

(J57)

(J58a)

(J59)

(J60)

(J61)

(J62)

(J63)

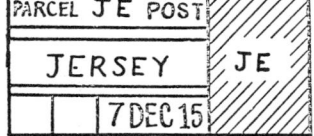

(J64)

Reduced by half

(J66)

PARCEL POST	1

JERSEY
(ST. HELIERS)
CHANNEL ISLANDS

(J67)
J67 reduced by half

PARCEL POST
JERSEY
26 MAR .75
CHANNEL ISLANDS

(J68)

F
JERSEY
(ST HELIERS)

(J70)

JERSEY
CHANNEL ISLANDS

(J71)

JERSEY

(J73)

JERSEY
1
27   DEC
CHANNEL ISLANDS

(J74)

JERSEY
12 JLY 60
10.45 AM
CHANNEL ISLANDS

(J75)

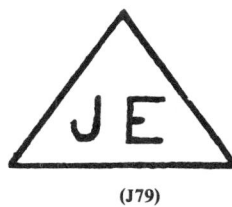
JERSEY
9 DEC 74
CHANNEL ISLANDS

(J76)

409

(J77)

409

(J78)

J E

(J79)

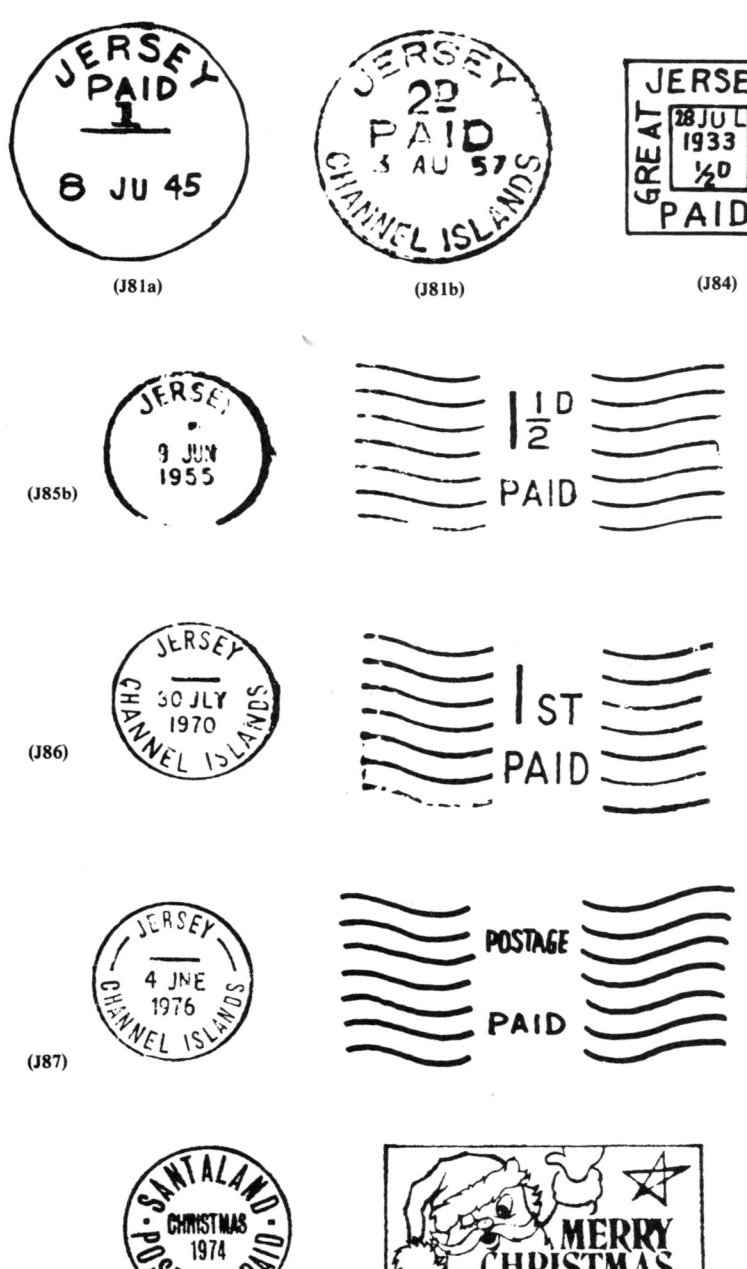

(J81a)

(J81b)

(J84)

(J85b)

(J86)

(J87)

(J89)

(J90)

(J91)

(J92)

Cat. No.	Type No.		Dates of use	Colour			Price on cover from
First Type							
JC47	**J33***		1830–43	Black	..	..	16·00
JC48			1843–45	Red ..	..	..	16·00
JC49	**J33a***	(recut, sans-serif)	1845–48	Red ..	..	..	16·00
JC50		(second recut)	1848–49	Red ..	..	..	16·00
	*On 1841 1d. red adhesive in black, dated 1841			*(off cover)*			£400
		in red, dated 1845		*(off cover)*			£750
Travelling Types							
JC51	**J34**	(with ornament)	1843	Black	..	..	£250
JC52	**J34a**	(no ornament)	1848	Red ..	..	..	£300
JC53	**J35**		1845	Red ..	..	..	£350
Double-arc Type							
JC54	**J36**		1849–58	Various	..	..	18·00
Early Single Circles							
JC55	**J37**	(name straight)	1858–90s	Black	..	..	1·00
JC56	**J38**	(name curved)	1870–1930s	Black	..	..	1·00
Squared Circles							
JC57	**J39**	(4 corner lines)	1881–84	Black	..	..	12·00
JC58	**J39a**	(3 corner lines)	1884–91	Black	..	..	9·00
JC59	**J39b**	("second circle")	1887–96	Black	..	..	6·00
JC60	**J39c**	(1 line, solid corner)	1892–1905	Black	..	..	6·00
Double Circles							
JC61	**J40**	(cross at foot)	1896–1929	Black	..	..	2·00
JC62	**J41**	(sans-serif 1)	1906–30	Black	..	..	1·00
JC63	**J42**	ST. HELIERS CHANNEL ISLANDS	1930–44	Black	..	..	1·00
JC64	**J43**	ST. HELIERS CH. IS.	1938–62	Black	..	..	50

Cat. No.	Type No.		Dates of use	Colour			Price on cover from
JC65	J44	JERSEY. CHANNEL ISLANDS/1	1928–34	Black	..	..	5·00
JC66		JERSEY. CHANNEL ISLANDS/3	1952–	Black	..	..	30
JC67	J44a	JERSEY. CHANNEL ISLANDS/1	1950s–	Black	..	..	30
JC68		JERSEY. CHANNEL ISLANDS/2	1950s–	Black	..	..	30
JC69		JERSEY. CHANNEL ISLANDS/4	1950s–	Black	..	..	30
JC70	J45	JERSEY. CHANNEL ISLANDS	1934–48	Black	..	..	2·00
JC71	J46	JERSEY C.I./1	1945–	Black	..	..	30
JC72		JERSEY C.I./2	1946–	Black	..	..	30

Modern Single Circles

JC73	J47		1935–	Black	..	..	30
JC74	J48	JERSEY CHANNEL ISLANDS, 1–16	1938–	Black	..	..	30
JC75	J48a	JERSEY CHANNEL ISLANDS, 21 or 22		Black	..	..	50
JC76	J49	JERSEY CHANNEL IS.		Black	..	..	50

Machine Cancellations

JC77	J50	JERSEY 18–19mm	1923–28	Black	..	..	3·00
JC78		(time omitted)	1923–28	Black	..	..	6·00
JC79	J50a	JERSEY 14–16mm	1928–30	Black	..	..	3·00
JC80	J51	(6 wavy lines)	1930–31	Black	..	..	1·00
JC81	J51a	(5 wavy lines)	1931–35	Black	..	..	80
JC82	J51b	(7 wavy lines)	1935–37	Black	..	..	50
JC83		(re-use)	1948–53	Black	..	..	35
JC84		(locally made figures)	1942–43	Black	..	..	1·00
JC85	J51c	(7 wavy lines segmented)	1937–40	Black	..	..	50
JC86		(re-use)	1946–48	Black	..	..	35
JC87		(locally made figures)	1943–46	Black	..	..	1·00
JC88	J52	(datestamp without arc)	1953–60	Black	..	..	15
JC89	J53	(larger letters)	1960–69	Black	..	..	15
JC90	J53a	(small letters)	1960s	Black	..	..	15
JC91	J54	(straight-lined box)	1969—	Black	..	..	10

Crown Registered Mark

JC92	J55		1855–59	Black	..	..	90·00
JC93	J56	(different crown)	1859–70	Red ..	..	..	70·00
JC94			1864	Black	..	..	60·00

Registration Cancellations

JC95	J57	JERSEY	1879–1936	Black	..	3·00
JC96	J58	JERSEY Channel Islands	1936	Black	..	1·50
JC97	J58a	JERSEY CHANNEL IS.	1939	Black or violet ..		1·00
JC98	J58b	(larger letters)	1947	Black or violet ..		1·00
JC99	J59	JERSEY CHANNEL ISLANDS 2	1954—	Black	..	1·00
JC100		JERSEY CHANNEL ISLANDS 3	1954—	Black	..	1·00
JC101		JERSEY CHANNEL ISLANDS 4	1954—	Black	..	1·00
JC102	J60	REGISTERED, no date	1939–46	Black	..	2·00

Money Order Office Cancellation

JC103	J61		1900–08	Black	..	20·00

Parcel Post Cancellations

JC104	J62	Barred oval 27mm	1886–1911	Black	..	20·00
JC105	J62a	(larger, 30mm)	1890	Black	..	30·00
JC106	J63	Double ring	1892–1916	Black or violet ..		4·00
JC107	J64	PARCEL JE POST/JERSEY	1915–17	Black	..	8·00
JC108	J64a	PARCEL JE POST/JERSEY/1	1917	Black	..	8·00
JC109	J65	JERSEY/date/CHANNEL ISLAND	1930s—	Black	..	2·00
JC110	J65a	(ISLANDS plural)	1960	Black	..	2·00

Cat. No.	Type No.		Dates of use	Colour			Price on cover from
JC111	**J66**	JERSEY/CHANNEL ISLANDS/1	1930s—	Black	..	..	2·00
JC112		JERSEY/CHANNEL ISLANDS/2	1930s—	Black	..	..	2·00
JC113		JERSEY/CHANNEL ISLANDS/3	1956—	Black	..	..	1·00
JC114	**J67**	JERSEY/(ST. HELIERS)	1950s	Violet	..	..	5·00
JC115	**J68**	Single circle	1970—	Black	..	..	30

Cancellations for Small Packets

JC116	**J69**	F/JERSEY	1893	Black	..	..	20·00
JC117	**J70**	F/JERSEY/(ST. HELIERS) 30mm	1898–1909	Black	..	..	20·00
JC118	**J70a**	(larger, 42mm)	1951	Black	..	..	8·00
JC119	**J71**	JERSEY/bars/CHANNEL ISLANDS					
			1952	Black	..	..	5·00
JC120	**J72**	Rectangular cancel	1938	Black	..	..	8·00
JC121	**J73**	Roller cancel	1957	Black	..	..	15·00
JC122	**J74**	JERSEY 1/CHANNEL ISLANDS	1938–52	Black or violet	..		50
JC123		JERSEY 2/CHANNEL ISLANDS	1938–52	Black or violet	..		50
JC124	**J74a**	JERSEY 1/CH. IS.		Black	..	..	50
JC125	**J75**	JERSEY/CHANNEL ISLANDS	1960s	Black	..	..	50
JC126	**J76**	Date between lines	1969—	Black	..	..	50

Triangles

JC127	**J77**	409 in small triangle	1909—	Black	..	..	15·00
JC128	**J77a**	(with wavy lines)	1934—	Black	..	..	3·00
JC129	**J78**	409 in larger triangle	1930s	Black	..	..	1·00
JC130	**J78a**	(with wavy lines)	1952—	Black	..	..	3·00
JC131	**J79**	JE in triangle	1939—	Black	..	..	1·00

"Paid" Handstamps

JC132	**J80**	½d., without					
		CHANNEL ISLANDS	1919—	Red	..	..	12·00
JC133	**J81***	Various values with					
		CHANNEL ISLANDS, 29mm	1919—	Red	..	..	1·00
JC134	**J81a**	½d. modified as 1d.	1945	Red	..	..	20·00
JC135	**J81b**	As Type **J81**, but 32mm	1956—		..	..	1·00
		*Used in lieu of adhesives					
		(1d., 2½d., 3d., 5d.)	1941–45		..	..	15·00

Machine "Paid" Markings

JC136	**J82**	JERSEY/PAID ½d./date	1926–29	Red	..	..	4·00
JC137	**J83**	GREAT BRITAIN added	1929	Red	..	..	4·00
JC138	**J84**	½d. boxed type	1932	Red	..	..	5·00
JC139	**J85***	(Value)/PAID between wavy lines	1937–68	Red	..	..	50
JC140		as above	1958	Black	..	..	1·00
JC141	**J85a**	GT. BRITAIN removed; with arc	1951	Red	..	..	50
JC142	**J85b**	New c.d.s., no arc	1955	Red	..	..	50
JC143	**J86**	1st PAID between wavy lines	1968–71	Red	..	..	20
JC144		2nd PAID between wavy lines	1968–71	Red	..	..	20
JC145	**J87**	POSTAGE PAID between wavy lines	1971—	Red	..	..	20
JC146	**J88**	POSTAGE R PAID between wavy lines	1972—	Red	..	..	50
JC147	**J89**	SANTALAND/POSTAGE PAID	1974–75	Red	..	..	3·00
JC148		(Santa in sleigh)	1976—				2·00
		*1D/PAID used in lieu of adhesive	1942–45		..	..	10·00

Cat. No.	Type No.		Dates of use	Colour			Price on cover from
Postal Administration "Paid" Marking							
JC149	**J90**		1969—	Black	..	..	10
Meter Stamp Neopost No. 8							
—		Used in lieu of adhesives (½d., 1d., 1½d., 2½d.),	1941–45		..	..	.. 10·00
Philatelic Bureau Cancellations							
JC150	**J91**	PHILATELIC BUREAU	1970—	Black	..	..	30
	(**J92**	PHILATELIC SERVICE: c.t.o. on adhesives only)					
		"First Day of Issue": *see* Section 15.					
		Prices for Nos. JC 104–126 refer to markings *on piece*.					

GUERNSEY

Guernsey datestamps show many similarities to the Jersey types and can be considered under the same headings.

First Type

The first Guernsey datestamp (Type **G20**) is recorded in the P.O. Proof Books as having been dispatched on 31 May 1830 and it was in use in June. It was recut, a new stamp (Type **G20a**) being dispatched on 29 July 1843: the letter N appears to have been repaired and a new set of figures supplied with the 4's sans-serif. The Postmaster faced a problem in 1844 with this datestamp, through shortage of numerals. When a 4 occurred in the day of the month he had to substitute an inverted 7 for the first 4 of 1844 (Type **G20b**).

Travelling Types

While the datestamp Type **G20** was away for its recut in 1843 a "skeleton" or "travelling" type was evidently put into use, since a strike is recorded on 28 July 1843 (Type **G21**).

In 1847 Type **G20a** finally gave out. For a period from the end of July until mid-August another "travelling" type saw service (Type **G22**). Dates between 29 July and 13 August 1847 have been recorded.

Double-arc Type

On 15 August 1847 the G.P.O. dispatched a double-arc datestamp (Type **G23**) lettered A, B or C. It appears to have been in use till 1853, although a replacement was supplied on 27 December 1851 (Type **G23a**). In turn a new datestamp (Type **G23b**) was sent on 14 October 1853.

Type **G23** had arcs less than 3mm apart. The other types (arcs 3mm apart) are distinguished from the position of the letters G and Y of GUERNSEY in relation to a line drawn across the bottom of the date (month and day). In Type **G23a**,

G–Y falls below the base of the date; in Type **G23b** G–Y stands above the base of the date.

Numerous colours are found in strikes of this stamp. It started with black in 1847, changed to blue in 1849, then to various shades of yellow from January 1853, reverted to black via a rust colour in 1854, went to a dirty green in 1856, and ended in blue-black in 1858.

Early Single Circles

A small circular datestamp 19mm in diameter (Type **G24**) was introduced in 1858. An example is recorded in the Proof Books as having been dispatched on 29 January 1858. It was used as a backstamp on letters arriving in the island and is found lettered A, B or C. Three slightly different types were used between 1858 and 1872. The letters signify time of arrival—morning, afternoon or evening.

Other single-circle datestamps (Type **G25**) ranging from 19 to 25mm in diameter with the name GUERNSEY in small or large letters round the top and the date in two lines across the centre were used between 1870 and the 1930s. They are known with the following letters above the date: A, B, C, D and P; also with an asterisk or without any letters at all. From 1889 the letters were replaced by the actual time of the collection.

Squared Circles

The "combined obliterator", often termed the "squared circle" by collectors, was introduced in 1887 (Type **G26**). It started with four lines outside the circle and was lettered A, B, C or D. In 1896 the letters were replaced by the time of posting. In 1902 a slightly smaller type (**G26a**) was taken into use, having only three corner lines, and this continued until 1905.

Double Circles

A double-circle datestamp (Type **G27**) with solid bars separated by a cross was put into service in 1905 (earliest date recorded 24 March). There are several sub-types with different sizes of letters and cross, and with bars of different thickness. Type **G27** remained in use up to 1929. Up to 1914 all Guernsey datestamps had the month preceding the day but from then onwards the day precedes the month.

In 1929 a double-circle datestamp worded GUERNSEY (ST. PETER PORT)/CHANNEL IS. was introduced (Type **G28**), the earliest recorded date of use being 20 December. It was replaced in 1937 by a similar type in which CHANNEL IS. has been abbreviated to CH. IS. (Type **G28a**) and this remained in use until 30 September 1969 along with one having CHAN. IS. at the bottom (Type **G28b**).

A variant was introduced in 1963 (Type **G29**), still worded GUERNSEY (ST. PETER PORT) but containing thin bars in the lower arcs and containing a numeral.

Other double-circle datestamps seen (Type **G30**) are GUERNSEY C.I./1 and GUERNSEY C.I./2 with black bars each side of the numeral, which is at the foot. They are believed to date from 1945 for use in case the cancelling machine broke down.

Modern Single Circles

The late 1930s saw the introduction of new single-circle cancellations and they remained in use until 30 September 1969. They were 23–24mm in diameter and had GUERNSEY at the top and CHANNEL ISLANDS at the bottom (Type **G31**). An asterisk appears above the date. A variety occurs in 1941 with a stop between CHANNEL and ISLANDS.

In 1948 numbers from 5 to 11 are found inserted in place of the asterisk and such cancellers were for use at the counter on registered mail and postal orders. In August 1954 the numbers were replaced by letters running from E to M (except I).

In contrast to Type **G31** there is a single-circle cancellation, Type **G32**, in which the words GUERNSEY CHANNEL ISLANDS read right round the circumference. This is also known with figure 1 at the foot (Type **G33**).

A rare type (**G34**), used for short periods in 1945 and 1946 as a cancelling stamp, has GUERNSEY CH. IS. at the top and PARCEL DEPOT at the bottom. It was probably meant for internal use on dockets.

From 1952, and mainly for such rush times as Christmas, a canceller numbered 12 and reading GUERNSEY (ST. PETER PORT) CHAN. IS. has seen service (Type **G35**).

When the Bailiwick of Guernsey became postally independent on 1 October 1969 there was a complete revision of all datestamps then in use.

The Head Office counter received the single-circle Type **G36**, diameter 26½mm, the individual cancellers being lettered E to N (less I) to which one lettered P was later added. The Sorting Office was issued with the same style of datestamp; this shows no identifying letter, or the time above the date, or an asterisk in place of the time.

Very similar cancellers, which show an island or town name at the foot, are from sub-offices and these are listed in Section 14.

At its opening on 2 June 1971 the Postal Museum was provided with a special single-circle datestamp and this is still in use (Type **G37**). It features the Guernsey scroll marking of pre-adhesive days (*see* Section 3).

Machine Cancellations

A Krag machine was introduced in Guernsey in June 1923, giving a cancellation of five wavy lines in conjunction with square datestamps reading GUERNSEY and (below) the date in one line. This Type **G38** is a continuous impression of datestamps and lines.

A Universal machine replaced it in December 1931 (Type **G39**) and this consisted of a circular datestamp flanked by five wavy lines.

In 1936 Type **G39a** was put into use, the wavy lines increased to seven in number and now broken in two places such that the centre portion was removable. This type saw service until 1938.

In 1937 another type (**G39b**) was introduced in which the seven wavy lines were continuous and this remained in service throughout the German Occupation. In 1941 the figure 0 was split to make the final 1 of the year; in 1942, 1943, 1944 and 1945 the last two figures of the date were made locally.

In May 1945 the machine was refitted with a new datestamp lacking the lower arc below GUERNSEY and having seven wavy lines in the segmented style (Type **G40**). However, in mid-1947 the wavy lines were changed to the continuous form (Type **G40a**).

A new datestamp came into use in May 1948 (Type **G41**). This had tall thin letters occupying half the circle and the other half filled with an arc; it developed a crack in November. The seven wavy lines were segmented. From February 1949 until January 1955 the old datestamp first used for Type **G39a** in 1936 was pressed into service again.

A completely new datestamp (Type **G42**) took its place in January 1955 and it was in turn replaced in 1959 (Type **G42a**) and again in 1960 (Type **G43**). The seven segmented wavy lines were still employed. The time is sometimes replaced by a line.

Postal independence in 1969 saw the wording of the datestamp altered to GUERNSEY POST OFFICE with an arc at the foot. This single circle of 22mm diameter (Type **G44**) has the time and date in three lines (the time sometimes replaced by a line) and the seven segmented wavy lines continue as before. As from 1972 the wavy lines have given way to two parallel thin bars 50mm long and 8mm apart (Type **G45**).

Slogans

The wavy lines of the machine cancellations have been replaced from time to time by slogans. The first was the EP and "lover's knot" used extensively in the British Isles to celebrate the Wedding of (the then) Princess Elizabeth in 1947. A priced list for that slogan and subsequent ones is given in Section 15.

Crown Registered Mark

A mark showing a crown above the word REGISTERED is known used in Guernsey in 1852 and is struck in blue (Type **G46**). It is rare.

Registration Cancellations

A marking on cover recorded in 1900 is a large R in an oval with FEE PAID below (Type **G47**).

Oval registration cancellations are known from 1938 measuring about 40 × 25mm and reading REGISTERED/GUERNSEY with date in one line across the centre (Type **G48**). A slightly wider stamp, 40 × 28mm, occurs struck on the back of a cover dated 1940 (Type **G48a**).

During the Occupation a rubber stamp was made locally (Type **G49**), a 30 × 19mm box inscribed GUERNSEY struck in violet. In the centre the registration number is added by numbering machine in red.

An undated marking (Type **G50**) was put into use in 1945. It measures 38 × 25mm and reads GUERNSEY at the top and CHANNEL ISLANDS at the bottom. The word REGISTERED occurs across the centre between parallel lines and the whole stamp is in the shape of a flattened oval.

A new oval registered datestamp was introduced in 1948 (Type **G51**) and reads REGISTERED/date/GUERNSEY CH. IS. It measures 38 × 28mm.

The coming of postal independence led to another design of oval handstamp, namely Type **G52**. This is inscribed "Guernsey Post Office/Registered" in upper and lowercase letters and is for use in the Sorting Office. Type **G53**, in which the words are transposed, so that "Registered" is at the top, is the handstamp employed at the Head Office counter.

Money Order Office Cancellation

A datestamp of the Money Order Office, reading GUERNSEY at the top and M.O.O. at the bottom, is known cancelling stamps at various dates between 1886 and 1913 (Type **G54**).

Parcel Post Cancellations

The first parcel post cancellation (Type **G55**), issued in 1886, is a single circle inscribed GUERNSEY in the centre and the circle filled with three lines above and three below. In the autumn of 1889 the more familiar double-ring rubber cancel (Type **G56**) superseded it, again inscribed simply GUERNSEY. Between 1889 and 1905 seventeen cancellers in this design were supplied. It remained in use until 1915 when replaced by the large "label" design. It has been recorded used on postage stamps, though this was obviously not its proper function.

Of the seventeen cancellers of Type **G56** one had serifed letters and all the others were sans-serif. Variations in the sizes of the letters and the disposition of the inner arc can be distinguished.

About 1910 Type **G57** is recorded, in which the wording within the double ring is now GUERNSEY/ST. PETER PORT in two lines.

Types **G56** and **G57** remained in concurrent use until the introduction of the first of the large "label" types in 1915. This was Type **G58**, the right-hand third of which shows the letters GU in a background of diagonal lines. The remaining space is divided horizontally in three and worded PARCEL GU POST/GUERNSEY/date. In 1925 the wording was altered to give Type **G59**. In this, GU in the right-hand third now reads PARCEL POST while the left-hand space is filled with GUERNSEY/CHANNEL ISLANDS in two lines in the upper part and the date below.

Further label types are known after the Second World War, but as mentioned above under "Modern Single Circles" an internal marking saw a rare usage in 1945–46 cancelling *letters*. This is the GUERNSEY CH. IS./PARCEL DEPOT c.d.s. (Type **G34**).

Dating from 1948 is Type **G60**, a label cancellation copiously worded and elaborately subdivided. The right-hand third is in three parts, the bottom one being shaded, the middle reading PARCEL POST and the top either blank or (Type **G60a**) containing a numeral. The left-hand space has GUERNSEY/(ST. PETER PORT)/CHAN. IS. (SMITH STREET) filling the upper two-thirds with the lower third consisting of more shading and a box for the date.

A somewhat smaller and less elaborate rectangular cancel came into use in the 1950s (Type **G61**). The main area is filled with GUERNSEY/CHANNEL ISLANDS, but above this is a narrow box enclosing PARCEL POST and a numeral.

The large-label design came back into use in 1956 and persisted until the newly independent Guernsey Post Office reorganised all cancellations in 1969–70. The layout of the "label" has again been altered with Type **G62**. In three of the corners (top and bottom left and bottom right) are diagonal lines of shading. At the left and right are panels with PARCEL reading upwards at the left and POST reading upwards at the right. The centre is divided into three panels, the middle one showing the date. The top and bottom panels have the variant wordings which distinguish the cancellers.

Type **G62**, issued in 1956, read SMITH STREET (above) and GUERNSEY/(ST. PETER PORT) CHAN. IS. (below). It was soon withdrawn, perhaps because the emphasis on SMITH STREET was a mistake. Early in 1957 the words are redistributed (Type **G62a**) and now read: GUERNSEY (above) and (ST. PETER PORT)/CHAN. IS. (SMITH ST.) (below).

Another revision took place in 1961, the final wording becoming ST. PETER PORT (above) and GUERNSEY/CHANNEL ISLANDS (below). This is Type **G63**.

Wholly new cancellations were put into use in Guernsey in 1970 for the parcel post. The box-type marking (Type **G64**) reads GUERNSEY POST OFFICE/PARCEL POST above the date and HEAD OFFICE below. It was introduced on 20 July 1970. The similar stamps supplied to Guernsey sub-offices are dealt with in Sections 13 and 14.

Cancellations for Small Packets

Various rubber stamps have seen service in cancelling small packets and they tend to be short-lived. The following are noted from 1938.

Type **G65** is a circular stamp, diameter 30mm. It reads GUERNSEY at the top and CHANNEL ISLANDS at the bottom with the date (and sometimes the time) across the centre.

Type **G66** is a similar circle but the wording is GUERNSEY ST. PETER PORT round the top and CHANNEL IS. round the bottom.

Type **G67** is a rectangle measuring 50 × 20mm with GUERNSEY/date/CHANNEL ISLANDS in three lines.

A marking from 1952 is a single circle worded GUERNSEY/CHANNEL ISLANDS in two lines across the centre (Type **G68**).

A roller cancel (Type **G69**) was introduced in 1957, reading GUERNSEY/(ST. PETER PORT)/CHAN. ISLES (SMITH ST.) between double lines and repeated endlessly.

A new rubber handstamp for small packets was part of the complete revision of cancellations at the time of postal independence in 1969. This is Type **G70** in which "Guernsey Post Office" appears (in upper and lowercase) at the top, with a star between dashes at the foot. The date and time are shown in two lines in the centre. By 1972 this datestamp had been modified so that GUERNSEY POST OFFICE is now in capital letters (Type **G71**).

Triangles

The triangular cancellations are for use on bulk postings of circulars. Type **G72** is GU in a large triangle and began to be used in 1939. In 1940 Type **G73** was introduced, namely 324 in a smaller triangle. It replaced the datestamp in the cancelling machine and the centre section of the wavy lines was simultaneously replaced by PAID. This 324 in a triangle began to be used from 1952 with the wavy lines of the machine cancellation but omitting the inserted PAID (Type **G73a**).

"Paid" Handstamps

Two PAID handstamps were sent to Guernsey on 10 August 1920. One had a fixed ½d. (Type **G74**) and the other had movable values (Type **G75**). They were single circles with GUERNSEY around the top and CHANNEL ISLANDS around the bottom (this latter was absent on the fixed-value ½d. stamp). Below GUERNSEY appear in three lines the value, the word PAID and the date.

The PAID handstamps were struck in red. The ½d. saw use till 1940 when rising postal rates made it obsolete. During the Occupation the year figures were made locally and, as they did not fit well, sometimes printed poorly or did not show at all. The PAID handstamps were pressed into service if adhesives ran short, when letters prepaid in cash at Head Office were franked by this method. This is reported as having occurred in January, October and November 1943 and from April 1945.

In the 1950s a new type, 32mm diameter, reading GUERNSEY/GREAT BRITAIN with the value/PAID/date across the middle came into use (Type **G75a**). It also occurs without the date and value, thus simply reading PAID across the centre (Type **G75b**).

The independent Postal Administration introduced the single-circle Type **G76** in 1969, reading Guernsey Post Office/PAID/date and of 32mm diameter. A 30mm type (**G76a**) has GUERNSEY POST OFFICE in capitals.

Machine "Paid" Markings

A new die for use in the Krag cancelling maching (Type **G38**) was introduced in 1926. This is Type **G77** in which the words GUERNSEY/PAID ½D/date appear in three lines flanked by five wavy lines. In 1929 the words GREAT BRITAIN were added to the die in a line below GUERNSEY (Type **G78**).

A different die was fitted in 1932, to give Type **G79**. In this boxed type there was an inner square containing ½D with the date in two lines below. The outer square read GUERNSEY/PAID (top and bottom) and GREAT/BRITAIN (left and right, both reading upwards).

The Universal machine came into use in 1936 with segmented wavy lines, seven in number. The centre part could be fitted with the PAID indication (Type **G80**) as, for example, ½D/PAID. The circular datestamp read GUERNSEY/GT. BRITAIN with the date in two lines across the centre. A similar cancel used from 1945 omitted the GREAT BRITAIN and so was inscribed simply GUERNSEY (Type **G80a**).

During the German Occupation the machine PAID marking was used in a similar way to the PAID handstamps to denote prepayment of postage in cash at various times of shortage of adhesives from 1942 to 1945.

When two-tier postage was instituted in 1968 value figures were taken out and dies reading 1st PAID and 2nd PAID used instead (Type **G81**).

With postal independence in 1969 the datestamp was modified to read GUERNSEY POST OFFICE (Type **G82**). Then with decimalisation on 15 February 1971 the two-tier system was abandoned and in consequence the 1st PAID and 2nd PAID became simply PAID (Type **G83**).

Philatelic Bureau Cancellations

In June 1971 a new States Philatelic Bureau with adjacent offices was opened in St. Peter Port next to the Head Post Office. It gives many services to collectors and may be contacted at: States Philatelic Bureau, Head Post Office, Guernsey.

For its own mail the Bureau uses a single-circle handstamp (Type **G84**) which reads (upper and lowercase) "Guernsey Post Office/Philatelic Bureau" around the circumference and the date (in capitals) in one line across the centre. There are two cancellers diameter 26½mm; they differ in the size of the words "Philatelic Bureau" but each has an asterisk above the date. A third 26½mm canceller is without the asterisk. Its fourth canceller is slightly larger (27½mm diameter) and has the asterisk. This rubber handstamp (Type **G84a**) is used only on registered mail.

In September 1978 the Guernsey Post Office Board announced that it would supply, when requested, stamps cancelled to order ("that is, stamps cancelled without being affixed to envelopes so that the gum is retained"). The cancellation is Type **G85**, also reading GUERNSEY POST OFFICE/PHILATELIC BUREAU.

"First Day of Issue" markings are dealt with in Section 15.

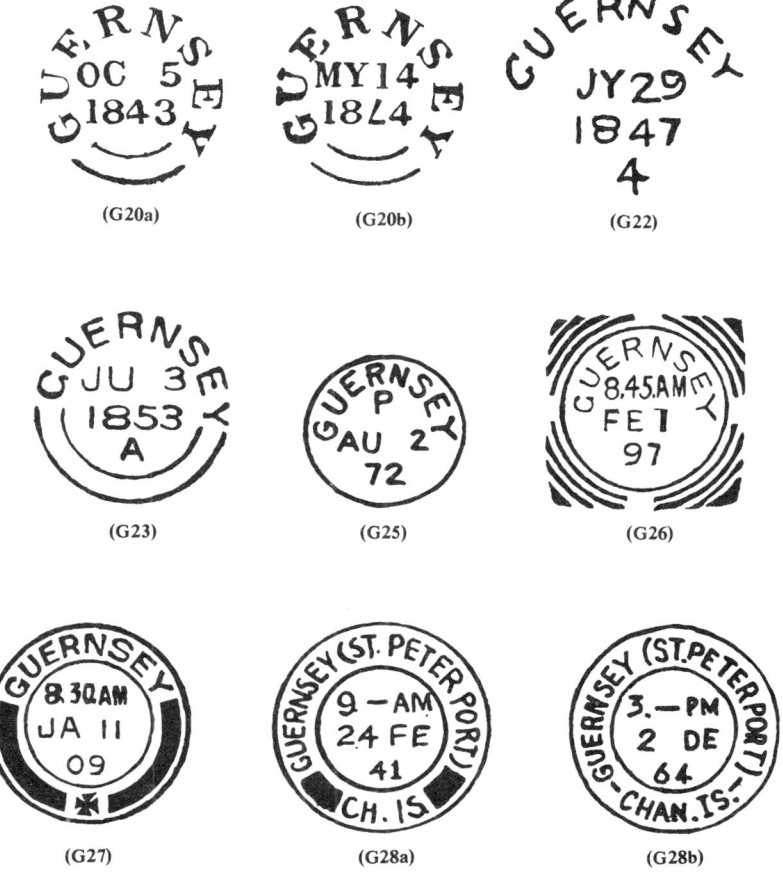

(G20a)   (G20b)   (G22)

(G23)   (G25)   (G26)

(G27)   (G28a)   (G28b)

(G31)

(G32)

(G34)

(G36) No. GC60

(G37)

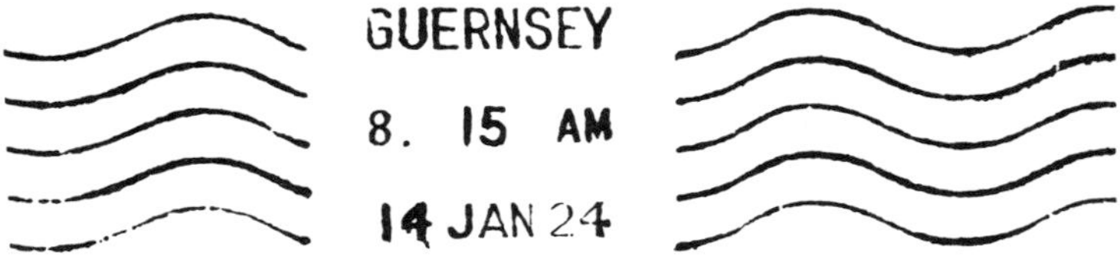

GUERNSEY

8 . 15 AM

14 JAN 24

(G38)

(G39b) c.d.s.

(G40) c.d.s.

(G41) c.d.s.

(G42a) c.d.s

(G43) c.d.s.

(G44-45) c.d.s.

GUERNSEY
R1162

(G49)

(G51)

(G52)

(G55)

(G56)

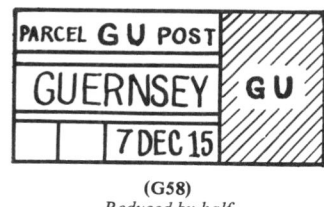

(G58)
Reduced by half

(G60) *Reduced by half*

(G62) *Reduced by half*

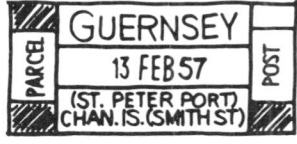

(G62a) *Reduced by half*

GUERNSEY POST OFFICE
PARCEL POST

2 SEP 1975

HEAD OFFICE

(G64)

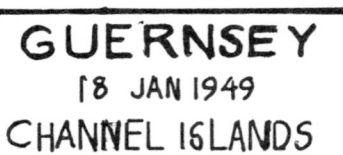

(G67)

(G70)

(G72)

(G73a) Die

(G75a)

(G76)

(G77)

(G79) Die

(G80a)

(G82)

Cat. No.	Type No.		Dates of use	Colour			Price on cover from
First Type							
GC29	G20		1830–47	Black	..	..	25·00
GC30	G20a	(recut)	1843–47	Black	..	..	30·00
GC31	G20b	(inverted 7 in year)	1844	Black	..	..	45·00
Travelling Types							
GC32	G21		1843				£375
GC33	G22		1847	Black	..	..	£275
Double-arc Type							
GC34	G23		1847–53	Black or blue		..	18·00
GC35	G23a		1852–58	Various	..	..	18·00
GC36	G23b		1853–58	Various	..	..	18·00
Early Single Circles							
GC37	G24	(19mm diameter)	1858–72	Black	..	..	10·00
GC38	G25	(19–25mm diameter)	1870–1914	Black	..	..	4·00
GC39		(25mm diameter)	1915–30s	Black	..	..	2·00
Squared Circles							
GC40	G26	(four lines)	1887–1902	Black	..	..	8·00
GC41	G26a	(three lines)	1902–05	Black	..	..	8·00
Double Circles							
GC42	G27	(cross at foot)	1905–29	Black	..	..	1·00
GC43	G28	ST. PETER PORT/CHANNEL IS.	1929–37	Black	..	..	1·00
GC44	G28a	ST. PETER PORT/CH. IS.	1937–69	Black	..	..	1·00
GC45	G28b	ST. PETER PORT/CHAN. IS.	1960s	Black	..	..	1·00
GC46	G29	(thin bars)	1963–69	Black	..	..	1·00
GC47	G30	GUERNSEY C.I./1	1945–63	Black	..	..	1·00
GC48		GUERNSEY C.I./2	1945–63	Black	..	..	1·00
Modern Single Circles							
GC49	G31	GUERNSEY/CHANNEL ISLANDS	1930s–69	Black	..	..	1·00
GC50		same, numbered 5–11	1948–54	Black	..	..	1·50
GC51		same, lettered E–M	1954–69	Black	..	..	1·50
GC52		locally made year figures	1942–45	Black	..	..	2·00
GC53	G32	GUERNSEY CHANNEL ISLANDS	1930s–69	Black	..	..	1·00
GC54	G33	GUERNSEY CHANNEL ISLANDS/1					
			1930s–69	Black	..	..	1·50
GC55	G34	PARCEL DEPOT	1945–46	Black	..	..	15·00
GC56	G35	GUERNSEY (ST. PETER PORT)	1952–69	Black	..	..	2·00
GC57	G36	Guernsey Post Office, E–P	1969—	Black	..	..	30
GC58		same, no letter	1969—	Black	..	..	30
GC59		same, with time	1969—	Black	..	..	30
GC60		same, with asterisk	1969—	Black	..	..	30
GC61	G37	POSTAL MUSEUM	1971—	Black	..	..	20
Machine Cancellations							
GC62	G38	Square datestamp	1923–31	Black	..	..	3·00
GC63	G39	(5 wavy lines and c.d.s.)	1931–36	Black	..	..	50
GC64	G39a	(7 wavy lines segmented)	1936–38	Black	..	..	30
GC65		(datestamp re-used)	1949–55	Black	..	..	30
GC66	G39b	(7 wavy lines continuous)	1937–45	Black	..	..	30
GC67		(split 0 for 1)	1941	Black	..	..	1·00
GC68		(locally made figures)	1942–45	Black	..	..	1·00
GC69	G40	(c.d.s. no arc, segmented lines)	1945–47	Black	..	..	50
GC70	G40a	(c.d.s. no arc, continuous lines)	1947–48	Black	..	..	1·00
GC71	G41	(c.d.s. tall letters, seg. lines)	1948–49	Black	..	..	1·00
GC72	G42	(c.d.s. short arc, seg. lines)	1955–60	Black	..	..	50

Cat. No.	Type No.		Dates of use	Colour	Price on cover from
GC73	G42a	(c.d.s. small letters, arc exceeds semicircle)	1959	Black	50
GC74	G43	(c.d.s. shorter arc, seg. lines)	1960–69	Black	30
GC75	G44	GUERNSEY POST OFFICE	1969–72	Black	50
GC76	G45	(two parallel bars)	1972—	Black	20

Crown Registered Mark

GC77	G46		1852	Blue	£125

Registration Cancellations

GC78	G47	R in oval/FEE PAID	1900	Black	20·00
GC79	G48	Oval REGISTERED/GUERNSEY	1938	Black	2·00
GC80	G48a	(wider oval)	1940	Black	2·00
GC81	G49	Local rubber stamp	1944	Violet with red ..	5·00
GC82	G50	REGISTERED between lines	1945	Black	2·00
GC83	G51	Oval REGISTERED/GUERNSEY CH. IS.	1948–69	Violet	2·00
GC84	G52	Guernsey Post Office/ Registered	1969	Black	3·00
GC85	G53	Registered/Guernsey Post Office	1970	Black	2·00

Money Order Office Cancellation

GC86	G54		1886–1913	Black	25·00

Parcel Post Cancellations

GC87	G55		1886–89	Black ..	25·00
GC88	G56	GUERNSEY sans-serif	1889–1915	Black or red ..	3·00
GC89		GUERNSEY serifed	1890	Black	10·00
GC90	G57	GUERNSEY/ST. PETER PORT	1910–15	Black	7·00
GC91	G58	PARCEL GU POST/GUERNSEY	1915–25	Black	15·00
GC92	G59	GUERNSEY/CHANNEL ISLANDS	1925	Black	5·00
GC93	G60	GUERNSEY/(ST. PETER PORT)	1948	Black	2·00
GC94	G60a	(with numeral)			3·00
GC95	G61	PARCEL POST/GUERNSEY	1950s	Violet	4·00
GC96	G62	SMITH STREET above	1956	Black	10·00
GC97	G62a	SMITH ST. below	1957–61	Black	2·00
GC98	G63	ST. PETER PORT	1961–69	Black	1·00
GC99	G64	GUERNSEY POST OFFICE	1970	Black or violet ..	30

Cancellations for Small Packets

GC100	G65	GUERNSEY/CHANNEL ISLANDS c.d.s.	1938–52	Black or violet ..	50
GC101	G66	GUERNSEY ST. PETER PORT	1938–52	Black or violet ..	1·00
GC102	G67	Rectangular cancel	1938–52	Black or violet ..	1·00
GC103	G68	GUERNSEY/CHANNEL ISLANDS s.c.	1952	Black or violet ..	2·50
GC104	G69	Roller cancel	1957	Black	15·00
GC105	G70	Guernsey Post Office c.d.s.	1969	Black	30
GC106	G71	GUERNSEY POST OFFICE c.d.s.	1972	Black	30

Triangles

GC107	G72	GU in triangle	1939–69	Black	5·00
GC108	G73	324, wavy lines and PAID	1940	Red	5·00
GC109	G73a	324 and wavy lines	1952–69	Black	2·00

"Paid" Handstamps

GC110	G74	½d. without CHANNEL ISLANDS	1920–40	Red	3·00
GC111	G75*	With CHANNEL ISLANDS, various values	1920–69	Red	3·00

Cat. No.	Type No.		Dates of use	Colour	Price on cover from
GC112	**G75a**	GUERNSEY/GREAT BRITAIN, various values	1950s	Red	1·00
GC113	**G75b**	GUERNSEY/PAID/ GREAT BRITAIN	1950s	Red	1·00
GC114	**G76**	Guernsey Post Office	1969	Red	30
GC115	**G76a**	GUERNSEY POST OFFICE	1969—	Red	30
		*Used in lieu of adhesives (1d., 2½d.)	1943–45	.. .. ..	10·00

Machine "Paid" Markings

Cat. No.	Type No.		Dates of use	Colour	Price on cover from
GC116	**G77**	GUERNSEY/PAID ½D/date	1926–29	Red	8·00
GC117	**G78**	GREAT BRITAIN added	1929–32	Red	6·00
GC118	**G79**	½d. boxed type	1932–36	Red	5·00
GC119	**G80***	(Value)/PAID between wavy lines	1936–68	Red	1·00
GC120	**G80a**	GREAT BRITAIN omitted	1945–46	Red	1·00
GC121	**G81**	1st PAID between wavy lines	1968–69	Red	1·00
GC122		2nd PAID between wavy lines	1968–69	Red	1·00
GC123	**G82**	GUERNSEY POST OFFICE 1st PAID	1969–71	Red	50
GC124		GUERNSEY POST OFFICE 2nd PAID	1969–71	Red	50
GC125	**G83**	GUERNSEY POST OFFICE PAID	1971—	Red	20
GC126		(*error*) Used as canceller	1974	Black	2·00
		*Used in lieu of adhesives	1942–45	.. ..	10·00

Philatelic Bureau Cancellations

Cat. No.	Type No.		Dates of use	Colour	Price on cover from
GC127	**G84**	26¼mm c.d.s.	1971—	Black	30
GC128		26¼mm, larger wording	1971—	Black	30
GC129		26¼mm, no asterisk	1971—	Black	30
GC130	**G84a**	27¼mm, c.d.s.	1971—	Black	30
	(**G85**	PHILATELIC BUREAU: c.t.o. on adhesives)			

"First Day of Issue": *see* Section 15.

Prices for Nos. GC 87–106 refer to markings *on piece*.

10. Postage Due and Instructional Marks

Instructional marks may be separated into three groups:
(1) Marks which indicate that a certain amount of postage due is to be collected;
(2) Marks explaining the reason for a charge and which often include the amount due;
(3) Marks detailing some irregularity in transmission which does not involve an extra charge.

Instructional markings have been in use generally throughout the British Isles and so can only be allocated to a particular office where a cover bears other identifying features. Such general markings are not considered here.

As mentioned in Section 8, the replacement of the Maltese Cross cancellation in 1844 led to offices receiving an identifying number. In the course of this, Jersey was given 409 and Guernsey 324. These numerals will be found in some of the instructional marks.

Colours of Strikes. There was a procedure for the colour of ink to be used but it has by no means always been adhered to. The office of dispatch should normally impress on underpaid letters a mark in red indicating the charge to be collected and the reason for it. If an underpayment was first noticed at the office of arrival the mark should have been applied in black.

Jersey (409) usually did this correctly, but Guernsey (324) nearly always used black ink only.

Marks in the third group, where no charge is involved, were usually struck in violet or green, though black is very common, too.

Manuscript Marks. A number of early letters from Jersey and Guernsey have manuscript endorsements and the following are recorded:
1. "Missent to (Jersey datestamp of 1848)".
2. "Not found" in red on a Jersey letter of 1842.
3. "Not known" in red on a letter from the Isle of Wight to Guernsey in 1857.
4. "Now residing in London/Address not known" in red on a letter from Newark to Guernsey in 1841.
5. "Left for St. Malow from (Guernsey datestamp of 1855)".
6. "More to pay" and large figure 2 in black on letter from Guernsey to Jersey of 1856.

(*Prices of manuscript markings on entire*: simple charge marks, £10–£20; instructions—Not known, etc., £20–£40; instructions plus a datestamp, £80–£100.)

Weymouth Marking. One of the consequences of postal independence for Jersey and Guernsey is the action taken in the Islands to deal with mail continuing to be prepaid with withdrawn British stamps. This is outlined in the sub-sections following.

But the converse of this problem exists. Many people arriving back in Weymouth after a holiday in the Islands mistakenly affix Jersey or Guernsey stamps to letters posted on the mainland, where they have no validity. Weymouth Post Office (whose number is 873) have accordingly applied a postage due marking in black or green since 1972. This measures 60 × 25mm and the charge is completed in manuscript. It reads "Channel Island/stamps not/admissible when/posted on U.K./mainland".

(*Price on cover* £1.)

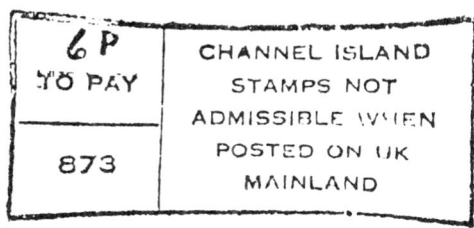

Postage due marking of Weymouth

JERSEY

Instructional marks specifically from Jersey are now considered, classified into the three groups mentioned. They are priced in the list at the end of this sub-section and the catalogue numbering system adopted is:

    (1) Postage due indicators . . . . *prefix* JD
    (2) Explanations for charges . . . . JE
    (3) Irregularities in transmission . . . . JT

(1) Postage Due

The earliest charge marks recorded in the G.P.O. Proof Books are for ½d. and 1d. of a type common to many provincial towns. The date was December 1880, but as they bore no identifying numbers they are excluded here.

A stamp specifically for Jersey was dispatched in February 1883 and though in use till 1900 it is rare on cover. This Type **1** has a large 2d. with 409 below, all enclosed in an oval frame.

Beginning in 1902 numbers of similar markings were introduced (Type **2**), showing a large figure of amount due together with the number 409, but now without a frame. The 1d. was the first (1902), followed by 2d. and 3d. sent in 1914, and the 4d. and 5d. in 1921. The 2d. is known in 1914 with a ½ added by a separate handstamp, so making a 2½d. rate. It is on a postcard to France. The 1d. has been seen lacking the 409; it is on a postcard from France to Guernsey via Jersey dated May 1904.

A new type of charge marking incorporating the words "To Pay" was inaugurated in 1918 (Type **3**). This read "1d./To Pay/409" and it was followed by 4d. in 1921, 1¼d. in 1922, and 2½d. and 3½d. in 1957.

A "To Pay" marking of quite different style (Type **4**) is the boxed 1p introduced in 1972 and now omitting the numeral 409.

Postage Due on Foreign Mail. A large letter T (for Taxe) has been used internationally in conjunction with the U.P.U. system of reckoning the amount due in centimes (5c. = ½d.). Around the turn of the century postcards and letters passing between Jersey and France may be found with a hexagonal marking (Type **5**) which showed a figure below the T and (beneath the frame) the letters JE for Jersey. The figures denoting centimes are 5 and 15 known from 1903; the 20, 30, 40 and 50 of this hexagonal type were sent on 28 September 1907. Some of the 5c. cards have in addition a 1d. charge marking (Type **2**) to show how much was to be collected in Jersey. The 1d. is computed from the U.P.U. rule which has been in operation since 1878, namely that a postage due charge equals twice the postage deficiency.

When the scheme for assessing postage due on underpaid mail was initially agreed by U.P.U. countries the currency standard adopted was a "franc" (= 100 centimes) of the Latin Monetary Union; this was replaced after the First World War by a "gold franc". But general monetary instability and constantly revised postage rates amongst member-countries made calculations connected with postage due increasingly complicated. A new and easier system was accordingly adopted from 1 January 1966 and revised in 1976.

Stated amounts in centimes have now been replaced by a fractional indicator. The originating country shows in its Taxe marking a fraction whose denominator is the basic foreign letter rate in its own currency. From 1966 to 1976 it put a figure in the numerator for twice the amount by which the letter was underpaid, again in national currency. The receiving administration then multiplied the resulting fraction by its own foreign rate and collected this amount from the addressee in its own money.

The first of these fractional markings (Type **6**) appears to have been used in Jersey from 1971. The denominator is 5 contained in a large box with T for Taxe. The figure below the fraction bar became 8 in 1974 and then 10 in 1977, reflecting changing rates.

The system in use since 1976 (and its associated marking) is explained at the end of the following sub-section.

(2) Explanations for Charges

Jersey has had numbers of markings whose wording makes clear the reasons for making charges on underpaid or unpaid mail.

A very early marking, found on letters from the Continent in the late 1860s, is an unframed "Insufficiently/Stamped" (Type **1**).

The G.P.O. Proof Books show the dispatch in February 1882 of a framed mark (Type **2**) "More to pay/above _____oz/409". The similar Type **3**, "Liable to Letter Rate/409", is known in 1903–05 struck on postcards from France that were intended for internal use only.

The early 1920s were a time of several changes in the rates for letters and postcards and these are reflected in markings of the period. The framed Type **4**, with a large 1d. and the message "To pay/Liable to/Postcard Rate/409", is often met and refers to a rate change from 1d. to 1½d. for postcards bearing a conventional message. A comparable "1d. To pay/Liable to/Letter Rate/409" also exists as Type **5**.

More markings connected with rates appeared in the 1930s. Type **6** is a boxed "To pay/Liable to/Letter/Rate/409" with a manuscript figure of amount inserted. Two sizes are reported, with different styles of lettering. Similar boxed types read: (Type **7**) "More to pay/Letter Rate above ...... oz./409" and (Type **8**) "To pay/Contrary to Regulations/Liable to/......Rate/409", again with amounts in manuscript.

Type **9** is the commonest mark found on unstamped letters and is a boxed "To pay/Posted/Unpaid/409" with the amount in manuscript or stamped at a separate operation. It is also known with fixed denomination of 5d. in 1963 and 6d. (1964) struck in green (Type **9a**). A similar boxed marking (Type **10**) reads "To pay/Posted/Out of/Course/409". The words "out of course" refer to registered mail posted in a letterbox instead of being handed over a post office counter.

Markings for unpaid and underpaid mail continue in Jersey under the independent postal administration but completely new types have been introduced. The simple rectangular handstamp (Type **11**) was put into use in 1971 reading "Posted/Unpaid". The amount due is indicated by letter P (for pence) with a figure below, in this case 4, and the mark is struck in violet or blue. Increases in postage rates have extended the range over the years: a 5p and 6p in 1972; 7p in 1974; 8p and 10p in 1975; 14p in 1976 and 12p in 1978. The 7p has the old British numeral "409" in the bottom right corner.

A comparable boxed type (**12**) has the words "To Pay/Underpaid". Beginning in 1972 with the amount to be inserted below P (for pence), fixed-amount stamps were introduced subsequently: 1p and 2p in 1975 and 4p in 1976.

Before Jersey became postally independent in 1969 British and Regional stamps were in use. They were withdrawn from sale on 30 September but continued to be accepted for postage for another month until 31 October 1969 when they were invalidated in the island. (The Regionals remained on sale on the mainland at British Philatelic Counters till 30 September 1970 and were finally invalidated because of decimalised currency as from 1 March 1972.)

Jersey put a label on all its letterboxes which read ONLY JERSEY STAMPS VALID, but dealt with mail which nevertheless bore invalidated issues by handstamping it with an unframed "Stamp Void" (Type **13**) and charging double postage. In 1970 a framed handstamp reading "Stamp Invalid" (Type **14**) replaced it and this in turn gave way to boxed markings with the same wording but including the amount charged.

The first of these (Type **15**) read "Stamp Invalid/8d to pay" and appeared in 1970. After decimalisation in 1971 there were two further marks, "Stamp Invalid/......to pay/409" (Type **16**), notable in including the numeral 409 in spite of independence. The amounts chargeable were 5p (1971) and 6p (1972). Later additions to the series omit the 409 (Type **16a**) and these have been 7p (in 1974), 8p (1975), 10p (1975) and 14p (1976), reflecting changes in postal rates.

When franked letters are posted with an incomplete meter stamp a special handstamp is used. Two types have seen service. Type **17** is worded all in capitals "To pay/Postage cannot be/prepaid by means/of an incomplete/franking impression/Liable to ......rate". There is a box to the left headed with letter D for pence and in which the charge was filled in by hand. Type **17** was used in the 1960s and was somewhat modified from 1971 with the advent of decimalisation to give Type **17a**. The D was now shown as P for new pence and the numeral

409 placed at bottom left. The wording was the same as before except that the concluding "Liable to ......rate" was omitted.

The previous sub-section mentioned the fractional markings for postage due on letters from abroad. The system was revised in 1976 and since then the numerator has indicated the actual deficiency. This fraction of the foreign rate (rounded down to the nearest penny) is collected from the recipient plus a fixed surcharge, formerly 8p, then 11p and raised in 1978 to 15p. A large box mark, 56 × 39mm, is stamped on the letter; it has compartments headed "To pay/Underpaid", "+ Surcharge" and "Total/to/Pay", the amounts being written in by hand (Type **18**).

(3) Irregularities in Transmission

The first marking in this category is pre-adhesive. Letters from London posted "too late" to catch the mailboat were so marked.

A handstamp with "too late" entirely in small lowercase letters (Type **1**) was used in 1831. A script "Too Late" is known from 1846 (Type **2**), struck first in green but in red in 1849 and in black in 1903 and 1905.

A group of markings came into use in 1879–80 to deal with the regulations that anything sent at a lower rate than that for letters had to be left open at the ends and not contain any enclosure. The four marks in question (Types **3–6**) each include the Jersey number 409.

The first, from December 1879, reads "Contains a communication/of the nature of a Letter/409". The other three, from November 1880, read: "Contrary to regulations/409"; "Closed contrary/to regulations/409"; and "Prohibited enclosure/409". In each case the stamps are boxed.

The G.P.O. Proof Books for February 1882 have two similar markings but they have not been seen on covers before the 1900s. They are "Not known/409" (Type **7**) and "Gone away/409" (Type **8**).

Another marking of this nature may be found, "Posted out/of course" (Type **9**), for registered mail irregularly posted. The marking in this case is unframed.

Three missent marks are known. A "Missent to Jersey", measuring 5 × 32mm, is recorded in 1958 and a larger unframed type in 1975 (Types **10** and **10a**). Also in that year may be found a boxed "Missent to" with "Jersey" added in manuscript (Type **11**).

The 11 × 46mm handstamp GOREY (Type **12**) recorded on a card in 1960 wrongly addressed to St. Martin's, was replaced in 1967 by Type **13**, a boxed "Your correct postal address is/Gorey, Jersey/Any other form of address/may lead to delay". These were needed because there was confusion whether certain addresses were in Gorey or St. Martin's.

The Post Office began to make use in 1960 of a large boxed stamp (Type **14**) headed in capitals "Return to Sender/Undelivered for reason stated". The eight reasons were then set out in two columns of upper and lowercase above the numeral "409" and were: Gone away; Not known; Not occupied; No such address in; Deceased; Refused; Not called for; Insufficiently addressed. This stamp was meant to be ticked at the appropriate place. It was replaced in 1969 with a very similar type (**14a**) but this omits the "409", also "Undelivered For Reason Stated" is printed as upper and lowercase not capitals.

Letters marked "Airmail" but insufficiently prepaid receive a boxed marking (Type **15**) introduced in 1974. It reads "Insufficient postage paid for/Transmission by air./Diverted to surface route".

Cat. No.	Type No.	Dates of use	Colour	Price on cover

(1) Postage Due Indicators

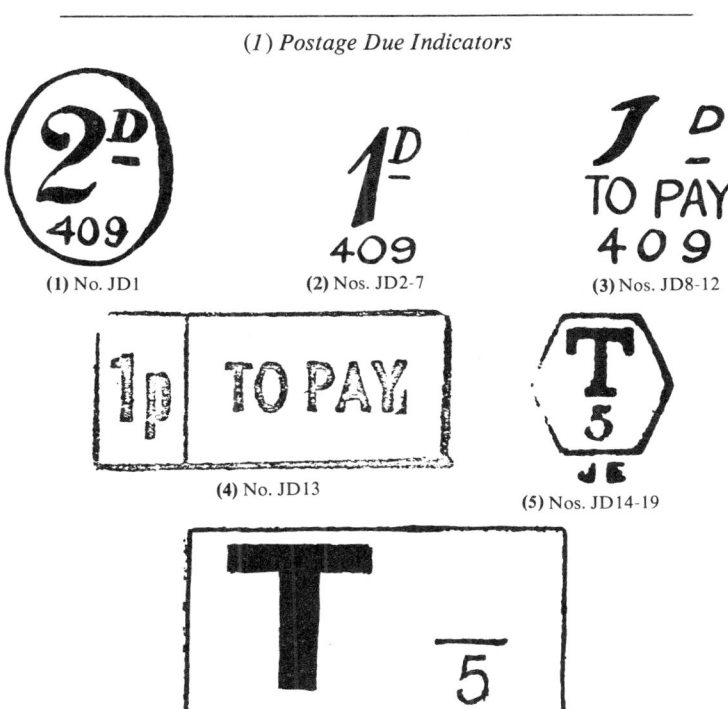

(1) No. JD1

(2) Nos. JD2-7

(3) Nos. JD8-12

(4) No. JD13

(5) Nos. JD14-19

(6) Nos. JD20-22

JD1	**1**	1883–1900	Black	£175
JD2	**2** (1d.)	1902	Black or red	3·00
JD3	(2d.)	1914	Black or red	3·00
JD4	(2d. + ½)	1914	Black	15·00
JD5	(3d.)	1914	Black or red	3·00
JD6	(4d.)	1921	Black or red	3·00
JD7	(5d.)	1921	Black or red	5·00
JD8	**3** (1d.)	1918	Black, red or green ..	3·00
JD9	(1¼d.)	1922	Black, red or green ..	7·00
JD10	(2½d.)	1957	Red	3·00
JD11	(3½d.)	1957	Red	3·00
JD12	(4d.)	1921	Black or red	3·00
JD13	**4** (1p)	1972–77	Violet	1·00
JD14	**5** (T5)	1903	Black	20·00
JD15	(T15)	1903	Black	20·00
JD16	(T20)	1907	Black	25·00
JD17	(T30)	1907	Black	30·00
JD18	(T40)	1907	Black	35·00
JD19	(T50)	1907	Black	40·00
JD20	**6** (T_5)	1971	Violet	2·00
JD21	(T_8)	1974	Violet	2·00
JD22	(T_{10})	1977	Violet	1·00

Cat. No.	Type No.		Dates of use	Colour	Price on cover

(2) Explanations for Charges

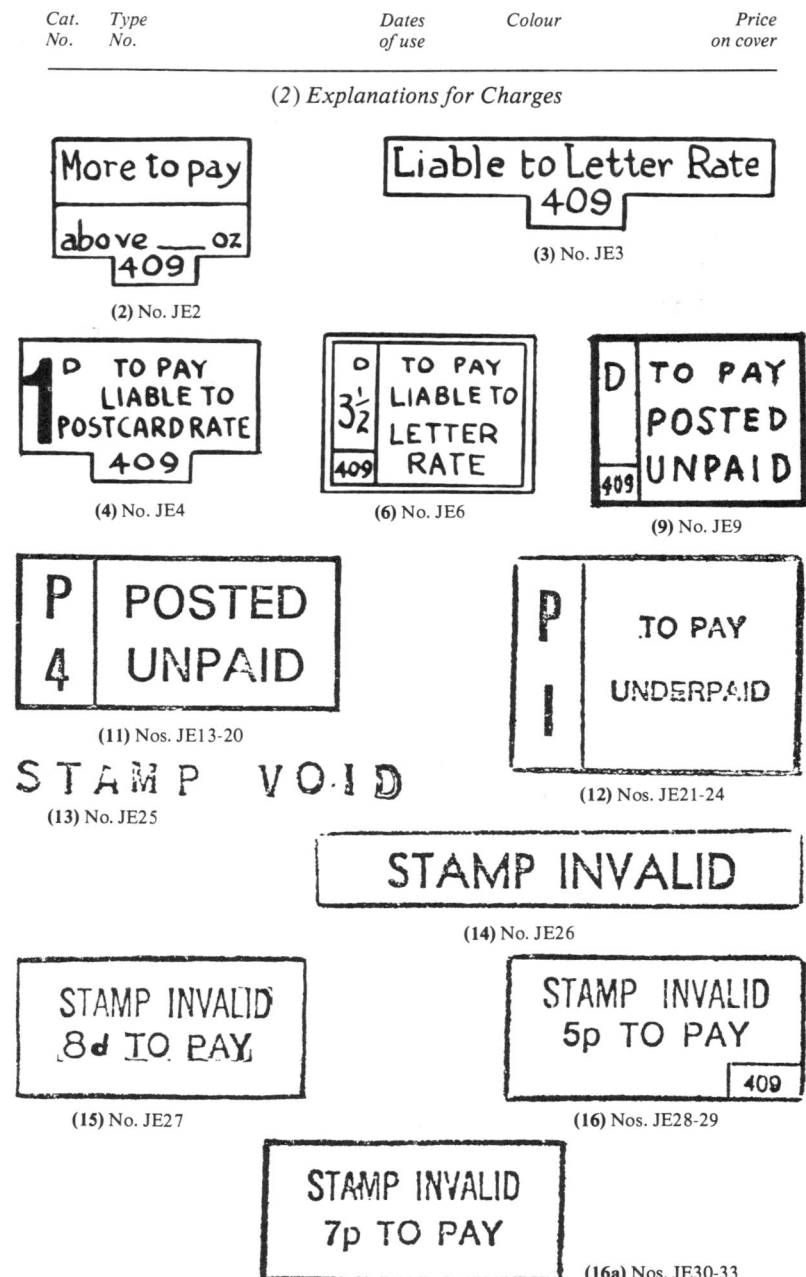

(2) No. JE2

(3) No. JE3

(4) No. JE4

(6) No. JE6

(9) No. JE9

(11) Nos. JE13-20

(12) Nos. JE21-24

(13) No. JE25

(14) No. JE26

(15) No. JE27

(16) Nos. JE28-29

(16a) Nos. JE30-33

Cat. No.	Type No.	Dates of use	Colour	Price on cover

(17) No. JE34

```
┌─────────────────────────────────────┐
│  D    │      TO PAY                  │
│       │  POSTAGE CANNOT BE           │
│       │  PREPAID  BY  MEANS          │
│       │  OF  AN  INCOMPLETE          │
│       │  FRANKINC IMPRESSION         │
│       │  LIABLE TO..........RATE     │
└─────────────────────────────────────┘
```

```
┌──────────────────────────┬──────────┐
│    TO PAY                 │  TOTAL   │
│    UNDERPAID              │   TO     │
│                          ─│  PAY     │
│             5             │          │
│                           ├──────────┤
│      +        8           │   13,    │
│   SURCHARGE FEE           │          │
└──────────────────────────┴──────────┘
```

(18) No. JE36

JE1	1		1860s	Black	.. .. .. 90·00
JE2	2		1882	Black	.. .. .. 25·00
JE3	3		1900s–59	Black	.. .. .. 15·00
JE4	4		1920s–60s	Black, red or green	.. 7·00
JE5	5		1920s	Black	.. .. .. 8·00
JE6	6		1930s–60s	Black, red or green	.. 1·00
JE7	7		1950s	Black or green	2·00
JE8	8		1950s	Black	.. .. .. 2·00
JE9	9		1930s–60s	Black, red or green	.. 1·00
JE10	9a	(5d.)	1963	Green	.. .. .. 3·00
JE11		(6d.)	1964	Green	.. .. .. 3·00
JE12	10		1950s	Black	.. .. .. 3·00
JE13	11	(4p)	1971—	Violet	.. .. .. 2·00
JE14		(5p)	1972—	Violet	.. .. .. 2·00
JE15		(6p)	1972–76	Violet	.. .. .. 2·00
JE16		(7p)	1974	Violet	.. .. .. 2·00
JE17		(8p)	1975–76	Violet	.. .. .. 2·00
JE18		(10p)	1975–76	Violet	2·00
JE19		(12p)	1978	Violet	.. .. .. 2·00
JE20		(14p)	1976–77	Violet or blue	.. .. 2·00
JE21	12	(P–)	1972—	Violet or black	.. .. 2·00
JE22		(1p)	1975–77	Violet	1·00
JE23		(2p)	1975—	Violet or blue	1·00
JE24		(4p)	1976—	Violet or blue	1·00
JE25	13		1969	Green or violet	.. .. 2·00
JE26	14		1970–75	Green or violet	2·00
JE27	15	(8d.)	1970	Green or violet	.. .. 1·00
JE28	16	(5p)	1971	Violet	.. .. .. 1·00
JE29		(6p)	1972	Violet	.. .. .. 1·00

Cat. No.	Type No.	Dates of use	Colour				Price on cover
JE30	**16a** (7p)	1974	Violet				1·00
JE31	(8p)	1975	Violet	..	..	..	1·00
JE32	(10p)	1975	Violet	..	..	..	1·00
JE33	(14p)	1976	Violet	..	..	..	1·00
JE34	**17**	1960s	Violet	..	..	..	3·00
JE35	**17a**	1971	Violet	..	..	..	2·00
JE36	**18**	1976—	Blue ..	..	..	..	1·00

(3) Irregularities in Transmission

too late

(1) No. JT1

(2) No. JT4

Not Known
409

(7) No. JT9

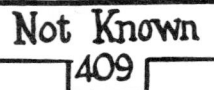

(8) No. JT10

POSTED OUT ·
· OF · COURSE

(9) No. JT11

YOUR CORRECT POSTAL ADDRESS IS
GOREY, JERSEY.
ANY OTHER FORM OF ADDRESS
MAY LEAD TO DELAY .

(13) No. JT16

(14a) No. JT18

Insufficient postage paid for
Transmission by air.
Diverted to surface route.

(15) No. JT19

Cat. No.	Type No.	Dates of use	Colour				Price on cover
JT1	**1** too late	1831	Black	..	..	..	£125
JT2	**2** Too late	1846	Green	..	..	..	80·00
JT3	as above	1849	Red	..	..	..	70·00
JT4	as above	1903–05	Black	..	..	..	50·00
JT5	**3** Contains a communication . . 409	1879	Black	..	..	..	65·00
JT6	**4** Contrary to regulations 409	1880–1959	Black	..	..	..	20·00
JT7	**5** Closed contrary to regulations 409	1880	Black	..	..	..	20·00
JT8	**6** Prohibited enclosure 409	1880	Black	..	..	..	40·00
JT9	**7** Not Known 409	1900s–59	Black or violet	..	..	8·00
JT10	**8** Gone away 409	1900s–59	Black or violet	..	..	6·00
JT11	**9** Posted out of course	1950s	Violet	..	..	..	8·00
JT12	**10** Missent to Jersey	1958	Violet	..	..	..	5·00
JT13	**10a** Missent to Jersey	1975	Violet	..	..	..	3·00
JT14	**11** Missent to	1975	Violet	..	..	..	2·00
JT15	**12** GOREY	1960	Black	..	..	..	4·00
JT16	**13** Your correct postal address.....	1967	Violet	..	..	..	10·00
JT17	**14** Return to sender......409	1960	Violet	..	..	..	2·00
JT18	**14a** Return to sender	1969—	Violet or blue	..	..	1·00
JT19	**15** Insufficient postage......	1974	Violet	..	..	..	1·00

GUERNSEY

The comparable instructional marks from Guernsey can be divided into the same three groups that were given for Jersey. Prices are given in a list at the end of this sub-section using as catalogue numbering system:

(1) Postage due indicators . . . . *prefix* GD
(2) Explanations for charges . . . . GE
(3) Irregularities in transmission . . . . GT

(1) Postage Due

A large 1d. with numeral 324 below (Type **1**) is known applied in 1897 but in 1928 it was replaced by the similar Type **2**. The 2d. in this latter style was added in the early 1900s. The 3d. and 4d. (Type **3**) include the words "To pay" below the amount; they are believed to date from the early 1920s but most examples known are on covers sent after 1940.

Hexagonal Taxe markings (Type **4**) follow the pattern outlined under Jersey. They have GU for Guernsey below the hexagon and are known with figures denoting centimes for 5, 10, 15, 20 or 40. The T15 occurs on a postcard to France dated 1893, when double this amount was collected at Caen and a postage-due adhesive affixed. The other markings in this series have been noted from the early 1900s.

(2) Explanations for Charges

The framed marking Type **1** reads "More to pay/above_____ oz/324" and came into use in the early 1900s, as did Type **2** "Liable to Letter Rate/324". This latter marking is also found on mail during the German Occupation.

Type **3** is worded "To pay/Liable to/Letter/Rate" and to the left is a space for the amount above the numeral 324, the whole enclosed in a double frame. It dates from the 1920s. From the 1900s comes Type **4**: "1d To Pay/Liable to/Postcard Rate/324". These reflect changes in postal rates and regulations governing class of mail.

Guernsey has made use of Type **5** on underpaid mail by a framed marking reading "MORE TO/PAY/LETTER RATE/ABOVE——— oz/324" or its similar Type **5a**, "More to pay/Letter rate above ——— oz/324" (upper and lowercase letters).

Unpaid mail was marked normally with the framed handstamp Type **6**. This had a space at left to insert the amount and read: "To pay/Posted/Unpaid/324". It probably went into use in the 1930s, but the earliest examples seen are in the 1940s. Types with a fixed 6d. or 8d. were introduced in the late 1950s (Type **6a**).

With the coming of postal independence the "324" has been dropped and the marking somewhat modified though reading the same: "To pay/Posted/Unpaid". In Type **7**, dating from 1969, the left-hand space has a "D" for pence and the amount is inserted in manuscript. With decimalisation in 1971 Type **8** was brought into service. The box is now a narrow rectangle whose left-hand half has "......p/To Pay" and its right-hand "Posted/Unpaid". The vertical bar broke about December 1976.

Analogous boxed markings (Types **9** and **10**) vary the wording to "Posted/Underpaid" so as to deal with deficiencies in postage. Type **10a** (1977) is unboxed and the words are now larger—5mm capitals instead of the 2mm size in Type **10**.

Postal independence also raised the problem of how to handle mail on which the public continued to affix British or Regional stamps, even though these were initially invalidated after 31 October 1969 (but extended to the end of March 1970 at the request of the Guernsey Hoteliers Association). Guernsey labelled all its pillar boxes "Guernsey Postage Stamps only may be used on items posted in this box" and prepared an unframed "Stamp Invalid" marking (Type **11**) struck in black or violet from 1969.

After the final invalidation (March 1970) double postage was charged, using the normal Type **7** applied in green. After decimalisation in 1971 a suitably worded framed handstamp (Type **12**) was substituted which said: "Stamp(s)/Invalid/——— p/To pay".

A large boxed marking applied to undelivered mail is Type **13**, dating from the 1930s. The wording is "Undelivered for/reason stated/Postage Due/for return/to/Sender". A series, of fixed amount, is recorded: 1d. and 1½d. struck in violet and the higher values 2d., 2½d., and 3d. in green. The 1d. differs somewhat in design: the words at the top are in upper and lowercase and there is no vertical line or 324.

Postal rate charges in the 1950s called for a framed handstamp (Type **14**) reading "Surcharge due/to increased/postal charges". To the left was the D for penny, a space for the amount and (below) the numeral 324 for Guernsey.

Letters franked with incomplete meter stamps are marked from the 1960s with a large boxed stamp (Type **15**): "To pay/Postage cannot be/prepaid by means/of an incomplete/franking impression/Liable to ......rate". Again, there is a panel to the left showing D (space) 324.

(3) Irregularities in transmission

A framed handstamp "Gone Away/324" was put into use in the 1900s (Type **1**) and there is an unframed "Found in course/of sorting" (Type **2**).

Two missent marks have been recorded. One used in 1954 is boxed with "Missent to Guernsey" in capital letters (Type **3**) and the other, seen in 1975, is unframed and has the same words in large upper and lowercase letters (Type **3a**).

An elaborate handstamp (Type **4**) has a column headed "Initials" for the postal officer, and the various reasons for non-delivery which can be ticked in a separate column are: Gone away; Address unknown; Road unknown; Name unknown; Insufficient address; No post town; Addressee deceased. The 324 is absent from this stamp but it is headed "Guernsey/Channel Islands".

A similar large box (Type **5**) is known, headed "Return to sender/Undelivered for reason stated". The reasons listed, in two columns with a space for a tick, are: Gone away; Not known; Not occupied; No such address in; No post town; Deceased; Refused; Not called for; Insufficiently addressed, and 324 is shown at the bottom. The whole of the text is in capital letters.

Type **4** dates from 1956 and Type **5** has been seen from 1960. A simple handstamp of 1973, size 3 × 45mm, reads "Returned Postal Packet" (Type **6**).

Cat. No.	Type No.	Dates of use	Colour	Price on cover

(1) Postage Due Indicators

(1) No. GD1   (2) Nos. GD2-3   (3) Nos. GD4-5   (4) Nos. GD6-10

Cat. No.	Type No.	Dates of use	Colour	Price on cover
GD1	1	1897–1928	Black	8·00
GD2	2 (1d.)	1928–69	Black or red	6·00
GD3	(2d.)	1900s–69	Black or red	6·00
GD4	3 (3d.)	1920s–69	Black or green	5·00
GD5	(4d.)	1920s–69	Black or green	5·00
GD6	4 (T5)	1900s	Black	25·00
GD7	(T10)	1900s	Black	30·00
GD8	(T15)	1893	Black	30·00
GD9	(T20)	1900s	Black	35·00
GD10	(T40)	1900s	Black	40·00

(2) Explanations for Charges

(2) No. GE2

(4) No. GE4

Cat. No.	Type No.	Dates of use	Colour	Price on cover

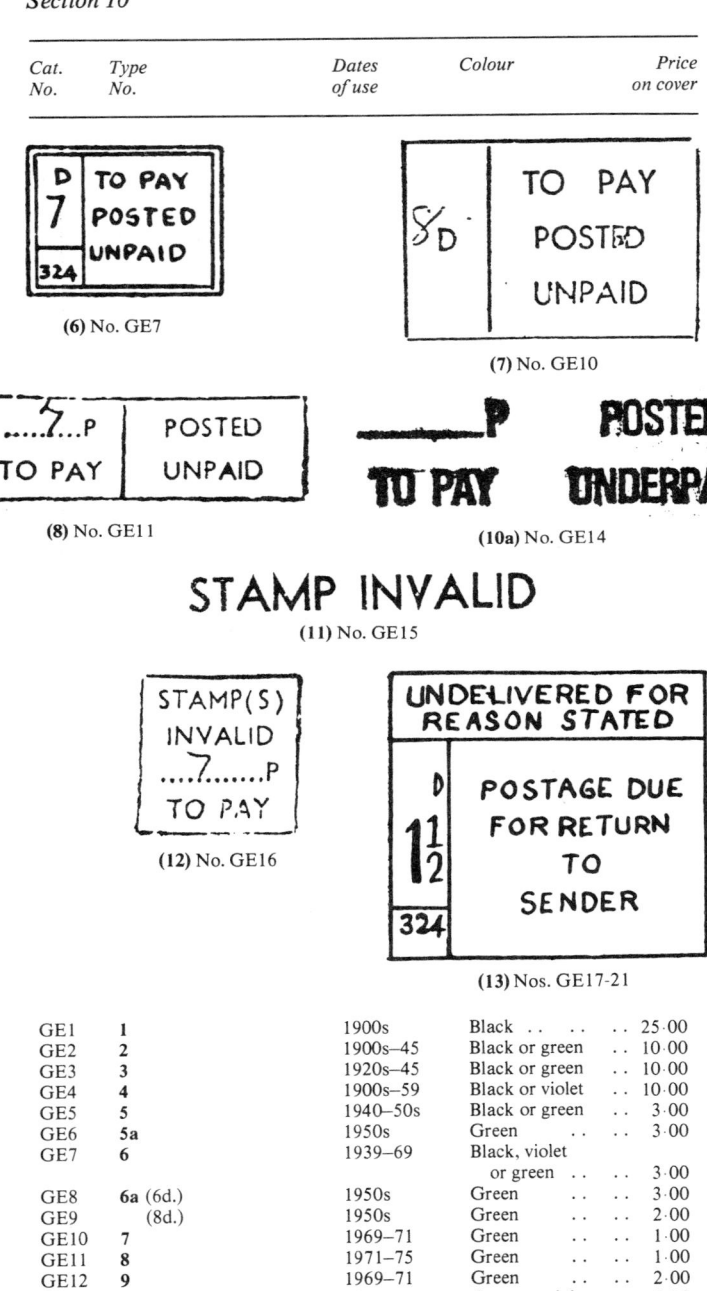

(6) No. GE7

(7) No. GE10

(8) No. GE11

(10a) No. GE14

STAMP INVALID
(11) No. GE15

(12) No. GE16

(13) Nos. GE17-21

GE1	1	1900s	Black	.. 25·00
GE2	2	1900s–45	Black or green	.. 10·00
GE3	3	1920s–45	Black or green	.. 10·00
GE4	4	1900s–59	Black or violet	.. 10·00
GE5	5	1940–50s	Black or green	.. 3·00
GE6	5a	1950s	Green ..	.. 3·00
GE7	6	1939–69	Black, violet or green ..	.. 3·00
GE8	6a (6d.)	1950s	Green ..	.. 3·00
GE9	(8d.)	1950s	Green ..	.. 2·00
GE10	7	1969–71	Green ..	.. 1·00
GE11	8	1971–75	Green ..	.. 1·00
GE12	9	1969–71	Green ..	.. 2·00
GE13	10	1971	Green or violet	.. 1·00
GE14	10a	1977	Violet	.. 1·00

Cat. No.	Type No.	Dates of use	Colour	Price on cover
GE15	**11**	1969	Black or violet	.. 2·00
GE16	**12**	1971	Violet	.. 1·00
GE17	**13** (1d.)	1930s–41	Violet	.. 3·00
GE18	(1½d.)	1930s–54	Violet	.. 3·00
GE19	(2d.)	1930s	Green ..	.. 3·00
GE20	(2½d.)	1930s	Green ..	.. 3·00
GE21	(3d.)	1930s	Green ..	.. 3·00
GE22	**14**	1950	Green ..	.. 5·00
GE23	**15**	1960s	Green ..	.. 5·00

(3) Irregularities in Transmission

(4) No. GT5

(5) No. GT6

GT1	**1** Gone away 324	1900s–60	Black or green	.. 8·00
GT2	**2** Found in course of sorting	1950s	Black or green	.. 12·00
GT3	**3** MISSENT TO GUERNSEY	1954	Violet	.. 20·00
GT4	**3a** Missent to Guernsey	1975	Violet	.. 2·00
GT5	**4** Non-delivery	1956–60	Violet	.. 3·00
GT6	**5** Return to sender	1960–69	Violet	.. 2·00
GT7	**6** Returned postal packet	1973	Black	.. 1·00

11. Military Mail

Guernsey Militia

During the Napoleonic Wars letters from the Guernsey Militia Headquarters and the replies were carried round the island by the chasseurs of the Militia. They are quite rare and no more than thirty examples have been recorded, most of these being endorsed "On Service" in manuscript. One is illustrated. Similar letters probably exist for Jersey, but we have not seen any.

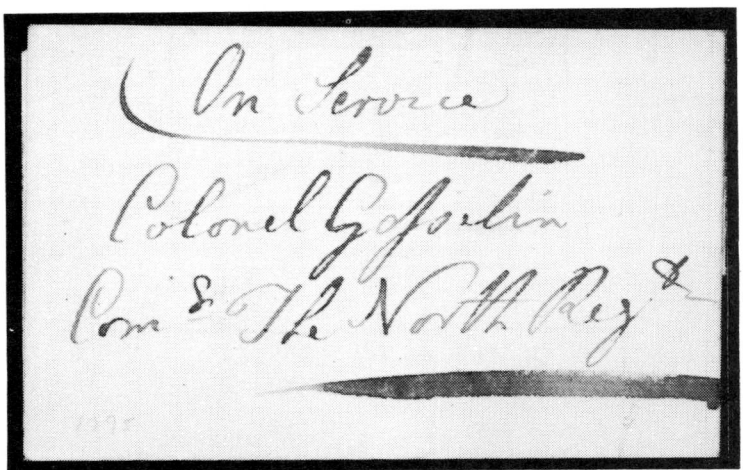

Guernsey Militia letter of 1795

Soldiers and Sailors Letters

Covers exhibiting the correct 1d. rate granted to soldiers and sailors by the Act of 1795 are sought after.

Similarly, letters written from Fort Regent in Jersey and Fort George in Guernsey during the times that they contained military garrisons are collectable, commanding a small premium. During the period 1854–70 such letters, although bearing adhesives, were often marked "On Her Majesty's Service".

Royal Jersey Militia Camp

Mail posted at a summer camp of the Royal Jersey Militia in 1908 was marked with a violet cachet consisting of a large double-circle inscribed MEDICAL CORPS/THE ROYAL MILITIA OF JERSEY, with a large cross in the centre. The postage stamps were cancelled at the head office.

Liberation 1945

After the Islands were liberated from German Occupation British Field Post Offices were established in Guernsey and Jersey. That for Guernsey was F.P.O. 138 and that for Jersey F.P.O. 302. They functioned from 9 May to 10 November 1945.

In Guernsey a circular rubber stamp with ARMY/POST OFFICE in the centre and six vertical bars at top and bottom was also used on parcels and small packets. This can only be identified as coming from Guernsey if the F.P.O. number is also used on the wrapper. A registration label then in use had 138 struck in violet after the printed "F.P.O. No."

Force Headquarters

The Military Headquarters in Jersey used a special boxed handstamp (50 × 18mm) on mail and an example is illustrated on a postcard sent on 8 June 1945. The card also shows the temporary 1d. Paid handstamp (Type **J81a**) made up from the ½d. value.

The card illustrated is now in the Occupation Museum at St. Peter's. The message on the reverse is interesting historically and reads: "Please cause the captured GERMAN horse loaned to you to be at St. Mary's Arsenal on 12th June 1945 at 11.30 a.m." This is under signature of an Army Officer.

Force Headquarters handstamp

MILITARY MAIL

Field Post Office markings

	Dates of use	Colour					Price
Guernsey Militia letters	1790–1815	—	..	..	..	*from*	50·00
Soldiers and Sailors Letters at 1d. rate	1795–1820	—	..	..	..	*from*	50·00
Royal Jersey Militia cachet	1908	Violet	..	..	*on cover*	60·00
F.P.O. 138 c.d.s. (Guernsey)	1945	Black	..	..	*on cover*	25·00
F.P.O. 302 c.d.s. (Jersey)	1945	Black	..	..	*on cover*	25·00
Army Post Office handstamp	1945	Violet	..	..	*on piece*	40·00
Force Headquarters handstamp	1945	Black	..	..	*on card*	40·00

For Prisoner of War mail *see* Section 21.

12. Paquebot Marks

Paquebot marks have been used in both Islands on mail landed from ships calling there. The letters or postcards have either been handed to the purser for delivery to the nearest post office, or posted in a special box provided on board. On arrival at the post office the stamps, usually foreign ones and mainly French, have been cancelled with a Jersey or Guernsey postmark and a PAQUEBOT stamp has also been applied.

JERSEY

The earliest example recorded for Jersey is of the omnibus type shown, issued to a number of ports, and has the word PAQUEBOT in sloping serifed letters measuring 5 × 36mm; it is struck in violet on a cover from Plérin dated 1896. The next type was similar, but measured 6 × 40mm and was struck in black in 1903–04 and in violet in 1904–05. A third type with upright letters measuring 4½ × 34mm was struck in violet in 1905. Also recorded for 1905 was a fourth type with sloping letters measuring 4½ × 30mm, struck in violet. These are usually found on mail from France.

We have not seen any paquebot marks used after 1905 until a new handstamp was prepared for Jersey in 1973. This has sans-serif letters measuring 4½ × 32mm. It is still in use and has been seen on mail bearing French, Swedish and British stamps.

Other Jersey marks with a maritime flavour were those used on board the Swedish-America Line's vessels *Kungsholm* and *Gripsholm* when they visited the island in 1970, 1971, 1972 and 1973. Special handstamps were used and are listed in Section 15.

GUERNSEY

The only early paquebot mark recorded for Guernsey is one struck in violet on two French postcards of 1903. It is of the omnibus type with sloping letters and measuring 4 × 34½mm. It can be distinguished from the Jersey mark by the tail to the Q, which is much rounder.

The next one which has been seen is slightly longer and has a curly top to the T. Only two examples are known, both on French cards used in 1928.

A sans-serif PAQUEBOT measuring 6 × 27mm is known struck in black on a number of French reply paid cards of 1969.

In 1972 the Guernsey Post Office Board introduced a new stamp with "Paquebot" in upper and lowercase letters. This is still current and is known struck in violet on mail bearing British, French and occasionally Guernsey postage stamps.

PAQUEBOT

Omnibus type of marking

Cat. No.	Dates of use	Colour	Measurements	Price on cover
Jersey				
JP1	1896	Violet	5 × 36mm (sloping)	£150
JP2	1903–04	Black	6 × 40mm (sloping)	£100
JP3	1904–05	Violet	6 × 40mm (sloping)	£100
JP4	1905	Violet	4½ × 34mm (upright)	£100
JP5	1905	Violet	4½ × 30mm (sloping)	£100
JP6	1973	Violet	4½ × 32mm (sans-serif)	2·00
Guernsey				
GP1	1903	Violet	4 × 34½mm (sloping)	£300
GP2	1928	Black	4 × 38mm (sloping)	£300
GP3	1969	Black	6 × 27mm (sans-serif)	25·00
GP4	1972	Violet	(upper & lowercase)	˙2·00

See also: "Hovermail flights" in Section 16 (Airmails and Hovercraft Mail) and "Carteret" in Section 17 (Mails between the Channel Islands and France).

13. The Smaller Islands

The smaller islands dealt with in this Section are: Alderney, Sark, Herm, Jethou, Brecqhou and Lihou.

ALDERNEY

When post offices were established in Guernsey and Jersey in 1794, no provision was made for Alderney and mail for that island was carried privately until 1812. In that year Sir John Doyle, Governor of Guernsey, wrote to Francis Freeling, Secretary of the Post Office, and offered to arrange carriage of mails by his "scouts". Freeling accepted this and instructed the Guernsey Postmistress to make up an Alderney bag whenever required. Some kind of post office was set up on Alderney by Le Mesurier, whose family were the hereditary governors.

The arrangement between Doyle and Freeling held good until 1815, when peace was signed between Britain and France, and the carriage of letters reverted to private ships. A private post office is thought to have survived in Alderney after this but no postal markings were used.

In August 1823 the States of Guernsey passed an Ordinance which set up a special office, known as the Foreign Post Office and run by George S. Syvret and Matthieu Barbet, to handle all mail addressed to or from Alderney and the neighbouring French coast. The masters of all ships were instructed to deliver their letters there and call for mail before sailing. The Ordinance was strengthened later in 1823 and again in 1833 and seems to have been intended to give a monopoly of letters for France and Alderney to one of the private offices still existing and to give official sanction to the position then obtaining, whereby payments of 1d. were made to the master of the ship carrying the letters and the agent at the port. The Ordinance was finally repealed in 1841 but the private post office apparently continued to function for several years afterwards.

On 21 July 1840 a Memorial from the inhabitants of Alderney praying for the establishment of a Government Post Office there was forwarded by the Hon. Fox Maule; also an application from Mr. Brown complaining of the extra charge on letters from Guernsey. The Postmaster General replied on 5 August saying that he could not consent, at present, to make any alterations to the existing arrangements for sending letters to Alderney. It was not until 1843 that a post office was established in the island.

The first cancellation used in Alderney is believed to have been that commonly known as the "Guernsey Cross". It is a Maltese Cross (Type 1) of quite distinctive shape, most noticeably in the outer cross cutting inward to four sharp points. It is extremely rare and there was no reason for it to have been used in Guernsey as the general English type was issued and used there (**G14**), as it was in Jersey (**J26**). Specialists have as yet no definite evidence to support its use in Alderney, but it can be stated that all but one of the known covers are without contents and only two of the nine recorded and examined bear a Guernsey datestamp. On the other hand, each bears an endorsement "Via Southampton per private steamer" or similar wording and has the Southampton

Ship Letter stamp on the back. Two letters have been seen marked as being written from *Jersey*, but this does not prove that they were posted there.

The railway had reached Southampton by 1840, but not Weymouth, so it was quicker to send mail via Southampton. A Guernsey Post Office notice of 1842 allowed this if the letters were endorsed as stated above.

Alderney was a sub-office of Guernsey and most mail passed through Guernsey where it received the ordinary Maltese Cross cancellation and the Guernsey datestamp. Letters were, however, occasionally sent direct to Southampton and it seems probable that the Alderney Postmaster considered that he should cancel such letters before dispatching them and made a special Maltese Cross for this purpose. This was used from 1843 to 1845 until, it is believed, a 324 obliterator of Guernsey replaced it.

On 8 January 1848 an undated stamp reading ALDERNEY in sans-serif letters round the top and having two concentric semi-circular arcs at the bottom was dispatched (Type **2**). A similar stamp with larger letters was sent from the G.P.O. on 17 May 1855. This type was not usually used for cancelling postage stamps but was placed on the envelope alongside them and the 324 used as a cancellation.

A double-arc handstamp (Type **2a**), now with date and code A was sent on 2 April 1851 and there are records of further examples being dispatched from the G.P.O. on 15 June 1855 (code A), also 9 September and 23 October 1857 (both code C). Types **2** and **2a** are rarely found on complete cover. Most of those known came from a solicitor's mail and all had the addresses torn off before they were released.

On 4 May 1848 the numeral obliterator 965 was dispatched from the G.P.O. Two types exist: Type **3**, used from 1848 to the mid-1860s, having four bars at top and bottom and Type **3a**, used from then to 1897. Type **3a** has three bars only at top and bottom; it measures 22mm across and the figures are slightly narrower than in Type **3**.

A "skeleton" type of datestamp, 30mm in diameter, with ALDERNEY at the top and the date across the centre was used in 1922 (Type **4**). An example is known dated 13 October.

Reverting to earlier history, the double-arc datestamp had been replaced in 1860 by a small single circle, 20mm in diameter with code A (Type **5**). The P.O. Proof Books record this as having been dispatched on 24 April 1860 and it is known used on 24 May of that year. Another example code A was dispatched on 8 November 1872. Examples with code C were sent on 31 December 1860 and 12 November 1884. This datestamp had a long life until 1910, but less than 30 examples have been traced, mostly of the 1872 type.

The single circle was revived about 1936 when a 24mm datestamp came into use (Type **6**). This is inscribed ALDERNEY at the top and CH. IS. at the bottom; the date is in two lines across the centre with an asterisk above it. The wording was changed in 1955 so that it now read ALDERNEY/GUERNSEY CHANNEL ISLANDS (Type **7**).

This remained in use until 1969 when the Guernsey Post Office became independent. On 1 October that year a new single-circle datestamp was introduced (Type **8**) measuring 22½mm in diameter. This had "Guernsey Post Office" at the top, "Alderney" at the bottom and the date in a single line across the centre with an asterisk, an A or a B above it. A similar type, but 26½mm in diameter, went into use in 1970 and is still current.

Since the turn of the century double circles have also seen service. The first (Type **9**) had ALDERNEY at the top and a small cross between thick bars at the bottom. The earliest date of use recorded is 14 July 1897. It has been seen with letter A above the date. Type **9a** has thinner bars and no code letter.

In 1930 there appeared Type **10**. This double-circle datestamp has ALDERNEY at the top and CH.IS between thin bars at the bottom. A similar type (**10a**) came into use about 1935 in which the bars are thicker and there is an asterisk above the date. A scarce usage of Type **10a** occurred in 1966 when, between 1 and 10 August, there can be found this marking with letter A or B instead of the asterisk. From 11 August 1966 a new double-circle type (**11**) came into use and this reads ALDERNEY/GUERNSEY CHANNEL ISLANDS, lettered A or B.

Since the period of postal independence a double-circle datestamp with GUERNSEY POST OFFICE/ALDERNEY in capital letters has been introduced in 1976 for counter work. This is Type **12**.

Parcel Post Cancellations

The first parcel post cancellation was a double-ring rubber type (**13**) with the name ALDERNEY across the centre. It was dispatched from the G.P.O. on 13 July 1911. The similar Type **14**, reading ALDERNEY/CHANNEL ISLANDS, is also known on Edwardian stamps but its date of introduction cannot be traced. It was probably about 1912 and seems to have been needed because Type **13** had quickly disintegrated in use. Both are scarce markings.

A large label type of parcel post cancellation (Type **15**) was issued to the island about 1947. The earliest date of use seen in 1949. In 1958 a new parcel stamp in the large label type was introduced and this is Type **16**. It has ALDERNEY at the top, the date across the centre and CHANNEL ISLANDS at the bottom; there are the words PARCEL at the left and POST at the right, both reading upward.

A somewhat smaller and simpler label type (**17**) dates from 20 July 1970, in the period of independence. This reads: GUERNSEY POST OFFICE/PARCEL POST/date/ALDERNEY.

Cancellations for Small Packets

Three single-circle cancellations for use on packets and small parcels are recorded. Type **18**, in use from 1955 to 1958, reads ALDERNEY GUERNSEY at the top and the unusual abbreviation CHAN. ISLES at the bottom. Between 1958 and 1970 a new rubber stamp was used (Type **19**) with the words ALDERNEY at the top and CHANNEL ISLANDS at the bottom. Since independence Type **20** has been introduced, the wording being "Guernsey Post Office/Alderney". This was issued on 16 June 1970 and is a rubber stamp of 30mm diameter.

Special Cancellations

A small First Day of Issue cancellation was used on 11 November 1970 when the first Christmas stamps were issued by Guernsey, the 4d. denomination of which featured St. Anne's Church, Alderney.

In 1975 another special cancellation was used to mark the visit of the Queen Mother.

Military Stamp

An unusual stamp made of rubber and sent to Alderney on 30 January 1907 is oval in shape and reads POST OFFICE at the top, R.E. OFFICE across the centre and ALDERNEY at the bottom. The R.E. probably stands for Royal Engineers and its seems likely that the stamp was intended to mark military mail posted by the garrison but not to cancel postage stamps. An example is known on an Edward VII ½d. on piece.

Occupation and Liberation Mail

During the German Occupation Alderney was completely evacuated of its civilian population, most of whom came to Britain just before the Germans arrived, and was heavily fortified by the Nazis. Russian P.O.W. labour was used.

In August 1943, 750 French Jews were taken to the island and a concentration camp was established at Camp No. 2 which was called "Norderney". The inmates of the camp were allowed to send and receive two letters per month but this privilege was sometimes withdrawn.

Letters were inscribed on the back with the internee's name, personal reference, registered number, hut number, and nature of employment. Some had the large red cachet of the *Insel Frontführer* of the Todt Organisation applied. They then had a 1f·50 Pétain stamp affixed and were handed in at the island office where they were put into sacks and sent by ship to France.

On arrival at Cherbourg the letters were taken to Paris where they arrived at St. Lazare station and were sent to the chief receiving office to be cancelled with the single-line obliterator PARIS CENTRALISATEUR.

Sometimes the mails went via St. Malo or Granville and were taken to Montparnasse station from where, after receiving the circular datestamp of the station, they were delivered in the normal way.

All the letters were censored by the Germans but it is not known whether this was done in Paris or in Alderney. Very few letters have survived.

Covers are known sent by German Occupation forces between 1940 and 1945.

The British Post Office in Alderney was closed from 22 June 1940 to 21 September 1945. The Army Postal Service provided postal facilities from May to September 1945 and from that date until 30 September 1946 an officer of the Guernsey Post Office was sent to Alderney and postal services were provided in the sub-office building. Colonel Marriette resumed his appointment as Sub-Postmaster on 1 October 1946.

Submarine Cover

On 16 May 1947 the submarine H.M.S. *Alderney* made a voyage to Portsmouth carrying six covers. They bear the Alderney single-circle datestamp of 16 May and the rectangular datestamp COMMANDING OFFICER/16 MAY 1947/H.M.S. ALDERNEY. The 2½d. postage stamp is cancelled with the Gosport, Hants, datestamp of 17 May 1947.

Local Carriage Labels

The Commodore Shipping Company and the Alderney Shipping Company

Ltd. have issued adhesive labels for prepayment of fees for carriage of parcels on their vessels plying between Guernsey and Alderney. The Alderney Parcel Delivery Service also issues adhesives for internal delivery of parcels. These, while interesting when properly used on pieces of parcel wrappings, are outside the scope of this Catalogue.

(1) (2) (2a)

(3) (3a)

(5) (6) (7) (8)

(9) (9a) (10a)

(11)

(13)

(14)

(15)

(*Above*) *Reduced by half*

(16)

(18)

(19)

(20)

1907 cachet

Cat. No.	Type No.	Dates of use		Price on cover

Nos. AC1–28: All struck in black

Prices for Nos. AC 19–26 refer to markings on piece

AC1	1*	Maltese Cross	1843–45	£4000
		*Large portion of cancellation on adhesive	.. .. (off cover)	£750
AC2	2	ALDERNEY double arc	1847–55	£400
AC3	2a	dated double arc	1851–60	£300
AC4	3	Numeral obliterator, 4 bars	1848–60s	£175
AC5	3a	same, 3 bars	1860s–97	£175
AC6	4	Skeleton datestamp	1922	£200

Single circles

AC7	5	ALDERNEY	1860–1910	25.00
AC8	6	ALDERNEY/CH. IS.	1936–55	3.00
AC9	7	ALDERNEY/GUERNSEY CHANNEL ISLANDS	1955–69	2.00
AC10	8	Guernsey Post Office/Alderney, 22½mm	1969—	1.00
AC11		same, 26½mm	1970—	75

Double circles

AC12	9	ALDERNEY, thick bars, cross at foot	1897–1932	15.00
AC13	9a	same, thinner bars	1930	15.00
AC14	10	ALDERNEY/CH. IS., thin bars	1930–35	5.00
AC15	10a	ALDERNEY/CH. IS., thick bars, asterisk	1935–66	5.00
AC16		ALDERNEY/CH. IS., thick bars, A or B	1966 (1–10.8)	20.00
AC17	11	ALDERNEY/GUERNSEY CHANNEL ISLANDS	1966—	2.00
AC18	12	GUERNSEY POST OFFICE/ ALDERNEY	1976—	50

Parcel Post cancellations

AC19	13	ALDERNEY double ring	1911	40.00
AC20	14	ALDERNEY/CHANNEL ISLANDS	1912—	35.00
AC21	15	Label, date at foot	1947–58	3.00
AC22	16	Label, date in centre	1958–70	2.00
AC23	17	Box type	1970—	1.00

Single circles (Small Packets)

AC24	18	ALDERNEY GUERNSEY/CHAN. ISLES	1955–58	2.00
AC25	19	ALDERNEY/CHANNEL ISLANDS	1958–70	2.00
AC26	20	Guernsey Post Office/Alderney	1970—	75

Special cancellations

| AC27 | — | First Day of Issue (11 Nov.) | 1970 .. .. .. | 1.50 |
| AC28 | — | Visit of Queen Mother | 1975 .. .. .. | 1.00 |

CACHETS, ETC.
Struck in colours indicated

1907	Oval POST OFFICE/R.E. OFFICE/ALDERNEY. Violet .. .. (on piece)	50.00
1942–44	"Insel Frontführer/ALDERNEY/TODT Bei Cherbourg" in red unframed circle	60.00
1943	As above on Jewish Concentration Camp Mail	75.00
1943	Jewish Concentration Camp covers, with manuscript endorsement on back	60.00

Dates of use		Price on cover

CACHETS, ETC. (CONTD.)

1947	Boxed COMMANDING OFFICER/16 MAY 1947/H.M.S. ALDERNEY.	
	Black	15·00
1957	Visit of Queen and Duke of Edinburgh, large boxed type. Black	4·00
1962	577 (HAMPSHIRE) FIELD SQN. R.E. (T.A.) (date) Territorial Camp.	
	Violet	3·00
1962	"Alderney THE Channel Island", publicity cachet States of Alderney.	
	Blue	1·00
1971	Oval REGIMENTAL HEADQUARTERS/30th SIGNAL REGT./4 SEPT. 1971.	
	Red	3·00
1972	Boxed "Alderney Welcomes/H.R.H. PRINCESS ANNE/May 25th".	
	Blue	2·50
1974	Small oval ALDERNEY/CHANNEL ISLANDS. Black	1·00
1975	Small double-circle POSTED IN/ST. ANNES/ALDERNEY.	
	Red or violet	50
1975	Boxed CHRISTMAS/GREETING/FROM/ALDERNEY and lion.	
	Black or red	50
1975	Double-circle POSTED DURING/ALDERNEY WEEK. Red	50
1975	Boxed STATES OF GUERNSEY/ALDERNEY AIRPORT. Blue	50

SARK

Prior to the establishment of a post office in Sark in 1857, letters were carried between the island and Guernsey by boatmen, who usually charged ½d. per letter. Letters are known dated around 1718 but none of them bears a charge mark of any kind.

(Price from £100.)

When Peter Le Pelley was Seigneur of Sark in 1838 he tried to introduce a Post Office and the idea was discussed by the Chief Pleas on several occasions, but it was too revolutionary to be accepted. In those days very few letters were written on the island and most of those were by the Seigneur and the Vicar, and so the boatmen continued to carry the mail in their fishing baskets.

The question was raised again in 1857 and, after long consideration, it was agreed to establish a post office at La Hêche, in a thatched cottage and store belonging to a Mr. Queripel, who became the first Sub-Postmaster. Once a day Mr. Queripel carried the mail from La Hêche to the Creux Harbour and returned with the incoming mail. In the first year of the post office 1500 letters were posted in Mr. Queripel's letterbox.

An undated double-arc handstamp (Type **1**) was dispatched to Guernsey on 15 July 1857. An example of this mark is known on a letter sent to Gibraltar in 1858 and a second example is also reported to exist.

The first datestamp was the single-circle Type **2**. It was probably introduced in 1885 when the Sark post office was created a Money Order Office. It is recorded as being in use by 1890, but does not appear to have been used to cancel postage stamps until 1904. Examples are known used up to 1932 and again in 1940. Those lettered B are scarce.

A rubber stamp of 29mm diameter, shown as Type **3**, was dispatched in 1885. Only one example has been seen used, in 1888, struck in violet.

On 17 March 1960 a single-circle type (**4**) of 24mm diameter was put into use with SARK · GUERNSEY/CHANNEL ISLANDS round the circumference and the date in two lines in the centre with an asterisk above.

The Guernsey Post Office Board issued new datestamps to all its sub-offices when it became independent on 1 October 1969 and they were uniform single-circle types. That for Sark reads "Guernsey Post Office/Sark"; it has the date in two lines in the centre with A, B or asterisk above and is 22½mm in diameter (Type **5**). It was replaced by a larger one (26½mm diameter) on 11 November 1970.

A single-circle rubber stamp of 30mm diameter (Type **6**) was issued for use on small packets on 16 June 1970. It reads GUERNSEY POST OFFICE/SARK.

As for the double-circle cancellations, Type **7** was introduced in 1927. An interesting usage is that it may be found on covers prepared during the Occupation when bisecting of postage stamps was officially permitted. The 2d. Postal Centenary stamp bisected is thus recorded on cover or card cancelled with Type **7**. The cancel was in use throughout the whole period of Occupation and so can be found with locally made figures for the year date.

In the autumn of 1947 this cancellation was replaced by a similar one (Type **8**) having an asterisk instead of the A above the date and it continued in use until 1966.

A new double-circle type (**9**) was introduced in that year with SARK at the top and GUERNSEY CHANNEL ISLANDS at the bottom. It has a thin bar on each side of SARK and is lettered A or B or has an asterisk above the date.

Sark has one of the new-style parcel post cancellations (Type **10**), rectangular in shape and reading GUERNSEY POST OFFICE/PARCEL POST/date/SARK. It was issued to the island on 20 July 1970.

Special Cancellations

A small First Day of Issue cancellation was used on 11 November 1970 when the first Christmas stamps were issued in Guernsey, the 9d. denomination of which featured St. Peter's Church, Sark.

In 1975 another special cancellation was used to mark the visit of the Queen Mother.

German Military Mail

During the Occupation German Army mail received an appropriate unit stamp containing the Kenn. number and was then taken to Guernsey for cancelling with the *Feldpost* datestamp.

Letters from naval personnel received a handstamp reading "Kriegsmarine/Sark/Hafenuberwachung Stelle" in a 35mm single circle with the eagle and swastika emblem in the centre. There was also a similar handstamp with "Kriegsmarine" removed.

Sark Quatercentenary

The quatercentenary (400th anniversary) of the British settlement of Sark was celebrated in 1965. Letters posted from 1 June received a boxed handstamped cachet reading ISLE OF SARK/1565 CHARTER 1965/QUATER CENTENARY. The adhesives were cancelled in the normal way.

The Dame of Sark also authorised the issue of pictorial labels inscribed ISLE DE SERK. Although they bear denominations of 3d., 6d., 9d. and 1s. they performed no postal service.

Local Carriage Labels

Adhesive labels issued by the Commodore Shipping Co. and the Isle of Sark Shipping Co. for carriage of parcels between Guernsey and Sark are outside the scope of this Catalogue.

(1)

(2)

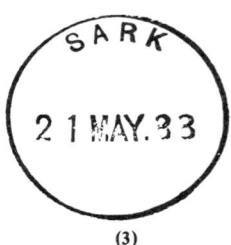

(3)

(4)

(5)

(6)

(7)

(8)

(9)

ISLE OF SARK
1565 CHARTER 1965
QUATER CENTENARY

1965 cachet

Cat. No.	Type No.	Dates of use				Price on cover
		Nos. SC1–14: All struck in black (except No. SC4 = violet)				
SC1	1	SARK double arc	1858	..	.. ..	£1500
Single circles						
SC2	2	SARK, lettered A	1885–1940		.. ..	15·00
SC3	2*	SARK, lettered B		..	.. .. ..	80·00
		*Large portion of cancellation on adhesive			.. .. (*off cover*)	40·00
SC4	3	SARK rubber stamp	1888	..	.. ..	£100
SC5	4	SARK GUERNSEY/ CHANNEL ISLANDS	1960–69	..	.. ..	4·00
SC6	5	Guernsey Post Office/Sark, 22½mm	1969—	..	.. ..	75
SC7		same, 26½mm	1970—	..	.. ..	75
SC8	6	GUERNSEY POST OFFICE/SARK, 30mm	1970—	.. (*on piece*)		1·00

Cat. No.	Type No.		Dates of use					Price on cover

Double circles

SC9	7*	SARK, GUERNSEY/						
		CHANNEL ISLANDS, letter A	1927–47	..	..	..		9·00
SC10		same, locally made figures in year	1941–45	..	..	..		15·00
		*On Postal Centenary 2d. bisect		..	..	..	..	50·00
SC11	8	similar to Type 7, asterisk	1947–66	..	..	..		4·00
SC12	9	SARK/GUERNSEY CHANNEL						
		ISLANDS, thin bars	1966–69	..	..	..		2·00

Parcel Post cancellation

SC13	10	Box type	1970—	.. *(on piece)*	1·50

Special cancellations

SC14	—	First Day of Issue (11 Nov.)	1970	..	..	..		1·50
SC15	—	Visit of Queen Mother	1975	..	..	..		1·00

CACHETS
Struck in black

1942–44	Single circle "Kreigsmarine/Sark/Hafenuberwachung Stelle"	..	..	50·00
1942–44	As preceding without "Kriegsmarine"	.. ..	..	50·00
1957	Boxed Visit of Queen and Duke of Edinburgh	.. .. ..	..	4·00
1965	Boxed ISLE OF SARK/1565 CHARTER 1965/QUATER CENTENARY		..	4·00
1972	Boxed "Sark Welcomes/H.R.H. PRINCESS ANNE"	.. .. ..	..	2·50

HERM

A few early letters are known from Herm dated from about 1820, but these were carried privately.

(*Price from* £150.)

In the early 1900s several Guernsey vessels ran day excursions to Herm and a postcard is known with an unframed HERM struck in black on the picture side and posted on arrival in Guernsey.

When Sir Percival (later Lord) Perry, the Chairman of Ford's, purchased the lease of Herm from Sir Compton Mackenzie in 1925 he took a large staff with him to the island and the Head Postmaster of Guernsey agreed to open a sub-office there. It was in the Mermaid Tavern and was open for only half an hour each day. A special datestamp was provided (Type **1**) and went into use on 1 May 1925. Special registration labels were also provided. The office was closed down on 30 November 1938 for lack of business.

The island was purchased by the States of Guernsey from the Crown in 1946 and in 1948 it was leased to a Mr. A. G. Jefferies, who tried to get the sub-office reopened, but this was refused on the grounds of insufficient business. Mr. Jefferies therefore instituted a local carriage service, for which special stamps were issued, and this was continued by his successor, Major A. G. Wood, until suppressed by the Guernsey Post Office Board on 1 October 1969. These local stamps are outside the scope of this Catalogue.

Following Guernsey's postal independence a new sub-office was established in Herm and a 22½mm single-circle datestamp (Type **2**) was issued on 1 October 1969. It was replaced by a similar one diameter 26½mm on 6 January 1971.

A single-circle rubber stamp of 30mm diameter was provided on 16 June 1970 for cancelling small packets (Type **3**).

On 20 July 1970 Herm also received the rectangular-style parcel post cancellation (Type **4**) reading GUERNSEY POST OFFICE/PARCEL POST/date/HERM ISLAND.

The first Christmas stamps of Guernsey in 1970 included a 1s. 6d. denomination featuring the St. Tugual Chapel, Herm. A special cancellation reading HERM ISLAND, FIRST DAY OF ISSUE/NOV. 11, 1970 was put into use to mark the event.

On 1 May 1975 the Guernsey Post Office provided a commemorative cancellation for the 50th anniversary of the opening of the first sub-office in Herm in 1925. This was used in Guernsey (*not* in Herm) and is listed under "Special handstamps" in Section 15 (Guernsey).

(1)

(2)

Cat. No.	Type No.		Dates of use				Price
		Nos. HC1–6: All struck in black					
HC1	1*	HERM GUERNSEY/CHANNEL ISLANDS	1925–38	..	..*cover*		£250
		*Large portion of cancellation on adhesive (*off *cover)*		..	..	.. ..	30·00
HC2	2	Guernsey Post Office/Herm Island, 22½mm	1969–71	..	..*cover*		1·00
HC3		same, 26¼mm	1971—	..	..*cover*		75
HC4	3	Small-packet rubber stamp	1970—	..	..*piece*		1·00
HC5	4	Parcel Post box type	1970—	..	..*piece*		1·50
HC6	—	First Day of Issue (1 Nov.)	1970	..	..*cover*		1·50
		CACHET					
1903	HERM handstamp. Black	.. ..	.. ..	..	..*postcard*		40·00

JETHOU

The island of Jethou is owned by the Crown and for over 200 years has been leased to private tenants. They have made their own arrangements for dispatch and collection of mail. One or two letters are known dated in the 1820s.

(Price from £150.)

Excursion trips were made to the island from Guernsey around the turn of the century and picture postcards sold on the vessels sometimes had a rubber cachet applied at the time of sale. A two-line unframed type reading JETHOU ISLAND/20 MAR.07 is known on a picture postcard of the island with Guernsey datestamp of the same day. Two examples are recorded also of a circular cachet, which was struck in violet, with the date (day and month only) applied by a second stamp. One is on an unused card and the other on one bearing an Edward VII ½d. adhesive cancelled Guernsey, 6 September 1909.

When Group Captain W. H. Cliff was tenant of Jethou he opened the island to the public and issued local carriage labels in 1960. Two showing the islets of Fauconniere and Crevichon carried their names instead of Jethou. Carriage labels were continued by his successor, Mrs. Susan Faed, until they were suppressed by the Guernsey Post Office Board from 1 October 1969. These issues are outside the scope of this Catalogue.

1909 cachet

CACHETS

1907	Two line JETHOU ISLAND/date. Black	45·00
1909	Circular JETHOU ISLAND/date/CHAN. ISLES. Violet	40·00

BRECQHOU

Brecqhou, a small island off Sark leased to a tenant, is in the Guernsey Bailiwick. No postal markings or identifying cachets exist, except in connection with a set of local carriage labels valid for one day only (30 September 1969) then suppressed by the new independent Guernsey postal authority the next day. The labels are outside the scope of the Catalogue.

LIHOU

Lihou is off St. Saviour's, Guernsey, to which it is joined by a causeway at low tide. No postal markings or identifying cachets exist until 1966. In that year the tenant issued local carriage labels but these and subsequent items were withdrawn on 30 September 1969 when the independent Guernsey postal authority was set up. The labels are outside the scope of the Catalogue.

14. Sub-offices of Jersey and Guernsey

The sub-office cancellations of Jersey and Guernsey can be divided into fourteen main types, illustrated below as Types **A** to **P**.

Some of the datestamps vary slightly in details. For example, Type **C** can be found with the name of the island at the bottom, with or without the letters c.i., and in sizes from 22mm to 24mm in diameter. A variety of code letters, asterisks and the time of collection are inserted into the datestamps.

Type **B** is found on the early registration labels and not usually cancelling stamps.

Types **H**, **K** and **M** vary somewhat: CHANNEL ISLANDS may be in full or abbreviated, according to the length of the name of the sub-office. In Type **K** the sectors marking off the office name are sometimes shown as solid black circles.

Parcel post labels allocated to many of the sub-offices in Jersey and Guernsey are known used from the 1880s to the 1950s. Several have strikes of the rarer parcel post cancellations and may bear denominations of postage stamps not otherwise found on cover.

(Prices in Section 23.)

Telegraph forms used from the sub-offices of Guernsey and Jersey are known from the 1880s.

(Prices from £3.)

Small circular handstamps (seals), diameter 21–30mm, were issued in many parts of the British Isles during the early 1900s for use primarily on mail bag labels. Some Jersey sub-offices used these in error to cancel stamps. The seals are of "negative" appearance (white letters on black background), with crown in the centre; around the circumference are (top) name of office and (bottom) JERSEY.

During the early 1900s, also, Head Post Offices sometimes held small stocks of registration labels with a blank space where the town number of an office would normally be printed. These were issued occasionally to offices whose stocks had run out and the office entered its respective town number in manuscript on the label each time one was affixed to an envelope. Examples are known at a few Jersey offices.

Bisected 2d. stamps of King George V and King George VI are known used at the following Guernsey sub-offices during the authorised period (27 December 1940 to 22 February 1941): Braye Road, Cobo, Les Gravées, Market Place, St. Andrew, St. Martin's, St. Peter in the Wood, St. Sampson's, St. Saviour's, The Vale and Ville au Roi (and, by favour, Beresford Street, Jersey).

Cancellations not seen. Sub-offices recorded as having been opened, but for which no cancellations have yet been seen, are: *Jersey*—Great Union Road (1904–24), Pier (1891), Pontac (1902–04); *Guernsey*—Bouet (1889–93), Catel Church (1899), La Moye (1891–96).

Rubber datestamps of Type **F** are recorded in the G.P.O. Proof Books as having been supplied to the following sub-offices but no examples of their use have yet come to light:

Jersey: St. Martin's, St. Mary's, St. Peter's.
Guernsey: Bouet, Catel Church, Les Gravées, Torteval, Vale.

Alderney, Sark and Herm. Cancellations of these sub-offices of Guernsey are dealt with separately in Section 13.

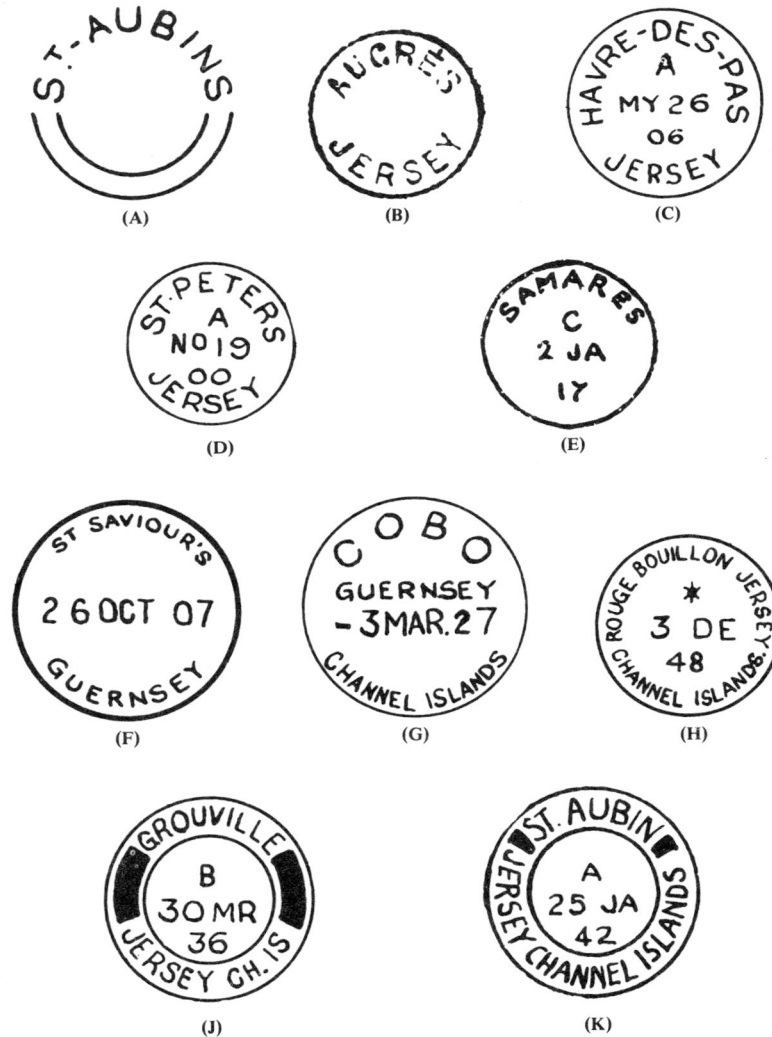

(A)   (B)   (C)

(D)   (E)

(F)   (G)   (H)

(J)   (K)

(L)

(M)

(N)
23½ mm diameter

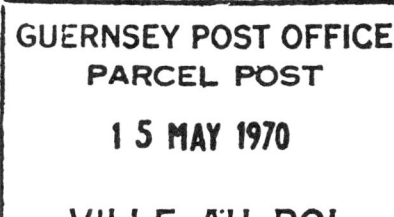

(P)

JERSEY

Prices are for these sub-office cancellations *on cover*, unless otherwise indicated.

Augrès

Opened 1893

1893	Type **B**, undated .. .. *on cover*		25·00
	on registration label		3·00
1908	Ditto, but with date		4·00
1930s	Type **H**		2·00

Beaumont

Opened 1853

1853	Type **A**, shades of blue, green or black		£120
1881	Type **D**		5·00
1892	Type **C**		2·50
1932	Type **K**		2·50

Beresford Street

Opened 1909, closed 25.3.72

1909	Type **C**	3·50
1909	Mailbag seal with crown in centre ..	25·00
1914	Manuscript "2" on registration label	3·00
1931	Rectangular parcel post cancellation as Type **J66** of Jersey, inscribed JERSEY (St. Heliers)/CHANNEL ISLANDS/BERESFORD STREET/ Parcel Post .. .. *on piece*	3·00
1930s	Type **H**	2·00
1950s	Ditto, but with code 2	1·50
1957	Rectangular parcel post cancellation as Type **J66** of Jersey, inscribed JERSEY/CHANNEL ISLANDS/ BERESFORD STREET/Parcel Post .. .. *on piece*	3·00
1961	Ditto, but with PARCEL POST at each end and date in centre *on piece*	3·00
1970	Ditto, but inscribed BERESFORD STREET/JERSEY/CHANNEL ISLANDS Parcel Post .. .. *on piece*	2·00

Carrefour Selous

Opened 1891, closed 30.6.44, reopened 1.1.46, closed 30.9.78

1891	Type **E**	.. ..	3·00
1891	Ditto, but *on registration label*	..	4·00
1946	Type **K**	.. ..	1·50

Central Market

Opened 1972

| 1972 | Type **M** (three different types) | .. | 1·00 |
| 1972 | Rectangular parcel post cancellation as Type **J66** of Jersey | *on piece* | 2·00 |

Cheapside

Opened 1890

| 1890 | Type **C** | .. .. | 4·00 |
| 1930s | Type **H** (two different types) | .. | 2·00 |

Colomberie

Opened 1906, closed April 1920

| 1906 | Type **C** | .. .. | 30·00 |

Conway Street

Opened by 1904, closed 1910

| 1904 | Type **D** | .. .. | 30·00 |

David Place

Opened 1874, closed July 1914

| 1874 | Type **C** | .. .. | 15·00 |

Faldouet

Opened 1893 (may have been closed for a few years from October 1919), closed finally 8.12.72

| 1893 | Type **E** | .. .. | 3·00 |
| 1930s | Type **J** .. | .. .. | 2·50 |

First Tower

Opened by 1885

1885	Type **E**	.. ..	3·00
1914	Skeleton, 36mm, black ..	.. ..	30·00
1914	As Type **E** but without code letter		2·00
1930s	Type **H**	.. ..	1·50

Five Oaks

Opened by 1890, closed 1932, reopened 1937, closed 23.7.47, reopened 3.4.50

1890	Type **D**	.. ..	3·50
1937	Type **K**	.. ..	1·50

Georgetown

Opened 1882, closed January 1927, reopened January 1935, closed 20.6.40, reopened 22.8.45

1882	Type **C** (two different types)	..	4·00
1935	Type **H**	.. ..	1·50

Gorey
A receiving house of the Jersey Penny Post was opened in 1830, using the boxed No. 2 handstamp, which carried on into the adhesive period. *See* Section 3 Jersey, Type **J8**.

Opened as a sub-office 1851

1851	Type **A**, blue, blue-green, dirty green or black (two different types) ..		£125
1873	Type **D**	.. ..	10·00
1882	Type **C**	.. ..	2·50
1906	30mm skeleton with code "x", black		30·00
1906	Type **D**, with code A	.. .. ..	2·00
1910	Parcel post Type **L**	.. *on piece*	25·00
1930s	Type **K**	.. ..	1·50
1960s	Rectangular parcel post cancellation as Type **J66** of Jersey	*on piece*	3·00

Gorey Village

Opened 1893, closed 20.6.40

1893	Type **C** (misspelt Corey)	.. ..	3·50
1930s	Type **H**	.. ..	7·50

Grands Vaux

Opened 5 December 1960

| 1960 | Type H | .. .. | 1·00 |

Greve d'Azette

Opened 1927, closed 28.6.74

1927	Type C, reading JERSEY C.I.	3·00
1927	Mailbag seal with crown in centre,	
	black	25·00
1940s	Type H	2·00

Grouville

Opened by 1857, closed about 1867, reopened 1890

1857	Type A (misspelt GRONVILLE), blue	£125
1890	Type E	3·50
1930s	Type J	3·00
1969	Type H	1·00

Havre des Pas

Opened by 1889, closed September 1962

| 1889 | Type C .. .. | 6·00 |
| 1930s | Type H .. .. | 2·50 |

La Rocque

Opened 1894

| 1894 | Type C .. .. | 3·00 |
| 1930s | Type K .. .. | 1·00 |

Le Squez

Opened 1 July 1974

1974	Temporary c.d.s. reading JERSEY,	
	CHANNEL IS. L.9	2·00
1975	Type H	1·00

Millbrook

Opened 1851, closed 1.1.44, reopened 10.9.45

1851	Type **A**, black or blue	£125
1873	Type **E**	10·00
1886	Type **C**	2·50
1930s	Type **K**	1·00

Pier

An office was opened temporarily in 1891 for six weeks during the potato season. A handstamp reading PIER/JERSEY in Type **D** was issued for use on telegrams but no example has yet come to light.

Quennevais

Opened 18 July 1950

1950	Type **M** (two different types).. ..	1·00
1971	As Type **M** but without arcs	1·00

Roseville Street

Opened by 1962

1962	Type **H**	1·00
1963	Type **H**, with figure "2" at base ..	1·00
1967	Rectangular parcel post cancellation as Type **J66** of Jersey *on piece*	1·00

Rouge Bouillon

Opened 1890

1890	Type **C**	5·00
1922	Manuscript "5" on registration label	3·00
1930s	Type **H**	1·00

St. Aubin

A receiving house of the Jersey Penny Post was opened in 1830, using the boxed No. 1 handstamp which carried on into the adhesive period. *See* Section 3 Jersey, Type **J7**.

Opened as a sub-office by 1851 (with name "St. Aubin's"), name changed to "St. Aubin" from 1902 (but note that spellings "St. Aubins" and "St. Aubyns" have also been used)

1851	Type **A**, ST. AUBINS, blue	£125
1865	Type **D**, ST. AUBINS	10·00
1870	Type **C**, ST. AUBYNS	10·00
1900s	Type **B**, undated *on registration label*	5·00
1903	Type **B**, with code and date inserted	2·00
1925	Skeleton, 30mm diameter	30·00
1925	Type **D**	2·50
1934	Type **K**	1·00
1958	As Type **K** but with figure "1" between arcs at bottom	1·00

St. Brelade's Bay

Opened 1890

1890	Type **F**, violet	30·00
1900s	Type **F** (different style of wording), violet	30·00
1913	Type **C**	2·00
1953	Type **M**	1·00

St. Clement's

A receiving house of the Jersey Penny Post was opened in 1830, probably using the boxed No. 4 handstamp, which carried over into the adhesive period. (*See* Section 3 Jersey, Type **J10**). An unframed St. Clement's handstamp in Type **A** was sent to this office but no example has yet been seen on cover.

St. John's

Opened 1852, closed by 1873, reopened 1881, closed January 1932

1852	Type **A**, black (two types)	£125
1881	Type **D**	3·50

St. John's Church

Opened 1891, closed 30.6.77, reopened 1.2.78

1891	Type **E**	2·50
1930s	Type **J**	2·00
1976	Temporary H.O. double circle, JERSEY CHANNEL ISLANDS, cancelling registration label	5·00
1976	Type **H**	6·00
1978	Type **H**, used again	1·00

St. Lawrence

Opened 1854, closed by 1860

1854	Type **A**, black or green	.. ..	£125

St. Martin's

Opened by 1850

1850	Type **A**, blue	..	..	..	..	£125
1897	Type **C**	..	..	..	..	2·00
1930s	Type **K**	..	..	..	..	1·00

St. Mary's

Opened by 1853

1880s	Type **C**	..	..	..	..	2·50
1930s	Type **K**, but solid black circles not					
	sectors	..	..	..	..	1·00

St. Ouen's

Opened by 1852 (with name "St. Owens"), name changed to present form in April 1922

1874	Type **E**, ST. OWENS	..	.. ..	5·00
1882	Type **D**, ST. OUENS	..	.. ..	5·00
1922	Type **C**, ST. OUENS	..	.. ..	2·50
1932	Type **K**, ST. OUEN'S	..	.. ..	1·00

St. Peter's

A receiving house of the Jersey Penny Post was opened in 1830, using the boxed No. 3 handstamp, which carried on into the adhesive period. *See* Section 3 Jersey, Type **J9**.

Opened as a sub-office 1851, closed 20.6.40, reopened 5.9.45

1851	Type **A**, blue	..	.. ..	£125
1874	Type **D**	.. ..	.. ..	5·00
1909	Skeleton, 25mm diameter		.. ..	30·00
1910	Skeleton, 36mm diameter		.. ..	30·00
1910	Type **D** (stop under T of ST.)		..	2·50
1933	Type **K**	..	.. ..	2·00
1968	Type **H**	..	.. ..	1·00

St. Saviour's

A receiving house of the Jersey Penny Post was opened in 1830, probably using the boxed No. 5 handstamp, but no example has yet been seen. *See* Section 3, Jersey.

Samares

Opened 1887

1887	Type **E**	.. ..	2·50
1930s	Type **K**	.. ..	1·00

Sion

Opened January 1932, closed 22.4.77

1932	Type **K**	2·50
1976	Temporary H.O. double circle, JERSEY CHANNEL ISLANDS with code letter N, with registration label of this office	5·00
1976	Type **H**	6·00

Stopford Road

Opened 1914, closed 10.8.73

1914	Type **C**	4·00
1914	Mailbag seal with crown in centre, black	25·00
1930s	Type **H**	2·00
1970s	Type **M** (without side arcs)	2·50

Town Mills

Opened 1904, closed October 1921, reopened 1973

1904	Type **C**	6·00
1973	Temporary c.d.s. reading JERSEY, CHANNEL IS. Z9	2·00
1974	Type **H**	1·00

Trinity
A receiving house of the Jersey Penny Post was opened in 1830, probably using the boxed No. 6 handstamp, which may have carried on into the adhesive period. *See* Section 3, Jersey.

Opened as a sub-office by 1852, closed by 1867, reopened 1891

1852	Type **A**, black, blue-black or dark blue	£125
1893	Type **F**, violet	30·00
1893	Type **F**, blue	35·00
1930s	Type **K**	1·00

GUERNSEY

Prices are for these sub-offices cancellations *on cover*, unless otherwise indicated.

Braye Road

Opened 1938, closed 9.2.43, reopened 1.5.47, closed 31.3.76

1938	Type **H**	.. ..	6·00
1969	Type **N**	.. ..	1·00
1970	Parcel post Type **P**	.. *on piece*	1·00

Camp du Roi

Opened 1925, closed 1.7.40

1925	Type **K**	.. .. .. *on piece*	10·00

Catel

Opened by 1849, closed 19.6.40, reopened 1.5.53

1849	Type **A**, black or green	.. ..	£125
1896	Type **E**	.. ..	3·00
1953	Type **H**	.. ..	2·00
1969	Type **N**	.. ..	1·00
1970	Parcel post Type **P**	.. *on piece*	1·00

Cobo

Opened 1888

1888	Type **F**, black	.. ..	14·00
1911	As Type **F** but larger lettering, purple	.. ..	14·00
1911	Ditto, but black or grey	.. ..	10·00
1918	Type **F**, 38mm, black	.. .. ..	75·00
1918	Type **F**, black	.. .. ..	10·00
1927	Type **G**, black	.. ..	20·00
1930	As Type **G** but smaller lettering, black	.. ..	20·00
1935	Type **K**	.. ..	2·50
1969	Type **N**	.. ..	1·00
1970	Parcel post Type **P**, black	.. .. *on piece*	2·00
1974	Ditto, but smaller lettering, purple	.. .. *on piece*	1·00

Collings Road

Opened 1974

1974	Skeleton, 30mm, black		35·00
1974	Type **N**		1·00
1974	Parcel post Type **P** ..	*on piece*	1·00

Forest

Opened 1893, closed 1896, reopened 1899, closed 29.9.78

1899	Type **F**, violet		14·00
1899	Type **F**, crimson		20·00
1911	As Type **F** but larger lettering, purple or black (*shades*)		10·00
1917	As Type **F** but FOREST larger, purple or black		12·00
1925	Type **G** (two types)		25·00
1930s	Type **J**		3·00
1969	Type **N**		1·00
1970	Parcel post Type **P** ..	*on piece*	1·00

L'Islet

Opened 1888, closed 29.6.40, reopened 1.11.45

1891	Type **C**		3·00
1891	Type **F**, violet		45·00
1930s	Type **K**		2·50
1969	Type **N**		1·00
1970	Parcel post Type **P** ..	*on piece*	2·00
1976	Ditto, but smaller lettering	*on piece*	1·00

Les Baissieres

Opened 1.2.52, closed 8.7.68

1952	Type **H**		8·00

Les Gravées

Opened by 1890

1891	Type **C**		2·50
1949	Type **H**		2·00
1969	Type **N**		1·00
1970	Parcel post Type **P** ..	*on piece*	2·00
1973	Ditto, but name misspelt LES GRAVES	*on piece*	5·00
1975	Ditto, but name corrected and smaller datestamp ..	*on piece*	1·00

Market Place

Opened 1883, closed 21.9.42, reopened 17.12.45

1883	Type **C**	6·00
1911	Type **L** (MARKET PLACE/GUERNSEY)	
	.. .. *on piece*	30·00
1936	Type **H**	3·00
1958	Parcel post as Type **15** of Alderney	
	.. .. *on piece*	2·00
1969	Type **N** (with code letter E)	1·00
1970	Ditto, but 26½mm (with code letter F)	1·00
1970	Parcel post Type **P** .. *on piece*	1·00
1977	Ditto, but slightly different sizes	
	overall .. .. .. *on piece*	1·00

Mount Row

Opened by 1895, closed by 1897

1895	Type **F**, violet *on parcel post label* 60·00

Pleinmont Road

Opened 1958, closed 1965

1958	Type **H** .. .. 6·00

Quay Branch Office

Opened June 1932, closed September 1939, reopened 1.9.48, closed 30.5.53

1932	Type **K** .. .. 10·00
1934	Type **H** .. .. 10·00

Rocquaine

Opened 11.7.67, closed 31.12.69

1967	Type **H** .. .. 6·00

St. Andrew's

Opened 1887, closed 26.3.43, reopened 1946

1887	Type **E**	10·00
1904	Type **C**	1·50
1930s	Type **K**	2·00
1969	Type **N**	1·00
1970	Parcel post Type **P** .. *on piece*	1·00

St. John's

Opened January 1935, closed 22.6.40, reopened 8.7.48

1935	Type **H**		2·50
1969	Type **N**		1·00
1970	Parcel post Type **P**	*on piece*	2·00
1975	Ditto, but slightly larger datestamp	*on piece*	1·00

St. Martin's

Opened by 1849, closed 1858, reopened 1.5.86

1849	Type **A**, black or dark blue		£125
1886	Type **C**		4·00
1930s	Type **K**		3·00
1960s	Type **H**		2·00
1969	Type **N**		1·00
1970	Ditto, but 26½mm, code A		1·00
1970	Parcel post Type **P**	*on piece*	2·00
1974	Ditto, but smaller, purple	*on piece*	1·00

St. Peter in the Wood

Opened by 1852 under the name "St. Peters", closed 1857, reopened 1876, name changed to present form on 1.5.86

1852	Type **A** (ST. PETERS), black, greenish blue or dirty grey		£125
1876	Type **C** (ST. PETERS)		10·00
1886	Type **E**		3·00
1930s	Type **K**, but solid black circles not sectors		2·00
1969	Type **N**		1·00
1970	Parcel post Type **P**	*on piece*	2·00
1974	Ditto, but smaller, purple	*on piece*	1·00

St. Sampson's

Opened 1849

1849	Type **A**, red or blue	£125
1865	Type **D**	10·00
1871	Type **C**	10·00
1886	Type **E**, 19mm with various codes	1·50
1895	Type **E**, 21mm	1·50
1911	Type **L** (ST. SAMPSONS)	35·00
1930s	Type **K**	2·50

1948	Type **H**, code F		1·50
1950s	Type **H** (GUERNSEY CH. IS., code E)		1·50
1954	Parcel post as Type **15** of Alderney (GUERNSEY/CHANNEL ISLANDS/ ST. SAMPSONS)	*on piece*	3·00
1957	Ditto, but ST. SAMPSONS/GUERNSEY/ CHANNEL ISLANDS ..	*on piece*	3·00
1969	Type **N** (code F)		1·00
1969	Ditto, but 26½mm (two types, codes E and G)		1·00
1970	Parcel post Type **P** ..	*on piece*		2·00
1973	Ditto, but wider size and broader lettering	*on piece*|	1·00

St. Saviour's

Opened 1906

1906	Type **F**, violet		9·00
1911	As Type **F** but larger lettering, no apostrophe in place name, purple or black		14·00
1917	Ditto, but in crimson		25·00
1920	Type **G**		25·00
1926	Ditto, but GUERNSEY larger		25·00
1930s	Type **K**		2·50
1969	Type **N**		1·00
1970	Parcel post Type **P** ..	*on piece*		1·00

Torteval

Open by 1911, closed 21.6.40, reopened 12.2.46

1946	Type **J**		2·50
1969	Type **N**		1·00
1970	Parcel post Type **P** ..	*on piece*		1·00

Vale

Opened as The Vale in 1893, name changed to present form in 1969

1893	Type **E**		4·00
1931	Type **K**		2·50
1969	Type **N** (VALE)		1·00
1970	Parcel post Type **P**	*on piece*		2·00
1974	Ditto, but larger lettering of VALE	*on piece*		1·00

Vale Road

Opened 1895, closed 22.6.40, reopened 1.12.45

1895	Type **C**	..	..	..	..	..	4·00
1930s	Type **K**	..	..	..	..	..	3·00
1950s	Type **H**	..	..	..	..	..	2·00
1969	Type **N**	..	..	..	..	..	1·00
1970	Parcel post Type **P**			..	*on piece*		1·00

Ville au Roi

Opened January 1936, closed 30.6.42, reopened 2.2.48

1936	Type **H**	..	..	..	..	..	3·00
1969	Type **N**	..	..	..	..	..	1·00
1970	Parcel post Type **P**			..	*on piece*		1·00

15. Cachets, Slogans and Special Markings

The Section is subdivided for Jersey and Guernsey as follows:
- **(A)** Cachets
- **(B1)** Slogans
  - **(B2)** Annual and periodic slogans
- **(C)** "First Day of Issue" markings
- **(D1)** Special handstamps
  - **(D2)** Philatelic exhibition markings

JERSEY

(A) Cachets

Large numbers of official and private cachets have been used by hoteliers, merchants, the organisers of local fairs and bazaars, railway companies, foreign consulates, etc. Many are of considerable interest to collectors and they are sought after.

Cachets are normally collected on complete cover or postcard. The prices below should be *added* to the value of the item to take account of the presence of the cachet clearly struck.

JERSEY CACHETS

1843	A. Edouard Lozey/Jersey. Oval. Black	4·00
1845	As preceding, but red	4·00
1848	P. Beghin & Cie/Negts/a Jersey. Oval. Black	4·00
1850	As preceding, but blue	4·00
1872	W. T. Pugsley/Ship & Insurance Broker/& Commission Agent/ Jersey. Large oval. Blue	4·00
1893–1903	Consulado de la Republica de Colombia/Jersey, with arms. Large oval. Black or violet	5·00

1901	Hotel du Palais de Cristal/J. Parison/Proprietaire/Jersey. Double circle	4·00
1901	Grand Hotel du Palais de Cristal/J. Parison/nouvou Proprietaire/ Jersey Iles de la Manche. Large serrated oval. Purple	5·00
1903	As preceding, but "nouvou" removed	5·00
1903	Millbrook Station, on postcard. Violet	7·00
1904–05	Hotel/de la Pomme d'Or/Jersey. Unframed. Black or blue	2·00
1905	As preceding, but violet	2·00
1905–06	Hotel/Jersey/Continental. Scroll-type oval. Violet, black or red	3·00
1906	Per Train, on postcard. Purple	6·00
1908	Crystal Palace Hotel/Jersey/J. Parison/Proprietor. Scroll. Blue	4·00
1908	S. Heliers/Sep. 1908/Bazaar. Double circle. Violet	35·00
1909	Grove Place/Wesleyan Bazaar/Aug. 5.09. Violet	6·00
1910	Boule d'Or. Violet	3·00
1910	Grand Hotel/de la Pomme d'Or/Jersey. Unframed. Violet	1·00
1911	Hotel de l'Europe/Jersey. Oval. Violet	1·00
1913	Wolf Caves/St. Johns/Jersey. Double circle. Violet or red	8·00
1915	The "Alexander" Hotel/St. Peters/Jersey. Violet	2·00
1917	Vice-Consulat de France/Jersey, with allegorical figure. Violet	2·00
1917	Censors Office/Jersey. Double oval. Violet	—
1939	Consulat de France aux Iles Anglo-Normandes/Jersey, with allegorical figure. Blue	2·00
1940	Air Raid Precaution Office/Jersey. Oval. Black	3·00
1941	Jersey-Guernsey/Mailboat/Channel Islands. Oval. Black or violet	40·00
1943	Correspondant/de/l'Aero-Club/de/France. Circle. Black	10·00
1950s—.	The Museum/Library/Jersey. Serrated double circle. Black	30
1950s—.	German Underground Hospital/Jersey, with open cross and swastika. Circle. Black or violet	40
1957	Visit of the Queen and Duke of Edinburgh. Boxed	3·00
1960s	Parish of St. Clement Jersey, with anchor in central shield. Double circle	50
1960s	Latvijas Republikas Vjce Konsulats/Jersey, with arms. Double circle. Violet	1·00
1960s	Librarie Francais/Jersey C.I./13–15 Hilgrove St. Double oval. Blue	50
1960s	Consultat de France a Jersey, with allegorical figure. Double circle. Black	1·00
1960s	Angenzia Consolare d'Italia/Jersey, with arms. Double circle	1·00
1963	Keeper & Steward/Royal Cabins/H.M. Yacht Britannia, on cover posted during visit of Queen Mother. Boxed. Black	8·00
1970	British/Railways/(date)/Jersey (T). Boxed. Violet	25
1970	British Railways/date/Jersey. Boxed. Red	60
1972	Jersey Welcomes/H.R.H. Princess Anne. Boxed. Red	1·50
1972	States of Jersey Airport, with arms. Unframed oval	50
1973	Posted Jersey Eastern Railway Guard's Van/La Hougue Bie	50
1973	Le Couperon de Rozel/Hotel/Jersey C.I. Black	20
1975	Flag Officer/Royal Yachts, on Royal Visit cover	5·00
1975	Commander's Office Royal Yacht Britannia, on Royal Visit cover	5·00
1975	Parish of Grouville/Jersey, with arms. Violet	30
1976	Posted/at/Jersey/Postal Museum/Fort Regent. Boxed. Violet	20
1970s	Finnish Vice-Consulate, Jersey, with lion. Oval. Violet	50
1970s	Netherlands Vice-Consulate St. Helier, with arms. Circle. Black	50
1970s	From the Portuguese Consulate/43 Hill Street, Jersey C.I. Unframed. Black	30
1970s	Passed by (date) Jersey Customs. Double oval. Violet	20
1970s	Royal Norwegian Consulate/Jersey, with arms. Double circle. Violet	50
1970s	Royal Swedish Consulate in St. Helier, with arms. Oval. Violet	50
1970s	Kgl. Dansk Konsulat, Jersey, with arms. Oval. Violet	50
1970s	Honorar. Konsul/der Bundesrepublik Deutschland/St. Helier. Unframed. Black	30

(B1) Slogans

Jersey has frequently replaced the wavy lines of the Universal machine cancellation (Section 9) with slogans, as below. Those slogans which are repeated at intervals are listed separately for convenience.

The prices are for complete covers showing clear strikes of the slogan and its associated datestamp, franked with postage stamps of the letter rate current at the time the slogan was applied. Cut-outs from covers and cards are worth one-quarter of the corresponding item on cover. Where the stamp is already catalogued at a higher figure in used condition, however, the slogan price shown below is to be *added* when valuing the entire.

JERSEY SLOGANS

Dates of use	Wording	Price on cover
	1931	
	The Best Investment a Telephone	4·00
	1946	
20.5.46 to 15.6.46	Don't Waste Bread Others Need It	50
1.7.46 to 31.7.46	Take No Chances Keep Death off the Road	50
9.9.46 to 8.10.46	Britain Can Make It Exhibition—1946	50
	1947	
23.5.47 to 21.6.47	Volunteer for a Forces Career	50
29.9.47 to 27.10.47	Save for the Silver Lining	50
20.11.47 to 30.11.47	EP and Wedding Bells	50
	1948	
3.5.48 to 27.5.48	A Distinguished Career Nursing	25
	1949	
3.1.49 to 31.1.49	Join the Volunteer Forces	50
1.4.49 to 29.4.49	Mind How You Go On The Road	50
	National Savings Week	50
20.5.49 to 20.6.49	Fly by British Airlines	50

Dates of use	Wording	Price on cover
	1950	
1.3.50 to 31.3.50	Road Users Please Mind The Children	50
	1953	
3.6.53 to 30.6.53	Long Live The Queen	50
	1955	
7.4.55 to 6.5.55	Please Check Address If Wrong Advise Writer	20
	1959	
1.4.59 to 2.5.59	Correct Addressing What a Blessing Saves us Guessing	20
	1960	
1.1.60 to 8.1.60	World Refugee Year 1959–1960 (with hand)	80
7.4.60 to 4.5.60	World Refugee Year (revised)	50
	1961	
	Buy Stamps in Books	20
16.9.61 to 25.10.61	Post Office 1861–1961 Savings Bank	50
26.10.61 to 1.11.61	Postal Order Gift Cards Make Gay Gift Messengers	30
2.11.61 to 30.11.61	B.B.C. tv Jubilee 1936–1961	40
	1962	
	Remember Road Accidents Can Be Caused By People	
14.7.62 to 31.7.62	Like You!	20
1.8.62 to 31.8.62	World Health Organisation Fights Malaria	30
1.9.62 to 16.9.62	Recorded Delivery Cheap Effective 6d	20
	1966	
1.10.66 to 31.10.66	Channel Islands 1066–1966 Les Isles Normandes	50
	1970	
31.7.70 to 4.8.70	Jersey Welcomes the Archbishop of Canterbury	20
	1971	
4.2.71	Opening of Jersey's New Postal H.Q. February, 1971	50
	1972	
18.3.72 to 2.4.72	Christian Crusade 72 March 18th to April 2nd	50
22.5.72	Visit of H.R.H. The Princess Anne	1·00
22.5.72	Ditto, with boxed datestamp in blue MAIL OFFICE H.M. YACHT BRITANNIA	6·00
	1973	
11.6.73 to 18.6.73	Plant a Tree in '73	20
and 25.6.73 to 30.6.73	Ditto, but in red	1.00
19.6.73 to 24.6.73	Cancer Research Campaign Cancer Will Yield	25
3.9.73 to 16.10.73	Taste The Sunshine in Jersey Tomatoes	25
9.11.73 to 24.11.73	Jersey Eisteddfod 50th Festival	25
	1974	
5.3.74	Safety is no Accident	25
14.10.74 to 20.10.74	Fire Safety Week	25
	Safety at Work Week	25
	1975	
5.5.75 to 10.5.75	Channel Islands 1940–1945 Official History 8th May	25
30.5.75	Visit of H.M. Queen Elizabeth The Queen Mother	40
	1976	
10.3.76	Maison Variety Official Opening	20
10.3.76 to 16.3.76	Jersey Telecommunications Salute World Telephone Service 1876–1976	20
18.3.76	Launch of H.M.S. *Jersey* by H.R.H. The Princess Anne	50

Dates of use	*Wording*	*Price on cover*
21.3.76 to 27.3.76	Mothers' Union 1876–1976	20
19.4.76 to 23.4.76	Army Benevolent Fund Jersey Appeal	20
24.4.76 to 4.5.76	Links With America Bicentenary Issue	20
5.5.76 to 11.5.76	7th West European and Mediterranean Conference, Commonwealth Parly. Assocn.	20
18.5.76 to 31.5.76	100 Years of Tea Packing in Jersey	20
12.7.76 to 7.8.76	High Value Definitive Stamps Issue	20
24.9.76 to 20.9.76	Jersey Welcomes 28th AIPH Congress 1976	20
19.11.76 to 23.11.76	25th Anniversary of Assembliee d'Jerriais (applied only to locally addressed mail)	30
10.10.76	Sir George Carteret Memorial Plaque	30
1.11.76	Samaritans	20
1.12.76 to 19.12.76	Christmas Greetings	20
20.12.76 to 2.2.77	Silver Jubilee Stamp Issue	25

1977

14.2.77 to 21.3.77	Currency Reform Centenary	20
29.3.77 to 23.6.77	St. John Ambulance Centenary	20
11.4.77 to 23.4.77	Deaf Children's Week	20
29.6.77 to 28.9.77	125th Anniversary of Founding of Victoria College	20
18.7.77 to 23.7.77	Occupational Centre Flag Day	20
1.11.77 to 12.11.77	Poppy Appeal	20
21.11.77 to 4.12.77	Post Your Christmas Greetings Early	20

1978

1.2.78 to 27.2.78	Royal Jersey Golf Centenary Issue	20
1.3.78 to 30.4.78	Europa Issue	20
1.4.78 to 7.4.78	Good Food Festival	20
	Jersey Stamps Worth Collecting	20
	Operation Drake	20
	Flag Day of Jersey Lifeboat Guild	20
6.11.78 to 2.12.78	Plant a Tree—Now Now Now	20

(B2) Annual or Periodic Slogans

The wording of the slogan is followed by the dates of use; exact dates are given where known, otherwise the years only.

The Telephone Makes Life Easier	
1932, 1933	2 00
Post Early For Christmas	
1946, 1947	25
1948, 1949, 1950, 1951, 1952, 1953, 1954, 1955, 1956, 1957, 1958, 1959, 1960, 1961, 1962, 1963, 1964, 1965, 1966, 1967, 1968	20
Blood Donors are Still Urgently Needed	
1947	25
1948, 1949, 1950, 1951, 1952, 1953, 1954, 1955	20
Civil Defence Join Now	
1951, 1952, 1953, 1954, 1955, 1956, 1962	20
Postage on Letters For Europe 4d	
1952, 1954	20
Have You Taken Out Your Licence For Radio-TV?	
1957, 1958, 1959, 1960, 1961, 1962, 1963	20
Express Good Wishes By Greetings Telegrams	
1958, 1959, 1960, 1961	20
Cheap Rate Trunk Calls 6PM–6AM	
1959, 1960	20
King George's Jubilee Trust	
1960, 1961	20
Jersey For A Happy Springtime Holiday	
1964, 1965, 1966, 1967, 1968, 1969, 1.1.70 to 31.3.70, 1.1.71 to 31.3.71, 3.4.72 to 30.4.72, 2.4.73 to 29.4.73, 1.4.74 to 28.4.74, 1975	20
Jersey for Summer Holidays	
1.4.70 to 30.6.70, 1.4.71 to 30.6.71	20
Jersey For Sunny Autumn Holidays	
1964, 1965, 1966, 1967, 1968, 1.7.69 to 12.10.69, 1.7.70 to 18.10.70, 1.7.71 to 16.10.71, 1.7.72 to 31.8.72, 2.7.73 to 2.9.73, 1.7.74 to 1.9.74, 1975..	20
Jersey For Sunshine In The Winter	
1964, 1965, 1966, 1967, 1968, 1969, 1970, 1971, 1972, 1973, 1974, 1975	20
Jersey For Christmas Holidays	
1965, 1966, 1967, 1968, 13.10.69 to 31.12.69, 19.10.70 to 31.12.70, 1971, 1972, 1973, 1974, 1975	20
Jersey New Potatoes Are Available	
1972, 13.5.73 to 9.6.73	20
Royal Silver Wedding Jersey's Stamp Issue 1 November 1972	
1.10.72 to 31.10.72	50
Next Stamp Issue [with date and name of issue]	
2.1.73 to 20.1.73, etc.	50
Please Remember The Joint Christmas Appeal	
3.12.73 to 30.12.73, 29.11.74 to 26.12.74, 23.11.75 to 20.12.75, 5.12.77 to 16.12.77	20
Jersey Lions Club Swimarathon	
9.2.76 to 13.2.76, 12.2.77 to 18.2.77, 6.2.78 to 11.2.78	20

(C) "First Day of Issue" Markings

With the 2½d. Regional stamps of 8 June 1964 (S.G. 9) Jersey began using the machine cancellation introduced generally in the British Isles, namely the words FIRST DAY OF ISSUE shown on an envelope and printed as a slogan alongside a circular datestamp (Type **A**). The datestamp is 21mm in diameter and includes the time of posting. It was originally inscribed JERSEY at the top and an arc below but a later version has the arc replaced by CHANNEL ISLANDS.

Normally the datestamp is to the left and the slogan to the right, but the positions have been transposed (examples noted in 1969). The independent Jersey postal administration have continued using this envelope-type slogan from time to time, primarily to cancel single adhesives on covers posted on the first day of issue.

The 4d. and 5d. Regional definitives of 4 September 1968 (S.G. 12 and 14) had a new cancellation (Type **B**). This was a 26mm circular datestamp made of rubber inscribed FIRST DAY OF ISSUE at the top, CHANNEL ISLANDS at the bottom and the date and JERSEY in two lines across the centre.

With the Liberation issue of 9 May 1970 a single-circle handstamp, diameter 24mm and inscribed FIRST DAY OF ISSUE/JERSEY CHANNEL ISLANDS, was put into use. In three lines across the centre are:

(Type **C**) date/PHILATELIC/BUREAU or
(Type **D**) date/PHILATELIC/SERVICE.

These centre details have been modified in Type **E**, which now gives only the date (in two lines). The wording around the circumference remains as in Types **C** and **D** but the diameter is now 22mm. This single-circle Type **E** was introduced in 1974.

Pictorial Handstamps. For the Inauguration issue of the independent postal administration a handstamp in the form of a shield was applied on the first day, 1 October 1969. Since then many issues have had special first day cancellations of a pictorial character related to the designs of the stamps. They are normally applied to covers bearing full sets only, the prices for which are given with Part 2 of this Catalogue.

Incomplete Sets. Incomplete sets passed through the post on the first day still give rise technically to "first day covers", though by philatelic custom this term, without further qualification, is normally understood to imply the presence of a complete set.

The covers can nevertheless still be valued from the table below. This shows by how much the total catalogue value of the stamps in used condition should be increased by virtue of the first day cancellation.

Type **A**	Slogan to right	25
	Slogan to left	20
B		60
C		*nil*
D		*nil*
E		*nil*

A
A

B

C

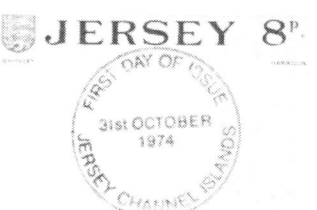

D

E

Jersey first-day cancellations

(D1) Special Handstamps

Numerous special handstamps have been used by the independent postal administration in Jersey. Prices are for covers, each franked with postage stamps of the letter rate current at the time. Where the postage stamp is already catalogued at a higher figure in used condition, this should be *added* to the price given below. Markings for philatelic exhibitions overseas are listed separately for convenience.

JERSEY SPECIAL HANDSTAMPS

Dates of use	Event	Price on cover
5.5.70 and 28.9.70	Visit of M.V. *Kungsholm* to Jersey	75
20.5.70	Trustee Savings Bank Conference	1·00
19.6.70	Dunkirk Veterans Association	60
14.8.70	Visit of M.V. *Gripsholm* to Jersey	75
18.8.70	Interlink Development Ltd. (Used Type **C**)	1·00
26.10.70	Railway Centenary Exhibition	60
1.4.71	30th Anniversary of Jersey's first 1d. stamp	40
6.5.71, 15.8.71 and 1.10.71	Posted on board M.V. *Kungsholm*	40
6.5.71	Imperial Life of Canada Convention	40
7.8.71	Posted on board M.V. *Gripsholm*	40
1971	Normacol Golden Jubilee (in violet)	60
15.5.71	Re-enactment of Siege of Gorey Castle	50
12.6.71	Visit of Cardinal Heenan	20
1.10.71 and 18.10.71	Exhibition of Postal History Société Jersiaise	40
2.10.71	Postal History Society Conference	40
1971	Commonwealth Postal Conference Visit to Jersey ..	50
2.11.71	21st Birthday of Channel Islands Specialists' Society ..	30
1972	Last day of £.s.d. stamps	30
1972	Visit of M.V. *Kungsholm* to Jersey	50
1972	Visit of M.V. *Gripsholm* to Jersey	40
1972	Re-enactment of Battle of Port de la Mare	30
16.5.73	50th Anniversary Aero Philatelic Club	30
29.5.73	Engagement of Princess Anne	1·50
1973	Posted on board M.V. *Gripsholm*	40
5.8.73	Posted on board M.V. *Kungsholm*	40
15.9.73	33rd Anniversary of Battle of Britain	30
26.9.73	Lions Club	30
1.10.73	Opening of new Post Office in Broad Street, St. Helier	30
1.11.73	65 Years of Scouting in Jersey	30
1973	Opening of Jersey Philatelic Bureau, Broad Street	15
5.3.74	Royal Artillery Association Jubilee	30
20.4.74	French Rotary Conference	30
24.4.74	La Corbière Lighthouse Centenary	30
27.4.74	21st National Assembly of Skal Clubs	30
20.7.74	Opening of St. Ouen's Manor	30
31.7.74	Sir Winston Churchill Centenary	40
31.7.74	150th Anniversary of R.N.L.I.	50
12.9.74	50th Anniversary of La Hougue Bie Tomb	30
14.9.74	Battle of Britain	50
30.9.74	Greetings from A. W. Pope Travel Bureau	30
30.11.74	Centenary of Birth of Churchill	40
16.1.75	Swearing-in of new Bailiff	30
15.3.75	25th Anniversary of Channel Islands Specialists' Society	30
9.5.75	30th Anniversary of Liberation	30

Dates of use	Event	Price on cover
2.8.75	Siege of Gorey Castle	30
4.8.75	75th Birthday of Queen Mother	75
8.9.75	European Architectural Heritage Year	30
29.9.75	Hans Christian Andersen Exhibition	30
1975	Launching of Lifeboat	40
26.2.76	230 Squadron, R.A.F.	40
5.3.76	40th Anniversary of first flight of Spitfire	30
29.5.76	Visit of Lord Mayor of London	30
31.10.76	Houdini Jubilee	30
1.3.77 to 4.3.77	Reunion of Association des Parlementaires de Langue Française	30
27.3.77	Official Visit of H.M.S. *Jersey*	25
7.6.77	Jersey Silver Jubilations	30
16.2.78	Jersey Scottish Society Jubilee	25
14.4.78	Multi District 105 Lions Convention	25
18.4.78	Inauguration of Sea Rangers Group	25
13.5.78	Good Food Festival	25
15.5.78	Sub-Postmasters' Federation Conference	25

(D2) Philatelic Exhibitions Overseas

At many of the world's philatelic exhibitions since 1971 the Jersey stand has provided special markings for covers (franked with Jersey stamps) presented for postmarking.

In the list below, (H) signifies a handstamp used for cancelling the stamps; the others are cachets, i.e. commemorative markings for the envelope.

Date of use	*Event*	*Price on cover*
12.3.71	Interpex, New York (H)	5·00
4.6.71 to 14.6.71	Basle Philatelic Exhibition	2·00
24.4.71 to 9.5.71	Foire de Paris	2·00
25.9.71 to 26.9.71	Assindia, Essen	2·00
17.3.72 to 19.3.72	Interpex, New York (H)	3·00
24.6.72 to 9.7.72	Belgica, Brussels	2·00
1972	St. Erick's Fair, Stockholm	2·00
1.11.72	BPE, London	50
2.3.73 to 4.3.73	Expo 73, Anaheim	3·00
9.3.73 to 11.3.73	Interpex, New York	3·00
11.5.73 to 20.5.73	Ibra, Munich	2·00
25.5.73 to 27.5.73	Compex 73, Chicago	2·00
31.10.73 to 3.11.73	BPE, London	1·00
26.2.73 to 3.3.73	Stampex, London	1·00
7.6.74 to 16.6.74	Internaba Exhibition	2·00
29.7.74 to 31.7.74	Philatex, Bournemouth	1·00
21.9.74 to 29.9.74	Stockholmia	2·00
30.10.74 to 2.11.74	BPE, London	1·00
22.11.74 to 24.11.74	ASDA, New York	1·00
29.11.74 to 1.12.74	Stamp Expo North, San Francisco	1·00
4.4.75	España 75, Madrid (H)	2·00
6.6.75	Arphila 75, Paris (H)	2·00
21.11.75 to 23.11.75	ASDA, New York	50
13.12.75	Themabelga, Brussels (H)	2·00
29.5.76	Interphil, New York	50
20. 8.76	Hafnia 76 (H)	50
14.10.76	Italia 76, Milan (H)	50
29.10.76	Rhein–Ruhr Posta 76, Essen (H)	50
19.11.76 to 21.11.76	ASDA, New York	50
1977	San Marino 77	30
1977	NPSS, New York	50
20.5.78 to 25.5.78	Naposta 78	50
9.6.78 to 18.6.78	Capex, Toronto	50
1978	Riccione	30

GUERNSEY

(A) Cachets

Interesting cachets are to be found on mail from Guernsey and they are popular with collectors.

Cachets are normally collected on complete cover to postcard. The prices below should be *added* to the value of the item to take account of the presence of the cachet clearly struck.

1865	Governor/Guernsey, with Royal Arms and Crown. Vertical oval. Blue	25·00
1871	Eugens Tillot/Guernsey. Oval. Blue	3·00
1872	Eugene Cadic/Guernsey, with fleur-de-lis. Oval. Black	6·00
1893	L. S. Constantine/Guernsey/Ile Anglaise. Oval. Red	5·00
1905	Army Pay Office/date/Guernsey. Boxed. Violet	3·00
1907	Cow Lane/St. Martin's/Old Guernsey, used at Old Guernsey Fair on 3.4.07. Black	15·00
1911	D.A.A.G. (Militia) Guernsey & Alderney. Double oval. Black	25·00
1914	Chapelle/Wesleyenne/Route Victoria. Oval. Black	3·00
1915	Great Western Railway/Agent's Office/(date) Guernsey. Violet	4·00
1917	Office of the/Guernsey/Tribunal. Double oval. Black	8·00
1920–21	Via/Mail Boat. Black	2·00
1940	Guernsey Railway Company Ltd., on 3d. bus ticket on cover. Violet	8·00
1957	Visit of the Queen and Duke of Edinburgh. Black	2·50
1965	Lieutenant Governor Guernsey, with Crown. Oval	40
1966	Maison de Victor Hugo & Hauteville House. Black	1·50
1970	Director of Postal Services. Boxed. Violet	50
1970	On Postal Service. Boxed	25
1970	Service des Postes. Boxed	25
1971	Ville/de/Paris/Hauteville House. Vertical oblong. Black	50
1972	Guernsey Welcomes/H.R.H. Princess Anne. Boxed. Green	2·50
1973	National Trust of Guernsey, used at La Viaer Marchi, Saumarez Park 9.7.73	30

(B) Slogans

The wavy lines of the Universal machine cancellation (Section 9) have from time to time been replaced by slogans, as under.

The prices are for complete covers showing clear strikes of the slogan and its associated datestamp, franked with postage stamps of the letter rate current at the time the slogan was applied. Cut-outs from covers and cards are worth one-quarter of the corresponding item on cover. Where the stamp is already catalogued at a higher figure in used condition, however, the slogan price shown below is to be *added* when valuing the entire.

GUERNSEY SLOGANS

Dates of use	Wording	Price on cover
	1947	
20.11.47 to 30.11.47	EP and Wedding Bells	50
	1966	
1.11.66 to 12.12.69	Guernsey British Holiday Abroad	20
	1970	
26.5.70 to 25.1.71	Obesity Shortens Life Treat It Seriously	3·00
	1971	
1.2.71 to Dec. 1972	Stamp Out Overweight	2·00
12.5.71 to 18.5.71	Royal Liver Friendly Society Annual Conference	50
21.5.71 to 2.7.71	First Class Mail	1·00
11.9.71	Guernsey Scout Association 1911–1971 Diamond Jubilee	1·00
	1972	
10.4.72 to 15.4.72	Guernsey TSB/150 Years of Service/Savings Week/10–15 April, 1972	40
	1973	
	Guernsey Issues/Stained Glass Windows/24 Oct. 1973	10·00
	1974	
	Guernsey Issues/R.N.L.I./15 Jan. 1974	10·00
	Guernsey Issues/Second Series/Low Value Definitives/2 April 1974	10·00
	1975	
	Channel Islands 1939–45 Occupation History May 8 ..	25
	1976	
	Beau Sejour Leisure Centre	25

The slogans of 1970 and 1971 about obesity and overweight were used on various occasions for bulk postings arranged by Medical Mailing International.

The First Class Mail slogan of 1971 was introduced because some mail at the 2½p rate to England was wrongly thought to be prepaid only second class by mainland offices.

The slogans of 1973 and 1974 about forthcoming stamps were printed in red additionally to a PAID handstamp (Type **G76a**). They appeared on official correspondence sent out from such Government offices as the Income Tax Department.

(C) "First Day of Issue" Markings

A 2½d. Regional stamp (S.G.6) issued in Guernsey on 8 June 1964 saw the introduction of the general machine cancellation of Great Britain. This is Type **A**, having the words FIRST DAY OF ISSUE on an envelope and printed as a slogan to the right of a circular datestamp inscribed GUERNSEY and containing an arc. After postal independence Type **A** saw further use, though the datestamp now read GUERNSEY POST OFFICE, with the Brock issue on 1 December 1969. On 12 August 1970 (Agriculture issue) and later the envelope slogan has been transposed to the left.

The 4d. and 5d. Regional definitives of 4 September 1968 (S.G. 10 and 12) were given first day cancellations from a rubber handstamp of 26mm diameter. This is a single circle (Type **B**) reading FIRST DAY OF ISSUE around the top and CHANNEL ISLANDS around the bottom. The date and GUERNSEY are across the centre in two lines.

With postal independence on 1 October 1969 Guernsey introduced a new circular datestamp, Type **C**. This is 23½mm in diameter inscribed in upper and lowercase with "Guernsey Post Office" around the top and "First Day of Issue" around the foot. The date appears in one line in the centre, while below this are "Philatelic/Bureau" in small letters.

Guernsey first-day cancellations

Pictorial Handstamps. Specially designed cancellations, often pictorial, have been used on first day covers for later issues beginning with the 1970 Christmas stamps depicting churches.

Incomplete Sets. Incomplete sets passed through the post on the first day still give rise technically to "first day covers", though by philatelic custom this term, without further qualification, is normally understood to imply the presence of a complete set.

The covers can nevertheless still be valued from the table below. This shows by how much the total catalogue value of the stamps in used condition should be increased by virtue of the first-day cancellation.

Type **A**	Slogan to right of GUERNSEY c.d.s.	25
	Slogan to right of GUERNSEY POST OFFICE c.d.s.	30
	Slogan to left of GUERNSEY POST OFFICE c.d.s.	20
Type **B**		60
Type **C**		*nil*

(D1) Special Handstamps

The first special handstamp was introduced in 1967 for a philatelic occasion, the 23rd Annual Conference of the Postal History Society. It was rectangular and reproduced the Guernsey scroll (Type **G2**). Since then numerous other markings, circular or rectangular, have been used. Prices for covers are given below, each franked with postage stamps of the letter rate current at the time. Where the postage stamp is already catalogued at a higher figure in used condition, this should be *added* to the given price.

Markings for philatelic exhibitions overseas are listed separately for convenience.

GUERNSEY SPECIAL HANDSTAMPS

Dates of use	Event	Price on cover
21.10.67	Postal History Society 23rd Annual Conference	1·00
9.2.70	Oldest Pillar Box in British Isles	30
18.2.71	30th Anniversary of Guernsey's first 1d. stamp	40
7.4.71	30th Anniversary of Guernsey's first ½d. stamp	40
4.9.71 to 5.9.71	Guernsey Power Boat Race	75
2.11.71	21st Birthday of Channel Islands Specialists' Society ..	30
25.1.72	150th Anniversary of Trustee Savings Bank	25
1973	Guernsey Variety Club Charter Day	30
15.3.75	25th Anniversary of Channel Islands Specialists' Society	30
1.5.75	Herm Island 50th Anniversary of Sub-office	50
1975	30th Anniversary of Liberation	30
1975	Visit of Queen Mother	75
1975	75th Anniversary Guernsey Rifle Association	30
1975	European Architectural Heritage Year	30
7.6.77	Silver Jubilee	25
1977	Police Open Day	25
1977	Commissioning of H.M.S. *Guernsey*	25
1978	60th Anniversary of R.A.F.	25

(D2) Philatelic Exhibitions Overseas

Guernsey participates in many philatelic exhibitions around the world and special markings are applied to covers (franked with Guernsey stamps) presented for postmarking.

Dates of use	Event	Price on cover
9.3.73 to 11.3.73	Interpex, New York	1·00
4.7.73 to 7.7.73	Apex, Manchester	1·00
1975	Arphila, Paris	50
1976	Interphil 76	75
29.10.76 to 1.11.76	Briefmarken-Messe, Essen	4·00
1976	Italia 76	75
1977	San Marino	50
1977	España 77	50
1978	Naposta 78	40
1978	Riccione 78	40
1978	Torino 78	40
1978	Roma 78	40
1978	Essen 78	40
1978	Capex, Toronto	40

16. Airmails and Hovercraft Mail

Early Airmail Flights (to 1969)

Ballons Montés from Paris are known addressed to Guernsey and Jersey, as are covers flown from London to Windsor on the 1911 Coronation Aerial Post, but the first airmail from the Channel Islands was flown from the French Navy's seaplane base in St. Peter Port, Guernsey in 1917. The various experimental and official airmail services between 1917 and 1969 are described below, and are listed and priced at the end of this Section.

French Seaplane Base in Guernsey, 1917–18.

A French seaplane base was established in Guernsey at the Southern end of St. Peter Port harbour in July 1917. Huts were erected by the Royal Navy and a Bessonau shed was sent from France.

The base was under the command of Lieutenant de Vaisseau Le Cour Grandmaison. There were three pilots (Lambert, Bourgault and Sylvestre) of whom one was an officer, and three observers (Rolin, Parmentier and Boissand). It was intended to have twelve seaplanes at the base but only two were sent in July. In September it was decided that the strength of the base be raised to sixteen patrol aircraft.

Bad weather in the winter caused real difficulties. On 19 December 1917 the motor launch was lost. The commander of the Normandy squadrons was unable to supply the torpedo boat that the base needed. The position was bad for take-off and landing and, because of the winds, the roofs of the portable hangers were in a very bad state. In view of this the Commandant recommended that the base be transferred to Cherbourg.

In January 1918 the strength of the base was eleven Telliers and ten F.B.A.s. In February and March activity was much reduced because of damage to the crane.

Enseigne de Vaisseau Flandrin replaced Lieutenant Le Cour de Grandmaison as commanding officer of the base.

The seaplane base remained in Guernsey until December 1918, when the aircraft were flown to Cherbourg and the 150 men attached to the base left the island.

Two cachets were used on mail sent from the base, which was carried to Cherbourg by seaplanes of the squardon and posted there. The first cachet (Type 1) is unframed and reads, in three lines, CENTRE d'AVION/MARITIME/de GUERNESEY. An example is known struck in violet on a card dated 1 December 1917 bearing Christmas greetings. The second cachet has an anchor in the centre and ESCADRILLE D'AVIATION MARTIME DE GUERNESEY in a double circle (Type 2). This is known struck in blue on several cards from members of the squadron and on a cover addressed to Croydon bearing a British stamp.

It is interesting to note that L. V. Lambert, one of the pilots, became French Consul in Guernsey many years later.

CENTRE d'AVIATION MARITIME ᴅᴇ GUERNESEY.

(1)

(2)

Southampton–Guernsey Flight, 1919. The earliest recorded flight from England to the Channel Islands was on 5 October 1919, during the Railway Strike period, when an unsuccessful attempt was made to carry *Lloyds Weekly News* from Southampton to Guernsey, the pilot of the machine being compelled to alight on the sea near Alderney. Papers were imprinted "By Seaplane, Special Edition", and after the accident were overprinted with a message from the pilot apologising for his failure.

Experimental Flight, 1935. In an effort to demonstrate to the postal authorities how great a saving of time could be effected by carrying mail by air to the Channel Islands, Whoopee Sports Ltd. had a small quantity of covers (less than 100) addressed to Roborough Aerodrome, Plymouth, and posted locally at 5 p.m. on Friday, 27 June 1935. These were flown to Jersey at noon on 28 June and arrived at 1.15 p.m., landing on the beach. The letters were then re-stamped and re-addressed with a grey label covering the old address and were re-posted in Jersey, receiving the 4.15 p.m. cancellation on the same day. The service, however, proved unsuitable for mail-carrying purposes, due to the non-existence of an aerodrome and the fact that the time-table varied with the tides.

Official Flight, 1937. An aerodrome was constructed in Jersey in 1937 and a contract for the transport of first-class mail was awarded to Jersey Airways, the first flights taking place on 1 June. The plane from Jersey left at 6.25 a.m. and arrived at Southampton at 7.37 a.m. with 335lb of mail. That from Southampton left at 7.50 a.m., arriving at Jersey at 8.50 a.m. with 229lb of mail.

An angular cachet (Type **3**) reading JERSEY AIRWAYS LTD/FIRST/AIR/MAIL/FLIGHT/1st JUNE/1937 was applied to covers handled at the Company's offices in London, Jersey or Southampton. Each office used a distinctive coloured ink as follows: London — green, Jersey — blue, Southampton — violet. A similar cachet struck in red was used by a well-known dealer, A. Phillips, on letters from Newport, Monmouthshire. The Jersey and Southampton covers were also endorsed FROM JERSEY or FROM SOUTHAMPTON in the same coloured ink as the cachet.

Covers with meter stamps of Jersey Airways are scarcer than those with adhesives. The slogan attached to the Jersey Airways meter stamp read JERSEY (emblem) AIRWAYS/VICTORIA RLY STATION PHONE VICTORIA 5692/5/1½ HRS − − LONDON − FARE £5/OR FROM/EXETER − SOUTHAMPTON − BRIGHTON. After "£5" the letters "RTN" are inserted vertically in tiny type.

(3)

(4)

(5)

(*Illustrations reduced*)

Covers addressed to the town office of Jersey Airways Ltd. received on arrival a straight-line cachet reading "for Jersey Airways Limited/1 JUN 1937" in blue. Covers addressed to the London office of the airline received on arrival a circular cachet in black reading LONDON/1 JUN 1937/OFFICE.

Guernsey Flights, 1939. The Southampton–Guernsey service by Guernsey Airways Ltd. commenced on 8 May 1939, a plane leaving Southampton at 8 a.m. and arriving at Guernsey at 8.59 a.m. Flown covers usually bear the 11.45 p.m. postmark of Southampton dated 7 May 1939, but twenty covers dispatched from London bear the 12.45 a.m. postmark of London dated 8 May 1939. Some covers received the cachets shown as Types **4** and **5**, the rectangular cachet usually being struck in purple and the circular in green. The aircraft was RMA G-ACZP and the pilot B. Walker.

The first flight from Guernsey took place on 22 May 1939. The plane left Guernsey at 6.28 a.m. and arrived at Southampton at 7.25 a.m. The pilot was J. B. W. Pugh. The usual postmark seen on flown covers is St. Peter Port, Guernsey, 5 a.m. 22 May 1939. Covers have been seen bearing both cachets (Types **4** and **5**) with the dates altered, struck very faintly in black. Privately printed souvenir covers of several kinds exist.

Jersey–Guernsey Flight, 1939. Also on 22 May, mail was flown for the first time from Jersey to Guernsey, the plane leaving Jersey at 6 a.m. and arriving at Guernsey 15 minutes later. No special cachets were applied and genuine flown covers are rare. They normally bear the 5 a.m. Jersey postmark of 22 May 1939. The aircraft was RMA G-ADVK and the pilot J. B. W. Pugh.

The return flight from Guernsey to Jersey did not take place until 10 July 1939. Details of time of departure, etc., are not known. Very little mail was carried owing to inadequate notice being given of the institution of the service. The usual postmark is that of Guernsey timed 5 a.m. on 10 July 1939. Regular services continued until war was declared on 3 September 1939, when all air services between Southampton and the Islands ceased.

Shoreham–Channel Islands Service, 1939. A service between Shoreham and the Islands was resumed on 8 November 1939, running to Jersey and Guernsey on Mondays, Wednesdays and Fridays, and from the Islands on Tuesdays, Thursdays and Saturdays. Daily services operated from 11 December, until the German Occupation on 1 July 1940, when all services were suspended.

Resumption of Air Services, 1945. On 10 September 1945 air services between Southampton and Jersey and Guernsey were resumed in both directions, and also the inter-island services. Special souvenir covers were prepared and were flown from Southampton at 6.30 a.m., Jersey at 9.20 a.m., and

(6)

(7)

Guernsey at 10.05 a.m. Some covers received a circular cachet (Type **6**) in purple applied in Jersey on mail to and from the island, or a rectangular one (Type **7**) in blue applied to mail entering Guernsey. Some covers sent from Guernsey to Jersey also received the rare GUERNSEY CH. IS. PARCEL DEPOT cancellation (Type **G34**) dated 10 SP 45.

Guernsey–Alderney Service, 1946. The first flight from Guernsey to Alderney took place on 18 June 1946 and the return flight was made on the same day. No special markings were applied to letters flown, of which there were eleven from Guernsey to Alderney and forty from Alderney to Guernsey, but they were initialled by the Sub-Postmaster and backstamped with the Alderney datestamp.

B.E.A. Take-over, 1947. When the airlines were nationalised in 1947 the Channel Islands services were taken over by British European Airways and the rectangular datestamps of the Jersey, Guernsey and Southampton offices were applied to letters carried on some flights under the new regime from 1 April. The Jersey stamp was in violet and was lettered A at the bottom; the Guernsey stamp was in violet and was lettered T at the bottom; and the Southampton one was in red and was lettered A at the bottom. Last-day covers under the old service on 31 March have a circular cachet of Channel Islands Airways. This was the parent company of both Jersey and Guernsey Airways and was formed in 1934.

First Alderney–Southampton Direct Mail, 1947. On 20 May 1947 a direct flight was made from Alderney to Southampton and twelve letters were carried by arrangement with the pilot and the Sub-Postmaster of Alderney. They were autographed by the pilot and posted on arrival at Southampton.

Scottish Airlines Flight, 1952. Scottish Airlines inaugurated a regular passenger service between Prestwick and Jersey in the summer of 1952, and on the first flight on 14 June 1952 the pilot, Captain J. C. Grant, carried seven letters which were posted on arrival in Jersey. The covers were stamped in four lines in violet SCOTTISH AIRLINES/PRESTWICK–JERSEY/FIRST FLIGHT/14 JUN 1952 and were signed by the pilot. Covers on the return flight bear a three-line cachet in black SCOTTISH AIRWAYS/JERSEY–PRESTWICK/14 JUN 1952.

B.E.A. Airway Letter Services, 1953. On 20 October 1953 British European Airways extended their Airways Letter Service to the Channel Islands, using the then current B.E.A. stamps for prepayment of their charges. The rates charged were 7d. for letters up to 2oz, 1s. from 2oz to 4oz, and 1s. 6d. from 4oz to 1lb, in addition to the ordinary inland postage. Letters had to be properly stamped and handed into the B.E.A. office or airport endorsed "To be called for" or "To be posted on arrival". The letters were then flown to the destination and those marked "To be posted on arrival" were dropped into the nearest pillar box and the postage stamps were cancelled by the Post Office. A letter from London to Jersey would have the B.E.A. stamp cancelled in London and the postage stamp would be cancelled in Jersey by B.E.A., either with the rectangular datestamp of the local office, with a rubber stamp reading CANCELLED, or by pen. The flights were made between Jersey and London, Guernsey and London, Jersey and Guernsey, and Guernsey and Alderney.

On 25 November 1953 the B.E.A. rates were raised to 8d., 1s. 2d., and 1s. 9d. and new stamps were issued. The rates were raised to 9d., 1s. 3d. and 1s. 11d. on 1 September 1954, using stamps of the same design with the values printed in black instead of in the colour of the stamps.

On 27 June 1956 the rates were increased to 10d., 1s. 5d., and 2s. 2d. and new stamps of smaller format were issued. When the rates were raised again on 1 July 1957, to 11d., 1s. 6d., and 2s. 4d., stamps of the same design were used.

The reason for the almost annual increases in rates was the increased railway freight charges. The charge for airway letters must be the same as that for railway letters and when British Rail put their charges up the Postmaster General insisted that British European Airways do the same.

Only during the 1953 and 1954 rate increases were first day covers flown between London and Guernsey and London and Jersey, although, of course, genuine commerical covers can be found flown on later dates.

Because of difficulties with H.M. Customs at London Aiport, British European Airways were forced to suspend their Airway Letter Service to

London from Jersey and Guernsey from 24 July to 2 September 1956, and then discontinue it altogether. There has been no embargo on the carriage of letters to the Islands from Britain. Some covers handed in at Guernsey on 24 July were marked "Received before embargo" and were carried in the normal way.

The rate was increased from 11d. to 1s. on 4 October 1961 and 100 covers were flown from London to Jersey. They bear the datestamps of the Air Mail Branch, London, and Jersey Airport.

A new series of Airway Letter stamps was issued in 1964 and covers bearing the 1s. stamp were flown from London to Jersey on 27 May.

A further series was issued in 1970 and letters bearing the 3s. 7d. stamp were flown from London to Guernsey and Jersey on 1 May. On 15 February 1971 covers with decimal 18p, 21p and 26p stamps were flown to Guernsey and Jersey.

Throughout its existence B.E.A. used several four-lined boxed or unboxed datestamps to cancel the Airway Letter Service stamps, either at the Guernsey and Jersey airports or at the town offices. Although each datestamp differed slightly they were all of a similar design which read B.E.A./date/GUERNSEY (or JERSEY)/AIRPORT and B.E.A./date/JERSEY (or GUERNSEY)/TOWN. Violet was the normal colour of ink, but black and red are also recorded.

Cambrian Airways Flight, 1964. On 2 December 1964 Cambrian Airways carried letters from Bristol to Guernsey and from Cardiff to Jersey. Special 1s. Cambrian Airways Air Letter stamps were used.

Helicopter Flight, 1965. On 1 November 1965 B.E.A. carried 100 covers from Jersey to Guernsey and 100 covers from Guernsey to Jersey by helicopter. They carried 1s. B.E.A. Airway Letter stamps cancelled at the airports. The covers from Jersey had a black rectangular cachet featuring a helicopter and inscribed FIRST SCHEDULED HELICOPTER FLIGHT/JERSEY – GUERNSEY. The covers from Guernsey had a similar cachet in green inscribed GUERNSEY – JERSEY.

British United Airways Flight, 1966. On 5 August 1966 British United Airways carried a dozen covers from Paris to Jersey. They were franked by French 60c. stamps and carried a red boxed cachet reading BRITISH UNITED/PARIS JERSEY/5 Aout 1966. On arrival in Jersey they received the British United datestamp of Jersey Airport.

Modern Flights (from 1969 onwards)
The flights from 1969 onwards are too numerous to describe in detail and, with certain exceptions, are less important. They are included in the priced list at the end of this Section.

Anniversary of First Airmail, 1969. To commemorate the thirtieth anniversary of the first airmail from Guernsey to England, special covers were flown on 22 May by L. E. Batchelor in a Cessna 172. The aircraft first called at Jersey to carry mail from Jersey to Guernsey and there picked up mail for England. The flight terminated at Thruxton. There were 150 matched pairs of covers signed by the pilot and a further 350 unsigned covers. A few of the original 1939 covers were also reflown.

Inauguration of New Postal Administrations, 1969. To commemorate the inauguration of the new Jersey and Guernsey Postal Administrations, British European Airways carried 1000 covers from each island to Heathrow. Both covers carry the B.E.A. insignia and the inscription "1st October 1969 British European Airways Commemorate the Inauguration of the States of Jersey Postal Administration (States of Guernsey Post Office)".

The Jersey covers bear the Jersey 2s. 6d. stamp featuring the airport and cancelled with the special Jersey first-day postmark. They also have the boxed B.E.A. Jersey Airport datestamp of 1 October 1969. The Guernsey covers have the Guernsey ½d., 1d., 1½d. and 5d. stamps cancelled with the special Day of Issue postmark.

Hovermail Flights
Channel Islands hovermail first started in 1969. The Hovermail Collectors' Club organised the majority of these first flights and, with one exception, less than 100 covers were carried on each flight. The one exception was the visit to the Islands by VT1.001 of Vosper Thorneycroft Ltd. in 1971. This craft carried out six special flights and several thousands of dealers' covers were on board although the craft also carried a very limited number of private covers and official mail of Hovertravel Ltd.

From 1976, hovermail posted in the waters around the Channel Islands has been dealt with in the same manner as paquebot mail, the first usage for mail posted at sea on board hovercraft. Apart from this paquebot mail which has been handled in accordance with U.P.U. regulations, no official mail has been carried either to or from the Channel Islands by hovercraft.

JERSEY AIRMAIL COVERS

*Inter-island flight. For convenience of reference the cover is listed under *both* islands and marked with an asterisk.

	1870	
	Ballons Montés from Paris, addressed to Jersey .. ..*from*	£200

	1911	
9/15.9.11	Coronation Aerial Post, London to Windsor, addressed to Jersey .. ..*from*	30·00

	1935	
28.6.35	Whoopee Sports Ltd. experimental flight	45·00

	1937	
1.6.37	Jersey Airways Ltd. (Type **3**). Blue	8·00
1.6.37	As above, but violet (Southampton)	8·00
1.6.37	As above, but green (London)	10·00
1.6.37	As above, but red (Newport, Mon., applied by A. Phillips)	9·00
1.6.37	Jersey Airways London. Meter stamp on first flight cover	12·00
1.6.37	"For Jersey Airways Limited/1 June 1937" straight-line cachet. Blue	15·00
1.6.37	LONDON/1 JUN 1937/OFFICE circular cachet. Black	8·00

	1939	
22.5.39*	Jersey to Guernsey inter-island, no cachets	25·00
10.6.39*	Guernsey to Jersey inter-island, no cachets	30·00

	1945	
10.9.45	Resumption of air services souvenir cover, no cachets	10·00
10.9.45	Circular cachet JERSEY/AIRWAYS (Type **6**). Purple	12·00

	1946	
	First Flight of Bristol Wayfarer, Filton–Jersey. Signed by pilot, J. Pegg	20·00

	1947	
1.4.47	B.E.A./JERSEY/A rectangular datestamp. Violet. In use from this date ..	8·00

	1948	
10.5.48	B.E.A. Advertising letter sent in f.d.c. of Channel Islands Liberation Issue. Envelope imprinted BRITISH EUROPEAN AIRWAYS	8·00

	1952	
14.6.52	SCOTTISH AIRLINES/PRESTWICK–JERSEY. Violet	40·00
14.6.52	SCOTTISH AIRWAYS/JERSEY–PRESTWICK, unframed. Black	30·00

	1953	
	B.E.A./JERSEY/AIRPORT, boxed datestamp. Black	5·00

	1954	
1.9.54	National Institute of Oceanography card dropped in the Atlantic by R.A.F. washed ashore on Jersey	25·00

	1961	
	B.E.A./JERSEY/AIRPORT boxed datestamp. Red	5·00

	1964	
17.7.64	Large double-circle FREEDOM/GROUP datestamp, on cover to Jersey ..	20·00
2.12.64	First Flight by Cambrian Airways from Cardiff to Jersey. With special 1s. Airway Letter stamp cancelled with boxed Cambrian Airways Ltd. cachet	14·00

	1965	
1.11.65	FIRST SCHEDULED HELICOPTER FLIGHT/JERSEY–GUERNSEY and helicopter. Black	10·00

1966

5.8.66   BRITISH UNITED/PARIS JERSEY boxed datestamp. Red .. .. 35·00

1968

28.5.68   B.E.A./JERSEY/AIRPORT boxed datestamp. Blue. BRITISH EUROPEAN
AIRWAYS/FRET/ORLY circular cachet. Violet .. .. 20·00

1969

22.5.69*   Jersey–Guernsey–England Airmail 30th Anniversary Flight .. .. 8·00
31.5.69   Re-introduction of Jersey to Portsmouth service. CHANNEL AIRWAYS/
PORTSMOUTH AIRPORT, HANTS boxed cachet .. .. 10·00
31.5.69   Re-introduction of Portsmouth to Jersey Service. CHANNEL AIRWAYS/
PORTSMOUTH AIRPORT, HANTS boxed cachet .. .. 10·00
13.7.69   Jersey–Caen Flight. BRITISH UNITED/ISLAND AIRWAYS/JERSEY AIRPORT
datestamp in black and FIRST FLIGHT/JERSEY CAEN unframed cachet   5·00
13.7.69   As above, but with unframed cachet PREMIER VOL/CAEN JERSEY and
date. Black .. .. 5·00
1.10.69   B.E.A. commemoration of new postal administration. Boxed B.E.A./
JERSEY/AIRPORT datestamp in violet on f.d.c. to London .. .. 3·00
2.12.69   50th Anniversary England-Australia Flight, with Inauguration stamp
and special circular cancellation .. .. 12·00

1970

24.2.70   Jersey–Derby Flight. British Midland Airways/JERSEY unframed
datestamp .. .. 5·00
28.3.70   Plymouth–Jersey Flight WESTWARD/AIRWAYS LTD unframed cachet.
Black .. .. 5·00
29.3.70   Jersey–Plymouth Flight WESTWARD/AIRWAYS LTD unframed cachet.
Black .. .. 5·00
1.5.70   New B.E.A. Airway Letter stamps (3s. 7d., 4s. 3d., 5s. 2d.) on flown
cover Heathrow–Jersey .. .. 2·00
2.5.70   Jersey–Manchester Flight BRITISH UNITED/JERSEY/AIRPORT boxed
datestamp. Blue .. .. 5·00
7.5.70   R.A.F. Flight. Red oval datestamp H.Q. OPERATIONS WING/R.A.F.
WADDINGTON .. .. 10·00
8/9.5.70   Plymouth–Guernsey–Jersey Flight by Aurigny Air Services, with
Aurigny Airport cachets in blue. Signed by pilots .. .. .. 10·00
9.5.70   25th Anniversary of Liberation of Channel Islands f.d.c. flown by
B.E.A. .. .. 6·00
5.6.70   Jersey–Quimper Flight. Four-line unframed cachet in black .. .. 9·00
20.6.70   25th Anniversary of re-opening of civil airways in Jersey. B.E.A./
JERSEY/AIRPORT .. .. 1·00
13.9.70   Jersey–Lessay Flight. Boxed BRITISH/ISLAND AIRWAYS/JERSEY
AIRPORT datestamp in black .. .. 9·00

1971

20.1.71   Southampton–Jersey Flight by B.E.A. Vickers Viscount. Boxed six-line
cachet with flight details. Black. Also two B.E.A. boxed datestamps
in red and black. Posted on first day of Postal Strike .. .. .. 2·00
24.1.71   Jersey–Paris Flight. With BIA cachet in blue .. .. 2·00
3.4.71   Jersey–Manchester Flight. With boxed BRITISH ISLAND/AIRWAYS
Duty Officer/Jersey Airport datestamp in black and ten-line undated
flight details in violet .. .. 2·00
3.4.71   Jersey–Staverton Flight. With INTRA/JERSEY/AIRPORT unframed
datestamp and ten-line flight details in violet .. .. 2·00
3.4.71   Staverton–Jersey Flight with INTRA AIRWAYS LTD/STATES AIRPORT
/ST. PETER/JERSEY cachet in red and ten-line flight details in violet .. 2·00
9.4.71   Cambrian Airways First Jet Flight, Heathrow–Jersey. Six-line unframed
cachet. Black .. .. 4·00
14.5.71   Portsmouth–Jersey Flight. With unframed J.F. AIRLINES four-line
cachet in blue .. .. 2·00
14.5.71   As above, but with eight-line cachet in violet .. .. 2·00

14.5.71	As above, but with eight-line cachet in violet and signed by pilot	3·00
12.6.71	Jersey–Brest Flight by Rousseau Aviation. With unframed eight-line cachet in blue	4·00
3.7.71	Jersey–Le Havre Flight by Rousseau Aviation. With unframed seven-line flight cachet in blue	4·00
6.7.71	FIRST TRISLANDER TO JERSEY straight-line cachet in black	5·00
6.7.71	Jersey–La Baule Flight by Rousseau Aviation. With unframed eight-line cachet in black	2·00
6.7.71	As above, but with ten-line unframed flight details in blue	2·00
1.10.71*	First scheduled Jersey–Guernsey Trislander Flight. With boxed AURIGNY/AIR datestamp in black, four-line unframed red cachet and one-line cachet in green	7·00
1.10.71*	First scheduled Guernsey–Jersey Trislander Flight. Cachets as above but one-line cachet is in red	7·00
1.11.71	Jersey–Gatwick Flight. With black BRITISH ISLAND/AIRWAYS boxed datestamp and four-line unframed cachet in green	2·00

1972

10.1.72	First Jersey–Rennes Flight. With eight-line unframed cachet in red ..	3·00
10.1.72	As above, but airmail envelope with four-line unframed cachet in red	6·00
29.2.72	Jersey–Southend last Channel Airways, 29 Feb. First Flight reflown Southend–Jersey by British Midland Airways, 2 March. With six-line black cachet	4·00
2.4.72	B.E.A. 25th Anniversary Flight. With boxed black cachet (London–Jersey)	2·00
2.4.72	As above but signed by pilot	4·00
2.4.72	As above, but with green cachet (Jersey–London)	2·00
2.4.72	As above, but signed by pilot	4·00
4.4.72	First Southend–Jersey Flight by British Midland. Four-line black cachet	4·00
7.4.72	50th Anniversary R.A.F. Regt. B.F.P.O. 1282 Jersey, on pictorial cover with 4p stamp	1·00
7.4.72	As above, but with 9p stamp and signed B. P. Young	3·00
21.4.72	Jersey–Caen First Flight by Intra Airways. With nine-line unframed cachet in black	2·00
7.5.72	Jersey–Amsterdam First Flight. With boxed cachet in violet	10·00
7.5.72	As above, but green cachet (Amsterdam–Jersey)	10·00
10.5.72	Jersey–Cambridge First Flight. With seven-line unframed black cachet	2·00
14.5.72	Jersey–Coventry First Flight by British Air Ferries. With five-line cachet in blue	4·00
27.5.72	Swansea–Jersey First Flight by Dan-Air. With six-line cachet in green and SWANSEA AIRPORT in blue	2·00
27.5.72	Carlisle–Jersey First Flight by Dan-Air. With five-line cachet in red and DAN-AIR NEWCASTLE in blue	2·00
18.6.72	First Flight Plymouth–Jersey by Brymon Aviation. With nine-line unboxed cachet in red	2·00
18.6.72	As above, but green cachet (Jersey–Plymouth)	2·00
1.7.72	B.E.A. 50p stamp on flown f.d.c. to Jersey from Heathrow	2·00
26.8.72	Brymon Aviation Flight to Jersey by Islander for 60th Anniversary of first aircraft to land in Jersey. With five-line cachet in black and special Jersey Air Race 1912 booklet	3·00
26.9.72	Jersey–Paris by B.E.A. to British Exhibition. With diamond-shaped cachet in black	1·50
26.9.72	Jersey–Paris by B.I.A. to British Exhibition. With red EX-POSITION/ GRANDE-/BRETAGNE/B.I.A. cachet	2·00

1973

2.1.73	Bournemouth–Jersey First Cargo/Mail Flight by Intra Airways. With four-line cachet in red and BOURNEMOUTH AIRPORT boxed datestamp	2·00
2.1.73	As above, but official Intra Airways postcard with four-line cachet in blue	2·00
2.1.73	Jersey–Dinard Inaugural Flight by Intra Airways. With eight-line cachet in blue	2·00

16.4.73	Morlaix–Jersey Inaugural Flight by Intra Airways. With boxed five-line cachet in blue	2·00
17.4.73	Portsmouth–Jersey Inaugural Flight by J.F. Airlines Islander. With nine-line cachet in blue	4·00
17.4.73	Jersey–Portsmouth Inaugural Flight by J.F. Airlines Islander. With four-line violet cachet	4·00
17.4.73	Portsmouth–Jersey Inaugural Flight by J.F. Airlines Trislander. With four-line red cachet and AURIGNY/JERSEY datestamp in black	4·00
17.4.73	As above, but Jersey–Portsmouth and black four-line cachet	4·00
22.4.73	Jersey–Newquay first scheduled flight by Brymon Airways. With BRYMON/22 APR 1973/NEWQUAY datestamp in black	1·00
12.5.73	Jersey–Ashford Inaugural Flight by Dan-Air Skyways Ltd. With eight-line cachet in red and BRITISH MIDLAND AIRWAYS/12 MAY 1973/JERSEY datestamp in blue	1·00
12.5.73	As above, but Ashford–Jersey Flight	1·00
12.5.73	Jersey–Ostend Inaugural Flight by Intra Airways. With eight-line cachet in red	1·00
15.5.73	40th Anniversary of First Official Airway Letter Service, Heathrow–Jersey. With five-line boxed cachet in green	1·00
16.5.73	Paris–Jersey Flight by B.I.A. With boxed nine-line cachet in green ..	1·00
16.5.73	Jersey–Heathrow Flight by B.E.A. With hexagonal blue cachet	1·00
16.5.73	Balloon Flight U.S. airletter with Jersey stamp. With cachet FLIGHT CANCELLED	1·00
16.5.73	Jersey Balloon Post Flight for Children's Aid, special card	4·00
19.5.73	Belfast–Jersey Inaugural Flight by British Midland Airways. With five-line cachet in blue and British Midland Belfast datestamp	1·00
19.5.73	Jersey–Stanstead Inaugural Flight by British Midland Airways. With five-line cachet in blue and British Midland datestamp of Jersey and Stanstead	1·00
22.5.73	Jersey–Deauville First Flight by Intra Airways. With seven-line cachet in green	1·00
	Jersey–Orly Flight by B.E.A. freight. With red circular cachet BRITISH EUROPEAN AIRWAYS/ORLY/FRET, and JERSEY AIRPORT in black	1·00
5/6.6.73	Balloon Flight airletter of 16 May. Reflown Iserlohn 5 and 6 June. With red balloon cachets	3·50
7.6.73	First day cover Aviation issue of 16.5.73 flown Jersey–Manchester by B.E.A. on 7 June. With special Aero-Philatelic Club 50th Anniversary cancellation of Jersey	1·00
15.9.73	Jersey–Coltishall Flight by R.A.F. With Battle of Britain cancellation	1·00
15.9.73	As above, but signed by pilot	2·00
27.10.73	Jersey–Caen–Exeter Flight by Intra Airways. With red and black cachets	2·00
27.10.73	As above, but return flight	2·00
31.10.73	Jersey–Heathrow last scheduled Vanguard flight by B.E.A. With four-line black cachet and signed by pilot	2·00
3.11.73	Jersey–Bournemouth Flight by B.I.A. With five-line blue cachet	1·00
3.11.73	As above, but return flight. With six-line green cachet	1·00
19.12.73	40th Anniversary Portsmouth–Jersey air service. Signed by pilot ..	2·00

1974

5.3.74	Jersey–Bournemouth Flight by Dan-Air. With four-line red cachet ..	1·00
1.4.74	New 55p B.E.A. Airway Letter stamp on flown cover from Heathrow to Jersey	1·00
19.4.74	Jersey–Luton Flight by British Midland. With four-line black cachet ..	2·50
19.4.74	As above, but return flight	2·50
20.4.74	Jersey–Bournemouth Flight by Dan-Air. With three-line blue cachet ..	1·00
24.4.74	Jersey–Bournemouth Flight by Dan-Air. With three-line red cachet ..	1·00
27.4.74	Jersey–Bournemouth Flight by B.I.A. With three-line blue cachet ..	1·00
7.6.74	Jersey–London Flight by British Airways. With U.P.U. set	2·00
19.6.74	Jersey–St. Brieuc Flight by Intra Airways. With five-line red cachet ..	2·00

28.6.74	British Airways Inaugural B.A.C. 1-11 Flight Birmingham–Jersey. With four-line red cachet	2·00
28.6.74	As above, but return flight	2·00
28.6.74	Birmingham–Jersey Flight by British Airways B.A.C. 1-11. With four-line cachet in black	2·00
20.7.74	Jersey–Luton Flight by British Midland. With five-line cachet in blue	1·00
	Battle of Britain Week cover flown over Jersey by Red Arrows. With typewritten inscription and signed by pilot	20·00
31.7.74	Jersey–Bournemouth Flight by B.I.A. With three-line cachet in violet	1·00
19.9.74	Battle of Britain R.A.F.A. card with two-line cachet in red. Flown from Bournemouth to Jersey	1·00
29.10.74	Jersey–Cherbourg First Flight by Aurigny. With four-line blue cachet and three-line red cachet	1·00
29.10.74	Jersey–Cherbourg by Aurigny. With two-line black cachet	1·00
29.10.74	As above, but return flight. With two-line green cachet	1·00
	1975	
16.1.75	Jersey–Bournemouth by Dan-Air. With boxed four-line cachet of Dan-Air Hurn Airport in black	75
29.3.75	Air Anglia First Scheduled Flight Humberside–Jersey. With four-line cachet in brown	75
29.3.75	As above, but Jersey–Humberside. With four-line cachet in blue	75
30.4.75	British Airways Last Scheduled Merchantman Flight, Heathrow–Jersey. With five-line cachet in violet and signed by pilot	2·00
30.4.75	As above, but Jersey–Heathrow	2·00
2.5.75	British Airways Inaugural Flight Jersey–Düsseldorf. With five-line cachet in green	3·00
2.5.75	As above, but Düsseldorf–Jersey	3·00
5.5.75	British Airways First Trials Flight Heathrow–Jersey by BAC 1-11. With six-line cachet in red	3·00
10.5.75	First Scheduled Flight by Air Anglia Aberdeen–Jersey. With four-line blue cachet	75
10.5.75	As above, but return flight. With four-line cachet in yellow	75
10.5.75	Air Anglia Humberside–Jersey Flight for Amy Johnson Festival	75
17.5.75	British Airways First Passenger Flight by Super 1-11 Heathrow–Jersey. With four-line blue cachet	2·00
17.5.75	As above, but return flight. With four-line red cachet	2·00
18.5.75	First Scheduled BAC 1-11 Flight Jersey–Gatwick by Dan-Air. With four-line purple cachet	75
18.5.75	As above, but return flight. With four-line green cachet	75
24.5.75	First Scheduled Flight Dan-Air Lydd–Jersey	75
30.5.75*	First Operational Flight of Trislander G-BCVX Alderney–Jersey	1·00
4.6.75	British Airways First Passenger Flight by Super 1-11 Manchester–Jersey. With four-line black cachet	2·00
18.9.75	Battle of Britain Week cover flown over Jersey by Red Arrows. With typewritten inscription and signed by pilot	10·00
30.10.75	10th Anniversary of Red Arrows. R.A.F. Museum cover with Jersey 25p stamp cancelled with special datestamp and signed by the team	3·00
30.10.75	10th Anniversary of Red Arrows. Jersey airletter flown to Bournemouth by Dan-Air	6·00
17.12.75	INRA Special Flight for 40th Anniversary of first Dakota flight from Jersey to Dinard	1·00
21.12.75	No. 56 Squadron R.A.F., R.A.F. Museum cover with Jersey 4p stamp	1·00
	1976	
20/21.1.76	Jersey–Bahrain via London on Concorde Inaugural Flight B.A.C. cover	2·50
29.1.76	Jersey first day of issue of 11p definitive of Jersey Airport, flown by British Airways to Heathrow	50
5.4.76	Commemorating Opening of British Caledonian Airways Jersey Airport Office, flown from Gatwick to Jersey by B.C.A.	75
15.4.76	R.A.F. 320 British Squadron special Jersey postmark on R.A.F. cover flown 19.5.76	50

18.4.76	Jersey–Carlisle. First Scheduled Flight by Dan-Air Services Ltd. ..	50
18.4.76	Carlisle–Jersey. First Scheduled Flight by Dan-Air Services Ltd. ..	50
1.5.76	British Airways first day of issue of £1 Airway Letter Service stamp, flown London to Jersey	1·50
23/24.5.76	Jersey–Washington via London on Concorde Inaugural Flight, B.A.C. cover	1·75
29.5.76	Jersey first day of issue of Links with America 11p, flown by British Airways to London and New York	1·75
8.6.76	R.A.F. 60th Anniversary of 56 Squadron. Special Jersey postmark on R.A.F. flown cover	50
27.10.76	Jersey–Leeds. First Scheduled Flight by Air Anglia	50
27.10.76	Leeds–Jersey. First Scheduled Flight by Air Anglia	50

1977

7.2.77	Jersey first day of issue of Silver Jubilee set, flown by British Airways to London	1·00
1.3.77	Dinard to Jersey, cover flown by Intra Airways with French Delegation	50
10.3.77	40th Anniversary of Jersey Airport, flown by B.I.A. from Southampton to Jersey	50
10.3.77	40th Anniversary of Jersey Airport, flown by British Caledonian Airways from Gatwick to Jersey	50
10.3.77*	40th Anniversary of Jersey Airport, flown by Aurigny from Alderney to Jersey	50
28.4.77	R.A.F. Introduction of the Hawk, special Jersey postmark on R.A.F. flown cover	50
14.5.77	Jersey–Amsterdam. First Scheduled Flight by Air Anglia	50
14.5.77	Amsterdam–Jersey. First Scheduled Flight by Air Anglia	50
18.5.77	Jersey–Brussels. First Scheduled Flight by Intra Airways Ltd.	50
18.5.77	Brussels–Jersey. First Scheduled Flight by Intra Airways Ltd.	50
2.6.77	R.A.F. Honouring 60 Squadron, special Jersey postmark on R.A.F. flown cover	50
7.6.77*	Silver Jubilee Celebration Day Flight by Aurigny Air Services, flown Guernsey to Jersey	1·50
11.8.77	Battle of Flowers special Jubilee cover, flown by Busybodies Hot Air Balloon	1·00
19/22. 11.77	Jersey–New York via London on Concorde Inaugural Flight B.A.C. cover	3·00
8/9.12.77	Jersey–Singapore via London on Concorde Inaugural Flight B.A.C. cover	3·75

1978

21.3.78*	Jersey–Guernsey–Jersey Inaugural Inter-Island Service by Intra Airways	60

GUERNSEY AIRMAIL COVERS

*Inter-island flight. For convenience of reference the cover is listed under *both* islands and marked with an asterisk.

	1870	
	Ballons Montés from Paris, addressed to Guernsey .. ..*from*	£350
	1911	
9/15.9.11	Coronation Aerial Post London to Windsor, addressed to Guernsey .. ..*from*	35·00
16.9.11	Coronation Aerial Post Windsor to London addressed to Guernsey .. ..*from*	60·00
	1917	
	CENTRE d'AVION/MARITIME/de GUERNESEY three line. Violet (Type 1)	£100
	1918	
	Circular ESCADRILLE D'AVIATION MARITIME DE GUERNESEY (Type 2). Blue and violet	70·00
	1919	
5.10.19	Newspaper with BY/SEAPLANE/SPECIAL/EDITION	25·00
	1939	
8.5.39	Southampton–Guernsey GUERNSEY AIRWAYS (Type 4). Purple or black	10·00
8.5.39	Southampton–Guernsey GUERNSEY AIRWAYS (Type 5). Green or black	10·00
8.5.39	Southampton–Guernsey (Type 4) on London dispatch cover	20·00
22.5.39	Guernsey–Southampton. Souvenir cover	10·00
22.5.39	As above but with Type **4** and Type **5** cachets	15·00
22.5.39*	Jersey to Guernsey inter-island, no cachets	25·00
10.6.39*	Guernsey to Jersey inter-island, no cachets	30·00
	1945	
10.9.45	Resumption of Air services Souvenir cover, no cachets	10·00
10.9.45	JERSEY AIRWAYS (Type 7). Blue	14·00
	1946	
18.6.46*	Guernsey to Alderney, no cachets	45·00
18.6.46*	Alderney to Guernsey, no cachets	20·00
	1947	
31.3.47	Large double-circle CHANNEL ISLANDS/AIRWAYS/GUERNSEY OFFICE. Black	12·00
1.4.47	B.E.A. GUERNSEY T rectangular datestamp. Violet. In use from this date	8·00
1.4.47	B.E.A. SOUTHAMPTON A rectangular datestamp. Red. In use from this date	80
	1953	
	B.E.A./GUERNSEY/AIRPORT boxed datestamp. Violet	5·00
	B.E.A./GUERNSEY/TOWN boxed datestamp. Violet	5·00
	1954	
7.8.54	Herm Island B.E.A. Feeder Service	10·00
	B.E.A./GUERNSEY/AIRPORT boxed datestamp. Black	5·00
1.9.54	National Institute of Oceanography card dropped in Atlantic by R.A.F. washed ashore on Guernsey	25·00
1.9.54	As above, but washed ashore on Sark	35·00
	1956	
	B.E.A./GUERNSEY/TOWN boxed datestamp. Black	5·00

1964
	B.E.A./GUERNSEY/AIRPORT datestamp, unframed, Black	5·00
2.12.64	First Flight by Cambrian Airways from Bristol to Guernsey. With 1s. Airway Letter stamp cancelled with boxed CAMBRIAN AIRWAYS LTD. datestamp	14·00
2.12.64	Cambrian Airways Flight from Guernsey to Jersey. With 1s. Airway Letter stamp cancelled with B.E.A. GUERNSEY AIRPORT unframed datestamp	14·00

1965
1.11.65	FIRST SCHEDULED HELICOPTER FLIGHT/GUERNSEY–JERSEY and helicopter. Green	10·00

1969
31.3.69	B.E.A./GUERNSEY/AIRPORT, large boxed datestamp in violet and B.E.A./LAST FLIGHT/JERSEY–GUERNSEY, unframed cachet in black. On last inter-island flight by B.E.A.	10·00
22.5.69*	Guernsey–England Airmail 30th Anniversary Flight to Thruxton	8·00
1.10.69	B.E.A. commemoration of new postal administration on f.d.c. to London. Circular first day postmark	3·00

1970
1.5.70	New B.E.A. Airway Letter stamps (3s. 7d., 4s. 3d., 5s. 2d.) on flown cover Heathrow–Guernsey	2·00
9.5.70	25th Anniversary of Liberation of Channel Islands f.d.c. flown by B.E.A.	6·00
10.11.70	Manston–Guernsey flight by Invicta Air Cargo. With single-line INVICTA AIR CARGO (1969) LIMITED. Black	8·00

1971
16.1.71	Guernsey–Heathrow flight by Vickers Viscount for 20th Anniversary of B.E.A. Air Letter stamp. Six-line unframed cachet in red	4·00
20.1.71	Gatwick–Guernsey flight by B.E.A. Vickers Viscount with boxed six-line cachet with flight details in black, and B.E.A. four-line unframed datestamp in black. Posted on first day of Postal Strike	2·00
23.5.71	Guernsey–Staverton Flight by Intra Airways. With ten-line green cachet	2·00
23.5.71	As above, but return flight	2·00
1.6.71	Portsmouth–Guernsey Flight by J.F.A. With eight-line violet cachet	2·00
1.6.71	As above, but signed by pilot	3·00
12.6.71	Guernsey–Cherbourg Flight by Rousseau Aviation. Eight-line unframed cachet in black with flight details	4·00
18.6.71*	25th Anniversary of first airmail Guernsey–Alderney and return. No cachets	2·00
5.7.71	FIRST TRISLANDER TO JERSEY, straight-line cachet in black. Cover with Guernsey postage stamp but posted in Jersey	5·00
1.10.71*	First scheduled Guernsey–Jersey Flight by Trislander. Four-line cachet in red and single-line GUERNSEY–JERSEY SERVICE in red. Boxed AURIGNY/AIR datestamp. Black	7·00
1.10.71*	First scheduled Jersey–Guernsey Flight by Trislander. Cachets as above but single-line cachet is in green	7·00
1.11.71	Guernsey–Alderney–Southampton First Flight by Trislander. Six-line unframed cachet in green	4·00

1972
1.4.72	B.E.A. 25th Anniversary Flight. With boxed red cachet (London to Guernsey)	2·00
1.4.72	As above, but signed by pilot	4·00
1.4.72	As above, but with black cachet (Guernsey to London)	2·00
1.4.72	As above, but signed by pilot	4·00

1.7.72	B.E.A. 50p stamp on flown f.d.c. to Guernsey from Heathrow ..	2·00
1.7.72	As above, but flown from Manchester	6·00
1.7.72	As above, but flown from Birmingham	6·00
4.8.72	Operation Redskin airletter flown from Guernsey to Hurn, Bournemouth, during airlift of tomatoes by Saggittair. With large red cachet	5·00
24.8.72	Guernsey Battle of Flowers Balloon Flight airletter. With five-line cachet in red	2·00
26.9.72	Guernsey–Paris Flight by B.E.A. to British Exhibition. With diamond-shaped cachet in black	1·50
26.9.72	Guernsey–Paris Flight by B.I.A. to British Exhibition. With red EXPOSITION/GRANDE/BRETAGNE B.I.A. cachet	2·00

1973

21.1.73	No. 201 Squadron R.A.F. cover with special cancellation from Guernsey to Kinross via St. Mawgan (Newquay)	1·00
21.1.73	As above, but signed by pilot	3·00
21.1.73	As above, but cover flown round world and signed by pilot	5·00
7.3.73	Guernsey–Bristol Flight. New 6½p airletter flown by Cambrian Airways Viscount via Cardiff. With red Cambrian Airways label and seven-line cachet in black	5·00
17.4.73	Portsmouth–Guernsey Inaugural Flight by Islander. With seven-line black cachet	1·00
17.4.73	Portsmouth–Guernsey Flight by J.F. Airlines	1·00
21.4.73	Guernsey–Plymouth Flight by Brymon Airways. With two-line BRYMON/PLYMOUTH cachet	2·00
21.4.73	As above, but return flight. With boxed BRYMON/GUERNSEY cachet	1·00
3.5.73	Guernsey–Amsterdam First Flight by B.E.A. With seven-line boxed cachet in violet	8·00
3.5.73	As above, but Amsterdam–Guernsey. With seven-line boxed cachet in green	8·00
4.7.73	Guernsey–Gatwick Flight by B.I.A. With Guernsey Aviation set and commemorative cancellation; plus five-line cachet in black	1·50
4.7.73	Guernsey–Manchester flight by B.E.A. Guernsey Aviation stamps on f.d.c. with special APEX cancellation and six-line cachet in green	1·50
25.9.73	Southampton–Guernsey. 50 Years of Aviation in Guernsey. Flight by B.E.A., pictorial cover	2·50
25.9.73	As above, but signed by pilot	5·00
25.9.73	Guernsey–Southampton Flight by B.I.A. With eight-line boxed cachet in black on airletter. Signed by pilot	3·50
25.9.73	Guernsey–Southampton Flight by Aurigny. With large pictorial cachet in black on airletter	2·00
1.11.73	Guernsey–Bournemouth Flight by B.I.A. With five-line cachet in green	1·00
1.11.73	As above, but Bournemouth–Guernsey	1·00
31.12.73	Guernsey–Portsmouth, Last Flight by J.F. Airlines Ltd., airletter signed by pilot	10·00
31.12.73	As above, but printed cover with five-line cachet in blue	1·00
31.12.73	As above, but return flight. With green cachet	1·00

1974

1.4.74	First Flight by British Airways Guernsey–London. With printed flight details	1·50
1.4.74	New 55p B.E.A. Airway Letter stamp on flown f.d.c.	1·00
30.5.74	Last commercial D.C. Flight Guernsey–Bournemouth. With six-line black cachet. Signed by pilots	3·00
12.6.74	Southampton–Guernsey Flight by B.I.A.	1·00
16.10.74	Diamond Jubilee 201 Squadron R.A.F. Special Flight cover	1·00
16.10.74	As above, but signed cover	1·50

1975

2.5.75	British Airways Jersey–Düsseldorf First Flight. With five-line green cachet. Flown to Jersey for flight by Aurigny	3·00
2.5.75	As above, but return flight. With red cachet	3·00

1976

20/21.1.76	Guernsey–Bahrain via London on Concorde. Inaugural Flight. B.A.C. Cover	2·50
1.5.76	British Airways first day of issue of £1 Airway Letter stamp, flown from London to Guernsey	1·50
22/24.5.76	Guernsey–Washington via London on Concorde. Inaugural flight. B.A.C. Cover .. .. *	1·75
18.6.76*	30th anniversary of first Guernsey–Alderney Mail Flight, flown by Aurigny	75
18.6.76*	30th anniversary of first Alderney–Guernsey Mail Flight, flown by Aurigny	75
1.7.76	Guernsey–Dinard by Bretagne Air Services	50
2.7.76	Dinard–Guernsey by Bretagne Air Services	6·00
3.8.76	Guernsey first day of issue of Views 5p stamp, flown by B.I.A. to Gatwick	50
14.10.76	Guernsey first day of issue of Historical Buildings 11p stamp, flown by British Airways to London and Milan	50

1977

8.2.77	Guernsey first day of issue of Silver Jubilee of Queen set, flown by British Airways to London	1·00
7.6.77*	Silver Jubilee Celebration Day Flight by Aurigny Air Services, flown Guernsey to Jersey	1·50
19/22.11.77	Guernsey–New York via London on Concorde. Inaugural Flight. B.A.C. Cover	3·00
8/9.12.77	Guernsey–Singapore via London on Concorde. Inaugural Flight. B.A.C. Cover	3·75

1978

21.3.78*	Jersey–Guernsey–Jersey Inaugural Inter-Island Service by Intra Airways	60
2.5.78	Guernsey first day of issue of 25th anniversary of Coronation 20p, flown Guernsey to Heathrow	75

ALDERNEY AIRMAIL COVERS

*Inter-island flight. For convenience of reference the cover is listed under *both* islands and marked with an asterisk.

	1946	
18.6.46*	Guernsey to Alderney, no cachets	45·00
18.6.46*	Alderney to Guernsey, no cachets	20·00
	1947	
20.5.47	First Flight Alderney–Southampton	35·00
	1953	
20.10.53	B.E.A. ALDERNEY TOWN boxed datestamp. Violet	5·00
	1954	
1.9.54	National Institute of Oceanography card dropped in Atlantic by R.A.F. washed ashore on Alderney	30·00
	1970	
16.11.70	Inaugural Flight by Aurigny Air Services, Alderney–Cherbourg and return	3·00
2.12.70	Return of the Islanders to Alderney. AURIGNY/ALDERNEY/AIRPORT unframed datestamp in black	3·00
	1971	
18.6.71*	25th Anniversary of the first airmail Guernsey–Alderney and return. No cachets	2·00
	1972	
20.5.72	25th Anniversary First Flight Southampton–Alderney, with Aurigny boxed eight-line cachet in blue	1·00
20.5.72	As above, but return flight	1·00
20.5.72	As above, but Aurigny Air Services cover, with six-line boxed cachet in black	3·00
	1975	
7.4.75	Brymon Airways First Flight Plymouth–Alderney, with three-line cachet in green	1·00
7.4.75	First Flight Aurigny Trislander Southampton–Alderney with ten-line cachet in black	1·00
30.5.75*	Trislander G-BCVX First Operational Flight Alderney–Jersey, with blue six-line cachet. Cancelled Jersey	1·00
	1976	
18.6.76*	30th Anniversary of first Guernsey–Alderney Mail Flight, flown by Aurigny	75
18.6.76*	30th Anniversary of first Alderney–Guernsey Mail Flight, flown by Aurigny	75
	1977	
10.3.77*	40th Anniversary of Jersey Airport, flown by Aurigny from Alderney to Jersey	50

CHANNEL ISLANDS HOVERMAIL COVERS

	1969	
4.5.69	Gorey–Carteret by J4 amateur-built hovercraft	15·00
	1970	
27.1.70	Carteret–Gorey by SR.N6 024 of Hoverwork Ltd.	13·00
27.1.70	Gorey–Carteret by SR.N6 024 of Hoverwork Ltd.	13·00
3.2.70	Jersey–Ryde I.O.W. by SR.N6 024 of Hoverwork Ltd.	15·00
20.4.70	Browndown (Gosport)–Alderney by SR.N6 XV614 of 200	
	Hovercraft Trials Squadron RCT	15·00
24.4.70	Alderney–Browndown by SR.N6 XV616 of 200 Hovercraft Trials	
	Squadron RCT	15·00
	1971	
4.1.71	Gosport–Jersey by VT1.001 of Vosper Thorneycroft Ltd.	
	Dealer's cover	1·50
4.1.71	As above. Signed by Captain	2·50
4.1.71	As above, but Hovertravel official cover with Hovertravel Ltd.	
	cachet in red	5·00
6.1.71	Jersey–Guernsey by VT1.001 of Vosper Thorneycroft Ltd. Dealer's	
	Cover	2·00
6.1.71	As above, but private cover signed by Commander	5·00
6.1.71	Guernsey–Jersey by VT1.001 of Vosper Thorneycroft Ltd. Dealer's	
	cover	2·00
6.1.71	As above, but private cover signed by Commander	5·00
7.1.71	Jersey–Dinard by VT1.001 of Vosper Thorneycroft Ltd. Dealer's	
	cover	1·50
7.1.71	As above, but Hovertravel official cover with Hovertravel Ltd.	
	circular cachet in red	5·00
7.1.71	Dinard–Jersey by VT1.001 of Vosper Thorneycroft Ltd. Dealer's	
	cover	1·50
7.1.71	As above, but Hovertravel official cover with Hovertravel Ltd.	
	circular cachet in blue	5·00
4.2.71	Jersey–Gosport by VT1.001 of Vosper Thorneycroft Ltd. Dealer's	
	cover with special Postal Strike Hovercraft stamp	1·50
4.2.71	As above, but Hovertravel official cover with Hovertravel Ltd.	
	cachet in green	5·00
4.7.71	Jersey–Alderney by SR.N5 XT492 of Interservice Hovercraft Unit	8·00
5.7.71	Alderney–Lee-on-the-Solent by SR.N5 XT492 of Interservice	
	Hovercraft Unit	13·00
	1972	
26.4.72	Browndown–Herm by SR.N6 XV614 of 200 Hovercraft Trials	
	Squadron, Royal Corps of Transport	8·00
26.4.72	Herm–Sawsonport by SR.N6 XV614 of 200 Hovercraft Trials Squ.	
	RCT	8·00
27.4.72	Sawsonport–Alderney by SR.N6 XV614 of 200 Hovercraft Trials	
	Squ. RCT	8·00
27.4.72	Herm–Sark by SR.N6 XV614 of 200 Hovercraft Trials Squ.	
	RCT	8·00
27.4.72	Sark–Jersey by SR.N6 XV617 of 200 Hovercraft Trials Squ.	
	RCT	8·00
28.4.72	Herm–Browndown by SR.N6 XV617 of 200 Hovercraft Trials	
	Squ. RCT	8·00
	1974	
27.2.74	Browndown–Alderney by SR.N6 MK5 XT657 of 200 Hovercraft	
	Trials Squ. RCT	7·50
1.3.74	Alderney–Browndown by SR.N6 MK5 XT657 of 200 Hovercraft	
	Trials Squ. RCT	7·50
17.6.74	Lee-on-the-Solent–Guernsey by SR. N6 XV859 of Interservice	
	Hovercraft Unit	7·50

19.6.74	Guernsey–Lee-on-the-Solent by SR.N6 XV859 of Interservice Hovercraft Unit	7·50
	1975	
25.6.75	Southampton–Jersey by HM2 303 of International Hoverservices Ltd. Posted at sea, receiving Jersey Paquebot on G.B.	7·50
26.6.75	Jersey–Carteret by HM2 303 of International Hoverservices Ltd. on charter to Hovercross Ltd.	3·00
26.6.75	Carteret–Jersey by HM2 303 of International Hoverservices Ltd. on charter to Hovercross Ltd.	3·00
1.7.75	Carteret–Jersey by HM2 303 of International Hoverservices Ltd. on charter to Hovercross Ltd. (first passenger operations) ..	3·00
18.7.75	Carteret–Sark by HM2 303 of International Hoverservices Ltd. on charter to Hovercross Ltd.	3·00
	1976	
12.7.76	Southampton–Jersey by HM2 GH-2018 of International Hoverservices Ltd. Posted at sea, receiving Jersey Paquebot on G.B.	5·00
14.7.76	Carteret–Jersey by HM2 GH-2018 of International Hoverservices Ltd. on charter to Hovercross Ltd. Posted at sea in French waters, receiving Jersey Paquebot on French	7·50
4.8.76	Jersey–Sark by HM2 GH-2018 of International Hoverservices Ltd. on charter to Hovercross Ltd. Posted at sea in international waters, receiving Sark postmark and Guernsey Paquebot on G.B.	7·50
4.8.76	As above, but posted in Jersey waters, receiving Sark postmark and Guernsey Paquebot on Jersey	7·50
4.8.76	Sark–Jersey as above, but posted in Sark waters, receiving Jersey postmark and Paquebot on Guernsey	7·50
13.9.76	Jersey–Cherbourg by HM2 GH-2018 of International Hoverservices Ltd. Posted at sea in Jersey waters, receiving Cherbourg Paquebot on Jersey	10·00
15.9.76	Jersey–Le Havre by HM2 GH-2018 of International Hoverservices Ltd. Posted at sea in Jersey waters, receiving Le Havre Paquebot on Jersey	10·00
18.9.76	Jersey–Southampton by HM2 GH-2018 of International Hoverservices Ltd. Posted at sea in Jersey waters, receiving Southampton Paquebot on Jersey	5·00
	1977	
23.5.77	Jersey–Carteret by HM2 GH-2018 of International Hoverservices Ltd. on charter to Hovercross Ltd. Posted at sea in Jersey waters, receiving Carteret Paquebot on Jersey	5·00
8.8.77	Sark–Carteret by HM2 GH-2018 of International Hoverservices Ltd. on charter to Hovercross Ltd. Posted at sea in Sark waters, receiving Carteret Paquebot on Guernsey	5·00
8.8.77	Carteret–Sark by HM2 GH-2018 of International Hoverservices Ltd. on charter to Hovercross Ltd. Posted at sea in French waters, receiving Sark postmark and Guernsey Paquebot on French	6·00
	1978	
28.6.78	Poole–Alderney by HM2 2023 of International Hoverservices Ltd. Posted at sea in international waters, receiving Alderney postmark and Guernsey Paquebot on G.B.	6·00
28.6.78	Alderney–Poole by HM2 GH-2023 of International Hoverservices Ltd. Posted at sea in Alderney waters, receiving Bournemouth and Poole Paquebot on Guernsey	6·00

17. Mails between the Channel Islands and France

Prior to 1843 letters were carried privately between the Channel Islands and France and were handed to agents on either side of the Channel for onward transmission. The agent would hand them to the captain of a ship who, in turn, would hand them to another agent at the port of arrival. For this service a fee of 3d. (or 3 decimes in France) was charged, 1d. going to each agent and 1d. to the captain of the ship.

The Foreign Post Offices
By Ordinance of the Royal Court of Guernsey dated 23 August 1823 a Foreign Post Office was set up in Guernsey for the purpose of dealing with letters to and from Alderney and the neighbouring coast of France. Two Guernseymen, Georges S. Syvret and Matthieu Barbet, held the monopoly of this service, making a charge of 2d. per letter, payable by the addressee, 1d. of which went to the Master of the ship bringing it. The Ordinance was twice strengthened, first on 13 December 1823 and again in March 1833, and was not repealed until January 1841.

According to a report made by George Louis, a Post Office Surveyor, who visited Jersey in 1829, a similar office (known as the French Post Office) was functioning there. It was run by Theodore Fontaine, and was concerned with the collection and dispatch of mails between St. Helier, Granville and St. Malo.

Louis believed this office to be sanctioned in some way by the French Government and a letter exists which seems to confirm that this office was in fact an official agency of the French Post Office.

The letter was written by Theodore Fontaine on 4 May 1842 to the Director-General of Posts, Paris, and requested "that as he (Fontaine) had to dispatch express packets every day to the Postmasters of St. Malo and Granville which called for the use of large quantities of wrapping paper, could he be supplied with some for the use of his office, also some wax".

On the front of the letter is the address and the word Service, also the red Outremer–St. Malo datestamp of 4 Mai 1842 (Type **16**); inside is yet another datestamp, this time in blue and reading Cabinet Particulier (Postes) 6 Mai 1842.

Both Foreign Post Offices were officially suppressed on 1 June 1843 in consequence of a new Anglo–French Postal Convention which came into force on that date. Under this Convention all mail to or from France was to be delivered to the British Post Office, and the French Postal Authorities agreed that it should not be sent through any other channels. Neither of the Foreign Post Offices used any postal markings.

French Ports of Entry and Departure
The huge field of markings for French maritime mail has implications for the Channel Islands. Postal history is rich in two centuries of cancellations and markings used to record ports of entry for foreign mail and ports of departure

for letters leaving France on the high seas. (Paquebot mail, involving ports of call for letters posted on board ship, is dealt with in Section 12.)

The first marking known to have been used on mail from the Channel Islands is D'JARSEY, unframed and measuring 21 × 3mm, applied at St. Malo in 1683 (Type 1). It appears to have been little used, as only two examples are known. A type (2) reading DE S'MALO was used in 1698.

Another marking found is D'ANGLETERRE struck in black from 1699 to 1720 and used on letters from England as well as from the Channel Islands (Type 3). This was followed in 1720 by a larger ANGLETERRE which can be found struck in red, blue or black until 1802 (Type 4).

From 1823 letters routed via England are found marked ANGLETERRE PAR BOULOGNE (or CALAIS or ROUEN) in two lines (Type 5). Letters going direct from the Islands to the adjacent French ports have GRANDE BRETAGNE/PAR GRANVILLE (or CHERBOURG or ST. MALO) in two lines (Type 6). This latter mark was used on letters from the Channel Islands only. The St. Malo mark exists with damage (a misshapen G to GRANDE) after about 1830.

Other markings are found on letters from Jersey and Guernsey, but are not, of course, restricted to mail from those islands; they may be described as follows.

Type 7 is SMALO in black measuring 27 × 4mm and recorded on letters from Guernsey dated 1776 and 1777. A similar version (with full stop) reads S. MALO and is known used 1755.

Type 8 is ST. MALO in black measuring 28 × 3½mm and is known on a letter from Guernsey dated 1790. In the same type is GRANVILLE in black and this measures 36 × 4mm (the G is slightly larger, 6mm high). It is recorded on a letter from Jersey of date 1781. MORLAIX in Type 8 is known on a letter of 1816.

Type 9 is a two-line marking. A letter from Guernsey of 1793 is known struck with 34/ST. MALO in black (dimensions 5 × 3½mm and 28 × 3½mm). Another Guernsey letter, dated 1817, bears 34/ST. SERVAN in this type (8 × 5mm and 38 × 5mm). Recorded 1823–29 is 48/CHERBOURG.

The 34/ST. SERVAIN in Type 9 exists on a letter from Sark of 1819 with the words "Colonies par" written in manuscript above it.

The figures "34" and "48" are French Departmental numbers, which occur in further markings. Type 10 reads DEB 48/CHERBOURG (known 1815) and there is also DEB 34/ST. MALO (known 1828–30). DEB probably means "Deboursé" (expended, disbursed). Type 11 is P21P/ST. BRIEUC (known 1820) and, similarly, P34P/ST. MALO (known 1828–31).

In 1788 the French had begun designating marks of entry for mail arriving by sea with the words COLONIES PAR and the name of the port. In relation to Channel islands mail are recorded (Type 12); St. Malo, Cherbourg, Granville and Le Havre.

These are unframed. One of the scarcest French pre-adhesive marks is Type 13, used in 1818, a boxed COL. PAR CHERBOURG.

The postal designation COLONIES was dropped in 1828 in favour of PAYS D'OUTRE MER and name of port (e.g. PAYS D'OUTRE MER/PAR NANTES). Such boxed markings were in use till 1831 though none is so far recorded on Channel Islands mail.

In August of 1831 the name of the port was deleted and the framed PAYS D'OUTREMER (Type 14) in black or red was used in conjunction with a large circular datestamp (Type 15). These have fleurons at each side and the French Departmental number at the foot.

Small circular datestamps, 20mm in diameter, struck in black or red were brought into use in March 1839 (Type **16**). These read OUTRE-MER at the top and ST. MALO (or GRANVILLE or CHERBOURG or LE HAVRE) at the bottom with the date in three lines across the centre. They are found on letters from the Channel Islands as well as from many other places abroad.

A distinctive mark, similar in size to the Outremer datestamp but worded ILES-C at the top (Type **17**), was introduced in June 1843. It was struck in red (a St. Malo strike in black is known) and remained in use until about 1879. The ports at which it was used were Cherbourg (rare), Granville and St. Malo. A variety of the St. Malo datestamp has ILES-C in larger letters with a full stop after C.

A mark made especially for use on letters from Jersey and Guernsey was a flat-topped 3 (Type **18**), indicating the 3 decimes ship charge due and struck in red at Granville and St. Malo.

Handstruck 6, 7 and 8 decime marks (Type **18**) can be found on letters from the Islands. They are usually struck in black and denote the amount of postage due, calculated at double rates. When struck on covers from the *Boîte Mobile* service they are extremely rare, since the entires were usually prepaid.

The Postal Conventions

The Postal Convention of 1843 provided for official exchange of mail between various British and French ports and for Packets between the Channel Islands and St. Malo. It also provided for mails to be carried by private steamers between Jersey and Guernsey and Cherbourg, Granville and St. Malo. The service between Jersey and Cherbourg was suppressed in 1845. Rates of postage were 5d. per $\frac{1}{2}$oz from England and 3d. per $\frac{1}{2}$oz from the Channel Islands. This was the rate to the French port of arrival and an additional 5 decimes per $\frac{1}{4}$oz was added for the French inland rate.

The Convention also provided for *boîtes mobiles* (movable boxes) in which letters could be posted and cancelled at the port of arrival. At a number of English ports special handstamps bearing the framed letters M.B. were applied to letters, but although it seems likely that similar ones were issued to the Channel Islands none has so far been recorded. On the French side, however, letters from the Channel Islands were marked with a small circular datestamp reading ILES-C at the top and bearing the name of the port, Cherbourg, Granville or St. Malo at the bottom (Type **17**). The "C" stands for "Channel", a curious mixture of French and English. This was also used on ordinary letters to France not posted in the movable box.

Two covers are known from this first *boîte mobile* service. One is from Jersey to France and has a single G.B. 1855 4d. on blue paper cancelled with the 3176 small-figures lozenge of St. Malo and the ILES-C ST. MALO c.d.s. of 8 January 1856. The other cover is addressed from Jersey to St. Malo. It bears a pair of the G.B. 1855 4d. on blue paper cancelled with the 1441 small-figures lozenge of Granville and the ISLES-C GRANVILLE c.d.s. of 10 May 1856.

In January 1855 the rate of postage from both the Channel Islands and England was standardized at 4d. per $\frac{1}{2}$oz. The 4d. letter was therefore a single one and the 8d. a double letter.

In 1856 a new Anglo–French Postal Convention was signed which provided for another *boîte mobile* service, of which full details are given later in this

Section. This service came into force on 1 January 1857 and rates of postage were:

1855—30.6.1870	4d per ½oz.
1.7.1870—31.12.1875	3d. per ½oz.
1.1.1876—11.6.1921	2½oz per 1oz.
12.6.1921—1939	3d. per 1oz.

It is interesting to note that the 1856 Convention reduced the rate from England to France from 6d. to 4d. but abolished the reduced Channel Islands rate of 3d.

The use of adhesive stamps on letters from the U.K. to France was not made compulsory until the 1856 Convention. Postage could be paid in cash on dispatch instead, but if this was not done stampless covers were charged to the recipient at twice the correct postage rate.

The Boîte Mobile Service

Under Article II of the Postal Convention between Great Britain and France dated 24 September 1856, in addition to the regular mail service, letters were to be exchanged between several British and French ports, such mails being carried by private vessels of either country, a gratuity of 1d. being paid on each letter. This means of communication became so constant that all the vessels carried a *boîte mobile* (movable box) on board for collecting such letters, and postmarks were brought into use for letters so posted.

The steamers of the London & South Western Railway ran from St. Helier to St. Malo and Granville on alternate weekdays, carrying the regular mails between the Islands and France. They also carried a movable letterbox in which letters, which had not passed through the Post Office, could be posted up to the time of sailing, and afterwards by passengers on board. On arrival at the destination these boxes were taken to the Post Office, where the letters were removed for cancelling.

There appears to have been no Guernsey movable box on this service. Letters were carried direct to St. Malo from Guernsey for many years by the *Fawn*, a 47-ton cutter. The captain was given letters by the Post Office and also received them from private persons. There is no evidence that the cutter *Fawn*, or the steamer by the same name, had a movable box on board.

The *Boîte Mobile* service ceased at the outbreak of war in 1939.

Letters from the Channel Islands. Letters from Jersey and Guernsey had the British stamps cancelled with the normal French numeral obliterator (lozenge of dots). In addition the covers received a dated postmark, at first octagonal (Type **20**) and later circular (Type **21**). These read ANGL. B.M. at the top and name of the port below.

For Type **20** the ports recorded are: St. Malo, Cherbourg, Granville and Le Havre. For Type **21** they are: St. Malo, Granville, Plérin and Port-Bail. A variant of the Plérin Type **21** has ANGLETERRE in place of ANGL. B.M.

The lozenge of dots obliterators contained different figures identifying the ports. Small figures (Type **22**) were used at first, but when the French post offices were renumbered on 1 January 1863 larger figures were introduced

(Type **23**). The numbers for the major ports were:

	Small Figures	Large Figures
Cherbourg	842	1002
Granville	1441	1706
Le Havre	1495	1769
St. Malo	3176	3734

In the large-figure series, in addition, Binic was numbered 480 and 3553 was St. Brieuc (though this latter has not been seen). The large 1769 for Le Havre, normally in black, is known in red, but only on a loose adhesive. The 3734 obliterator occurs in small figures, transferred to St. Malo and used as a supplementary cancellation to the large-figure 3734, above.

Mails to Cherbourg and Le Havre probably went by French ships from Guernsey. There was also a service from Southampton to Le Havre which has no connection with the Channel Islands.

The lozenge obliterations went out of use generally in April 1876. After that ordinary town datestamps were used (the special ANGL. B.M. Types **20** and **21** had already ceased); prices are given for complete covers cancelled with such datestamps and bearing British stamps.

About 1906 St. Malo brought into use a single-circle datestamp ANG. B.M./SAINT-MALO (Type **24**) in place of the ordinary town cancellation and this remained the case until the Second World War.

Letters from the French Ports. On arrival at St. Helier, letters from France had the stamps cancelled with the Jersey "409" obliterator and Type **25** worded JERSEY/FRANCE/MB was applied to the cover clear of the stamps. The letters "MB" refer, of course, to "movable box" and, because of its shape the cancellation is called a "milestone". It was dispatched from the G.P.O. on 24 March 1857 and the earliest recorded date of use is 26 April 1858.

On 25 July 1873 a similar datestamp (Type **26**) was sent to Jersey. The lettering is larger and the wider-spaced M.B. now has a stop between M and B. The cancellation originally had straight sides but it became distorted in use through its long life, the last recorded date being 24 August 1939. Before 1914 the month preceded the day in the date-line; thereafter their positions were transposed, as illustrated (Type **26a**). (This change was made in all cancels throughout the U.K.) The cancellation, normally in black, is known used in red in 1938 on a single stamp but this was probably accidental.

The Proof Book in the Post Office Records shows an M.B. datestamp as having been dispatched to Guernsey at the same time (1857) as the one to Jersey. So far no stamps or covers are known bearing this marking, however. Instead the French stamps were cancelled with a Guernsey barred-oval obliterator ("324") in a single or duplex or an ordinary datestamp.

For Jersey French stamps up to the "Peace and Commerce" types, first issued 1876, are found cancelled by the barred oval "409" in single or duplex with the "milestone" (Type **25**) struck on the cover. Later issues are found cancelled with the "milestone" alone. The Bordeaux issues of France (1870–71) are particularly desirable items on *boîte mobile* covers. A single French *Ballon Monté* is also known with the M.B. milestone mark.

In general, French stamps with Jersey and Guernsey cancellations are much scarcer than British stamps cancelled in France.

Boîte Mobile from Smaller Ports

Several ports cancelled mail from movable boxes though there was no reference to them in the 1856 Convention which had covered only St. Malo, Cherbourg, Granville and Le Havre. They are specifically mentioned here for that reason.

Port-Bail. Port-Bail is on the west coast of the Cotentin peninsula and from about 1868 to 1885 letters were sent there from Gorey in Jersey. Little is known of the mail service; the sailings are believed to have been irregular and concentrated on summer excursion steamers, which ceased when the port became silted up in 1885.

Port-Bail possessed a circular datestamp Type **21** since it is known on a letter from Jersey dated 14 April 1869 and which arrived in France next day.

Few covers or loose stamps with Port-Bail markings are known.

Plérin. Plérin, in the Bay of St. Brieuc, is another port at which mail from the Channel Islands was occasionally landed. It had a circular datestamp Type **21** and this is known on covers from Guernsey dated 1872–80.

Binic. Another small port in the Bay of St. Brieuc near Plérin, Binic also received mail from the Islands. Sailings were made from Guernsey by the cutter *Reindeer* and later by the *Echo*. Early in this century the *Fawn*, belonging to the St. Malo and Binic Steamship Co. Ltd., also made regular sailings to the port.

A part cover from Guernsey to Binic dated 1872 is known bearing a pair of the 1858 1d. red cancelled with Type **23**, the "480" large-figures lozenge of Binic.

A number of postcards from Guernsey to Binic exist bearing Edward VII stamps cancelled with the Binic/Côtes-du-Nord datestamp of 1907–08. An oval B.M. stamp is applied to each card (Type **27**), a marking of a land *boîte mobile* occasionally used on mail arriving from the Islands. Such an oval stamp is also known from St. Malo.

Carteret. The little port of Carteret is situated on the west coast of the Cotentin peninsula, near to Port-Bail. From about 1900, letters were carried from Gorey by the vessels of the Compagnie Rouennaise de Navigation, the paddle-steamers *Cygne* and *Jersey*. In recent years letters have been carried by the *Torbay Belle* and *Les Deux Léopards*, belonging to the Compagnie Navigation Carteret, but only if they bear French stamps.

Two types of cancellation (of equal value) are known on British stamps used on postcards routed via Carteret. The first consists of three concentric circles, the outer one being made up of dots, with the word CARTERET at the top, MANCHE at the bottom and the date in three lines in the centre. Examples are known from 1903 to 1908. The second type consists of a single circle 26½mm in diameter, with CARTERET at the top, MANCHE at the bottom and the date in three lines in the centre. Examples are known used from 1908 to 1913.

Two types of PAQUEBOT stamp are known used on the cards: both are of the French omnibus type. The first measures $4\frac{1}{2} \times 30\frac{1}{2}$mm and was used from 1903 to 1912. The second measures 4×30mm and was used in 1912–13.

For some time ordinary bags of mail were also carried between Jersey and Carteret and letters to and from France are known with the Carteret transit mark.

St. Brieuc. For a number of years in the late nineteenth and early twentieth centuries there were regular shipping services between the Channel Islands and St. Brieuc, in the Côtes du Nord. It seems likely that mail was carried on these services and British stamps with the "3533" large-figures lozenge and with later St. Brieuc datestamps may possibly exist.

The P-F and P-D Handstamps

As a result of the 1843 Convention P-F and P-D handstamps were issued to the Jersey and Guernsey Post Offices. Letters going beyond France could only be prepaid for the English and French postage—hence P-F (Paid to Frontier). The marking P-D indicate Paid to Destination.

It is probable that Jersey had a P-F stamp but no example has yet been recorded. The oval P-D stamp (Type **28**) was used from 1843 to 1862 and is known struck in red, black, blue and a dirty green. The circular P D stamp (Type **29**) was used from 1863 to 1875, generally in black, occasionally in red. In 1875 a small oval type (**30**) was struck in black or red. It had sloping letters and neither type has a hyphen between them. A replacement for this was sent from the G.P.O. on 16 July 1879.

Guernsey had an oval P-F. stamp (Type **31**) in use in 1843–44, which was struck in dull red. An oval P-D. stamp (Type **32**) was in use from 1843 to 1856, struck in red at first and then in the colour of the datestamp. It is also known in black on a cover from Guernsey to St. Malo dated 12 August 1872, with damage to the top. The circular P D stamp (Type **33**) was used from 1856 to 1874 and was struck in the colour of the datestamp, blue or black.

Letters to France from Jersey and Guernsey via Calais and Boulogne in 1856–57 are known with a larger circular P D stamp with thicker letters and in 1866 with a smaller type in red or black. These were almost certainly applied in London. Some of these covers have a large handstruck PAR LONDRES. This was privately applied by P. Beghin of Jersey. Small square or rectangular P D marks on letters *to* the Islands were sometimes applied on dispatch and so are French markings.

D 'J A R S E Y

(1)

GRANDE BRETAGNE
PAR GRANVILLE

(6)

SMALO

(7)

ST MALO

(8)

34
S⟋ SERVAN

(9)

COLONIES PAR
S⟋ MALO

(12)

PAYS D'OUTREMER

(14)

(15)

(16)

(17)

3

(18)

Cat. No.	Type No.		Dates of use	Colour		Price on cover
CF1	1	D'JARSEY	1683	Black	.. ..	£1000
CF2	2	DE S'MALO	1698	Black	.. ..	£150
CF3	3	D'ANGLETERRE	1699–1720	Black	.. ..	30·00
CF4	4	ANGLETERRE	1720–1802	Red, blue or black	.. ..	25·00
CF5	5	ANGLETERRE PAR BOULOGNE	1823–30	Black	.. ..	40·00
CF6		ANGLETERRE PAR CALAIS	1823–30	Black	.. ..	50·00
CF7		ANGLETERRE PAR ROUEN	1823–30	Black	.. ..	80·00
CF8	6	GRANDE BRETAGNE/PAR GRANVILLE	1823–25	Black	.. ..	£120
CF9		GRANDE BRETAGNE/PAR CHERBOURG	1823	Black	.. ..	£200
CF10		ditto	1823	Red-brown	..	£150
CF11		GRANDE BRETAGNE/PAR ST. MALO	1823–33	Black	.. ..	75·00
CF12	7	SMALO	1776–77	Black	.. ..	80·00
CF13		S. MALO	1755	Black	.. ..	40·00
CF14	8	ST. MALO	1790	Black	.. ..	30·00
CF15		GRANVILLE	1781	Black	.. ..	30·00
CF16		MORLAIX	1816	Black	.. ..	40·00
CF17	9	34/ST. MALO	1793	Black	.. ..	25·00
CF18		34/ST. SERVAN	1817	Black	.. ..	30·00
CF19		ditto, with manuscript "Colonies par"	1819	Black		£150
CF20		48/CHERBOURG	1823–29	Black	.. ..	40·00

Cat. No.	Type No.		Dates of use	Colour			Price on cover
CF21	10	DEB 48/CHERBOURG	1815	Black	..	..	40·00
CF22		DEB 34/ST. MALO	1828–30	Black	..	..	30·00
CF23	11	P21P/ST. BRIEUC	1820	Black	..	..	50·00
CF24		P34P/ST. MALO	1828–31	Black	..	..	35·00
CF25	12	COLONIES PAR/ST. MALO	1816–18	Black	..	..	50·00
CF26		COLONIES PAR/CHERBOURG	1821	Black	..	..	£100
CF27		COLONIES PAR/GRANVILLE	1823	Red	..	..	75·00
CF28		COLONIES PAR/LE HAVRE	1820s	Red	..	..	£120
CF29	13	Boxed COL. PAR CHERBOURG	1818	Black	..	..	£150
CF30	14	PAYS D'OUTREMER ⎱					
—	15	ST. MALO (34) c.d.s. ⎰	1830s	Black	..	..	30·00
CF31	14	PAYS D'OUTREMER ⎱					
—	15	GRANVILLE (48) c.d.s. ⎰	1830s	Black	..	..	30·00
CF32	16	OUTRE-MER/ST. MALO c.d.s.	1839	Black	..	..	60·00
CF33		ditto	1839–42	Red	..	..	40·00
CF34		OUTRE-MER/GRANVILLE c.d.s.	1839–41	Red	..	..	75·00
CF35		OUTRE-MER/CHERBOURG c.d.s.	1841	Red	..	..	£100
CF36		OUTRE-MER/LE HAVRE c.d.s.	1841	Red	..	..	45·00
CF37	17	ILES-C/CHERBOURG c.d.s.	1849	Red	..	..	£200
CF38		ILES-C/GRANVILLE c.d.s.	1843–79	Red	..	..	75·00
CF39		ILES-C/ST. MALO c.d.s.	1843–56	Red	..	..	50·00
CF40		ditto	1856–79	Red	..	..	40·00
CF41		ditto, ILES-C larger	1871	Red	..	..	30·00
CF42		ILES-C/ST. MALO	1848	Black	..	..	75·00
CF43	18	Flat-topped 3	1839–45	Red	..	..	10·00
CF44	19	Handstruck 6	1850s	Black	..	..	20·00
CF45		Handstruck 7	1850s	Black	..	..	20·00
CF46		Handstruck 8	1850s	Black	..	..	20·00

(20)

(21)

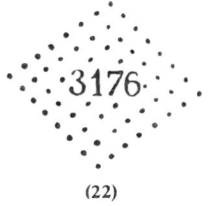

(22)

(23)

(24)

(25)

(26a)

(28)

 (31)

(29)

 (32)

(30)

(33)

Cat. No.	Type No.		Dates of use	Colour				Price on cover
Octagonal datestamps								
CF47	**20**	St. Malo	1857–67	Red	..	..	..	£130
CF48		Cherbourg	1857	Red	..	..	..	£250
CF49		Granville	1857–70	Red	..	..	..	£150
CF50		ditto	1906–08	Black		..	..	50·00
CF51		Le Havre	1857–67	Red	..	..	..	£200
Circular datestamps								
CF52	**21**	St. Malo	1867–68	Red	..	..	..	£100
CF53		Granville	1870	Red	..	..	..	£150
CF54		Plérin	1872–80	Red	..	..	..	£250
CF55		Angleterre Plérin	1881	Black		..	..	£200
CF56		Port-Bail	1869	Red	..	..	..	£200
Lozenge, small figures								
CF57	**22**	842 Cherbourg	1857	Black		..	..	—
CF58		1441 Granville	1856–62	Black		..	..	£300
CF59		1495 Le Havre	1857–62	Black		..	..	£350
CF60		3176 St. Malo	1856–62	Black		..	..	£200
CF61		3734 St. Malo	1863	Black		..	..	£400

Cat. No.	Type No.		Dates of use	Colour			Price on cover
Lozenge, large figures							
CF62	23	480 Binic	1872	Black	..	..	—
CF63		1002 Cherbourg	1863–76	Black	..	..	—
CF64		1706 Granville	1863–76	Black	..	..	£250
CF65		1769 Le Havre	1863–76	Black	..	..	£300
CF66		3734 St. Malo	1863–76	Black	..	..	£200
Ordinary French datestamps							
CF67	—	Binic c.d.s.	1907–08	Black	..	..	50·00
CF68	—	Carteret c.d.s.	1900–13	Black	..	..	45·00
CF69	—	ditto, with French Paquebot	1903–13	Black	..	..	60·00
CF70	—	Granville c.d.s.	1876–1939	Black	..	..	30·00
CF71	—	ditto, with French Paquebot	1912	Black	..	..	£100
CF72	—	St. Malo c.d.s.	1876–1906	Black	..	..	25·00
St. Malo datestamp							
CF73	24	ANG.B.M./SAINT-MALO	1906–39	Black	..	..	40·00
MB datestamps							
CF74	25	"Milestone" datestamp	1857–73	Black	..	..	£500
CF75	26	Larger lettering	1873–1900	Black	..	..	£120
CF76		ditto	1900–14	Black	..	..	90·00
CF77	26a	Day-month-year	1914–39	Black	..	..	90·00
Barred ovals on French stamps							
CF78	—	Guernsey "324"	1853–61	Black	..	..	—
CF79*	—	ditto	1862–71	Black	..	..	£275
		*For 1870–71 Bordeaux issue	.. .. ..	.. ..	..	..	£400
CF80	—	Jersey "409"	1853–61	Black	..	..	£275
CF81†	—	ditto	1862–79	Black	..	..	£250
		†For 1870–71 Bordeaux issue	.. .. ..	.. ..	..	..	£400
B.M. in oval							
CF82	27	Stamps cancelled St. Malo					40·00
CF83		Stamps cancelled Binic	1907–08				40·00
P–F and P–D handstamps							
CF84	28	Jersey oval P–D	1843–62	Red, black blue or green			40·00
CF85	29	Jersey circular PD	1863–75	Black or red		..	30·00
CF86	30	Jersey small oval PD	1875–79	Black or red		..	20·00
CF87	31	Guernsey P–F.	1843–44	Red ..	.. ..	..	60·00
CF88	32	Guernsey oval P–D.	1843–56	Red, black, blue or green		..	30·00
CF89		ditto	1872	Black	..	..	20·00
CF90	33	Guernsey circular PD	1856–74	Blue or black		..	15·00

Notes. In the case of lozenge obliterations (Types **22** and **23**), prices are for those on the 3d. and 4d. adhesives, which were the most commonly used values. Covers bearing other values are worth considerably more.

Types **20** and **21** were normally used in conjunction with Types **22** and **23**.

The value of Types **28** to **33** depends on the adhesives and the other postal markings on the cover.

Prices for markings on mail between the U.K./Channel Islands and France are for letters originating in or dispatched to the Islands. Those to or from the mainland are often worth less.

18. The German Occupation

German forces were in occupation of the Channel Islands between 1940 and 1945.

The Course of Events

The War Cabinet in London had decided to demilitarise the Islands. All British regular forces were withdrawn by 21 June 1940 and many civilians were evacuated to Britain by 23 June.

With the military evacuation the two Lieutenant-Governors (of Jersey and Guernsey) departed and civil administration had to be reorganised. Emergency bodies were accordingly set up to which many powers of the normal local government (the States) were transferred. In Guernsey the States of Deliberation set up a Controlling Committee with the Procureur (Major A. J. Sherwill) as President on 21 June. In Jersey the Assembly of the States formed a Superior Council under the Presidency of the Bailiff (A. M. Coutanche) and this first met on 24 June.

The first German troops flew into Guernsey on the evening of 30 June 1940 and the main forces arrived during the following day. On 1 July Jersey was occupied and on 2 July the island of Alderney. A detachment crossed from Guernsey to Sark on 4 July to complete the operation. Because of the demilitarisation the invasion proceeded without military opposition, though loss of life and casualties occurred through air-raids.

German military government became effective in August 1940 with the Channel Islands considered as part of France (*Département de la Manche*). *Feldkommandantur 515* (Field Command 515), responsible for all the Islands, was located in Jersey. It had a *Nebenstelle* (branch) on Guernsey and lesser organisations elsewhere. The *Kommandantur* itself had separate divisions for military and civil affairs; the *Wehrmacht* (armed forces) were, of course, a body separate from this military government organisation.

Since Jersey and Guernsey continued in allegiance to the British Crown the local civil administration remained. To recognise the reality of the Occupation new laws were henceforward approved by German *Kommandant* and Bailiff.

Currency

German currency was principally in circulation during the Occupation alongside British. When, some time after the invasion, the Germans eventually took control of the banks an official rate of exchange was fixed. This was 9·36 *Reichsmarks* to the pound, so that 1 RM was worth about 2s. 1¼d. Because of souvenir hunting and hoarding small change became scarce and the Islands printed notes of low denomination expressed in sterling.

Early Communications

The immediate result of the arrival of the Germans was that communication with the mainland of Britain abruptly ceased. Attempts were made by the islanders to make contact but very few messages can have arrived; there are only two known at present that did.

The method adopted was to send such letters in a cover addressed to the British Vice-Consul in Lisbon for forwarding. One Guernseyman who had a friend interned in France wrote to him by the same means, hoping that he might be able to pass on the news to England via the Red Cross (which was not yet functioning in Guernsey). This cover, which was handed in at the German Feldpost in the island, bore a strip of three 1d. stamps. These were not cancelled and one has been removed. As the internee died in camp it is not known if he ever received the letter, but the cover bears the censor stamp of *Front-Stalag 131* at St. Lô, France, which suggests it did reach its destination.

The other cover bears a 3d. Postal Centenary stamp (S.G. 484) that has been left uncancelled. These Vice-Consul, Lisbon, covers were outer wrappers and contained letters to be forwarded. This second example has the name and address of the sender, a Guernsey woman, on the back. It also bears the *Front-Stalag 131* censor stamp.

A method allowed to refugees in Britain wishing to communicate with their relatives in the Channel Islands was via P.O. Box 506, Lisbon, the address of Thomas Cook & Son, the official forwarding agents for mail within, to, and from enemy-occupied countries and Great Britain. They could write letters with severely limited contents and place them in stamped envelopes and send them under cover to Thomas Cook & Son, London, together with a 2s. postal order. The writers could not give any address but were to instruct their correspondents to write back c/o Post Box 506, Lisbon. Several covers sent by this service are in existence (*see* illustration) but bear a handstamp "Detained in France during German Occupation".

Mail via Lisbon with "detained" handstamp

From October 1940 communication with the Islands via the Red Cross organisation was established, but at first only the name and address of the enquirer could be transmitted. By the end of the year a message of not more than twenty-five words was allowed. No replies or messages from the Islands could be sent until 13 January 1941. On that date a Red Cross Bureau was opened in Guernsey. A Jersey Bureau was opened in March 1941. The Red Cross Message Service is dealt with in Section 19 of this Catalogue.

The Feldpost

The initial occupation of the Channel Islands by German forces was by elements of the 216th Infantry Division, which was part of the Army in France. The division's *Feldpostamt* (Field Post Office) was at Montmartin-sur-Mer, which had the Kenn. (code) No. 205 (the three digits to the left of the date in the datestamp). Mail from the forces in the Islands was collected and transported back to Montmartin-sur-Mer for cancelling.

There appears to have been a stationary military post office established in Jersey shortly after the initial occupation as a branch of *Feldpostamt 372* (which was at Cherbourg and used the Kenn. No. 447). It is reported to have had the Kenn. No. 405, but this was also used at St. Lô and at present we know of no covers from Jersey of this period using that number. The office was in Falle's shop at 12–14 Beresford Street.

The 319th Infantry Division moved into the Channel Islands on 19 April 1941 and replaced the elements of the 216th. The Kenn. number for the Jersey office was then changed to 712 (Type 1) and a Guernsey office was established at Le Jardinet, St. Martin's, and given the number 937. Local records in the Islands report the opening of both offices as 8 January 1941 and there are certainly philatelic covers from Jersey with a *Feldpost* cancellation (without the Kenn. number) known with this date sent by the late A. E. Le Gentil to friends in France. The cancellers used in Jersey had f, g or h above the date and those used in Guernsey d or e.

All civilian mail to any part of Occupied Europe had to go through the *Feldpost* at a charge of 25 pf. for letters and 15 pf. for postcards. German civilians were allowed to send their mail at the German internal rates of 12 pf. for letters and 6 pf. for postcards. German forces, of course, received free postage and quite a lot of official correspondence went back to Germany. This latter was often registered and only registered letters had the Kenn. number. It was also written on the registration labels. All military mail had a handwritten (or sometimes handstamped) five-digit *Feldpostnummer* to identify it.

Various covers are known with mixed German, French and British stamps or German and Channel Islands stamps. They are also known with airmail labels or with a red boxed handstamp MIT SCHNELLBOOT/BEFÖRDERT. These are all philatelic items and, although of some interest if they have the correct German postal rates and censor marks, are worth much less than genuine private correspondence.

One or two covers with Jersey and Guernsey stamps cancelled by a small oval handstamp inscribed JERSEY–GUERNSEY/MAIL BOAT/CHANNEL ISLANDS are reported to have been carried on the States of Jersey vessel s.s. *Spinell* to Granville and there handed over to the *Feldpost* (*see* Jersey Cachets, Section 15).

After the Allied landings in Normandy in June 1944 the *Feldpost* closed for several weeks. It was reopened on 1 August 1944, when it was stated that mail would be taken to the Continent by air. There is no evidence, however, that any got through and certainly, at the time of writing, no covers dated after June 1944 have been seen.

A small batch of philatelic registered covers accepted by favour from a Jerseyman (which was strictly against regulations) had the stamps cancelled with Type **1** dated 1 August 1944 and marked ZURÜCK (returned) in red. They were returned on 26 September. *See* No. GO4 in the Catalogue listing.

Radio Message Cards

A further consequence of the Normandy landings in 1944 was that German troops in the Channel Islands made use of radio to send messages to relatives in their homeland. Each man was allowed one very brief message a month to his next of kin. The Naval radio station at Wilhelmshaven received messages from several *Festungen* (fortified locations), including the Channel Islands, and special *Feldpost* postcards were prepared to forward these communications.

One such *Funknachrichtenkarte* (radio message card) was already preprinted with the origin *Dünkirchen–Kanalinseln* (Dunkirk–Channel Islands), either of which could be crossed out as appropriate.

Feldpost Overprints

Several German definitives of the Hitler head series are known overprinted "Deutsche feldpost/Kanalinseln" in a Gothic typeface. These may have been essays printed in Jersey, but are more likely to be bogus. Others overprinted by hand "Kanal-Inseln/Feld Post" are definitely bogus.

Jersey Mail Cancelled in France

On 12 August 1940 a German *Feldpost* unit arrived at the *Feldpostamt* at Montmartin-sur-Mer with Jersey civilian mail comprising some 1500 letters and 200 packets, which had not been cancelled in the island. For some unknown reason the Germans handed it over to the French postmistress, who, having in mind the English families awaiting news, cancelled all the letters with the normal Montmartin-sur-Mer datestamp and forwarded them with the French mail. What happened to them after that is not known, but it seems likely that most of the covers would have been destroyed by the recipients, if they ever received them. However, one 2½d. Postal Centenary stamp (S.G. 483) with this cancellation exists and is illustrated as Type **2**. The cancellation is a single circle of 26mm diameter with MONTMARTIN S/MER at the top, MANCHE at the bottom and the time and date in three lines in the centre.

Dienstpost

A *Dienstpost* functioned in the Channel Islands as it did in other German-occupied territories. Its purpose was to carry correspondence of an official nature which the authorities did not wish to entrust to the *Feldpost* or the civilian Post Office. Covers were handstamped in violet DEUTSCHE DIENSTPOST and were carried by military personnel.

Official Mail

German soldiers were supplied with green letter sheets headed "Feldpost", which went free of charge.

Letters from the German *Feldkommandantur* in Jersey had a two-line handstamp in black reading FELDKOMMANDANTUR 515/MIL VER. GR. A similar stamp was used in Guernsey.

Other marks used by the German *Feldkommandantur* are: a circular type with eagle in the centre inscribed FELDKOMMANDANTUR 515 and a similar type inscribed HAFENVEBERWACHUNGSSTELLE ST. HELIER.

Covers are known addressed to Germans in Jersey and bearing stamps cancelled with a circular handstamp with the swastika and eagle emblem in the centre and the inscription DIENSTSTELLE/FELDPOSTNUMMER 40517, but these are undoubtedly philatelic. A genuine cover of 1944 is known from Guernsey to Vienna having this handstamp numbered 24200. It is registered from *Feldpost* 937.

Official mail sent by the island Commandant in Jersey had a round handstamp reading INSELKOMMANDANTUR JERSEN with STANDORTKOMMANDANTUR typed across it. A swastika and eagle appeared in the centre. Various handstamps are also recorded reading DIENSTSTELLE/INSELKOMMANDANTUR/JERSEY.

Fakes

In 1969–70 a number of covers came from Germany with various fancy boxed cachets KANALINSELN, LUFTWAFFE GUERNSEY, LUFTWAFFE KANALINSELN, KRIEGSMARINE JERSEY, and unframed KANALINSELN in various sizes. These are fakes and in many cases have *Feldpost* marks which were never in the Channel Islands.

Guernsey Mission in France

From 16 August 1940 the States of Guernsey and Jersey maintained a joint Purchasing Commission in France, with headquarters at the Villa Hirondel, Granville.

The Guernsey representative was provided with special blue envelopes bearing the two-line inscription ETATS DE GUERNESEY/GRANVILLE. One such cover, addressed to the Aerated Water Co., Guernsey, is stamped with a German *Dienststelle* handstamp in black.

It is possible that a similar envelope may have been provided for the Jersey representatives, but none has yet been seen.

The Liberation

The Liberation of the Channel Islands was put in train when the German High Command accepted defeat in the Second World War and ordered active operations to cease at one minute past midnight on 9 May 1945. Victory-in-Europe (VE) Day was proclaimed in Britain for 8 May and Winston Churchill's speech on that day included the famous reference to the freeing of "our dear Channel Islands".

The local German Commandants in Guernsey and Jersey signed surrender documents on the morning of 9 May and British military and civilian detachments began arriving that afternoon. The main military forces moved into both islands on 12 May, when Royal Proclamations were made re-establishing the ancient institutions and privileges. A British military detachment went to Sark on 10 May and the German garrison was taken off as prisoners of war on the 17th. Troops from Guernsey crossed to Alderney on 16 May and prisoners of war were evacuated on the 20th. As a climax to these events the King and Queen visited Jersey and Guernsey on 7 June 1945.

The period of British military government ended on 25 August 1945 when Lieutenant-Governors were once again installed in both Bailiwicks. Field Post Offices had been in operation (*see* Section 11).

(1)   (2)

Cat. No.	Type No.		Dates of use	Colour			Price on cover
GO1	1	Feldpost (712)	1941–44	Black	..	.. ..	35.00
GO2		Feldpost (937)	1941–43	Black	..	.. ..	60.00
GO3		Feldpost (no number)	1941–44	Black	..	..*from*	25.00
GO4	—	Zurück handstamp	Aug. 1944	Red		.. ..	40.00
GO5	2	Montmartin-sur-Mer	12.8.40	Black	..	*on piece*	£100
Other handstamps							
GO6		Deutsche/Dienstpost	1941	Violet	..	.. ..	50.00
GO7		Feldkommandantur 515/Mil. Ver. Gr.	1942	Black	..	.. ..	25.00
GO8		Feldkommandantur 515 (circular)	1940	Blue	..	.. ..	40.00
GO9		Hafenveberwachungsstelle/St. Helier	1940s	Violet	..	.. ..	45.00
GO10		Inselkommandantur/Jersen	1942–43	Violet or black		..	40.00
GO11		Dienststelle Feldpostnummer 24200	1944	Black	..	.. ..	40.00
GO12		Dienststelle Inselkommandantur Jersey	1941–45	Violet or black		..	40.00
Radio Message Card							
GO13		Via Wilhelmshaven inscribed Kanalinseln	1944	—			£100
Special cover							
GO14		Etats de Guernesey/Granville	1941	—			40.00

German markings used in Alderney and Sark are listed in Section 13. For the adhesive postage stamps of the Occupation period *see* Part 2 of the Catalogue.

19. Red Cross Message Service

Through the Red Cross, civilians in the U.K. and overseas could send messages to friends and relatives in the Channel Islands and could receive replies, although by the time that arrangements were made in Jersey and Guernsey for handling these messages, a well-organised service on similar lines between the U.K. and Germany had already been in existence for about a year.

In Jersey, *ad hoc* arrangements were made to deal with messages received in December 1940 and January 1941. Later, a committee was set up under the Bailiff, and Mr. C. J. d'Authreau, the Assistant Postmaster, was seconded from his duties in March 1941 to take charge of the receipt and dispatch of messages. He opened an office in Halkett Place, St. Helier, known as the Bailiff of Jersey's Enquiry and News Service.

In Guernsey, an office to handle Red Cross messages was opened on 13 January 1941, with Mr. George A. Bradshaw in charge, assisted by Miss Leonie Trouteaud. (Mr. Bradshaw has in fact given his name to advice cards which his office posted to civilians in Guernsey to advise them that messages had been received and were awaiting collection. The cards were either sent inside window envelopes or on their own, but in either case were post free. The various types of card used are described and priced in a list at the end of this Section.) Mr. Bradshaw was deported in September 1942 and thereafter Miss Trouteaud was in charge.

U.K. residents could go to a Red Cross Bureau (usually situated in a Citizens' Advice Bureau, of which there was one in all the main towns) and leave a message of not more than twenty-five words. The messages were sent to Red Cross Headquarters in London, from there to the G.P.O. for censoring, then on to the Channel ports to be taken by sea to Lisbon. There, officials of the British Red Cross and of the International Red Cross dispatched the messages to Geneva, either by train via Spain and France or by sea via Marseilles.

When they arrived at Geneva the messages were checked by the International Red Cross, a cachet was applied, and the messages were put into window envelopes (a priced list of these appears at the end of this Section). The envelopes were put into boxes and sent to the headquarters of the German Red Cross in Berlin, where they were fed into the *Feldpost* system. Random censoring took place. Messages for the Channel Islands were sent from Berlin via Paris, where they were examined and had cachets applied by the French Commission of the German Red Cross. The German authorities in the Channel Islands advised the local authorities when the messages arrived and were available for collection. The same route (in reverse) was used for replies from the Channel Islands.

A Red Cross message from the U.K. to the Channel Islands would have the following marks:

(1) A British Red Cross local bureau cachet;

(2) One or two British censor marks;

(3) One or two International Red Cross Committee cachets;

(4) One or two cachets applied by the French Commission of the German Red Cross;

(5) One Guernsey or Jersey Red Cross cachet;
(6) Date stamps as applied;
(7) Chemical wash as applied.

The prices quoted are for forms showing the most common types of cachet. Those with the scarcer cachets command a premium, and prices for these can generally be calculated by adding to this basic price the price of the cachet (*see* separate list). Although message forms of foreign origin are listed, cachets applied in foreign countries are excluded.

Late in the war, after the Allied invasion of France closed the land route from Lisbon to Geneva, an arrangement was made between the British Red Cross, the German Red Cross and the International Red Cross Committee whereby messages arriving in Lisbon were transcribed on to a summary form which was forwarded to the Channel Islands by sea on the s.s. *Vega* (this ship is depicted on the 1s. 9d. Jersey "Liberation" commemorative stamp of 1970, S.G. 37).

In the following priced list of stationery and cachets, catalogue numbers are categorised:

Message forms	RXF
Summary forms	RXS
Window envelopes	RXE
Bradshaw Advice Cards	RXA
Cachets	RXC

RED CROSS MESSAGE STATIONERY

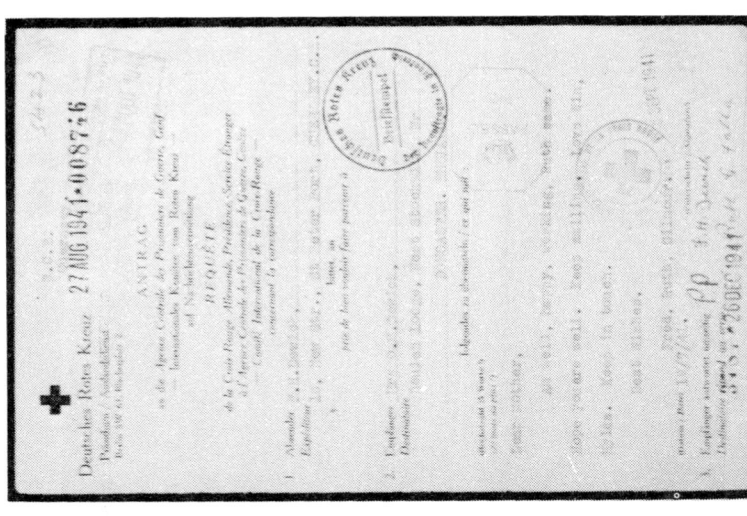

RXF5

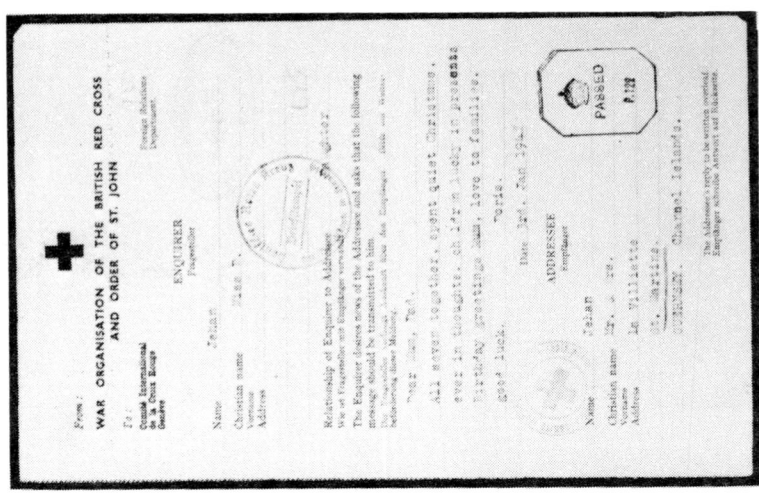

RXF2

Illustrations reduced

RXE 1

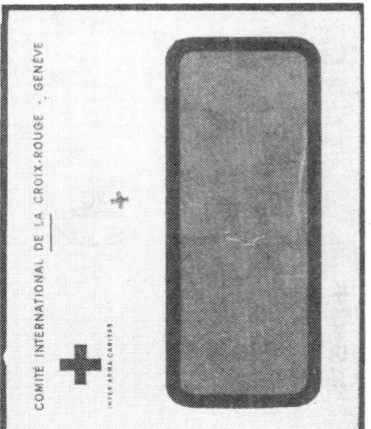

COMITÉ INTERNATIONAL DE LA CROIX-ROUGE . GENÈVE

INTER ARMA CARITAS

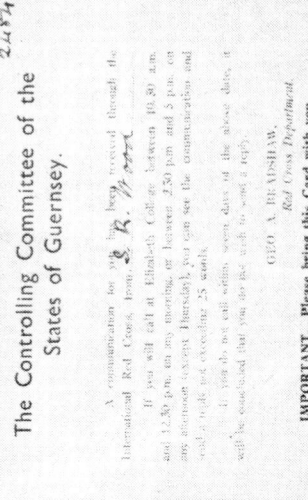

The Controlling Committee of the States of Guernsey.

2484

A communication for you, received through the International Red Cross, from ⟨handwritten⟩

If you will call at Elizabeth College between 10.30 a.m. and 12.30 p.m. on any morning, or between 2.30 p.m. and 5 p.m. on any afternoon (except Thursday), you can see the communication (and send a reply not exceeding 25 words).

If you do not call within seven days of the above date, it will be concluded that you do not desire to send a reply.

GEO. A. BRADSHAW.
Red Cross Department.

IMPORTANT. Please bring this Card with you.

RXA1 (reverse)

Illustrations reduced

RXS1

⊕ Red Cross Message Bureau

Summary of Civilian Message in sequence at Lisbon, Portugal.
Destined for the Channel Islands.

FROM Mrs. Bridle
Guernsey.

DATE OF MESSAGE 13.3.44.

MESSAGE

All well. Worry about Polly.
Dont know where Children are.
Love Girls.

(1) Message Forms from the United Kingdom
RXF1 — Sub-headed "Prisoners of War, Wounded and Missing Department" at top right. Bilingual (English and German) .. .. 4·00
RXF2 — Sub-headed "Foreign Relations Department" at top right. "The Addressee's reply to be written overleaf" (at foot). Bilingual (English and German) .. .. 4·00
RXF3 — As RXF2 but "(Not more than 25 words)." added at foot .. .. .. 2·50
RXF4 — Sub-headed "Foreign Relations Department" at top right. Trilingual (English, French and German) .. .. 2·50

(2) Message Forms from the Channel Islands
RXF5 — Bilingual (German and French). There are five varieties of this form, which differ only in minor typographic details. Supplied by the German authorities free of charge .. .. 2·50

(3) Message Forms from Overseas
RXF6 — Canadian form (although bearing no indication of country of origin). Size 224 × 143mm. Trilingual (English, French and German). Printed in black, except emblem and letters "C.I.R.C." in red .. .. .. 60·00
RXF7 — Ceylonese form, similar to RXF2 but headed "The Ceylon Branch of the British Red Cross Society" .. .. 40·00
RXF8 — Middle East form, used for messages from Middle East Forces. Six types exist, with differing sizes and typographical details .. .. 50·00
RXF9 — New Zealand form. Size 209 × 132mm, headed "The New Zealand Red Cross Society, Wellington, New Zealand" .. .. 60·00
RXF10 — Southern Rhodesian form, duplicated, size 254 × 203mm. No Red Cross emblem. Printed in black .. .. 60·00
RXF11 — As RXF10 but size 215 × 139mm and printed in red .. .. .. 80·00
RXF12 — Australian form, printed in red and headed "Australian Red Cross Society" .. .. 90·00
RXF13 — Indian form, headed "Indian Red Cross". In three slightly different types .. .. 90·00
RXF14 — French form .. .. 90·00
RXF15 — Irish form .. .. 20·00
RXF16 — Argentinian form .. .. 90·00
RXF17 — U.S. form .. .. 40·00
RXF18 — Dutch form £120
RXF19 — South African form £130

(4) Summary Form used at Lisbon
RXS1 — Size 217 × 139mm, headed "Red Cross Message Bureau. Summary of Civilian Message in suspence [sic] at Lisbon, Portugal. Destined for the Channel Islands" .. .. 30·00

(5) Window Envelopes used at Geneva
RXE1 — Grey, grey-green or grey-blue paper. Size 149 × 120mm. Window 119 × 43mm with 4mm carmine border .. .. 8·00
RXE2 — As RXE1 but window border is blue .. .. 20·00
RXE3 — As RXE1 but Red Cross and motto *above* COMITÉ ... GENÈVE instead of below it .. .. 10·00
RXE4 — As RXE3 but "No. 52" in very small print above upper right corner of window .. .. 6·00
RXE5 — As RXE4 but window border is scarlet .. .. 12·00
RXE6 — Size 162 × 115mm. Window 100 × 45mm .. .. 14·00
RXE7 — As RXE1 but without window .. .. 25·00

Other envelopes are known but these mainly carried official correspondence and are rare.

(6) Bradshaw Advice Cards
All these cards were printed by the Camp du Roi printing works, RXA1 to RXA4 on white, commercially printed postcards and RXA5 to RXA13 on coloured card. Three different versions of text were used and they read as follows:

Text A

The Controlling Committee of the
States of Guernsey.

_____1941

A communication for you has been received through the International Red Cross.
If you will call at Elizabeth College between 10.30 a.m. and 12.30 p.m. on any morning, or between 2.30 p.m. and 5 p.m. on any afternoon (except Thursday), you can see the communication and send a reply not exceeding 25 words.
If you do not call within seven days of the above date, it will be concluded that you do not wish to send a reply.

GEO. A. BRADSHAW,
Red Cross Department.

Text B

The Controlling Committee of the
States of Guernsey.

_____

A communication for you has been received through the International Red Cross, from _____
If you will call at Elizabeth College between 10.30 a.m. and 12.30 p.m. on any morning, or between 2.30 p.m. and 5 p.m. on any afternoon (except Thursday), you can see the communication and send a reply not exceeding 25 words.
If you do not call within seven days of the above date, it will be concluded that you do not wish to send a reply.

GEO. A. BRADSHAW,
Red Cross Department.

IMPORTANT—Please bring this Card with you.

Text C

The Controlling Committee of the
States of Guernsey.

_____

A communication for you has been received through the International Red Cross, from _____
If you will call at Elizabeth College between 10.30 a.m. and 12.30 p.m. on any morning, or between 2.30 p.m. and 5 p.m. on any afternoon (except Thursday), you can see the communication and send a reply not exceeding 25 words.
Please reply to this notice immediately. Even if you do **not** wish to answer the communication, **let the Red Cross Department know** or you will delay the return of many messages.

GEO. A. BRADSHAW,
Red Cross Department.

IMPORTANT—Please bring this Card with you.

CAMP DU ROI PRINTING WORKS.

RXA1   Commercially printed postcard ("POSTCARD/The address to be written on this side" printed on front) size 139 × 88mm, with text **A** printed in black on reverse. "Important—please bring this card with you" added at foot in manuscript .. .. 30·00

RXA2	As RXA1 but "IMPORTANT—Please bring this Card with you." printed at foot. "1941" at upper right printed in large italic type	20·00
RXA3	As RXA2 but "1941" in small upright type	20·00
RXA4	Commercially printed postcard ("PRINTED PAPER RATE", underlined, printed on front) size 138 × 88mm, with Text B printed in deep blue on reverse	16·00
RXA5	Printed on pink card. Address side blank. Text C on reverse (printer's imprint at lower left in upright type)	16·00
RXA6	As RXA5 but address altered (to 38 High Street) and opening hours altered (now 10 a.m. to 12.30 p.m. and 2 p.m. to 4.30 p.m.), both in manuscript	16·00
RXA7	Printed on cream card. As RXA5 but printed address now "38 High Street" and times reading "between 10 a.m. and 12.30 p.m. or between 2 p.m. and 4.30 p.m."	16·00
RXA8	Printed on green card, size 124 × 84mm. As RXA5 but printed address now "9–11 High Street" and times "between 10 a.m. and 1 p.m. or between 2 p.m. and 4 p.m.". Printer's imprint at lower centre in upright type	16·00
RXA9	As RXA8 with address changed to 1 Market Street in manuscript ..	16·00
RXA10	As RXA8 but grey card and printed address reads 1 Market Street ..	16·00
RXA11	As RXA10 but printed on blue card. Printer's imprint at lower left in italic type	16·00
RXA12	As RXA11 but printed on orange card	16·00
RXA13	As RXA12 but printed on blue card and printer's imprint at lower left in upright type	16·00

CACHETS APPLIED TO RED CROSS MESSAGES

RXC4

RXC11

RXC12

Deutsches Rotes Kreuz

Eing.:

Ausg.:

RXC13

RXC18

The Controlling Committee of the
States of Guernsey

Geo. A. Bradshaw.

Red Cross Department.

RXC24

STATES OF GUERNSEY

RED CROSS BUREAU

RXC25

RXC26

On behalf of the Bailiff
of Jersey's Enquiry and
News Service.

RXC29

PASSED
P. 263

RXC31

16 OCT 1942

RXC35

RXC36

Geprüft
Dienststelle
Feldpost Nr. 35372
I c

RXC40

Geprüft

RXC42

(1) Cachets used by the International Red Cross at Geneva

RXC1	Double circle, 29mm diameter, reading COMITÉ INTERNATIONAL DE LA CROIX ROUGE—GENÈVE. Red cross in centre	1·00
RXC2	As RXC1 but "de la" in lowercase letters	3·00
RXC3	Treble circle, 32mm diameter, otherwise similar to RXC1	8·00
RXC4	Treble circle, 34mm diameter, otherwise similar to RXC1	12·00
RXC5	Treble circle, 36mm diameter, otherwise similar to RXC1	6·00
RXC6	COUPON-REPONSE in single line, 34 × 3mm, in red	50·00
RXC7	TIMBRE-REPONSE in single line, 35 × 4mm	75·00

(2) Cachets used at the British Red Cross headquarters

RXC8	Double circle, 52mm diameter, reading BRITISH RED CROSS AND ST. JOHN WAR ORGANISATION. Red Cross in centre	15·00
RXC9	As RXC8 but 54mm diameter	16·00
RXC10	As RXC8 but 57mm diameter	12·00
RXC11	As RXC8 but 60mm diameter	12·00

(3) Cachets used in Paris by the French Commission of the German Red Cross

RXC12   Single circle, 36mm diameter, eagle and cross in centre, with wording "Deutsches Rotes Kreuz—Der Beauftragte für Frankreich". Cross in red, rest of cachet in blue (can be found in violet due to mixing of inks) .. ..   6·00

RXC13   Boxed cachet 46½ × 21mm divided horizontally into two sections. "Deutsches Rotes Kreuz" in upper section and "Eing." and "Ausg." in lower section. Roman type. In red .. ..   35·00

RXC14   As RXC13 but in Fraktur (Gothic) type, in blue or green £120

RXC15   As RXC13 but lower part of box omitted. In red, blue or green .. ..   3·50

RXC16   Single circle, 35mm diameter, reading "Deutsches Rotes Kreuz—Der Beauftragte in Frankreich" around outside and "Briefstempel" across centre, between two horizontal lines. Fraktur (Gothic) type. Struck in red, crimson, green, light blue, bright blue, purple-brown, violet or grey-black .. ..   2·50

RXC17   As RXC16 but Roman type. In maroon, brown or blackish purple ..   6·00

RXC18   Square, 39 × 39mm, containing single circle, 34mm diameter. Wording as RXC16. Roman type. Eagle at upper centre .. ..   8·00

(4) Cachets used in Berlin by the German Red Cross headquarters

RXC19   As RXC18 but reads "Präsidium" at foot .. ..   95·00

RXC20   Two-line cachet reading "Deutsches Rotes Kreuz/Präsidium" in Fraktur (Gothic) type. Unboxed, size 44 × 12mm. Indigo or violet ..   95·00

RXC21   Two-line cachet reading "Deutsches Rotes Kreuz" (in Roman) over date. Purple · .. ..   95·00

RXC19 and RXC20 are found only on official stationery.

(5) Cachets used by the Guernsey Red Cross

RXC22   Typewritten "The Controlling Committee of the States of Guernsey" with signature of George Bradshaw in manuscript and "Red Cross Dept." below .. ..   20·00

RXC23   As RXC22 but signature rubber-stamped .. ..   4·00

RXC24   As RXC22 but both wording and signature rubber-stamped. Size 85 × 23mm .. ..   3·00

RXC25   Boxed cachet 67½ × 24mm, reading STATES OF GUERNSEY/RED CROSS BUREAU. In black, blue, violet or green .. ..   2·50

(6) Cachets used by the Jersey Red Cross

RXC26   Embossed seal, 36mm diameter, with Arms of Jersey and wording S. BALLIVIE INSVLE DE IERSEYE .. .. *on its own*   20·00

RXC27   Double circle, 55mm diameter. Reads NACHFORSCHUNGS u. NACHRICHTEN-UEBERMITTELUNGS-STELLE around outside. Red Cross and DER BALIFF VON JERSEY in centre £150

RXC28   Unframed three-line cachet, 55 × 11mm, reading ON BEHALF OF THE BAILIFF/OF JERSEY'S ENQUIRY AND/NEWS SERVICE. In red, blue or violet .. ..   5·00

RXC29   Boxed cachet 68 × 23½mm reading as RXC28 but in upper and lowercase letters .. ..   2·75

RXC30   REPLY, 16 × 5mm, in black, blue-black or red .. ..   10·00

(7) British Censor Mark

RXC31   Octagonal cachet 36 × 26½mm containing crown, PASSED and reference number. Normally in red but known in other colours .. ..   2·50

(8) British Instructional Marks

RXC32   Four-line unboxed cachet 57 × 14mm reading NOT TO BE USED FOR REPLY/POST OFFICE WILL SUPPLY/ADDRESS OF CITIZENS ADVICE BUREAU/WHERE MESSAGE FORMS ARE AVAILABLE .. ..   18·00

RXC33   Wording as RXC32 but size 61 × 20mm. NOT TO BE USED FOR REPLY in capitals but rest of text in upper and lowercase letters .. .. ..   12·00

RXC34   Six-line cachet reading NOT TO BE USED FOR REPLY/POST OFFICE WILL SUPPLY/ADDRESS OF NEAREST RED/CROSS MESSAGE BUREAU WHICH/WILL DESPATCH A NEW MESS-/AGE FOR YOU. Size 68 × 27mm   12·00

(9) British Transit Mark applied at Brighton by the Royal Engineers

RXC35   Single circle, 29mm diameter, reading R.E. RECORD OFFICE/BRIGHTON. Date across centre   ..   ..   18·00

(10) German Civil Censor Marks

RXC36   Single circle, 28mm diameter, reading "Oberkommando der Wehrmacht—Geprüft", with eagle, swastika and code letter "b" for Berlin. In red   ..   ..   15·00

RXC37   As RXC36 but code letter "x" (Paris)   ..   ..   20·00

RXC38   Similar to RXC36 but 35mm diameter. In black   ..   ..   ..   20·00

RXC39   Gestapo censor mark, single circle 34mm diameter, reading "Zensurstelle—Geprüft" and with eagle and swastika in centre   ..   ..   18·00

(11) German Military Censor Marks

RXC40   Boxed cachet 46 × 29mm reading "Geprüft/Dienststelle/Feldpost" and number. In red   ..   ..   80·00

RXC41   As RXC40 but without number £120

(12) Censor Marks applied at German Internee Camps

RXC42   Biberach, double circle, 34mm diameter, reading "Internierungslager Biberach/Riß" above and "Postüberwachung" below, with "Geprüft" across centre   ..   ..   80·00

RXC43   Laufen oval cachet reading "Ilag VII Geprüft" with code letter "4" in centre. In violet   ..   ..   80·00

20. Internee Mail Service

Starting in September 1942 some 2000 British-born Channel Islands residents were deported and interned in Germany. They joined a handful of other civilians from the Channel Islands who had been detained on the Continent during the rapid German advance in 1940.

Following the outbreak of war in 1939 the International Red Cross Committee had sought and obtained the consent of the belligerents to treat internees as prisoners of war. One of the results of this arrangement was that interned civilians were allowed both to send and to receive correspondence. Although it had been instrumental in obtaining the consent of the belligerents, the Red Cross was not responsible for ensuring that a mail service operated.

Article 36 of the 1929 Geneva Convention, which governed the transmission of P.O.W. mail (and by the later agreement the mail of internees also), provided for the exchange of mail by post, by the shortest route and without fee. The belligerent countries arranged amongst themselves, generally by the channel of the Protecting Powers, for the exchange of mail. In Europe, throughout the greater part of the war, the exchange took place through the Swiss postal service, in particular via Basle.

The first deportees left Jersey on 17 September 1942 and Guernsey on 21 September 1942, both groups destined for Germany. The journeys were interrupted and a number of stops were made. During these stops the internees were not permitted to leave the trains in which they were travelling.

Mail is known from temporary camps (*Frontstalag*) at Compiègne and St. Denis in France from a few Channel Islanders who were caught in France and interned before the 1942 deportations, also from some women who were interned there for a short while in 1943 before being moved to Biberach/Riß. Additional mail is known to and from Stalag VIF, Dorsten, in north-west Germany, where internees were held in transit for six to seven weeks.

Ultimately all Channel Islands deportees were, as far as is known, interned in one or other of the six following internee camps: Biberach/Riß (Ilag VB) in Württemberg; Wurzach/Allgäu (Ilag VC) in Württemberg; Laufen Obb (Ilag VII) in Upper Bavaria; Kreuzburg (Ilag VIIIZ) in Upper Silesia; Libenau in Württemberg; and Walzburg – Weissenburg (Ilag XIII) in Bavaria.

The majority of mail is from Biberach/Riß or Laufen, addressed either to the Channel Islands or to the United Kingdom. Mail from the camps was written on "free-issue" pre-printed cards or lettersheets, the senders being restricted to a maximum of one per week.

Correspondence to the camps was sent in plain, unstamped envelopes, generally with the added manuscript annotations "Interniertenpost" when from the Channel Islands and "Kriegsgefangenenpost" when from the U.K., although "Interniertenpost" was sometimes used from the U.K. Fee-paid P.O.W. airletters are known from the U.K. and include the pre-printed 2½d. envelopes and the plain 5d. envelopes.

Correspondence to and from the Channel Islands effectively ceased in June 1944, but mail is known to have been carried by the Red Cross vessel s.s. *Vega* during the winter of 1944–45.

All mails were subject to censorship, most mails of camp origins bearing either a cachet or censor mark and some carrying additional German or British censor marks. Additional internee mail to the Channel Islands is known both from Italy and from the British camp on the Isle of Man, which held German internees.

All the official *Interniertenpost* stationery, when used, bears certain markings, which include postmarks, camp censor marks and camp cachets. The following listing allows for the card or lettersheet to bear a town or dumb cancel postmark, the cheapest variety of camp censor mark, and the cheapest variety of camp cachet. Any stationery bearing an additional or more expensive mark is priced at the value of the dearest mark.

Items of mail to or from Channel Islanders in concentration camps, in civil prisons in Germany and France or in internment camps in Switzerland for escaped prisoners of war is known but is very rare.

(Prices per item from £150.)

INTERNEE STATIONERY

Postcards. All cards of German origin are 149 × 96mm and, with four exceptions, are of similar format. The camp name is usually pre-printed in the sender's panel at the left. The cards were used from late 1942 until 1945.

(For cards in pristine condition add 20%.)

Cat. No.		To the C.I.	To the U.K.
IP1	Biberach/Riß *Interniertenpost* postcard	13·00	8·00
IP2	Wurzach/Allgäu *Interniertenpost* postcard	30·00	20·00
IP3	Ilag VII (Laufen Obb) *Interniertenpost* postcard	15·00	10·00
IP4	Ilag VII (Laufen Obb) Christmas card (1943). Picture of camp and "Christmas Greetings from Schloss Laufen"	25·00	20·00
IP5	Ilag VII (Laufen Obb) Christmas card (1944). Line-drawing of inside of canteen and "1944 A Merry Christmas and A Happy New Year Ilag VII 1945"	25·00	20·00
IP6	Ilag VII (Laufen Obb) special bilingual Polish/English postcard. Used in 1943–44 to notify internees' relatives of the receipt of a parcel through the Red Cross	35·00	30·00
IP7	Liebenau *Interniertenpost* postcard	†	£100
IP8	Wurzach/Allgäu, Oflag 55VD, *Kriegsgefangenpost* postcard (in German and French)	40·00	30·00
IP9	"Universal" *Kriegsgefangenenpost* postcard (in German only), from any internee camp	15·00	10·00
IP10	Postcard from Grande Caserne, Paris, used in 1941	£100	†

Lettersheets. All the lettersheets used were of the fold-over and tuck-in-type, and the overall dimensions of those of German origin are 286 × 146mm. As they are printed on chalk-surfaced paper they are generally found in poor condition.

(For examples in fine condition add 20%.)

Cat. No.		To the C.I.	To the U.K.
IP11	Biberach/Riß *Interniertenpost* lettersheet	13·00	8·00
IP12	Wurzach/Allgäu *Interniertenpost* lettersheet	30·00	20·00
IP13	Ilag VII (Laufen Obb) *Interniertenpost* lettersheet	15·00	10·00
IP14	Ilag VII (Laufen Obb) provisional lettersheet. "Kriegsgefangenenpost" obliterated and "Jnterniertenpost" [sic] substituted	25·00	20·00
IP15	Kreuzburg *Interniertenpost* lettersheet	50·00	40·00
IP16	"Universal" *Kriegsgefangenenpost* lettersheet	15·00	10·00
			To Unused Germany
IP17	*Interniertenpost* lettersheet from the Channel Islands, inscribed KANAL INSELN at foot	80·00	£100
			To the C.I.
IP18	Mail from Walzburg–Weissenburg	..*from*	£100
IP19	British lettersheets of Isle of Man origin addressed to Guernsey	..*from*	50·00

Airletters. The only airletters known to have been used are of British origin. They were first introduced on 21 July 1941 and were sold at 3d. each, including 2½d. postage (the European rate). Three types exist.

Cat. No.		To Germany
IP20	2½d. British airletter inscribed in English, French and German ..	20·00

Covers. This category includes all mail carried in commercial envelopes or newspaper wrappers, etc. Each piece would be expected to carry one, or more, of the following: an adhesive postage stamp where applicable, a town or dumb cancellation postmark, and the cheapest variety of censor mark, where applicable. Any cover bearing an additional or more expensive mark is priced at the value of the dearest mark (*see* the priced list of postmarks, censor cachets, camp cachets and instructional marks below).

Cat. No.		Price
IP21	From a German camp to Germany	60·00
IP22	From Germany to a German camp	60·00
IP23	From the U.K. to a German camp (free rate)	13·00
IP24	From the U.K. to a German camp (5d. airmail rate)	30·00

Cat. No.		Price
IP25	From a U.K. Isle of Man camp to Guernsey (5d. airmail rate)	90·00
IP26	From the Channel Islands to a German camp	50·00
IP27	Newspaper wrappers (1d. rate)	50·00
IP28	Fee-paid internee mail of Italian origin from *isolati* (British citizens living at liberty) addressed to the Channel Islands .. .. ..*from*	75·00

Unofficial Stationery. During periods of shortage during and immediately after the war, hand-made cards were produced by both internees and the camp authorities. These cards, hand written, are of the same format as the Official cards. They are only known from Ilag VII, Laufen.

Cat. No.		Price
IP29	Ilag VII (Laufen Obb)	50·00

MARKINGS

Postmarks, censor cachets, camp cachets and instructional marks. Because the operation of the mail service was the responsibility of the belligerents, nearly all pieces of mail bear a postmark from the place of origin, most of which are of no significance. One of the exceptions is mail of Channel Island origin, addressed to German camps, which does not usually bear a postmark. This may be recognised by the lack of both an adhesive postage stamp and a country or origin censor mark.

IPC 10

IPC 14

IPC 16

Internierungslager Biberach/Riß

IPC 18

IPC 31

 Geöffnet  Geöffnet

IPC 44

IPC 46

RETURNED FROM CONTINENT IN UNDELIVERED MAILS

IPC 53

Cat. No.		Price on entire

(1) German Postmarks

IPC1	German town cancel, with name of town and code. Double circle, 28mm diameter	13.00
IPC2	German "dumb" cancel (no place name shown), 28mm diameter. Used on Biberach mail	15.00
IPC3	As IPC2 but 29mm diameter and used on Kreuzburg mail	50.00
IPC4	TITTMONING town cancel with code "a" at foot, 28mm diameter. Used from 5 to 13 April 1943	50.00

(2) French Postmarks

IPC5	PARIS GARE DU NORD—PROVINCE A, single circle, 26mm diameter, used only during May 1944	£120
IPC6	POSTE AUX ARMEES, single circle, 27mm diameter, only known used 28 April 1945 on mail from Biberach/Riß. This date is *after* the liberation of Biberach/Riß by U.S. forces but *before* the liberation of the Channel Islands. Mail was processed by the French	80.00

Cat. No.		Price on entire

(3) Internee Camp Censor Marks

IPC7   Double circle, 33mm diameter, reading "Internierungslager Biberach/ Riß–Postüberwachung" around outside and "Geprüft" across centre. In violet, used from September 1943 to February 1945 .. .. ..   13·00

IPC8   "D 22" code, 5mm high. Censor mark used at Biberach/Riß. In blue-black or violet, used on mail from the U.K. from late 1944 onwards   .. ..   25·00

IPC9   Double oval, 38 × 24mm, reading "Ilag VII–Geprüft" and with code number in centre. In violet or blue-violet. Used from November 1942 to November 1944 .. ..   15·00

IPC10   Single circle, 32mm diameter, reading "Ilag VII–Geprüft" and with code number in centre. In violet or blue-violet. In use from November 1942 to November 1944 .. ..   15·00

IPC11   Similar to IPC10 but "Ilag" misspelt JLAG, and in capitals. Code number "13" in centre. In violet or blue-violet. Used only during October 1944   .. ..   25·00

IPC12   Double circle (outer circle has "cogwheel" effect), 29mm diameter. Code "2" in centre. Used at Kreuzburg in Spring 1944 .. ..   50·00

IPC13   Triangle 22mm high, reading "Ilag VIII Z/Geprüft" and code number. Used at Kreuzburg in the latter half of 1944 .. ..   50·00

IPC14   Shield type, 29mm high, reading "Ilag VIII/Geprüft" with code number. In scarlet. Used at Kreuzburg in Spring 1944 .. ..   50·00

IPC15   Single circle, 33mm diameter, reading "Oflag VD/geprüft" and code number in centre. In violet. Used until early 1943 ·· .. .. ..   75·00

(4) Internee Camp Cachets

IPC16   Single circle, 33mm diameter, reading "Internierungslager—Biberach/ Riß", and with eagle over swastika in centre. In violet. Used in December 1942 .. ..   30·00

IPC17   "Internierungslager/Biberach/Riß" in Fraktur (Gothic type) in two lines, size 59 × 9mm. In violet. Used early in 1943 .. ..   25·00

IPC18   As IPC17 but smaller type and in one line, 56mm long. In violet. Used in first half of 1943   .. ..   13·00

IPC19   "Zivilinternierungslager Biberach/Riß" in single line cachet, 61mm long. In violet. Used during second half of 1944   .. ..   30·00

IPC20   "Biberach an der Riß" in single line, 34mm long. Used during second half of 1944 .. ..   25·00

IPC21   As IPC16 but reading "Wurzach" at foot. Used in December 1942 ..   45·00

IPC22   "Internierungslager Wurzach (Württ.)", 64mm long, similar to IPC18. In violet. Used early 1943 to 1944 .. ..   30·00

IPC23   Similar to IPC16 but reading "Jlag VII" [*sic*] at top .. ..   75·00

IPC24   "Jlag VIII" [*sic*], 24mm long. In violet. Used in November 1942 and August 1943 .. ..   20·00

IPC25   "Laufen/Obb.", 49mm long. In violet. Used in November 1942 .. ..   30·00

IPC26   "Ilag VIII Z", 24mm long. Used at Kreuzburg in second half of 1944   55·00

(5) Internee Camp Instructional Marks

IPC27   "Jnternierten-Post" [*sic*], 67mm long. Used on mail from Laufen in November 1942 and August 1943   .. ..   20·00

IPC28   "Nicht im Ilag VIII", 35mm long. In violet. Used in April 1943 .. ..   60·00

(6) Transit Camp Censor Marks

IPC29   Double circle, 27mm diameter (outer circle with "cogwheel" effect), reading FR. STALAG/122/GEPRUFT. In scarlet. Used during 1943 .. ..   £100

IPC30   As IPC29 but with code "9" at foot. In violet. Used in 1943 .. ..   £100

IPC31   Diamond-shaped cachet, 58 × 28mm, reading "Frontstalag 122/ Geprüft". In violet £100

Cat. No.		*Price on entire*

IPC32 — Boxed cachet, 39½ × 15½mm, reading GEPRÜFT with code number "6" below. In violet. Used at Compiègne in 1943 .. .. — £100

IPC33 — As IPC32 but 41 × 19mm and with code number "2". In crimson. Used at St. Denis in 1944 .. .. — £100

IPC34 — As IPC32 but 40 × 18mm and code number "3". In crimson. Used at St. Denis in 1944 .. .. — £100

IPC35 — As IPC30 but 30mm diameter and code number "8". In violet. Used at St. Denis in July 1943 .. .. — £100

(7) British Censor Marks

Cachet RXC31 (*see* Section 19) is known on internee mail, also a censor label designated P.C.90, reading OPENED BY EXAMINER, etc.

(*Price* £13.)

A double-circle DEPUTY CHIEF FIELD CENSOR mark (21mm diameter) in black has been seen on post-liberation mail

(*Price* £60.)

Additional British censor marks struck in the Isle of Man internee camps are known

(*Price on mail addressed to Guernsey from* £75.)

(8) German Censor Marks

Cachets RXC36 and RXC37 (*see* Section 19) are known on internee mail, as well as similar cachets with code letters for different points of application. Indeed, the majority of German censor marks are identifiable from these code letters (fourteen different codes are known but not all were used on Channel Islands internee mail).

(*Price* £18.)

IPC36 — As RXC37 (*see* Section 19) but coded "y" for Bordeaux. In black. Only seen used on mail from Isle of Man internee camps to Guernsey .. .. — 90·00

IPC37 — Similar to IPC36 but 35mm diameter and coded "c" for Cologne. In red .. .. — 20·00

IPC38 — Similar to IPC36 but 35mm diameter and coded "e" for Frankfurt-am-Main. In red .. .. — 18·00

IPC39 — Similar to IPC36 but 35mm diameter and coded "d" for Munich. In red or blue .. .. — 18·00

IPC40 — Munich individual censor mark. Two-, three- or four-digit code number in rectangular box 27 × 15mm. In red. Usually present in pairs (i.e. two different code numbers) as the censors made a double check .. — 18·00

IPC41 — As IPC40 but 12 × 8mm .. .. — 18·00

IPC42 — Similar to IPC40/41 but 9 × 4mm, containing numeral code (Frankfurt-am-Main censor mark). In red or black .. .. — 18·00

IPC43 — "Geprüft/Dienststelle Feldpost 45190" (Paris censor mark), in two lines, 46mm long. In red. Used until December 1942 on internee mail from the U.K. to Guernsey .. .. — 75·00

IPC44 — Continuous censor tape 40mm wide. Coded "e" (for Frankfurt-am-Main) and printed in violet. Used on internee mail from the U.K. to Guernsey .. .. — 90·00

IPC45 — Continuous Frankfurt-am-Main censor mark, comprising single-circle cachets (19mm diameter) 79mm apart, linked by six parallel horizontal lines. Cachets read "Geprüft/Oberkommando der Wehrmacht", with code "e" and eagle and swastika in centre. In deep red. Used on internee mail from the U.K. to Guernsey .. .. .. — 90·00

Cat.	Price
No.	on entire

(9) Transit Marks

Cachet RXC1 (*see* Section 19) is known struck in red at Geneva on internee mail from November 1944.

IPC46	Single-circle cachet, containing code "Ab" (Berlin). Known 16mm, 20mm or 21mm diameter and in black, violet or red	55·00
IPC47	Similar to IPC46 but coded "Ae" (Frankfurt-am-Main). Diameter 19mm, 20mm or 21mm. In red or red-violet	35·00
IPC48	Similar to IPC46 but coded "Ax" (Paris). Diameter 19mm or 20mm. In red or red-brown	35·00
IPC49	Hexagonal Madrid airmail transit mark, 30mm across, reading CORREO AEREO/MADRID and date. In black. Used on internee mail from the U.K. Isle of Man camp to Guernsey	90·00
IPC50	Boxed cachet 56 × 26mm, reading BRITISH RED CROSS/AUSTRIA and cross. Used by British Red Cross commission in Austria on liberation mail from Ilag VII in 1945. In dull pink	60·00

(10) Instructional Marks

Cachet PW9 (*see* Section 21) has been seen used on internee mail as well as on P.O.W. mail.

IPC51	Rectangular boxed cachet, 62 × 18mm, reading UNDELIVERED FOR FOR REASON STATED/RETURN TO SENDER	20·00
IPC52	Rectangular boxed cachet, 74 × 17mm, reading "This letter/postcard has been returned by the/International Red Cross Committee at Geneva/who were unable to forward it". In violet. Used in conjunction with IPC51	25·00
IPC53	Rectangular boxed cachet, 75 × 18mm reading RETURNED FROM/ CONTINENT IN/UNDELIVERED MAILS. In violet	25·00
IPC54	Rectangular boxed cachet, 32 × 11mm, reading RETOUR/A L'ENVOYEUR. In black. Used in Paris in July 1944	25·00

21. Prisoner of War Mail

First World War

A P.O.W. Camp for German prisoners was opened at Blanches Banques in Jersey on 20 March 1915. For a few weeks, until an individual censorship cachet was provided, a standard type reading POST FREE/PRISONERS OF WAR/P.C. in a single circle was used. This can be found in black or magenta and the only proof of its use in Jersey is the name and address of the P.O.W. written on the back.

(*Price on cover* £40.)

In April 1915 a double-circle stamp with JERSEY at the top, CHANNEL ISLANDS at the bottom and P.C. in the centre was introduced. It is known in red for most of 1915 and then in violet. Covers usually bear, in addition, an oval black stamp inscribed PRISONERS OF WAR/INFORMATION BUREAU with a crown in the centre and the London "Official Paid" datestamp.

(*Price on cover* £50.)

Second World War

During the Second World War responsibility for the prisoner of war mail service rested with the belligerents, and the basic details have been outlined in Section 20 on internee mails.

Three distinct periods exist, the first being immediately after the Occupation, the second lasting until the end of the war, and the third following the cessation of hostilities. During the first period mails are known from British servicemen caught on the Islands and held in France. During the second period mails exist from many of the 150 German P.O.W. camps; additionally mails are known from Italian P.O.W. camps. Finally, during the third period mail is known to be addressed to a German serviceman held as a P.O.W. on Jersey.

Most of the mail originated in German camps and the following are the German names for the different types of camp: *Stammlager* or *Stalag*, prisoner of war camp; *Offizierlager* or *Oflag*, officer camp; *Marinelager* or *Marlag*, naval camp; *Luftlager* or *Stalag Luft*, air force camp; *Durchgangslager* or *Dulag*, transit camp; *Straflager* or *Stralag*, penal camp. The camps were identified by a code which was either a Roman numeral/alpha or an Arabic numeral (the Roman numeral was that of the German military district or *Wehrkreis*). From 1939 to 1945 an attempt was made to keep all locations secret and censorship regulations dictated that only "dumb" cancels (that is, those not showing the place of origin) to be used on P.O.W. mail; nevertheless, covers bearing town cancels do exist.

Each German camp had its own censor office which stamped all mail. The handstamps used were non-uniform, indeed within individual camps stamps were often of completely different form. The stamps usually bear the camp number and the individual censor's number and are known in a variety of colours.

Post Occupation Mails in July 1940. Two pieces are known. The first, from Cherbourg addressed to Jersey, is marked "P.G." (*Prisonnier de Guerre*) and also 'Inadmis/Retour a L'Envoyeur". After being returned to sender it was smuggled in by a Jersey fisherman. The second from Granville was carried to Jersey by a ship's pilot, it was manuscript marked "Geprüft" in red and stamped "Dienststelle/Inselkommandantur/Jersey" in violet.

(*Price* £120 *each piece.*)

Late 1940 to May 1945. Both inward and outward P.O.W. camp mail exists. The stationery used was similar to that on the internee mail service.

Cat. No.		Price
PW1	P.O.W. card or lettersheet from a *Stalag*	15·00
PW2	P.O.W. card or lettersheet from an *Oflag*	20·00
PW3	P.O.W. card or lettersheet from a *Marlag*	25·00
PW4	P.O.W. card or lettersheet from a *Luftlager*	25·00
PW5	P.O.W. card or lettersheet from a *Dulag*	30·00
PW6	P.O.W. card or lettersheet from a *Stralag*	40·00
PW7	Cover from the Channel Islands to a German P.O.W. camp	50·00
PW8	German town cancel on P.O.W. card or lettersheet	40·00
PW9	BRITANNIQUE, 42mm long, unframed. In violet or red on mail to a German camp ..*cover*	60·00
PW10	SHORT AND LEGIBLE LETTERS WILL RECEIVE PRIORITY, in two lines. 48mm long. In deep blue ..*cover*	20·00
PW11	Boxed cachet, 68 × 15mm, reading PAS DE LONGUES LETTRES/ ECRITURE TRES LISIBLE. In violet ..*cover*	20·00
PW12	BESETZTES GEBIET, single-line cachet in red. Applied by the German authorities to indicate mail which had originated in occupied territory ..*cover*	20·00
PW13	P.O.W. card from an Italian camp to Jersey or Guernsey (scarcer than German cards) ..*from*	40·00

Post-war Mails. After the surrender of the Channel Islands in May 1945, large numbers of German prisoners of war fell into Allied hands and some were held on the Islands. Only one item of mail is known, from Germany to a prisoner of war, bearing the Spremberg datestamp of 29 April 1946. It is addressed to "Liffz. Wilhelm Baigar, B. 167373, No. 802 P.O.W. Camp, Jersey, Great Britain, C.I."

(*Price* £120.)

22. Aerial Propaganda Leaflets

During the Second World War Allied propaganda leaflets were dropped over every occupied country. The Channel Islands were not forgotten and examples of leaflets dropped there make interesting reading. They are keenly sought after by collectors of Channel Islands stamps and postal history material. Two classes of leaflet were dropped, the first in English for the information and comfort of the civilian population and the second in German for the demoralisation of the occupying forces.

Leaflets for Civilians. In the first group are four leaflets, but only three were actually dropped. The first is headed "News from England" in Gothic letters, and is dated September 1940. It is inscribed "Distributed by the R.A.F." and has as its main feature a message from King George VI. It is numbered 600/1 and was dropped on the night of 23/24 September 1940.

The second is somewhat similar but bears the inscription "News from England" in Roman letters and is dated 30 September 1940. It is also inscribed "Distributed by the R.A.F." and "For the Channel Islands". It is numbered 600/2 and was dropped between 7/8 and 15/16 October 1940.

The third leaflet is a rather attractive one entitled "The Archbishop of York speaks to the people of the Channel Islands" and is printed in red and black. Its four pages contain the sermon preached by the archbishop on Sunday, 31 January 1943 in St. Martin-in-the-Fields Church, and broadcast in the B.B.C. Home Service. The archbishop took as his text the words from Isiah: "Comfort ye, comfort ye my people, saith your God." The leaflet also has pictures of the archbishop and of St. Martin-in-the Fields. It is numbered J1 and was dropped on 4/5 March 1943.

The fourth leaflet, which for some reason was never dropped, bears on one side the Royal Arms and in bold capitals "To the inhabitants of the Channel Islands", and on the other side is a statement made in the House of Commons by the Home Secretary, Mr. Herbert Morrison, on Tuesday, 12 December 1944. The statement deals with the sending of medicine, soap and food parcels to the islanders. The leaflet is numbered J2.

Leaflets for Occupation Forces. The second group of leaflets consists of a series of over 300 prepared by S.H.A.E.F. (Supreme Headquarters Allied Expeditionary Forces) and dropped almost daily, by the British and American Forces, behind the enemy front line and over isolated garrisons in the Channel Islands and elsewhere. They are the famous *Nachrichten* newspapers and gave the German forces latest details of the Allied war effort. Not every one of the series was dropped over the Channel Islands, and it is in any case virtually impossible to obtain all of them, so those interested are advised to include a representative selection, particularly the issues of April to August 1944, many of which were definitely disseminated on the Islands. The leaflets are numbered from T9 to T381.

One issue of the famous *Le Courrier de L'Air* series, which was dropped regularly over France, was actually dropped in Jersey. This was the issue for 23 March 1944.

A miniature German newspaper, *Front und Heimat* (Front and Home), was dropped over the Channel Islands by the Luftwaffe for the German Forces after they were cut off from France by the Allies.

A 12-page, sepia-coloured, illustrated booklet in English headed "We Protest", and with a picture of Field-Marshal Montgomery on the front, was distributed in Jersey by the Germans one night in 1944 after the Allied landings in Normandy. It purported to be a leaflet prepared by Allied soldiers, protesting at the politicians' presentation of the German soldier as a weakling. The text is rather crude and contains one or two obscene words.

Included in the disseminations for the German troops by the Allies were certain items of "black" propaganda, i.e. purporting to come from German sources. No details of these have been given officially, but known to have been dropped on the Channel Islands are certain small booklets having the appearance of genuine German stories but including a great deal of information, with illustrations, upon how to "go sick" and deceive the German Medical Officers so as to avoid fighting. It is interesting to note that similar information was dropped by the Germans on Allied troops in Italy.

Cat. No.	Leaflet	Price
PL1	*News from England*, 600/1	8·00
PL2	*News from England*, 600/2	8·00
PL3	*The Archbishop of York*, etc., J1	25·00
PL4	*To the inhabitants*, etc., J2	25·00
PL5	*Nachrichten* newspaper	*from* 3·00
PL6	*Le Courrier de L'Air*, 23 March 1944	2·00
PL7	*Front und Heimat*	1·00
PL8	*We Protest* booklet	10·00

23. Parcel Post Labels

Parcel post labels were introduced by the British Post Office on 1 August 1883. Sixteen different types (plus sub-types) have been issued, but not all are known used in the Channel Islands.

Most types show the name of the office, the head office, the telegraphic code address, with special panels in which details of the postage, registration and insurance could be entered, the adhesives stuck and the datestamp applied. Often the adhesives were cancelled with a different marking from the datestamp.

For example, the postage stamp might be cancelled with a double-ring parcel post marking (e.g. Jersey Type **J63**) and the space provided for "Office Stamp" or "Date Stamp" could show a sub-office c.d.s. (listed in Section 14).

The labels are mostly scarce or very scarce. They were affixed to the parcel, but they more often occur without stamps than with, either because the stamps were stuck elsewhere on the parcel or because they were later soaked off.

Eight different types are so far recorded for the Channel Islands, differing in details of wording in the upper parts. Those listed as PP5 and PP6 are unnamed and must, of course, be used with a Channel Islands c.d.s. The labels are of importance to specialists because they show examples of some of the scarcer sub-office datestamps; also because they often bear postage stamps not otherwise found on cover.

Prices are for labels only or for those with adhesives of little value. The value of high-denomination stamps must be added to that of the labels when these appear.

Cat. No.	Distinguishing wording, etc.	Dates of use		Price
PP1	PARCELS POST	1883	.. ..	50·00
PP2	PARCEL POST; italic *For Postage Stamps*	1884–95	..	20·00
PP3	Postage box headed S.D.; no space for Registration, etc.	1887–1905	..	10·00
PP4	Space provided for Registration, Express or Insurance Fee	1891–1920s	..	5·00
PP5	Label 50 × 40mm; coat of arms; no printed office name	1918–30s	..	5·00
PP6	Label 35 × 42mm; no coat of arms; no printed office name	1938–50s	..	2·00

Sub-offices. The earlier labels were printed in versions specifically for sub-offices. A typical example would thus read: PARCEL POST (either side of a coat of arms)/JERSEY/David Place.

Labels are so far recorded from the following:

Jersey: Beaumont, Beresford Street, Carrefour Selous, Cheapside, Colomberie, David Place, First Tower, Five Oaks, George Town, Gorey, Gorey

Village, Grouville, Havre-des-Pas, La Rocque, Millbrook, Rouge Bouillon, St. Aubin, St. Brelade's Bay, St. Martins, St. Owens, St. Peters, Samares and Town Mills.

Guernsey: Catel, Cobo, Forest, Les Gravées, L'Islet, Market Place, Mount Row, St. Andrew's, St. Martins, St. Peter-in-the-Wood, St. Sampson's, The Vale, Vale Road, *Alderney* and *Sark*.

Customs Duty Parcel Post Labels

On 1 November 1895 the British Post Office instituted a service whereby dutiable goods like tobacco sent from the Channel Islands to Britain could have charges prepaid with postage stamps. Special green labels with separate spaces for the stamps paying postage and those paying customs duty were brought into use and a handling charge of 1s. per parcel was made. The system was also used for prepayment of purchase tax in due course and it ceased on 30 September 1969.

The labels measure 89 × 108mm and are scarce. Victorian and Edwardian labels have the stamps paying postage cancelled with a datestamp and those paying duty cancelled with a double-ring rubber stamp normally used as a parcel post cancellation. Later issues have all the stamps cancelled with the same datestamp.

The labels in the upper part read PARCEL POST (either side of a coat of arms) below which is JERSEY (JE), GUERNSEY (GU) or ALDERNEY (ACK) with details of postage and registration or express fees in boxes to the right. Below these are boxes for postage stamps to be affixed and office datestamp to be applied. Below the boxes is the caption "Amount prepaid for Customs Dues .../(Stamps for this be affixed below)".

An Alderney label of 1936 is known overprinted for use in Jersey by means of a rubber stamp with JERSEY in a box. Perhaps the remaining Alderney stock was transferred to Jersey to meet a temporary shortage.

Cat. No.	Distinguishing wording, etc.	Dates of use			Price
Jersey					
CP1	Fee paid on/Registration; also "Office Stamp" (upper and lowercase)	1896	..	..	25·00
CP2	Fee paid on/Registration; also OFFICE STAMP	1901	..	..	25·00
CP3	Registration and/Express Fees; also OFFICE STAMP	1903	..	..	25·00
CP4	Registration and/Express Fees; also DATE STAMP	1917	..	..	20·00
Guernsey					
CP5	Registration and/Express Fees; also OFFICE STAMP	1905	..	..	25·00
CP6	ditto, but with DATE STAMP	1911	..	..	20·00
CP7	ditto, but with DATE STAMP and different arms	1914	..	..	15·00
CP8	Registration/and Express/Fees; also DATE STAMP	1952	..	..	15·00
Alderney					
CP9	Name in upper and lowercase	1910	..	..	40·00
CP10	Name in capitals	1936	..	..	30·00
CP11	As CP10 overprinted JERSEY by rubber stamp	1936	..	..	30·00

Forged Edward VII Stamp. The London stamp dealer, George Lowden (trading as George Ellis), was convicted in 1913 for selling photo-lithographed copies of the King Edward VII £1 green. These are on thinner paper than the genuine, have a roughly impressed crown watermark and are slightly deeper in colour.

Each has a forged Jersey postmark, since the £1 Edward was frequently used for payment of customs duty, as mentioned above.

Lowden had 2679 copies for sale but most were destroyed after the case.

(Price of forgery £250.)

Bibliography

Stanley Gibbons Catalogues
Great Britain Specialised Stamp Catalogue (Vol. 1, Queen Victoria; Vol. 2, King Edward VII to King George VI; Vol. 3, Queen Elizabeth II Pre-decimal Issues).
British Commonwealth Stamp Catalogue.
Elizabethan Specialised Catalogue of Modern British Commonwealth Stamps.
Collect Channel Islands Stamps.

Periodical Publications
Channel Islands Specialists' Society. *Bulletin*, 1950—
Channel Islands Specialists' Society. *Les Isles Normandes*, 1975—
Club of Channel Islands Collectors (New York). *The Channel Islands Reporter*
States of Guernsey Post Office Board. *Guernsey Philatelic News*, 1970—
Jersey Postal Administration. *Jersey Stamp Bulletin*, 1970—

General Works
R. C. ALCOCK AND F. C. HOLLAND. *The Postmarks of Great Britain and Ireland* (Cheltenham, 1940) and Supplements.
R. C. ALCOCK AND F. C. HOLLAND. *The Maltese Cross Postmarks* (Cheltenham, 1959). Revised edition as *Maltese Cross Cancellations of the United Kingdom* (1971).
O. G. BOWLBY. "Maritime Postal Markings." *The Philatelist*, November 1949.
H. L'ESTRANGE EWEN. *Priced Catalogue of Newspaper and Parcel Stamps issued by the Railway Companies of the United Kingdom, 1855–1906* (London, 1906).
FRANCIS J. FIELD. *Airmails of the British Isles* (Sutton Coldfield, 1946).
C. GRASEMANN AND G. W. P. McLACHLAN. *English Channel Packet Boats* (London, 1939).
JOHN G. HENDY. *The History of the Early Postmarks of the British Isles* (London, 1905).
JOHN G. HENDY. *The History of the Postmarks of the British Isles from 1840 to 1876* (London, 1909).
ROBSON LOWE. *The Encyclopaedia of British Empire Postage Stamps*, Vol. 1, Great Britain and the Empire in Europe, 2nd edition (London, 1952). Reprinted, inclusive of Supplements, as Vols. 34 and 35 of *Billig's Philatelic Handbook* (North Miami, Florida, 1973).
CYRIL R. H. PARSONS, COLIN G. PEACHEY AND GEORGE R. PEARSON. *Slogan Postmarks of The United Kingdom* (Aylesbury, Bucks, 1974). Two volumes, covering 1917–69 and 1970–73.
P. L. PEMBERTON. "British Stamps with French Postmarks." *Philatelic Journal of Great Britain*, July 1936, September 1936, December 1936, July 1937, July 1938, April 1939, June 1939.

ALAN W. ROBERTSON. *Maritime Postal History of the British Isles* (Pinner, Middlesex, 1955–64). Reprinted by Harry Hayes (Batley, Yorkshire, 1974).

RAYMOND SALLES. *La Poste Maritime Française*, Tome 1, Les Entrées Maritime et Les Bateaux à Vapeur (Paris, 1961).

ARNOLD M. STRANGE. *A List of Books on the Postal History, Postmarks and Adhesive Postage and Revenue Stamps of Great Britain*, 2nd edition (London, 1971).

R. M. WILLCOCKS. *The Postal History of Great Britain and Ireland; a Summarized Catalogue to 1840* (London, 1972).

R. M. WILLCOCKS. *England's Postal History to 1840* (London, 1975).

Channel Islands

Baker's Catalogue and Handbook of Stamps of the Channel Islands (Guernsey, 1943–49).

CHARLES CRUICKSHANK. *The German Occupation of The Channel Islands* (London, 1975). Official history, non-philatelic.

YVES MAXIME DANAN. *Emissions Locales et Affranchissements de Guerre des Iles de la Manche* (Paris, 1969).

YVES MAXIME DANAN. *Histoire Postale des Isles de la Manche*, Tome 1 and Tome 2 (Paris, 1976 and 1978).

R. A. HAYES. *Modern Channel Islands Flight Covers (from 1969)* (Jersey, 1974).

RICHARD MAYNE. *Mailships of the Channel Islands 1771–1971* (Chippenham, 1971).

DONALD McKENZIE. *The Red Cross Mail Service for Channel Island Civilians 1940–1945* (Chippenham, 1975).

HEINZ MÖHLE. *Die Briefmarken von den Kanal-Inseln; Guernsey und Jersey, Deutsche Besetzung 1940–45* (Frankfurt, 1970).

WILLIAM NEWPORT. *Stamps and Postal History of the Channel Islands* (London, 1972).

J. M. Y. TROTTER. "Early Guernsey Postal History and Private Agents for Guernsey Letters." *Transactions of the Société Guernesaise*, 1950. *Postal History Society Bulletin*, 1950.

PART TWO

Specialised Stamp Catalogue

1. THE GERMAN OCCUPATION

Types of British stamps overprinted or bisected for use in the Channel Islands during the German Occupation.

George V 1912–22 (Simple Cypher watermark) and 1924–26 (Block Cypher watermark) definitives

George V 1934–36 definitives

George VI 1937–39 definitives

1940 Stamp Centenary commemorative

A. GUERNSEY

Following the German Occupation the existing supplies of current British stamps continued in use until stocks became exhausted. It had earlier been decided that locally printed stamps should be supplied, but in the event these were not ready for issue until 18 February 1941. Faced with a dearth of 1d. stamps the authorities announced, on 27 December 1940, that bisected 2d. values would be allowed to do duty for 1d. stamps. The 2d. stamps available were the 1937 definitive and the 1940 Stamp Centenary commemorative. Examples of George V 2d. stamps bisected were also accepted by the Post Office, as were, in most instances, bisects of other values which had not been authorised.

The German Commandant had a swastika overprint applied to a number of the bisected 1940 Stamp Centenary 2d. stamps and submitted these to Berlin for approval, but this scheme was turned down, as was another which involved a similar overprint on the 1937 1d. value. Examples of both exist, but are very rare.

1940. Swastika overprints. *Stamps of Great Britain optd.*

(*a*) 1937 *Geo. VI definitive optd. with a number of small swastikas*
SW1 1d. scarlet £500

(*b*) 1940 *Stamp Centenary commemorative, intended for bisection, optd. with a swastika on each half of the stamp*
SW2 2d. orange £500

Nos. SW1/2 were prepared for use, but not issued. They are, therefore, only known unused.

Example of bisected 1940 Stamp Centenary 2d. stamp

1940 (27 Dec). *Stamps of Great Britain bisected.*

(*a*) *George V definitives*

			Price on cover
BS1	2d.	orange (1912–22 issue)	£175
BS2	2d.	orange (1924–26 issue)	£175
BS3	2d.	orange (1934 issue)	£175

(*b*) *George VI 1937–39 definitives*

BS4	1d.	scarlet	£350
BS5	2d.	orange	15·00

(*c*) 1940 *Stamp Centenary commemoratives*

BS6	1d.	scarlet	£350
BS7	2d.	orange	15·00
BS8	2½d.	ultramarine	£450

GS 1   Arms of Guernsey   "Loops" Watermark (*reduced to ½ size*)

(Designed by E. W. Vaudin)
(Printed in typography by Guernsey Press Co. Ltd.)

1941–44. *Rouletted.* (*a*) *White paper.* *No wmk.*

1	**GS1**	½d. light green (7.4.41)	2·50	1·00
		a. Emerald-green (6.41)	2·75	2·50
		b. Bluish green (11.41)	20·00	12·00
		c. Bright green (2.42)	6·00	1·75
		d. Dull green (9.42)	3·50	1·75
		e. Olive-green (2.43)	20·00	12·00
		f. Pale yellowish green (7.43 and later) (*shades*)	1·75	1·75
		g. Imperf. (pair)	£100	
		h. Imperf. between (horiz. pair) ..	£300	
		i. Imperf. between (vert. pair) ..	£400	
		j. Printed on the gummed side ..	80·00	
2		1d. scarlet (18.2.41)	1·50	45
		a. Pale vermilion (7.43) (etc.) ..	3·00	1·50
		b. Carmine ('43)	6·00	2·50
		c. Imperf. (pair)	85·00	60·00
		d. Imperf. between (horiz. pair) ..	£300	
		da. Imperf. vert. (centre stamp of horiz. strip of 3)		
		e. Imperf. between (vert. pair) ..	£400	
		f. Ptd. double (scarlet shade)		
3		2½d. ultramarine (12.4.44)	3·50	2·75
		a. Deep ultramarine (7.44)	3·00	2·75
		b. Imperf. (pair)	£200	
		c. Imperf. between (horiz. pair) ..	£500	

(*b*) *Bluish French bank-note paper. Wmk. loops.*

4	**GS1**	½d. bright green (11.3.42)	8·00	9·00
5		1d. scarlet (9.4.42)	6·00	9·00

The dates given for the shades of Nos. 1 and 2 are the months in which they were printed as indicated on the printer's imprints. Others are issue dates.

First Day Cover (No. 1)	3·00
First Day Cover (No. 2)	2·50
First Day Cover (No. 3)	4·00
First Day Cover (No. 4)	65·00
First Day Cover (No. 5)	35·00

Sheets: 60 (6 × 10).

IMPRINTS AND PRINTINGS
(Blocks of four)

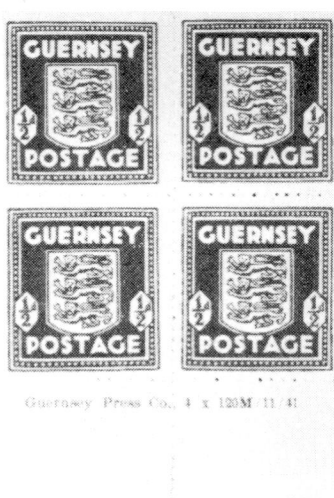

Guernsey Press Co., 4 x 120M/11/41

Imprint block of ½d. 4th printing

The various printings can be identified from the sheet imprints as follows:

½d. 1st Printing 240M/3/41 .. .. 15·00
2nd Printing 2 × 120M/6/41   .. .. .. 14·00
(a) Large white flaw above "G" of
"GUERNSEY" on bottom right stamp. 18·00
3rd Printing 3 × 120M/6/41   .. .. .. 12·00
4th Printing 4 × 120M/11/41 .. .. .. £110
5th Printing 5 × 120M/2/42   .. .. .. 35·00
6th Printing 6 × 240M/2/42   .. .. .. 35·00
7th Printing 7 × 120M/9/42   .. .. .. 12·00
8th Printing 8 × 120M/2/43   .. .. .. £110
9th Printing 9 × 120M/7/43   .. .. .. 10·00
10th Printing 10 × 120M/10/43 .. .. .. 10·00
11th Printing Guernsey Press Co., (*stop
and comma*)   .. .. 10·00
12th Printing Guernsey Press Co. (*stop only,
margin at bottom 23 to 27 mm*) .. .. 10·00
13th Printing Guernsey Press Co. (*stop only,
margin at bottom 15mm*) .. .. .. 10·00
1d. 1st Printing 120M/2/41 .. .. 18·00
2nd Printing 2 × 120M/2/41   .. .. .. 15·00
3rd Printing 3 × 120M/6/41   .. .. .. 10·00
4th Printing 4 × 120M/6/41   .. .. .. 15·00
5th Printing 5 × 120M/9/41   .. .. .. 16·00
6th Printing 6 × 240M/11/41 .. .. .. 16·00
7th Printing 7 × 120M/2/42   .. .. .. 30·00
8th Printing 8× 240M/4/42   .. .. .. 14·00

	9th Printing 9 × 240M/9/42	.. .. ..	10·00
	10th Printing 10 × 240M/1/43	.. .. ..	10·00
	11th Printing 11 × 240M/7/43	.. .. ..	20·00
	12th Printing Guernsey Press Co.	.. ..	25·00
	13th Printing PRESS TYP.	.. ..	9·00
	14th Printing "PRESS" (*inverted commas unlevel*)		9·00
	15th Printing "PRESS" (*inverted commas level, margin at bottom 28mm*)		14·00
	16th Printing "PRESS" (*inverted commas level, margin at bottom 12mm*)		5·00
2½d.	1st Printing Guernsey Press Co., ...		20·00
	2nd Printing "PRESS" (*inverted commas unlevel*)		18·00
	3rd Printing "PRESS" (*inverted commas level, margin at bottom 22mm*)		18·00
	4th Printing "PRESS" (*inverted commas level, margin at bottom 15mm*)		18·00

The numbered imprints occur in the left-hand corner, bottom margin on the 1st printing of the 1d., and central, bottom margin on all other printings of all three values.

In the numbered imprints, for example, 2 × 120M/6/41, the "2" indicates the number of the printing; "120M" denotes the number of stamps printed in thousands, in this case 120,000; and "6/41" denotes the date of the printing, June 1941.

In the first ten printings of the ½d. and the first eleven printings of the 1d. the printing details are prefixed by the name of the printer, "Guernsey Press Co."

Withdrawn and invalidated: 13.4.46.

B. JERSEY

Soon after Jersey was occupied by German troops the Commandant ordered the Postmaster to forward stocks of the currently available (British) stamps to Bigwoods, the Jersey printers, to be overprintd with a swastika and "JERSEY 1940". The Bailiff of Jersey protested at this action and, after reference to Berlin, the Commandant ordered the stocks of overprinted stamps to be destroyed. Only four complete sets and a few singles are known to have survived. One of the complete sets is in the Jersey Postal Museum.

Bigwoods also prepared a local 1d. stamp depicting the Arms of Jersey and inscribed "ETATS DE JERSEY", with and without an overprint of a swastika and "1940". These also were destroyed, except for two sheets of each which were cut up for collectors and a complete (but damaged) sheet with the overprint. A complete sheet of the unoverprinted stamp is in the National Postal Museum, London.

(JS 1)
(Overprinted by Bigwoods, States of Jersey Printers)

1940. Swastika overprints. *Stamps of Great Britain optd. with Type JS 1. (a) On* 1937–39
George VI definitives

SW1	½d.	green	.. ..	£160
SW2	1½d.	red-brown	.. ..	£160
SW3	2d.	orange	.. ..	£175
SW4	2½d.	ultramarine	.. ..	£175
SW5	3d.	violet	.. ..	£175
SW6	4d.	grey-green	.. ..	£175
SW7	5d.	brown	.. ..	£175
SW8	6d.	purple	.. ..	£175
SW9	7d.	emerald-green	.. ..	£175
SW10	8d.	bright carmine	.. ..	£175
SW11	9d.	deep olive-green	.. ..	£175
SW12	10d.	turquoise-blue	.. ..	£175
SW13	1s.	bistre-brown ..	.. ..	£175

(b) On 1940 *Stamp Centenary issue*

SW14	½d.	green	.. ..	£175
SW15	1½d.	red-brown	.. ..	£175
SW16	2d.	orange	.. ..	£175
SW17	2½d.	ultramarine	.. ..	£175
SW18	3d.	violet	.. ..	£175

As Nos. SW1/18 were prepared but not issued, they are only known unused.

Proofs: proof overprints made from a single block exist on the Edward VIII 1½d. and on the Stamp Centenary set (except the 1d.).

Forgeries: forgeries of the swastika overprints were reported in circulation in 1974. They are cruder in appearance and differ from the genuine examples as follows: (1) the swastika is much thinner on the forgeries and can be at the wrong angle; (2) the ink is much thinner, many forged overprints revealing large white patches under the glass; (3) the swastika and "JERSEY 1940" have been applied separately.

JS 2

(Designed by R. W. Cutland)
(Printed in typography by Bigwoods)

1940. *No wmk. Imperf. (a) Type* **JS 2**

SW19	1d.	scarlet	.. ..	£300

(b) Type **JS 2** *overprinted as Type* **JS 1** *but without* "JERSEY"

SW20	1d.	scarlet	.. ..	£300

Nos. SW19/20 were prepared but not issued. They do not exist in used condition.
Sheets: 30 (10 × 3).
A proof sheet of 6 (2 × 3) of No. SW20 exists on laid paper, ungummed and rouletted.

JS 3   Arms of Jersey

(Designed by Major N. V. L. Rybot)
(Printed in typography by *Evening Post*, Jersey)

1941–42.   *White paper (thin to thick).   No wmk.   P* 11.

1	**JS 3**	½d.	bright green (29.1.42)	.. .. ..	1·60	1·00
			a. Imperf. between (vert. pair)	..	£400	
			b. Imperf. between (horiz. pair)	..	£300	
			c. Imperf. (pair)	.. ..	75·00	
			d. On greyish paper	.. .. ..	2·50	3·00
2		1d.	scarlet (1.4.41)	.. ..	1·50	1·25
			a. Imperf. between (vert. pair)	..	£400	
			b. Imperf. between (horiz. pair)	..	£300	
			c. Imperf. (pair)	.. ..	£100	
			d. On chalk-surfaced paper	.. ..	30·00	30·00
			e. On greyish paper	.. .. ..	2·75	2·75

First Day Cover (No. 1)	3·00
First Day Cover (No. 2)	4·00

Sheets: 60 (6 × 10).

PLATE PROOFS
(Pairs)

½d. on thin paper in black £125
1d. on thick card in black .. .. 60·00

IMPRINTS
(Blocks of six)

½d. "EVENING POST", JERSEY, JANUARY 1942 .. 12·00
1d. "EVENING POST", JERSEY, 17/3/41 .. .. 12·00

Plate flaws: many plate flaws exist on these stamps and most are worth twice normal.
The white circles on the ½d. (No. 48) and 1d. (No. 42) are the best and worth three times
normal.
Numbers printed: ½d., 750,000; 1d., 1,000,000.
Withdrawn and invalidated: 13.4.46.

JS 4   Old Jersey Farm

JS 5   Portelet Bay

JS 6   Corbière Light-
house

JS 7   Elizabeth Castle

JS 8   Mont Orgueil
Castle

JS 9   Gathering Vraic
(seaweed)

(Designed by E. Blampied. Engraved by H. Cortot)
(Printed in typography by French Govt. Ptg. Works, Paris)

1943–44. *No wmk.   P* 13½.

3	**JS 4**	½d. green (1 June)	4·00	1·25
4	**JS 5**	1d. scarlet (1 June)	40	15
		a. On newsprint (28.2.44)	1·00	1·00
5	**JS 6**	1½d. brown (8 June)	1·00	1·50
6	**JS 7**	2d. orange-yellow (8 June)	1·00	1·50
7	**JS 8**	2½d. blue (29 June)	2·50	1·00
		a. Thin paper with design showing through back		
		b. On newsprint (25.2.44)	1·25	1·00
8	**JS 9**	3d. violet (29 June)	1·50	2·00
3/8		Set of 6	7·50	6·50

First Day Covers (3)	10·00

IMPRINTS AND PRINTINGS
(Blocks of six)

½d.	1st printing 1/5/43	32·00
	2nd printing 3/5/43	32·00
	3rd printing 6/10/43	32·00
1d.	1st printing 7/5/43	3·50
	2nd printing 8/5/43	3·50
	3rd printing 7/10/43	3·50
	4th printing 28/2/44	3·50
1½d.	1st printing 17/5/43	8·00
	2nd printing 18/5/43	8·00

2d.	1st printing 20/5/43	..	..	..	..	.. 8·00
	2nd printing 21/5/43	..	..	..	..	.. 8·00
2½d.	1st printing 31/5/43	..	..	..	..	.. 20·00
	2nd printing 25/2/44	..	..	..	..	.. 20·00
3d.	1st printing 4/6/43	..	..	..	..	.. 12·00
	2nd printing 5/6/43	..	..	..	..	.. 12·00

PROOFS

Die proofs in black on rough paper, signed Cortot		90·00
Colour proofs, signed Cortot	*from*	£100
Colour proofs, unsigned	*from*	90·00
Black presentation proofs on good quality wove paper		£140
Epreuves-de-luxe in issued colours, with imprint "Atelier de Fabrication des Timbres-Poste, PARIS" and covered with tissue paper		£110
Mise en train proofs in black on pink paper, ½d., 1d., 1½d. and 2d. only .. .. *each*		60·00
Half-size essays of ½d. and 1d. in single or two colours on wove or India paper *from (each)*		£110

Sheets: 60 (two panes 3 × 10).
Imprint: None.
Withdrawn and invalidated: 13.4.46.
The dates given for the newsprint varieties are those when they were printed. Other dates are those of issue.

Official Stamps

JS 10

1940 (July). *Typo. Imperf.*

O1 **JS 10** (—) black .. .. 50·00 50·00

No. O1 was used by Capt. Gussek, the first Jersey Commandant, on his official mail and occasionally on documents.

1940. *Inscr.* "HAFEN/KOMMANDANT/JERSEY" *with anchor in centre. Imperf.*

O2 (—) black .. .. 50·00 50·00

No. O2 was used by the Harbour Master.

2. THE LIBERATION COMMEMORATIVES

To commemorate the third anniversary of the Liberation of the Channel Islands, Great Britain issued two stamps on 10 May 1948, depicting vraicking (seaweed gathering). The stamps were issued in Jersey, Guernsey, Alderney and Sark and were also available at the G.P.O., London, and at Belfast, Birmingham, Bristol, Cardiff, Edinburgh, Leeds, and Manchester, remaining on sale until 30 September 1948. They were valid for postage throughout the British Isles and from many Field Post Offices abroad.

Multiple G vi R

CS 1 Gathering Vraic

CS 2   Islanders gathering Vraic

(Designed by J. R. R. Stobie (1d.), from drawing by E. Blampied (2½d.))
(Printed in photogravure by Harrison and Sons)

1948 (10 May). Third Anniversary of Liberation. *Wmk. Multiple* G vi R. *Perf. 15 × 14* (*C*).

C1	**CS 1**	1d.	scarlet	.. ..	10	10
C2	**CS 2**	2½d.	ultramarine	.. ..	15	15
			SV1. Crown flaw	.. .. ..	2·50	
			SV2. Blue line across wheel	..	2·50	
			SV3. "Broken" wheel	.. ..	2·50	

First Day Cover	4·50

Varieties

SV1 2½d. Left arm of centre cross on crown elongated (R.1/1)

SV2 2½d. Blue line across wheel of cart (R.6/1)

SV3 2½d. Irregular patch on wheel appears as a break (R. 20/5)

CYLINDER NUMBERS
(Blocks of six)

1d. Cyl. 2	.. ..	80
2½d. Cyl. 4	.. ..	1·20

Sheets: 120 (6 × 20).
Quantities sold: 1d., 5,934,000; 2½d., 5,398,000.

> *Sheet position of flaws.* The position in the sheet of stamps showing flaws is given by reference to the horizontal row. Thus R. 6/4 identifies the 6th horizontal row from the top and the 4th stamp along from the left-hand margin.

Postal Stationery

Postcard with "Official Paid" frank. Inscribed "Re-Occupation of Channel Islands". Issued to islanders after the Liberation to enable them to write to their relatives free of charge.

1945 (May).

SSC1	Franked postcard	6·00	30·00

3. THE REGIONAL ISSUES

In July 1956 the Postmaster-General announced that the Queen had agreed in principle to the issue of regional stamps for Britain and that Jersey and Guernsey were each to have a 2½d. stamp. Shortly afterwards advisory committees were formed to advise the Postmaster-General on the choice of subjects and artists for the new stamps. Designs (eight in Guernsey and several in Jersey) were submitted anonymously to the committees and from them the final selection was made.

In Guernsey a design by Eric Piprell, a Guernseyman, was chosen. It shows the Crown of William the Conqueror from the second silver penny of William I and the Guernsey lily as described in the book *The Lilium Sarniense*, by James Douglas, published in 1725. Before the stamp was ready postage rates had increased and the denomination was changed to 3d., the normal letter rate, otherwise the stamp would have been in almost the same colour as the Guernsey lily.

The Jersey stamp was designed by William M. Gardner, who chose the Mace presented to the island by Charles II in 1663, and the Arms of Jersey as his main subjects, with potato and tomato plant in the borders to emphasise the importance of the agricultural produce of the island.

Both stamps were issued on 18 August 1958.

A 2½d. was added for each island on 8 June 1964 for use on tourists' postcards. To save going back to the design committees it was decided to use the second-choice designs in the original competition. The Guernsey design was by Eric Piprell and featured a variation of the Lily and Crown theme. The Jersey design was by Edmund Blampied and featured the Arms and the Mace. One sheet of the Jersey stamp had the bottom row of stamps imperforate.

New 4d. denominations in blue, for the increased letter rate, were issued on 7 February 1966, in the designs of the 3d. stamps. In 1967 the 3d. and 4d. were both issued with phosphor lines.

When the two-tier letter post was introduced in September 1968, the colour of the 4d. stamps, for second-class mail, was changed to sepia and 5d. values were issued in Royal blue for the first-class rate on the fourth of the month. The colour of the 4d. was changed to vermilion on 26 February 1969, because of confusion between the 4d. and 5d. colours under artifical light. These three values were on unwatermarked paper with PVA gum.

Validity. Although specifically issued for regional use, these issues were initially valid for use throughout Great Britain.

The regional stamps were withdrawn from sale in Guernsey and Jersey on 30 September 1969, when the Islands established their own postal services. They continued to be accepted for postal use in both islands until 31 October 1969 (and then Guernsey granted a further extension for British and regional stamps till the end of March 1970).

The stamps continued to be valid in the United Kingdom although they were withdrawn from sale at the Philatelic Bureau and Counters on 30 September 1970, finally being invalidated from 1 March 1972.

Dates of Issue. Conflicting dates of issue have been announced for some of the regional issues, partly explained by the stamps being released on different dates by the Philatelic Bureau in Edinburgh or the Philatelic Counter in London and in the regions.

We have adopted the practice of giving the earliest known dates, since once released the stamps could have been used anywhere in the U.K.

All stamps are perf 15 × 14 and printed in photogravure by Harrison and Sons in sheets of 240 (12 × 20). Portrait by Dorothy Wilding Ltd.

The watermark used for the earlier issues was the "Multiple Crowns" type of Great Britain.

"Multiple Crowns" Watermark

A. GUERNSEY

GS 2   GS 3

(Designed by E. A. Piprell)

1958 (18 Aug)–67. *Watermark Multiple Crowns.*

6	**GS 2**	2½d. rose-red (8.6.64)	70	85
		Sa. Pale rose-red	85	85
7	**GS 3**	3d. deep lilac		
		Sa. Cream paper (18.8.58)	1·00	20
		Sb. Whiter paper (5.7.62)	60	10
		p. One centre phosphor band (24.5.67)	12	30
		pSa. Deep reddish lilac	20	30
8		4d. ultramarine (7.2.66)	25	15
		V128. Stem flaw	3·00	
		p. Two phosphor bands (24.10.67)	12	15
		p. V128. Stem flaw	3·00	

First Day Cover (No. 6)	..	..	..	..	..	4·00
First Day Cover (No. 7)	..	..	..	..	..	3·00
First Day Cover (No. 8)	..	..	..	..	..	2·00

No. 7 exists in a Presentation Pack together with the other stamps from different Regions issued in 1958 (*Price* £75).

Variety

V128
4d. Coloured line
across top of stem (Cyl
1 no dot R. 12/8).
Retouched on No. 11
(See V179).

CYLINDER NUMBERS
(Blocks of six, all No Dot)

2½d.	pale rose-red	.. 1	10·00	3d. phos.	 5	1·00
	rose red	.. 3	9·00	4d.	 1	2·50
3d.	cream paper	.. 4	9·00	4d. phos.	 1	1·00
	whiter paper	.. 4	5·00			
		.. 5	4·50			

Quantities sold (ordinary only): 2½d. 3,485,760; 3d. 25,812,360; 4d. 4,415,040.
Withdrawn: 31.8.66 2½d.
Sold out: 6.3.68 3d. and 4d. ordinary; 10.68 4d. phosphor; 11.68 3d. phosphor.

1968 (16 Apr)–69. *No watermark. Chalky paper. PVA gum. One centre phosphor band*
(*Nos.* 10/11) *or two phosphor bands* (*others*).

9	GS 3	4d.	pale ultramarine (16.4.68)	..	..	i0	40
			Sa. Phosphor omitted	..	..	.. 15·00	
			V128. Stem flaw	..	..	.. 3·00	
10		4d.	olive-sepia (4.9.68)	..	..	15	15
			Sa. Phosphor omitted	..	..	.. 10·00	
			Sb. Phosphor horizontal		..	.. 3·00	
			V128. Stem flaw	..	..	.. 3·00	
			V129. Retouched "4"	..	..	.. 3·00	
11		4d.	bright vermilion (26.2.69)	..	..	40	35
			V179. Stem flaw retouched	..		.. 4·50	
12		5d.	Royal blue (4.9.68)	..	..	35	15
			V130. Stamen flaw	..	..	.. 3·00	
			V234. Stamen flaw retouched		..	6·00	

First Day Cover (Nos. 10 and 12)	..	.. ..	1·00
First Day Cover (No. 11)	..	.. .. ..	1·00

No. 9 was not issued in Guernsey until 22 April.

PVA Gum. Polyvinyl alcohol was introduced by Harrisons in place of gum arabic in 1968. It is almost invisible except that a small amount of pale yellowish colouring matter was introduced to make it possible to see that the stamps have been gummed. Although this can be distinguished from gum arabic in unused stamps there is, of course, no means of detecting it in used copies. It should be noted that gum arabic is shiny in appearance, and that, normally, PVA gum has a matt appearance.

Varieties

V129
4d. Spot over "4" has been retouched (Cyl 1 no dot R. 16/10). Corrected on No. 11.

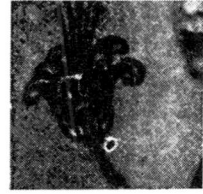

V179
Former flaw is now retouched but still shows as a smudge to right of stem (Cyl 1 no dot R. 12/8).

V130
5d. Large coloured spot over central stamen (Cyl 1 no dot R. 12/1).

V234
5d. Still visible after retouch on late printing.

Cylinder Numbers
(Blocks of six, all No Dot)

4d. pale ultramarine	1	1·00	4d. bright vermilion	1	3·25
4d. olive-sepia ..	1	1·25	5d.	1	2·75

Sold out: 3.69 4d. ultramarine.

Withdrawn: 30.9.69 (locally), 30.9.70 (British Philatelic Counters) 4d. olive-sepia, 4d. bright vermilion and 5d.

B. JERSEY

JS 13   JS 14

(Designed E. Blampied (2½d.), W. M. Gardner (others))

1958 (18 Aug)–67. *Watermark Multiple Crowns.*

9	**JS 13**	2½d. carmine-red (8.6.64)		70	85
		a. Imperf three sides (pair) ..		£375	
		V84. Thin "POSTAGE"		6·50	
10	**JS 14**	3d. deep lilac			
		Sa. Cream paper (18.8.58) ..		1·00	20
		V24. "Halberd" flaw		7·00	
		V85. Joined tomato		7·00	
		Sb. Whiter paper (23.9.62) ..		75	15
		V180. Scratched collar		7·00	
		p. One centre phosphor band (9.6.67)		12	15
		p. V180. Scratched collar		3·00	
		pSa. *Dull reddish lilac*		30	15
		pSa. V180. Scratched collar ..		6·00	
11		4d. ultramarine (7.2.66)		35	15
		V60. Leaf flaw		3·00	
		SV1. Neck flaw		2·50	
		p. Two phosphor bands		15	20
		p. SV1. Neck flaw		2·00	

First Day Cover (No. 9)					4·00
First Day Cover (No. 10)					3·00
First Day Cover (No. 11)					2·00

No. 10 exists in a Presentation Pack together with the other stamps from different Regions issued in 1958. (*Price complete* £75)

Varieties

Normal V84
2½d. Letters of "POSTAGE" are thinner resulting in more white showing in the "o" and "G" (Cyl 1 no dot R. 18/1).

V24
3d. "Halberd" flaw to left of mace (Cyl 1 no dot R. 20/3). Subsequently retouched.

V85
3d. Tomato on truss at left joined to leaf by white line (Cyl 1 no dot R. 19/9). Later retouched.

V180
3d. Diagonal scratch through Queen's collar at right (Cyl 2 no dot R. 9/8).

V60
4d. White flaw over top leaf at left (Cyl 1 no dot R. 3/6). Later retouched on ordinary and exists only retouched on the phosphor issue.

SV1
4d. White flaw on front of Queen's neck (Cyl 1 no dot R. 18/9)

CYLINDER NUMBERS
(Blocks of six, all No Dot)

2½d.	..	..	.. 1	12·00	4d.	 1	2·75
3d. cream paper	.. 1			8·00	4d. phos	 1	1·25
3d. whiter paper	.. 1			6·00			
	..	..	.. 2	24·00			
3d. phos (dp lilac)	2			90			
3d. phos (dull reddish lilac)	..	.. 2		2·25			

Quantities sold (ordinary only): 2½d. 4,770,000; 3d. 35,169,720; 4d. 6,623,040.
Withdrawn: 31.8.66 2½d.
Sold out: 10.67 3d. ordinary; 11.67 4d. ordinary; 10.68 3d. and 4d. phosphor.

1968 (4 Sept)–69. *No watermark. Chalky paper. PVA gum. One centre phosphor band (Nos. 12/13) or two phosphor bands (No. 14).*

12	**JS 14**	4d. olive-sepia	20	20
		SV1. Neck flaw	2·00	
13		4d. bright vermilion (26.2.69)	35	30
		SV1. Neck flaw	3·00	
14		5d. Royal blue	35	15
		V132. Leaf dot	4·00	
		V133. Shield flaw	4·00	

First Day Cover (Nos. 12 and 14)	1·00
First Day Cover (No. 13)	1·50

For PVA Gum *see* note after Guernsey No. 12.

Varieties

V132
5d. White dot above lowest leaf at right (Cyl 1 no dot R. 16/6).

V133
5d. Top leaf at right is joined to shield by white line (Cyl 1 no dot R. 19/12).

CYLINDER NUMBERS
(Blocks of six, all No Dot)

4d. olive-sepia	.. 1	90	5d.	.. ..	1	2·75
4d. bright vermilion	1	2·75			

Withdrawn: 30.9.69 (locally), 30.9.70 (British Philatelic Counters) 4d. olive-sepia, 4d. bright vermilion and 5d.

4. THE INDEPENDENT POSTAL ADMINISTRATIONS

In 1967 the Postmaster-General announced that the British Post Office would become a public corporation in 1969 and offered the Channel Islands and the Isle of Man the opportunity of establishing their own postal services, if they so wished. Guernsey and Jersey set up committees to investigate the possibilities, as they wished their postal services to remain under state control. A London firm of accountants was commissioned to report on the viability of independent postal administrations and, after receiving its reports, the States of both islands voted to opt for postal independence.

After the Postmaster-General had satisfied himself that proper arrangements had been made for the future of the staff, their pensions, etc., he agreed to the transfer of the services to the Island Administrations and this duly took place on 1 October 1969.

A. GUERNSEY

GS 4   Castle Cornet
and Edward the
Confessor

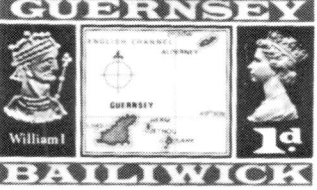

GS 5   Map and William I

GS 6   Martello Tower
and Henry II

GS 7   Arms of Sark
and John

GS 8   Arms of Alderney
and Edward III

GS 9   Guernsey Lily
and Henry V

GS 10 Arms of Guernsey
and Elizabeth I

GS 11 Arms of Alderney
and Charles II

GS 12 Arms of Sark
and George III

GS 13 Arms of
Guernsey and Victoria

GS 14 Guernsey Lily
and Elizabeth I

GS 15 Martello
Tower and John

GS 16 View of Sark

GS 17 View of Alderney

GS 18   View of Guernsey

Two Types of 1d. and 1s.6d.:

Type I. Latitude inscribed "40° 30' N"   Type II. Corrected to "49° 30' N"

(Designed by R. Granger Barrett)
(Printed in photogravure by Harrison & Sons Ltd. (½d. to 2s. 6d.) or Delrieu (others))

1969 (1 Oct)–70. *P* 14 (½d. *to* 2s. 6d.) *or* 12½ (*others*), *all comb.*

13	GS 4	½d.	deep magenta and black (a) ..	8	8
			V270. Nick in frame	1·50	
			V271. White patch in wall ..	1·50	
			Sa. Thin paper	3·00	3·00
			Sa. V270. Nick in frame ..	5·00	
			Sa. V271. White patch in wall ..	5·00	
14	GS 5	1d.	bright blue and black (I) (a) ..	10	15
			V173. Extra line of latitude ..	3·00	
			Sa. Thin paper (b)	60	60
			Sa. V174. Partly corrected line of latitude	4·50	
14b		1d.	bright blue and black (*thin paper*) (II) (eg)	50	50
			V218. Faint circle	2·75	
			V219. Dagger in shoulder ..	2·75	
15	GS 6	1½d.	yellow-brown and black (a) ..	10	10
16	GS 7	2d.	gold, bright red, deep blue and black (a)	10	10
			Sa. Thin paper (g)	25	25
17	GS 8	3d.	gold, pale greenish yellow, orange-red and black (a) ..	10	10
			a. Error. Wmk Block CA ..	£600	
			aSi. Wmk inverted	£600	
			Sb. Thin paper (g)	15	15
18	GS 9	4d.	multicoloured (a)	10	15

19	**GS 10**	5d. gold, bright vermilion, bluish violet and black (*a*)	25	25
20	**GS 11**	6d. gold, pale greenish yellow, light bronze-green & blk (*a*) ..	40	40
		Sa. Thin paper (*g*)	50	50
21	**GS 12**	9d. gold, brt red, crimson & black (*a*)	85	85
		Sa. Thin paper (*g*)	1·00	1·00
22	**GS 13**	1s. gold, brt verm, bis & blk (*a*) ..	85	85
		Sa. Thin paper (*g*)	1·50	1·50
23	**GS 5**	1s. 6d. turq-green & blk (I) (*a*) ..	90	90
		V173. Extra line of latitude ..	6·00	
		Sa. Thin paper (*d*)	3·00	3·00
		Sa. V174. Partly corrected line of latitude	6·00	
23*b*		1s. 6d. turquoise-green & black (*thin paper*) (II) (*eg*)	14·00	2·50
		V218. Faint circle	16·00	
24	**GS 14**	1s. 9d. multicoloured (*a*)	4·00	3·00
		Sa. Blue-green omitted		
		Sb. Thin paper (*g*)	7·00	5·00
		V175. Missing ear-ring	14·00	
25	**GS 15**	2s. 6d. brt reddish vio & blk (*a*) ..	8·00	6·00
		Sa. Thin paper (*g*)	12·00	10·00
26	**GS 16**	5s. multicoloured (*a*)	8·00	9·00
		SV1. Mauve "Balloon" flaw ..	14·00	
27	**GS 17**	10s. multicoloured (*a*)	40·00	30·00
		a. Perf 13 (*f*)	£150	£100
28	**GS 18**	£1 multicoloured (*a*)	14·00	15·00
		V220. White spot over "A" ..	25·00	
		a. Perf 13 (*fh*)	2·50	3·00
		a. V220. White spot over "A" ..	7·00	

First Day Covers (Nos. 13/28) (3)	65·00
Presentation Packs (Nos. 13/28, including both types of 1d. and 1s. 6d.) (3) (9.70)	70·00

In No. 24Sa the effect of the missing colour is that the stem of the lily shows yellow.

The thinner paper varieties result from a deliberate change as the thicker paper did not adhere well; it may be further distinguished by the gum which is white instead of creamy.

There was no postal need for the ½d. and 1½d. values as the ½d. coin had been withdrawn prior to their issue in anticipation of decimalisation. These values were only on sale at the Philatelic Bureau and at the Crown Agents as well as in the U.S.A.

Printings:

(*a*) 1.10.69 (*b*) 24.11.69 (*c*) 12.12.69 (booklets) (*d*) 1.70
(*e*) 4. 2.70 (*f*) 17. 3.70 (*g*) 18. 5.70 (*h*) 1971

Varieties

V270
½d. Nick in white frame
at left (Cyl. 1A–1A, R.
4/2).

V271
½d. White patch in wall
at left (Cyl. 1B–1B, R.
3/2).

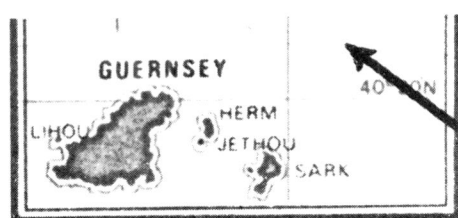

V173
1d. and 1s. 6d. Extra line above line of latitude (Cyl.
1A–1A, R. 1/2).

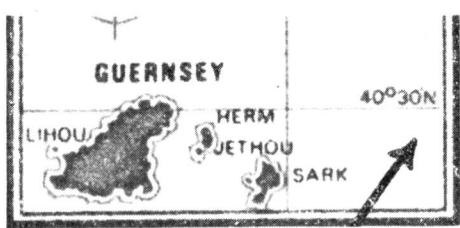

V174
1d. and 1s. 6d. Extra line of latitude partly removed
with diagonal line below "3" (Cyl. 1A–2A, R. 1/2).

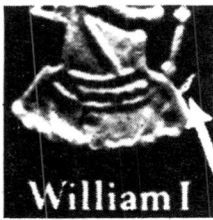

V219
1d. (14b). Dagger in
William's   shoulder
(Cyl. 2B–2B, R. 4/1).

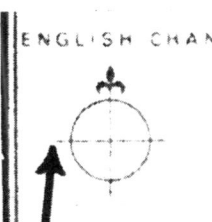

V218
1d. (14b) and 1s. 6d.
(23b). Faint circle to the
left of compass (Cyl.
2A–2A 1d. or 1A–2A
1s. 6d., R. 4/3).

Normal   V175
1s. 9d. Small patch of
white obscures ear-ring
so that it seems to be
missing (Cyl. 1A–1A,
R. 1/4).

SV1
5s. Mauve "Balloon"
above cliff (R. 5/4)

V220
£1 (28 and 28a). White
spot over "A" of
"BAILIWICK" (R. 6/3).

CYLINDER NUMBERS
(Blocks of four)

½d.	1A–1A	50	6d.	1A (×4)	2·40
	1B–1B ..	50		1B (×4)	2·40
1d. (I)	1A–1A	60	9d.	1A (×4)	5·00
	2A–2A (b)	3·50		1B (×4)	5·00
	2B–2B (b)	3·50	1s.	1A (×4)	5·00
(II)	2A–2A ..	3·00		1B (×4)	5·00
	2B–2B ..	3·00	1s. 6d. (I)	1A–1A ..	5·50
	3A–3A (g)	3·00		1B–1B ..	5·50
	3B–3B (g)	3·00		1A–2A (d)	18·00
1½d.	1A–1A ..	60		1B–2B (d)	18·00
	1B–1B ..	60	(II)	1A–2A ..	85·00
2d.	1A (×4)	60		1B–2B ..	85·00
	1B (×4)	60		2A–3A (g)	85·00
3d.	1A (×4)	60		2B–3B (g)	85·00
	1B (×4)	60	1s. 9d.	1A (×5)	24·00
4d.	1A (×5)	60		1B (×5)	24·00
	1B (×5)	60	2s. 6d.	1A–1A ..	48·00
5d.	1A (×4)	1·50		1B–1B ..	48·00
	1B (×4)	1·50			

The values printed by Delrieu are without cylinder numbers.

BOOKLET PANES

The booklet panes consist of single perforated stamps with wide margins all round intended to fit automatic machines designed for the Great Britain 2s. booklets. They are therefore found with three margins when detached from booklets or four margins when complete.

Booklet pane with complete margins

Issued in Booklets B1/6:

Face value	Cat. No.			
1d. Type II	14c. Booklet stamp with margins (*thick paper*) (*c*)	.. ..	55	55
4d.	18a. Booklet stamp with margins (*c*)		35	35
	a.V374. White spot	.. ..	3·00	
	ab.Yellow omitted ..	.. ..	£100	
	Sac. Blue-green omitted*	..	75·00	
5d.	19a. Booklet stamp with margins (*c*)		50	50
	ab. Gold (inscr. etc.) omitted		£175	

* This affects only the stem of the lily which shows as yellow. The 4d. has only been found in 4s. booklets containing panes of one and should not be confused with colour shifts of the blue-green which also show the stem in yellow.

Booklet Pane Variety

V374
4d. White spot by lily
(from booklets)

SET INFORMATION

Sheets: 60 (2 panes 5 × 6). Most sheets of the 5s., 10s. and £1 were divided into two panes before issue.

Imprint: Central, bottom margin (½d. to 2s. 6d.).

Quantities sold:

½d.	2,480,000	1s.	435,773
1d. (Nos. 14/14*b*)	1,560,971	1s. 6d. (Nos. 23/*b*)	627,003
1½d.	980,000	1s. 9d.	255,111
2d.	574,610	2s. 6d.	225,732
3d.	487,199	5s.	165,047
4d.	2,782,490	10s. (No. 27)	114,000
5d.	1,393,193	(No. 27a)	55,200
6d.	456,275	£1 (No. 28)	120,000
9d.	374,975		

Sold out: 8.71, 10s. (No. 27a).

Withdrawn: 6.10.69, ½d., 1½.; 4.2.70, 1d. (No. 14), 1s. 6d. (No. 23); others 14.2.72 (except for No. 28a which remained on sale with decimal definitives until 31.3.76).

Although officially withdrawn the 1d. and 1s. 6d. both Type I were subsequently included in Presentation Packs, whilst the ½d. and 1½d. remained on sale at the Philatelic Bureau until 14 February 1972.

GS 19   Isaac Brock as
Colonel

GS 20   Sir Isaac
Brock as Major-
General

GS 21   Isaac Brock as
Ensign

GS 22   Arms and Flags

(Designed by R. Granger Barrett)
(Printed in lithography by Format International Security Printers Ltd.)

1969 (1 Dec). Birth Bicentenary of Sir Isaac Brock. *P* $13\frac{1}{2} \times 14$ (2s. 6d.) *or* $14 \times 13\frac{1}{2}$
(*others*), *all comb.*

29	**GS 19**	4d. multicoloured	..	..	..	20	20
30	**GS 20**	5d. multicoloured	..	..	..	20	20
31	**GS 21**	1s. 9d. multicoloured		..	..	3·75	3·00
32	**GS 22**	2s. 6d. multicoloured		..	..	3·75	3·50

First Day Cover (Nos. 29/32)	6·00
Presentation Pack (Nos 29/32)	11·50

PLATE NUMBERS
(Blocks of four)

4d.	1A (×6)	..	1·25	1s. 9d.	1A (×5)	..	23·00
	1B (×6)	..	1·25		1B (×5)	..	23·00
	1C (×6)	..	1·25		1C (×5)	..	23·00
	1D (×6)	..	1·25		1D (×5)	..	23·00
5d.	1A (×7)	..	1·25	2s. 6d.	1A (×6)	..	23·00
	1B (×7)	..	1·25		1B (×6)	..	23·00
	1C (×7)	..	1·25		1C (×6)	..	23·00
	1D (×7)	..	1·25		1D (×6)	..	23·00

Sheets: 60 (2 panes 5 × 6) 2s. 6d.; (2 panes 6 × 5) others.
Imprint: Right-hand corner, bottom margin.
Quantities sold: 4d. 940,956; 5d. 732, 658; 1s. 9d. 224,157; 2s. 6d. 218,955.
Withdrawn: 30.11.70.

GS 23 Landing Craft
entering St. Peter's Harbour

GS 24 British War-
ships entering St. Peter
Port

GS 25 Brigadier
Snow reading the
Proclamation

(Designed and printed in photogravure by Courvoisier)

1970 (9 May). 25th Anniversary of Liberation. *Granite paper. P* 11½ (C).

33	**GS 23**	4d. blue and pale blue	.. .. ..	30	30
34	**GS 24**	5d. brown-lake and pale grey	.. ..	30	30
35	**GS 25**	1s. 6d. bistre-brown and buff	.. ..	6·00	6·00

First Day Cover (Nos. 33/5)	.. ..	6·00
Presentation Pack (Nos. 33/5)	.. ..	10·00

CYLINDER NUMBERS
(Blocks of four)

4d.	A1–1	..	1·75	1s. 6d.	A1–1	..	36·00
	B1–1	..	1·75		B1–1	..	36·00
5d.	A1–1	..	1·75			
	B1–1	..	1·75			

Sheets: 25 (5 × 5).

Imprint: Left-hand corner, top margin (4d., 5d.); bottom corner, left-hand margin (1s. 6d.).

Quantities sold: 4d. 968,873; 5d. 817,958; 1s. 6d. 248,532.

Withdrawn: 8.5.71.

GS 26   Guernsey
Tomatoes

GS 27   Guernsey Cow

GS 28   Guernsey Bull

GS 29   Freesias

(Designed and printed in photogravure by Courvoisier)

1970 (12 Aug). Agriculture and Horticulture. *Granite paper. P* 11½ (C).

36	**GS 26**	4d. multicoloured	.. ..	25	25
37	**GS 27**	5d. multicoloured	.. ..	25	25
38	**GS 28**	9d. multicoloured	.. ..	7·00	4·00
39	**GS 29**	1s. 6d. multicoloured	.. ..	9·00	6·00

First Day Cover (Nos. 36/9)	.. ..	10·00
Presentation Pack (Nos. 36/9)	.. ..	26·00

CYLINDER NUMBERS
(Blocks of four)

4d.	A1–1–1–1	1·50	9d.	A1–1–1–1	42·00
	B1–1–1–1	1·50		B1–1–1–1	42·00
	C1–1–1–1	1·50		C1–1–1–1	42·00
	D1–1–1–1	1·50		D1–1–1–1	42·00
5d.	A1–1–1–1	1·50	1s. 6d.	A1–1–1–1	55·00
	B1–1–1–1	1·50		B1–1–1–1	55·00
	C1–1–1–1	1·50		C1–1–1–1	55·00
	D1–1–1–1	1·50		D1–1–1–1	55·00

Sheets: 25 (5 × 5).
Imprint: Central, bottom margin.
Quantities sold: 4d. 1,082,608; 5d. 1,000,000; 9d. 237,685; 1s. 6d. 241,816.
Withdrawn: 11.8.71.

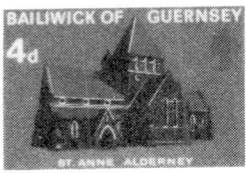

GS 30 St. Anne's
Church, Alderney

GS 31 St. Peter's
Church, Guernsey

GS 32 St. Peter's
Church, Sark

GS 33 St. Tugual
Chapel, Herm

(Designed and printed in photogravure by Courvoisier)

1970 (11 Nov). Christmas. Island Churches. *Granite paper.* P 11½ (C).

40	GS 30	4d. multicoloured	..	.. .. ..	25	20
		V217. Large "AS"	..	.. ..	1·00	
41	GS 31	5d. multicoloured	..	.. .. ..	25	25
42	GS 32	9d. multicoloured	..	.. .. ..	3·50	2·00
43	GS 33	1s. 6d. multicoloured	..	.. ..	6·00	4·00

First Day Cover (Nos. 40/3)	.. ..	6·00
Presentation Pack (Nos. 40/3)	.. ..	14·00

Variety

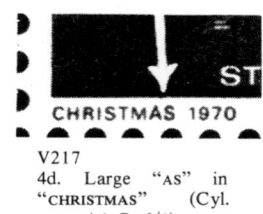

V217
4d. Large "AS" in
"CHRISTMAS" (Cyl.
    A1, R. 6/1).

CYLINDER NUMBERS
(Blocks of four)

4d.	A1–1–1–1	1·50	9d.	A1–1–1–1	21·00
	B1–1–1–1	1·50		B1–1–1–1	21·00
5d.	A1–1–1–1	1·50	1s. 6d.	A1–1–1–1	36·00
	B1–1–1–1	1·50		B1–1–1–1	36·00

Sheets: 50 (5 × 10) 4d., 5d.; (10 × 5) others.
Quantities sold: 4d. 815,737; 5d. 668,886; 9d. 236,833; 1s. 6d. 223,907.
Withdrawn: 10.11.71.

INVALIDATION OF £.s.d. STAMPS. Nos. 13/43 (except Nos. 28/a), and Nos. D1/7 were invalidated on 14 February 1972.

GS 34   Martello Tower and John

(Designed R. Granger Barrett)
(Printed in photogravure by Harrison (½p to 10p) or Delrieu (others))

1971 (6 Jan)–73. Decimal Currency. *Designs as before, but inscribed with face values in decimal currency as Type* **GS 34.** *Chalk-surfaced paper.* P 14 (½p *to* 10p) *or* 13 (*others*), *all comb.*

44	GS 4	½p deep magenta and black (*b*)	..	15	15
45	GS 5	1p bright blue and black (II) (*b*)	..	10	8
46	GS 6	1½p yellow-brown and black (*b*)	..	12	12
47	GS 9	2p multicoloured (*b*)	.. .. ..	12	12
		b. Glazed, ordinary paper (*b*)	..	20	20
48	GS 10	2½p gold, bright vermilion, bluish violet and black (*be*)	.. .. ..	15	5
		a. Bright vermilion omitted	..	£200	
49	GS 8	3p gold, pale greenish yellow, orange-red and black (*be*)	..	20	20
50	GS 14	3½p mult (*glazed, ord. paper*)(*b*)	..	20	20
51	GS 7	4p multicoloured (*b*)	.. .. ..	30	25
52	GS 5	5p turq-grn & black (II) (*b*)	.. ..	25	25
53	GS 11	6p gold, pale greenish yellow, lt bronze-green & black (*b*)	..	35	35
54	GS 13	7½p gold, bright vermilion, bistre and black (*b*)	.. ..	45	45
55	GS 12	9p gold, bright red, crimson and black (*b*)	.. ..	2·50	2·50
56	GS 34	10p bright reddish vio & blk (*a*)	..	2·50	2·50
		SV2. "Extra rock" flaw	.. ..	10·00	
		a. Ordinary paper. *Bright reddish violet and deep black* (*c*)	..	2·00	1·50
		a.SV2. "Extra rock" flaw ..	..	8·00	
57	GS 16	20p mult (*glazed, ord. paper*) (*af*)	..	2·00	2·00
		SV1. Mauve "Balloon" flaw	..	15·00	
		a. *Shade** (*d*)	..	75	75
		a.SV1. Mauve "Balloon" Flaw	..	5·00	
58	GS 17	50p mult (*glazed, ord. paper*) (*adg*)	..	2·50	2·00

First Day Covers (Nos. 44/58) (2)	.. .. ..	9·00
Presentation Packs (Nos. 28a, 44/58) (3) ..	..	12·00

* No. 57 has the sky in a pale turquoise-blue; on No. 57*a* it is pale turquoise-green.

Printings:
(*a*) 6.1.71; (*b*) 15.2.71; (*c*) 1.9.72; (*d*) 25.1.73; (*e*) 2.4.73; (*f*) 10.74; (*g*) 7.75

Variety

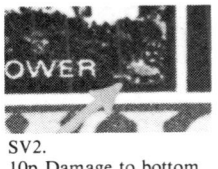

SV2.
10p Damage to bottom right of main design appears as "extra rock". (Cyl. 1A–1A; R. 5/1)

½p	1A–1A ..	..	90	4p	1A (×4)	..	1·75
	1B–1B ..	..	90		1B (×4)	..	1·75
1p	1A–1A ..	..	60	5p	1A–1A ..	..	1·50
	1B–1B ..	..	60		1B–1B ..	..	1·50
1½p	1A–1A ..	..	75	6p	1A (×4)	..	2·10
	1B–1B ..	..	75		1B (×4)	..	2·10
2p	1A (×5)	..	75	7½p	1A (×4)	..	2·75
	1B (×5)	..	75		1B (×4)	..	2·75
2½p	1A (×4)	..	90	9p	1A (×4)	..	15·00
	1B (×4)	..	90		1B (×4)	..	15·00
3p	1A (×4)	..	1·25	10p	1A–1A ..	..	15·00
	1B (×4)	..	1·25		1B–1B ..	..	15·00
3½p	1A (×5*)	..	1·25	20p	none		
	1B (×5)	..	1·25	50p	21–22–23–24		
					(*later ptgs only*)		50·00

* Only four "1A" Nos. are shown in the margin, the black "1A" being omitted in error.

BOOKLET PANES

These are in the same format as those issued with the 1969–70 definitive set.

Issued in Booklets B7/9 (stamps on glazed ordinary paper) or B10/12 (stamps on chalk-surfaced paper).

Face value	Cat. No.			
½p	44a.	Booklet stamp with margins		
		(*Glazed ordinary paper*)		
		(*b*)	15	25
		ab. Chalk-surfaced paper		
		(*e*)	15	25
2p	47a.	Booklet stamp with margins		
		(*Glazed ordinary paper*)		
		(*b*)	15	15
		ab. Chalk-surfaced paper		
		(*e*)	12	15
2½p	48b.	Booklet stamp with margins		
		(*Glazed ordinary paper*)		
		(*b*)	20	20
		ba. Chalk-surfaced paper		
		(*e*)	15	15

SET INFORMATION

Sheets: 50 (2 panes 5 × 5) ½p to 10p; 30 (5 × 6) others.
Imprint: Central bottom margin (½p to 10p).
Quantities sold:

½p	980,959	3p	2,245,560	7½p	322,905
1p	568,509	3½p	317,523	9p	349,211
1½p	559,576	4p	527,696	10p	538,153
2p	2,512,903	5p	511,742	20p	630,888
2½p	4,469,578	6p	346,255	50p	258,150

Withdrawn: 1.4.75 ½p to 10p (9p, 10p and Presentation Packs sold out previously); 31.3.76 20p and 50p.

GS 35   Hong Kong
2c. of 1862

GS 36   Great Britain
4d. of 1855–57

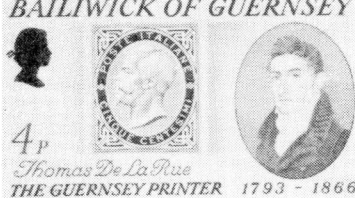

GS 37   Italy 5c. of 1862

GS 38   Confederate
States 5c. of 1862

(Designed and recess-printed by De La Rue & Co., Ltd.)

1971 (2 June). Thomas De La Rue Commemoration. P 14 × 13½ (C).

59	**GS 35**	2p dull purple *to* brown-purple*	..		50	20
60	**GS 36**	2½p carmine-red	..	.. .. ..	50	20
61	**GS 37**	4p deep bluish green	..	.. .. ..	7·50	3·00
62	**GS 38**	7½p deep blue ..	..	.. .. ..	7·50	3·00

First Day Cover (Nos. 59/62) ..	.. .. ..	6·00
Presentation Pack (Nos. 59/62)	.. .. ..	17·00

* These colours represent the extreme range of shades of this value. The majority of the printing, however, is in an intermediate shade.

PLATE NUMBERS
(Blocks of four)

2p	1A	.. ..	3·00	4p	1A	.. ..	45·00
	1B	.. ..	3·00		1B	.. ..	45·00
2½p	1A	.. ..	3·00	7½p	1A	.. ..	45·00
	1B	.. ..	3·00		1B	.. ..	45·00

Sheets: 25 (5 × 5).
Imprint: Central, bottom margin.
Quantities sold: 2p 897,742; 2½p 1,404,085; 4p 210,691; 7½p 199,424.
Withdrawn: 1.6.72.

GS 39 Ebenezer
Methodist Church, St.
Peter Port

GS 40 Church of St.
Pierre du Bois

GS 41 St. Joseph's
Roman Catholic
Church, St. Peter Port

GS 42 Church of St.
Philippe de Torteval

(Designed and printed in photogravure by Courvoisier)

1971 (27 Oct). Christmas. Island Churches. *Granite paper.* P 11½ (C).

63	**GS 39**	2p multicoloured	.. ..	40	20
64	**GS 40**	2½p multicoloured	.. ..	40	20
65	**GS 41**	5p multicoloured	.. ..	4·75	2·50
66	**GS 42**	7½p multicoloured	.. ..	4·75	3·50

First Day Cover (Nos. 63/6)	.. ..	6·00
Presentation Pack (Nos. 63/6)	.. ..	12·00

CYLINDER NUMBERS
(Blocks of four)

2p	A1–1–1–1	..	2·40	5p A1–1–1–1	..	29·00
	B1–1–1–1	..	2·40	B1–1–1–1	..	29·00
	C1–1–1–1	..	2·40	C1–1–1–1	..	29·00
	D1–1–1–1	..	2·40	D1–1–1–1	..	29·00
2½p	A1–1–1–1	..	2·40	7½p A1–1–1–1	..	29·00
	B1–1–1–1	..	2·40	B1–1–1–1	..	29·00
	C1–1–1–1	..	2·40	C1–1–1–1	..	29·00
	D1–1–1–1	..	2·40	D1–1–1–1	..	29·00

Sheets: 50 (two panes 5 × 5).
Imprint: Central, bottom margin (2p, 2½p) or left-hand corner, bottom margin (5p, 7½p).
Quantities sold: 2p 991,155; 2½p 916,004; 5p 223,412; 7½p 215,768.
Withdrawn: 26.10.72.

GS 43   *Earl of Chesterfield* (1794)

GS 44   *Dasher* (1827)

GS 45   *Ibex* (1891)

GS 46   *Alberta* (1900)

(Designed and printed in photogravure by Courvoisier)

1972 (10 Feb). Mail Packet Boats (1st series). *Granite paper. P* $11\frac{1}{2}$ (C).

67	**GS 43**	2p multicoloured	.. ..	25	20
68	**GS 44**	$2\frac{1}{2}$p multicoloured	.. ..	25	20
69	**GS 45**	$7\frac{1}{2}$p multicoloured	.. ..	2·75	3·00
70	**GS 46**	9p multicoloured	.. ..	2·75	3·00

First Day Cover (Nos. 67/70)	.. ..	7·00
Presentation Pack (Nos. 67/70)	.. .. ..	10·00

CYLINDER NUMBERS
(Blocks of four)

2p	A1–1–1–1	..	1·50	$7\frac{1}{2}$p	A1–1–1–1	.. 16·00
	B1–1–1–1	..	1·50		B1–1–1–1	.. 16·00
$2\frac{1}{2}$p	A1–1–1–1	..	1·50	9p	A1–1–1–1	.. 17·00
	B1–1–1–1	..	1·50		B1–1–1–1	.. 17·00

Sheets: 50 (2 panes 5 × 5).
Imprint: Central, bottom margin.
Quantities sold: 2p 973,503; $2\frac{1}{2}$p 954,263; $7\frac{1}{2}$p 288,929; 9p 289,340.
Withdrawn: 9.2.73.

GS 47   Guernsey Bull

(Printed in photogravure by Courvoisier)

1972 (22 May). World Conference of Guernsey Breeders, Guernsey. *Granite paper.* P
11½ (C).

71 **GS 47**   5p multicoloured .. ..   2·00   1·75

First Day Cover (No. 71)   ..   ..   2·50

CYLINDER NUMBERS
(Blocks of four)
5p A1–1–1–1   ..   ..   12·00
    B1–1–1–1   ..   ..   12·00

Sheets: 50 (2 panes 5 × 5).
Imprint: Central, bottom margin.
Quantity sold: 267,458.
Withdrawn: 21.5.73.

GS 48   Bermuda
Buttercup

GS 49   Heath Spotted
Orchid

GS 50   Kaffir Fig

GS 51   Scarlet
Pimpernel

(Designed and printed in photogravure by Courvoisier)

1972 (24 May). Wild Flowers. *Granite paper. P* 11½ (c).

72	**GS 48**	2p multicoloured	.. ..	15	15
73	**GS 49**	2½p multicoloured	.. ..	15	15
74	**GS 50**	7½p multicoloured	.. ..	1·25	1·25
75	**GS 51**	9p multicoloured	.. ..	2·00	1·50

First Day Cover (Nos. 72/5)	.. ..	3·00
Presentation Pack (Nos. 72/5)	.. ..	6·00

CYLINDER NUMBERS
(Blocks of four)

2p	A1–1–1–1	..	90	7½p	A1–1–1–1	.. 7·50
	B1–1–1–1	..	90		B1–1–1–1	.. 7·50
	C1–1–1–1	..	90		C1–1–1–1	.. 7·50
	D1–1–1–1	..	90		D1–1–1–1	.. 7·50
2½p	A1–1–1–1	..	90	9p	A1–1–1–1	.. 12·00
	B1–1–1–1	..	90		B1–1–1–1	.. 12·00
	C1–1–1–1	..	90		C1–1–1–1	.. 12·00
	D1–1–1–1	..	90		D1–1–1–1	.. 12·00

Sheets: 50 (2 panes 5 × 5).
Imprint: 2p, 7½p central, bottom margin; others left-hand corner, bottom margin.
Quantities sold: 2p 1,006,041; 2½p 1,028,826; 7½p 249,471; 9p 244,839.
Withdrawn: 23.5.73.

GS 52   Angels adoring
Christ

GS 53   The Epiphany

GS 54   The Virgin
Mary

GS 55   Christ

(Designed and printed in photogravure by Courvoisier)

1972 (20 Nov). Royal Silver Wedding and Christmas. Stained-glass windows from Guernsey Churches. *Granite paper. P* 11½ (C).

76	**GS 52**	2p multicoloured	..	..	..	..	10	10
77	**GS 53**	2½p multicoloured	..	..	..	..	15	15
78	**GS 54**	7½p multicoloured	..	..	..	..	80	75
79	**GS 55**	9p multicoloured	..	..	..	..	1·25	1·00

First Day Cover (Nos. 76/9)	..	..	..	..	2·10
Presentation Pack (Nos. 76/9)	..	..	..	..	4·25

CYLINDER NUMBERS
(Blocks of four)

2p	A1–1–1–1	.. 60	7½p A1–1–1–1	..	4·75
	B1–1–1–1	.. 60	B1–1–1–1	..	4·75
2½p	A1–1–1–1	.. 90	9p A1–1–1–1	..	7·50
	B1–1–1–1	.. 90	B1–1–1–1	..	7·50

Sheets: 50 (2 panes 5 × 5).
Imprint: Central, bottom margin.
Quantities sold: 2p 878,893; 2½p 1,037,387; 7½p 314,972; 9p 313,367.
Sold out by 31.3.73.

GS 56 *St. Julien*
(1925)

GS 57 *Isle of
Guernsey* (1930)

GS 58 *St. Patrick*
(1947)

GS 59 *Sarnia* (1961)

(Designed and printed in photogravure by Courvoisier)

1973 (9 Mar). Mail Packet Boats (2nd series). *Granite paper.* P 11½ (C).

80	**GS 56**	2½p multicoloured	..	..	..	..	12	12
81	**GS 57**	3p multicoloured	..	..	..	..	30	30
82	**GS 58**	7½p multicoloured	..	..	..	..	2·00	2·00
83	**GS 59**	9p multicoloured	..	..	..	..	2·00	2·00

First Day Cover (Nos. 80/3)	..	..	..	..	4·00
Presentation Pack (Nos. 80/3)	..	..	..	..	5·00

CYLINDER NUMBERS
(Blocks of four)

2½p	A1–1–1–1	..	75	7½p	A1–1–1–1	..	12·00
	B1–1–1–1	..	75		B1–1–1–1	..	12·00
3p	A1–1–1–1	..	1·75	9p	A1–1–1–1	..	12·00
	B1–1–1–1	..	1·75		B1–1–1–1	..	12·00

Sheets: 50 (2 panes 5 × 5).
Imprint: Central, bottom margin.
Quantities sold: 2½p 947,888; 3p 1,274,699; 7½p 278,998; 9p 263,569.
Withdrawn: 8.3.74; 3p sold out earlier.

GS 60   Supermarine
"Sea Eagle"

GS 61   Westland
"Wessex"

GS 62   De Havilland
"Rapide"

GS 63   Douglas
"Dakota"

GS 64   Vickers
"Viscount"

(Designed and printed in photogravure by Courvoisier)

1973 (4 July). 50th Anniversary of Air Service. *Granite paper.* P $11\frac{1}{2}$ (C).

84	**GS 60**	$2\frac{1}{2}$p multicoloured	..	..	..	12	12
85	**GS 61**	3p multicoloured	..	..	..	15	15
86	**GS 62**	5p multicoloured	..	..	..	25	25
87	**GS 63**	$7\frac{1}{2}$p multicoloured	..	..	..	85	85
88	**GS 64**	9p multicoloured	..	..	..	85	85

First Day Cover (Nos. 84/8)	.. ..	2·25
Presentation Pack (Nos 84/8)	.. ..	3·00

CYLINDER NUMBERS
(Blocks of four)

$2\frac{1}{2}$p	A1–1–1–1	..	75	$7\frac{1}{2}$p A1–1–1–1	..	5·00
	B1–1–1–1	..	75	B1–1–1–1	..	5·00
3p	A1–1–1–1	..	90	9p A1–1–1–1	..	5·00
	B1–1–1–1	..	90	B1–1–1–1	..	5·00
5p	A1–1–1–1	..	1·50			
	B1–1–1–1	..	1·50			

Sheets: 50 (two panes 5 × 5).
Imprint: Central, bottom margin.
Quantities sold: $2\frac{1}{2}$p 918,953; 3p 1,285,890; 5p 313,882; $7\frac{1}{2}$p 294,369; 9p 288,225.
Withdrawn: 3.7.74; 5p sold out earlier.

GS 65 The Good
Shepherd

GS 66 Christ at the
Well of Samaria

GS 67 St. Dominic

GS 68 Mary and the
Child Jesus

(Designed and printed in photogravure by Courvoisier)

1973 (24 Oct). Christmas. Stained-glass windows from Guernsey Churches. *Granite paper.* P 11½ (C).

89	**GS 65**	2½p multicoloured	..	..	..	..	10	10
90	**GS 66**	3p multicoloured	..	..	..	..	15	15
91	**GS 67**	7½p multicoloured	..	..	..	..	35	35
92	**GS 68**	20p multicoloured	..	..	..	..	80	80

First Day Cover (Nos. 89/92)	2·00
Presentation Pack (Nos. 89/92)	1·75

CYLINDER NUMBERS
(Blocks of four)

2½p	A1–1–1–1–1 ..	60	7½p	A1–1–1–1–1	2·10
	B1–1–1–1–1 ..	60		B1–1–1–1–1	2·10
3p	A1–1–1–1–1 ..	90	20p	A1–1–1–1–1	5·00
	B1–1–1–1–1 ..	90		B1–1–1–1–1	5·00

Sheets: 50 (two panes 5 × 5).
Imprint: Central, bottom margin.
Quantities sold: 2½p 1,284,342; 3p 1,285,851; 7½p 367,714; 20p 367,625.
Withdrawn: 23.10.74.

GS 69   Princess Anne
and Captain Mark Phillips

(Designed by G. Anderson)
(Printed in photogravure by Courvoisier)

1973 (14 Nov). Royal Wedding. *Granite paper. P* 11½ (C).

93	**GS 69**	25p multicoloured	1·00	1·10

First Day Cover (No. 93)	.. ..	1·25
Presentation Pack (No. 93)	.. ..	2·00

CYLINDER NUMBERS
(Blocks of four)

25p	A1–1–1–1	6·00
	B1–1–1–1	6·00

Sheets: 50 (two panes 5 × 5).
Imprint: Central, bottom margin of each pane.
Quantity sold: 392,767.
Withdrawn: 13.11.74.

GS 70 *John Lockett* (1875)

GS 71 *Arthur Lionel* (1912)

GS 72 *Euphrosyne Kendal* (1954)

GS 73 *Arun* (1972)

(Designed and printed in photogravure by Courvoisier)

1974 (15 Jan). **150th Anniversary of Royal National Life-boat Institution.** *Granite paper.*
P 11½ (C).

94	**GS 70**	2½p multicoloured	.. ..	10	10
95	**GS 71**	3p multicoloured	.. ..	15	15
96	**GS 72**	8p multicoloured	.. ..	50	50
97	**GS 73**	10p multicoloured	.. ..	50	50

First Day Cover (Nos. 94/7)	.. ..	1·25
Presentation Pack (Nos. 94/7)	.. ..	1·50

CYLINDER NUMBERS
(Blocks of four)

2½p	A1–1–1–1	..	60	8p	A1–1–1–1	.. 3·00
	B1–1–1–1	..	60		B1–1–1–1	.. 3·00
3p	A1–1–1–1	..	90	10p	A1–1–1–1	.. 3·00
	B1–1–1–1	..	90		B1–1–1–1	.. 3·00

Sheets: 50 (two panes 5 × 5).
Imprint: Central, bottom margin of each pane.
Quantities sold: 2½p 1,016,058; 3p 1,162,020; 8p 393,660; 10p 393,668.
Withdrawn: 14.1.75; 8p, 10p sold out earlier.

GS 74 Private, East
Regiment, 1815

GS 75 Officer, 2nd
North Regiment, 1825

GS 76 Gunner,
Guernsey Artillery,
1787

GS 77 Gunner,
Guernsey Artillery,
1815

GS 78 Corporal,
Royal Guernsey
Artillery, 1868

GS 79 Field Officer,
Royal Guernsey
Artillery, 1895

GS 80 Sergeant, 3rd
Regiment, 1867

GS 81 Officer, East
Regiment, 1822

GS 82 Field Officer,
Royal Guernsey
Artillery, 1895

GS 83 Colour-
Sergeant of
Grenadiers, East
Regiment, 1833

GS 84 Officer, North
Regiment, 1832

GS 85 Officer, East
Regiment, 1822

240 *Guernsey 1974*

GS 86 Field Officer,
Rifle Company, 1868

GS 87 Private, 4th
West Regiment, 1785

GS 88 Field Officer,
4th West Regiment,
1824

GS 89 Driver, Field
Battery, Royal
Guernsey Artillery,
1848

GS 90 Officer, Field
Battery, Royal
Guernsey Artillery,
1868

GS 91 Trooper, Light
Dragoons, 1814

(Printed in photogravure by Courvoisier (½p to 10p) or Delrieu (others))

1974 (2 Apr)–78. *Granite paper (½p to 10p). P* 11½ *(½p to 10p),* 13 × 13½ *(20, 50p) or* 13½
× 13 *(£1), all comb.*

98	**GS 74**	½p multicoloured (*aj*)	..	..	5	5
99	**GS 75**	1p multicoloured (*aci*)	..	..	5	5
100	**GS 76**	1½p multicoloured (*a*) ..	..	..	5	5
101	**GS 77**	2p multicoloured (*ak*)	..	..	5	5
102	**GS 78**	2½p multicoloured (*a*) ..	..	..	5	5
103	**GS 79**	3p multicoloured (*a*) ..	..	..	5	5
104	**GS 80**	3½p multicoloured (*a*) ..	..	..	5	8
105	**GS 81**	4p multicoloured (*abc*)	..	..	8	8
105*a*	**GS 82**	5p multicoloured (*f*)	..	..	8	10
106	**GS 83**	5½p multicoloured (*a*) ..	..	..	10	10

107	**GS 84**	6p multicoloured (*ae*)	.. ..	10	10
107*a*	**GS 85**	7p multicoloured (*f*)	.. ..	12	15
108	**GS 86**	8p multicoloured (*ag*)	.. ..	15	15
109	**GS 87**	9p multicoloured (*a*) ..	.. ..	20	20
110	**GS 88**	10p multicoloured (*ah*)	.. ..	20	20
111	**GS 89**	20p multicoloured (*d*) ..	.. ..	35	35
112	**GS 90**	50p multicoloured (*d*) ..	.. ..	85	85
113	**GS 91**	£1 multicoloured (*d*) ..	.. ..	1·75	1·75

First Day Covers (Nos. 98/105, 106/7, 108/13) (3)	5·00
First Day Cover (Nos. 105*a*, 107*a*)	25
Presentation Packs (Nos. 98/105, 106/7, 108/13) (3)	4·25
Presentation Pack (Nos. 105*a*/10) (*issued* 6.77)	1·10

The ½p and 2½p with red colour omitted were formerly listed as Nos. 98c and 102a. Since it is now known that the red can be removed chemically they have been deleted.

Printings:

(*a*) 2.4.74	(*b*) 10.74	(*c*) 12.74	(*d*) 1.4.75	(*e*) 12.75
(*f*) 29.5.76	(*g*) 7.76	(*h*) 11.76	(*i*) 8.2.77	(*j*) 7.77
(*k*) 12.77	(*l*) 7.2.78			

CYLINDER NUMBERS
(Blocks of four)

½p A1–1–1–1 ..	8	5p A1–1–1–1 ..	50	
B1–1–1–1 ..	8	B1–1–1–1 ..	50	
1p A1–1–1–1 ..	12	5½p A1–1–1–1 ..	60	
B1–1–1–1 ..	12	B1–1–1–1 ..	60	
1½p A1–1–1–1–1	15	6p A1–1–1–1–1	60	
B1–1–1–1–1	15	B1–1–1–1–1	60	
2p A1–1–1–1–1	25	7p A1–1–1–1 ..	75	
B1–1–1–1–1	25	B1–1–1–1 ..	75	
2½p A1–1–1–1 ..	25	8p A1–1–1–1 ..	90	
B1–1–1–1 ..	25	B1–1–1–1 ..	90	
3p A1–1–1–1 ..	30	9p A1–1–1–1 ..	1·25	
B1–1–1–1 ..	30	B1–1–1–1 ..	1·25	
3½p A1–1–1–1 ..	40	10p A1–1–1–1 ..	1·25	
B1–1–1–1 ..	40	B1–1–1–1 ..	1·25	
4p A1–1–1–1 ..	50	20p to £1 None		
B1–1–1–1 ..	50			

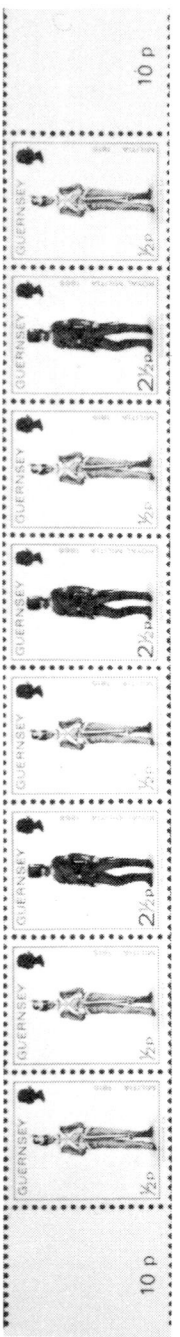

No. 98a

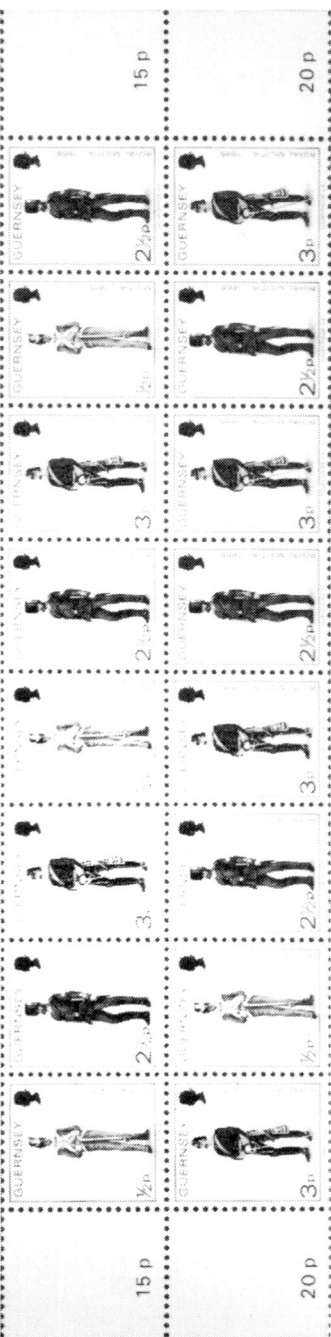

No. 98b

(illustrations reduced to ⅓ size)

(*illustrations reduced to ⅓ size*)

No. 99a

No. 99b

BOOKLET PANE AND STRIPS

Nos. 98a/b come from special booklets sheets of 88 (8 × 11), and Nos. 99a/b from separate booklet sheets of 80 (2 panes 8 × 5). These sheets were put on sale in addition to the normal sheets. The strips and panes have the left-hand selvedge stuck into booklet covers except for No. 99b which had the strip loose, and then folded and supplied in plastic wallets.

(*See list overleaf*)

Issued in Booklet B13

    98a. *Se-tenant* booklet strip of 8 (Nos. 98 × 5,

        102 × 3) (*a*)   30

Issued in Booklet B14

    98b. *Se-tenant* booklet pane of 16 (Nos. 98 × 4,

        102 × 6, 103 × 6) (*a*) .. .. .. 1·00

Issued in Booklet B15

    99a. *Se-tenant* booklet strip of 8 (Nos. 99 × 4,

        103, 105 × 2, 105*a*) (*i*)   35

Issued in Sachet SB1

    99b. *Se-tenant* sachet strip of 4 (Nos. 99, 101 ×

        2, 105*a*) (*l*) 20

BOOKLET SHEETS

Uncut examples of the special sheets used for the preparation of Booklets B13/15 and Sachet SB1 were sold by the Guernsey Philatelic Bureau to collectors.

    98aS. Booklet sheet containing No. 98a × 7 and

        No. 98b × 2   .. .. 5·00

    99aS. Booklet sheet containing No. 99a × 10 .. 3·75

    99bS. Sachet sheet containing No. 99b × 20 .. 4·00

SET INFORMATION

Sheets: 100 (two panes 10 × 5) ½ to 10p; 25 (5 × 5) others.

Imprint: Central, bottom margin of each pane.

GS 96 Badge of
Guernsey and U.P.U.
Emblem

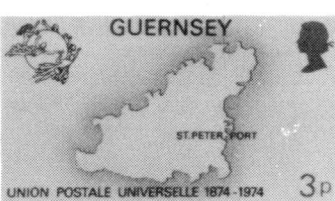

GS 97 Map of
Guernsey

GS 98 U.P.U.
Building, Berne, and
Guernsey Flag

GS 99 "Salle des
Etats"

(Printed in photogravure by Courvoisier)

1974 (7 June). Universal Postal Union Centenary. *Granite paper. P* 11½ (C).

114	**GS 96**	2½p brown-purple, black and yellow-green	5	5
115	**GS 97**	3p multicoloured	8	8
116	**GS 98**	8p black, red and yellow	35	40
117	**GS 99**	10p multicoloured	45	50

First Day Cover (Nos. 114/17)		1·00
Presentation Pack (Nos. 114/17)		1·25

CYLINDER NUMBERS
(Blocks of four)

2½p	A1–1–1	25	8p	A1–1–1	2·10
	B1–1–1	25		B1–1–1	2·10
3p	A1–1–1–1	50	10p	A1–1–1–1–1	2·75
	B1–1–1–1	50		B1–1–1–1–1	2·75

Sheets: 25 (5 × 5).
Imprint: Central, bottom margin.
Quantities sold: 2½p 1,231,657; 3p 1,839,674; 8p 345,271; 10p 356,501.
Withdrawn: 6.6.75.

GS 100   "Cradle Rock"

GS 101   "Moulin Huet Bay"

GS 102   "Au Bord de la Mer"

GS 103   Self-portrait

(Designed and printed in photogravure by Delrieu)

1974 (21 Sept). Renoir Paintings. *P* 13 (C).

118	**GS 100**	3p multicoloured	..	..	..		15	8
119	**GS 101**	5½p multicoloured	..	..	..		25	12
120	**GS 102**	8p multicoloured	..	..	..		50	50
121	**GS 103**	10p multicoloured	..	..	..		75	60

First Day Cover (Nos. 118/21)	.. .. ..	1·25
Presentation Pack (Nos. 118/21)	.. .. ..	2·25

Sheets: 25 (5 × 5).

Imprint: Right-hand corner, top margin (3p and 5½p) and bottom corner right-hand margin (others).

Quantities sold: 3p 670,648; 5½p 422,677; 8p 377,615; 10p 391,095.

Withdrawn: 20.9.75.

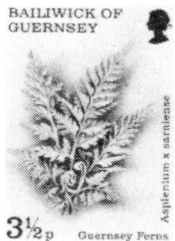

GS 104 Guernsey
Spleenwort

GS 105 Sand
Quillwort

GS 106 Guernsey
Quillwort

GS 107 Least
Adder's Tongue

(Designed and printed in photogravure by Courvoisier)

1975 (7 Jan). **Guernsey Ferns.** *Granite paper.* P 11½ (C).

122	**GS 104**	3½p multicoloured	.. .. ..	8	8
123	**GS 105**	4p multicoloured	.. .. ..	10	10
124	**GS 106**	8p multicoloured	.. .. ..	20	20
125	**GS 107**	10p multicoloured	.. .. ..	50	50

First Day Cover (Nos. 122/5) ..	.. .. ..	1·00
Presentation Pack (Nos. 122/5)	.. .. ..	1·00

CYLINDER NUMBERS
(Blocks of four)

3½p	A1–1–1–1 ..	50	8p	A1–1–1–1 ..	1·25
	B1–1–1–1 ..	50		B1–1–1–1 ..	1·25
	D1–1–1–1 ..	50	10p	A1–1–1–1–1	3·00
4p	C1–1–1–1 ..	60		B1–1–1–1–1	3·00
	D1–1–1–1 ..	60		D1–1–1–1–1	3·00

Sheets: 50 (two panes 5 × 5).
Imprint: Central, bottom margin.
Quantities sold: 3½p 1,089,142; 4p 1,370,743; 8p 430,672; 10p 443,636.
Withdrawn: 6.1.76.

GS 108   Victor Hugo
House

GS 110   United
Europe Oak,
Hauteville

GS 109   Candie
Gardens

GS 111   Tapestry Room,
Hauteville

(Designed and printed in photogravure by Courvoisier)

1975 (6 June). Victor Hugo's Exile in Guernsey. *Granite paper. P* 11½ (C).

126	**GS 108**	3½p multicoloured	.. .. ..	8	8
127	**GS 109**	4p multicoloured	.. .. ..	8	8
128	**GS 110**	8p multicoloured	.. .. ..	20	20
129	**GS 111**	10p multicoloured	.. .. ..	30	30

First Day Cover (Nos. 126/9)	1·00
Presentation Pack (Nos. 126/9)	75

CYLINDER NUMBERS
(Blocks of four)

3½p	A1–1–1–1 ..	50	8p	A1–1–1–1 ..	1·25
	B1–1–1–1 ..	50		B1–1–1–1 ..	1·25
4p	A1–1–1–1 ..	50	10p	A1–1–1–1 ..	1·75
	B1–1–1–1 ..	50		B1–1–1–1 ..	1·75

MINIATURE SHEET

GUERNSEY POST OFFICE

SOUVENIR OF VICTOR HUGO'S EXILE

IN GUERNSEY 1855 - 1870

Illustration reduced, actual size 114 × 143*mm*

MS130   Containing Nos. 126/9   . .   . .   . .   1·00   1·00

First Day Cover (**MS**130)	2·50

Sheets: 50 (5 × 10) 3½p, 10p; (10 × 5) others.
Imprint: Central, left-hand margin (3½p, 10p) or central, bottom margin (4p, 8p).
Quantities sold: 3½p 810,327; 4p 1,346,628; 8p 377,637; 10p 369,282; **MS**130 269,217.
Withdrawn: 5.6.76.

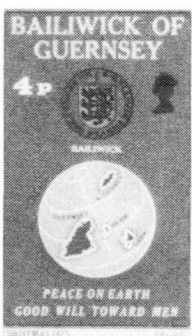

GS 112   Globe and
Seal of Bailiwick

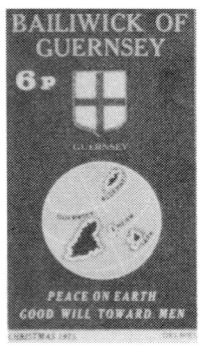

GS 113   Guernsey
Flag

GS 114   Guernsey Flag and Alderney
Shield

GS 115   Guernsey Flag and Sark Shield

(Designed and printed in photogravure by Delrieu)

1975 (7 Oct). Christmas. *P* 13 (C).

131	**GS 112**	4p multicoloured	..	..	..	8	10
132	**GS 113**	6p multicoloured	..	..	..	12	15
133	**GS 114**	10p multicoloured	..	..	..	20	20
134	**GS 115**	12p multicoloured	..	..	..	25	30

First Day Cover (Nos. 131/4)	1·00
Presentation Pack (Nos. 131/4)	80

Sheets: 50 (two panes 5 × 5).
Imprint: Central, left-hand margin (4p, 6p); central, bottom margin (others).
Quantities sold: 4p 678,619; 6p 667,413; 10p 392,529; 12p 361,548.
Withdrawn: 6.10.76.

GS 116   Les Hanois

GS 117   Les Casquets

GS 118   Quesnard

GS 119   Point Robert

(Designed and printed in photogravure by Courvoisier)

1976 (10 Feb). Lighthouses. *Granite paper. P* $11\frac{1}{2}$ (C).

135	**GS 116**	4p multicoloured	.. .. ..	10	10
136	**GS 117**	6p multicoloured	.. .. ..	15	15
137	**GS 118**	11p multicoloured	.. .. ..	25	25
138	**GS 119**	13p multicoloured	.. .. ..	30	30

First Day Cover (Nos. 135/8) ..	.. .. ..	1·00
Presentation Pack (Nos. 135/8)	.. .. ..	1·10

CYLINDER NUMBERS
(Blocks of four)

4p	A1–1–1–1 ..	60	11p	A1–1–1–1 ..	1·50
	B1–1–1–1 ..	60		B1–1–1–1 ..	1·50
6p	A1–1–1–1 ..	75	13p	A1–1–1–1 ..	2·00
	B1–1–1–1 ..	75		B1–1–1–1 ..	2·00

Sheets: 50 (two panes 5 × 5).
Quantities sold: 4p 846,362; 6p 900,899; 11p 366,468; 13p 348,358.
Withdrawn: 9.2.77.

GS 120   Milk Can   GS 121   Christening Cup

(Designed and printed in photogravure by Courvoisier)

1976 (29 May). Europa. *Granite paper.* P 11½ (C).

139	**GS 120**	10p	chestnut and greenish black	75	60
140	**GS 121**	25p	slate and deep dull blue	1·50	1·40

First Day Cover (Nos. 139/40)	..	..	..	2·75
Presentation Pack (Nos. 139/40)	..	..	..	2·25

Sheets: 9 (3 × 3).
Sold out: 4.6.76.

GS 122   Pine Forest, Guernsey

GS 123   Herm and Jethou

GS 124   Grande
Greve Bay, Sark

GS 125   Trois Vaux
Bay, Alderney

(Designed and printed in photogravure by Courvoisier)

1976 (3 Aug). **Bailiwick Views.** *Granite paper. P* 11½ (C).

141	**GS 122**	5p multicoloured	..	..	10	12
142	**GS 123**	7p multicoloured	..	..	15	15
143	**GS 124**	11p multicoloured	..	..	20	25
144	**GS 125**	13p multicoloured	..	..	25	30

First Day Cover (Nos. 141/4)	1·00
Presentation Pack (Nos. 141/4)	85

CYLINDER NUMBERS
(Blocks of four)

5p	A1–1–1–1 ..	60	11p	A1–1–1–1 ..	1·25
	B1–1–1–1 ..	60		B1–1–1–1 ..	1·25
7p	A1–1–1–1 ..	90	13p	A1–1–1–1 ..	1·50
	B1–1–1–1 ..	90		B1–1–1–1 ..	1·50

Sheets: 50 (two panes 5 × 5).
Quantities sold: 5p 661,771; 7p 1,016,350; 11p 349,773; 13p 336,027.
Withdrawn: 2.8.77.

GS 126   Royal Court
House, Guernsey

GS 127   Elizabeth
College, Guernsey

GS 128   La
Seigneurie, Sark

GS 129   Island
Hall, Alderney

(Designed and printed in photogravure by Courvoisier)

1976 (14 Oct). Buildings. *Granite paper. P* 11½ (C).

145	**GS 126**	5p multicoloured	..	..	10	12
146	**GS 127**	7p multicoloured	..	..	15	15
147	**GS 128**	11p multicoloured	..	..	20	25
148	**GS 129**	13p multicoloured	..	..	25	30

First Day Cover (Nos. 145/8)	1·00
Presentation Pack (Nos. 145/8)	85

CYLINDER NUMBERS
(Blocks of four)

5p	A1–1–1–1–1	60	11p	A1–1–1–1–1	1·25
	B1–1–1–1–1	60		B1–1–1–1–1	1·25
7p	A1–1–1–1–1	90	13p	A1–1–1–1–1	1·50
	B1–1–1–1–1	90		B1–1–1–1–1	1·50

Sheets: 50 (two panes 5 × 5).
Imprint: Central, bottom margin.
Quantities sold: 5p 1,097,445; 7p 1,051,184; 11p 371,155; 13p 352,347.
Withdrawn: 13.10.77.

GS 130   Queen Eliza-
beth II

GS 131   Queen Eliza-
beth II (half-length
portrait)

(Designed by R. Granger Barrett)
(Printed in photogravure by Courvoisier)

1977 (8 Feb). Silver Jubilee. *Granite paper. P* $11\frac{1}{2}$ (C).

149	**GS 130**	7p multicoloured	.. .. ..	15	15
150	**GS 131**	35p multicoloured	.. .. ..	70	80

First Day Cover (Nos. 149/50)	.. .. ..	1·10
Presentation Pack (Nos. 149/50)	.. .. ..	1·10

CYLINDER NUMBERS
(Blocks of four)

7p	A1–1–1–1–1	90	35p A1–1–1–1–1–1	4·25
	B1–1–1–1–1	90		

Sheets: 25 (5 × 5).
Imprint: Central, bottom margin.
Quantities sold: 7p 1,004,250; 35p 536,971
Withdrawn: 7.2.78.

GS 132   Woodland, Talbots Valley

GS 133   Pastureland, Talbots Valley

(Designed and printed in photogravure by Courvoisier)

1977 (17 May). Europa. *Granite paper.* P $11\frac{1}{2}$ (C).

151	**GS 132**	7p multicoloured	..	..	..	12	12
152	**GS 133**	25p multicoloured	..	..	..	45	50

First Day Cover (Nos. 151/2)	75
Presentation Pack (Nos. 151/2)	80

CYLINDER NUMBERS
(Blocks of four)

7p	A1–1–1–1–1	75	25p	A1–1–1–1–1	2·75
	B1–1–1–1–1	75		B1–1–1–1–1	2·75

Sheets: 50 (two panes 5 × 5).
Imprint: Right-hand corner, bottom margin.
Withdrawn: 16.5.78.

GS 134   Statue-
menhir, Castel

GS 135   Megalithic
Tomb, St. Saviour

GS 136   Cist, Tourgis

GS 137   Statue-
menhir, St. Martin

(Designed and printed in photogravure by Courvoisier)

1977 (2 Aug). Prehistoric Monuments. *Granite paper. P* 11½ (C).

153	**GS 134**	5p	multicoloured	.. .. ..	10	10
154	**GS 135**	7p	multicoloured	.. .. ..	15	15
155	**GS 136**	11p	multicoloured	.. .. ..	20	25
156	**GS 137**	13p	multicoloured	.. .. ..	25	30

First Day Cover (Nos. 153/6) ..	.. .. ..	1·10
Presentation Pack (Nos. 153/6)	.. .. ..	1·00

CYLINDER NUMBERS
(Blocks of four)

5p	A1–1–1–1 ..	60	11p A1–1–1–1 ..	1·25
	B1–1–1–1 ..	60	B1–1–1–1 ..	1·25
7p	A1–1–1–1 ..	75	13p A1–1–1–1 ..	1·50
	B1–1–1–1 ..	75	B1–1–1–1 ..	1·50

Sheets: 50 (2 panes 5 × 5).
Imprint: Central, right-hand margin (5p, 13p); central, bottom margin (others).
Withdrawn: 1.8.78.

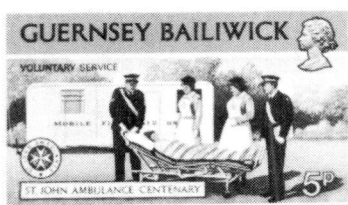

GS 138   Mobile First Aid Unit

GS 139   Mobile Radar Unit

GS 140   Marine
Ambulance *Flying
Christine II*

GS 141   Cliff Rescue

(Designed by P. Slade and M. Horder)
(Printed in photogravure by Courvoisier)

1977 (25 Oct). St. John Ambulance Centenary. *Granite paper.* P 11½ (C).

157	GS 138	5p multicoloured	..	..	..	8	10
158	GS 139	7p multicoloured	..	..	..	12	15
159	GS 140	11p multicoloured	..	..	..	20	25
160	GS 141	13p multicoloured	..	..	..	25	30

First Day Cover (Nos. 157/60)	..	..	..	1·00
Presentation Pack (Nos. 157/60)	..	..	..	95

CYLINDER NUMBERS
(Blocks of four)

5p	A1–1–1–1–1	50	11p	A1–1–1–1 ..	1·25
	B1–1–1–1–1	50		B1–1–1–1 ..	1·25
7p	A1–1–1–1 ..	75	13p	A1–1–1–1 ..	1·50
	B1–1–1–1 ..	75		B1–1–1–1 ..	1·50

Sheets: 50 (2 panes 5 × 5).

Imprint: Right-hand corner, bottom margin on each pane (5 and 7p); top corner, right-hand margin on each pane (others).

Withdrawn: 24.10.78.

GS 142 View from
Clifton, *c* 1830

GS 143 Market
Square, St. Peter Port,
c 1838

GS 144 Petit-Bo Boy,
c 1839

GS 145 The Quay, St.
Peter Port, *c* 1830

(Designed and printed in recess and lithography by De La Rue)

1978 (7 Feb). Old Guernsey Prints. *P* 14 × 13½ (C).

161	**GS 142**	5p black and pale apple-green	..	10	12
162	**GS 143**	7p black and stone		15	15
163	**GS 144**	11p black and light pink		25	25
164	**GS 145**	13p black and light azure		25	30

First Day Cover (Nos. 161/4)	90
Presentation Pack (Nos. 161/4)	1·00

PLATE NUMBERS
(Blocks of four)

5p	1A–1A	60	11p	1A–1A	1·50
	1B–1B	60		1B–1B	1·50
7p	1A–1A	90	13p	1A–1A	1·50
	1B–1B	90		1B–1B	1·50

Sheets: 50 (2 panes 5 × 5).
Imprint: Left-hand corner, bottom margin.
Withdrawn: 6.2.79.

GS 146 *Prosperity*
Memorial

GS 147 Victoria
Monument

(Designed by R. Granger Barrett)
(Printed in lithography by Questa Colour Security Printers Ltd.)

1978 (2 May). Europa. *P* 14½ (C).

165	**GS 146**	5p multicoloured	.. .. ..	10	12
166	**GS 147**	7p multicoloured	.. .. ..	15	15

First Day Cover (Nos. 165/6)	60
Presentation Pack (Nos. 165/6)	50

Sheets: 20 (5 × 4) 5p; (4 × 5) 7p.

GS 148   Queen Eliza-
beth II

(Designed by R. Granger Barrett, from bust by Arnold Machin)
(Printed in photogravure by Courvoisier)

1978 (2 May). 25th Anniversary of Coronation. *Granite paper.* P $11\frac{1}{2}$ (C).
   167 **GS 148**   20p black, grey and bright blue   ..   40   45

First Day Cover (No. 167)	70
Presentation Pack (No. 167)	60

CYLINDER NUMBERS
(Blocks of four)
20p A1–1–1   ..   ..   ..   2·40
       B1–1–1   ..   ..   ..   2·40

Sheets: 50 (2 panes 5 × 5).
Imprint: Right-hand corner, bottom margin.

GS 149 Queen Eliza-
beth II

(Designed by R. Granger Barrett, from bust by Arnold Machin)
(Printed in photogravure by Courvoisier)

1978 (28 June). Royal Visit. *Granite paper. P* 11½ (C).
   168 **GS 149**   7p black, grey and bright green ..   15   15

First Day Cover (No. 168)	.. ..	50
Presentation Pack (No. 168)	.. ..	40

CYLINDER NUMBERS
(Blocks of four)
      7p A1–1–1   90
           B1–1–1   90

Sheets: 50 (2 panes 5 × 5).
Imprint: Top corner, right-hand margin.

GS 150 Gannet

GS 151 Firecrest

GS 152 Dartford
Warbler

GS 153 Spotted Red-
shank

(Designed by John Waddington Ltd.)
(Printed in photogravure by Courvoisier)

1978 (29 Aug). Guernsey Birds. *Granite paper. P* 11½ (C).

169	**GS 150**	5p multicoloured	..	..	10	12
170	**GS 151**	7p multicoloured	..	..	15	15
171	**GS 152**	11p multicoloured	..	..	20	25
172	**GS 153**	13p multicoloured	..	..	25	30

First Day Cover (Nos. 169/72)	.. .. ..	1·00
Presentation Pack (Nos. 169/72)	.. .. ..	95

CYLINDER NUMBERS
(Blocks of four)

5p	A1–1–1–1	..	60	11p A1–1–1–1 ..	1·25
	B1–1–1–1	..	60	B1–1–1–1 ..	1·25
7p	A1–1–1–1	..	90	13p A1–1–1–1 ..	1·50
	B1–1–1–1	..	90	B1–1–1–1 ..	1·50

Sheets: 50 (2 panes 5 × 5).
Imprint: Right-hand corner, bottom margin.

GS 154   Solanum

GS 155   Christmas Rose

GS 156   Holly

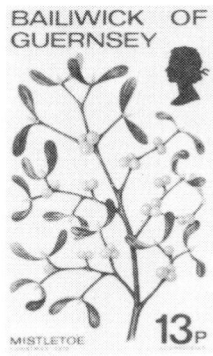

GS 157   Mistletoe

(Designed and printed in photogravure by Courvoisier)

1978 (31 Oct). Christmas. *Granite paper. P* 11½ (C).

173	**GS 154**	5p multicoloured	10	12
174	**GS 155**	7p multicoloured	15	15
175	**GS 156**	11p multicoloured	20	25
176	**GS 157**	13p emerald, yellow and olive-grey	25	30

First Day Cover (Nos. 173/6)	1·00
Presentation Pack (Nos. 173/6)	95

CYLINDER NUMBERS
(Blocks of four)

5p A1–1–1–1 ..	60	11p A1–1–1–1 ..	1·25
B1–1–1–1 ..	60	B1–1–1–1 ..	1·25
7p A1–1–1–1 ..	90	13p A1–1–1 ..	1·50
B1–1–1–1 ..	90	B1–1–1 ..	1·50

Sheets: 50 (2 panes 5 × 5).
Imprint: 5p, 7p central, bottom margin; others central right-hand margin.

POSTAGE DUE STAMPS

GSD 1 Castle
Cornet

(Designed by R. Granger Barrett)
(Printed in photogravure by Delrieu)

1969 (1 Oct). *Face value in black; background colour given.* P 12½ × 12 (C).

D1	**GSD 1**	1d.	plum	.. ..	1·00	1·00
D2		2d.	bright green	.. ..	1·50	1·00
D3		3d.	vermilion	.. ..	3·00	2·50
D4		4d.	ultramarine	.. ..	4·00	3·75
D5		5d.	yellow-ochre	.. ..	5·00	4·50
D6		6d.	turquoise-blue	.. .. ..	7·00	7·00
D7		1s.	lake-brown	.. ..	17·00	17·00

Sheets: 60 (10 × 6).
Quantities sold: 1d. 82,802; 2d. 75,340; 3d. 74,532; 4d. 74,659; 5d. 71,129; 6d. 72,912; 1s. 71,659.
Withdrawn and Invalidated: 14.2.72.

GSD 2 Castle
Cornet

(Designed by R. Granger Barrett)
(Printed in photogravure by Delrieu)

1971 (15 Feb)–76. Decimal Currency. *Face value in black; background colour given.* P 12½ × 12 (C).

D8	**GSD 2**	½p plum (a)	.. ..	8	8
D9		1p bright green (a)	.. .. ..	8	8
D10		2p vermilion (a)	.. .. ..	8	8
D11		3p ultramarine (a)	.. .. ..	8	10
D12		4p yellow-ochre (a)	.. .. ..	10	10
D13		5p turquoise-blue (a)	.. ..	10	10
D14		6p violet (c)	.. ..	12	15

D15	**GSD 2**	8p light yellow-orange (*b*)	..	..	20	20
D16		10p lake-brown (*a*)	..	.. ..	25	25
D17		15p grey (*c*)	.. ..	.. ..	30	35

Presentation Pack (Nos. D1/13, D16)	.. ..	60·00
Presentation Pack (Nos. D8/17)	.. .. ..	1·10

Printings: (*a*) 15.2.71; (*b*) 7.10.75; (*c*) 10.2.76.
Sheets: 60 (10 × 6).
Withdrawn: 1.8.78 (½p and 1p sold out by 6.78).

GSD 3   St. Peter Port
(Printed in photogravure by Delrieu)

1977 (2 Aug). *Face value in black; background colour given.* P 13 (C).

D18	**GSD 3**	½p lake-brown	.. ..	5	5
		SV3. Broken "A" ..	.. ..	1·00	
D19		1p bright purple	.. ..	5	5
		SV3. Broken "A"	.. ..	1·00	
D20		2p bright orange	.. ..	5	5
		SV3. Broken "A"	.. ..	1·00	
D21		3p vermilion	.. ..	5	5
		SV3. Broken "A"	.. ..	1·00	
D22		4p turquoise-blue	.. ..	8	8
		SV3. Broken "A"	.. ..	1·50	
D23		5p yellow-green	.. ..	8	10
		SV3. Broken "A"	.. ..	1·50	
D24		6p turquoise-green ..	.. ..	10	12
		SV3. Broken "A"	.. ..	2·00	
D25		8p brown-ochre	.. ..	15	15
		SV3. Broken "A"	.. ..	2·50	
D26		10p ultramarine	.. ..	20	20
		SV3. Broken "A"	.. ..	3·00	
D27		15p bright violet	.. ..	25	30
		SV3. Broken "A"	.. ..	3·50	

Presentation Pack (Nos. D18/27)	.. .. ..	1·25

Variety

SV3.
All values. There is a
break in the left-hand
side of the "A" in
"BAILIWICK" (R. 10/1).

Sheets: 50 (5 × 10).

STAMP BOOKLETS

Prices given are for complete booklets.

Type A   Military Uniforms

1969 (12 Dec). *White cover as Type A, printed in black. Stitched. Panes of one.*

> *Trooper, Royal Guernsey Cavalry (Light Dragoons) 1814.*
> B1   2s. booklet. Containing 3 × 4d. (No. 18a), 2 × 5d. (No. 19a) and 2 × 1d. (No. 14c)   ..   2·40
> *Officer, St. Martin's Company (La Milice Bleue), Guernsey, 1720.*
> B2   4s. booklet. Containing 6 × 4d. (No. 18a), 4 × 5d. (No. 19a) and 4 × 1d. (No. 14c)   ..   5·00
> *Colour Sergeant of Grenadiers and Rifleman, East (Town) Regiment, Guernsey 1833.*
> B3   6s. booklet. Containing 9 × 4d. (No. 18a), 6 × 5d. (No. 19a) and 6 × 1d. (No. 14c)   ..   7·50

> *Withdrawn:* 14.2.72.

1970 (29 June). *White Cover as Type A. Printed in black (B4), green (B5) or red (B6). Same composition as Nos.* B1/3. *Stitched. Panes of one.*

> *Officer, Royal Guernsey Horse Artillery, 1793.*
> B4   2s. booklet ..   ..   5·00
> *Gunner, Royal Guernsey Artillery, 1743.*
> B5   4s. booklet ..   ..   9·00
> *Sergeant, Royal Guernsey Light Infantry, 1832.*
> B6   6s. booklet ..   ..   15·00

> *Quantities sold:* B1 and B4 81,928; B2 and B5 23,817; B3 and B6 25,123.
> *Withdrawn:* 14.2.72.

1971 (15 Feb). *White cover as Type* A. *Printed in black (B7), green (B8) or red (B9). Stitched. Panes of one.*

> *Officer, Royal Guernsey Horse Artillery, 1850.*
> B7   10p booklet. Containing 2 × ½p (No. 44a), 2 × 2p (No. 47a) and 2 × 2½p (No. 48b)   ..   2·50

Sergeant, Guernsey Light Infantry (Grenadiers), 1826.

B8 20p booklet. Containing 4 × ½p (No. 44a), 4 ×
2p (No. 47a) and 4 × 2½p (No. 48b) .. 3·00

Sergeant and Bandsman, Royal Guernsey Light Infantry (North Regiment), 1866.

B9 30p booklet. Containing 6 × ½p (No. 44a), 6 ×
2p (No. 47a) and 6 × 2½p (No. 48b) .. 4·00

Withdrawn: 27.6.73 (B7); 12.3.75 (B8); 15.1.75 (B9)

1973 (2 Apr). *White cover as Type* A. *Printed in black* (B10), *green* (B11) *or red* (B12). *Stitched. Panes of one.*

Officer, Guernsey Horse Artillery.

B10 10p booklet. Containing 2 × ½p (No. 44ab), 2
× 2p (No. 47ab) and 2 × 2½p (No. 48ba) .. 80

Grenadier, Guernsey Light Infantry, 1792.

B11 20p booklet. Containing 4 × ½p (No. 44ab), 4
× 2p (No. 47ab) and 4 × 2½p (No. 48ba) .. 1·50

Insignia, Royal Guernsey Light Infantry.

B12 30p booklet. Containing 6 × ½p (No. 44ab), 6
× 2p (No. 47ab) and 6 × 2½p (No. 48ba) .. 1·75

Nos. B10/12 are inscribed "January 1973" on the back cover.
Withdrawn: 1.4.75.

Type B   Arms of Guernsey

1974 (2 Apr). *Silver* (B13) *or gold cover* (B14) *as Type* B.

B13 10p booklet. Containing 5 × ½p and 3 × 2½p in
se-tenant strip (No. 98a) 20

B14 35p booklet. Containing 4 × ½p, 6 × 2½p and 6
× 3p in *se-tenant* pane (No. 98b) 60

The strips and panes have the left-hand selvedge stuck into booklet covers and are then folded and supplied in plastic wallets.

1977 (8 Feb). *Green cover as Type* B.

B15 20p booklet. Containing 4 × 1p, 3p, 2 × 4p
and 5p *se-tenant* strip (No. 99a) 35

The note beneath B14 also applies here.

STAMP SACHET

Sachets have cardboard covers, contained in plastic wallets, the strips of stamps being folded and left loose inside.

1978 (7 Feb). *Blue cover as Type* B.

SB1 10p sachet. Containing 1p, 2 × 2p, 5p in *se-tenant* strip (No. 99b) 20

POSTAL STATIONERY

Airletters

All the following Guernsey airletters were photogravure-printed by McCorquodale & Co. Ltd., who also carried out the surcharging of SSA2/2a and the overprinting of SSA4. The "Postage Paid" roundels added to uprate air letters (for example SSA8) were printed locally.

SSA1

1969 (1 October). *Imprinted 9d. stamp showing St. Peter Port Harbour.*

SSA1	9d. blue	1·50	1·50
	a. Border round stamp	2·00	2·00

1971 (15 February). *SSA1 surcharged in decimal currency.*

SSA2	4p on 9d. blue	1·00	1·00
	a. Border round stamp	1·50	1·50

SSA3

1971 (1 July). *Imprinted 5p stamp showing Sark Harbour (design similar to* 1971 20p *definitive).*

SSA3   5p blue   .. ..   1·00   1·00

SSA4

1971 (11 September). *Diamond Jubilee of Guernsey Scout Association. SSA3 overprinted.*

SSA4   5p blue   .. ..   3·00   2·00

SSA5

1973 (3 March). *50th Anniversary of Rotary International in Guernsey. Imprinted 6½p stamp and Rotary emblem.*

SSA5	6½p gold and blue	.. ..	1·75	1·00

SSA6

1973 (7 March). *Large format. Imprinted 6½p stamp.*

SSA6	6½p blue	.. ..	1·00	60

1973 (10 September). *Provisional Airletters.*

SSA7	6p on 5p blue (SSA3 surcharged) ..	75	60
SSA8	7p blue (SSA6 with "Postage Paid ½p" roundel added)	75	60

As from 10 September 1973, SSA7 was sold with a 1p adhesive stamp attached (to uprate it to 7p) and SSA8 with a ½p adhesive attached (to uprate it to 7½p).

1974 (7 October). *Imprinted 6p and 7p stamps (designs similar to corresponding stamps in 1974 definitives).*

SSA9	6p blue (small format)	75	60
SSA10	7p blue (large format)	75	60

SSA9 and SSA10 exist in paler shades of blue.

1975 (17 March). *Provisional Airletters.*

SSA11	8½p blue (SSA9 with "Postage Paid 2½p" roundel added)	50	30
SSA12	9p blue (SSA10 with "2p Postage Paid" roundel added)	50	30
	a. Error. Printing missing but with uprating roundel	30·00	

Due to an increase in postal rates, SSA11 and SSA12 were from 29 September 1975 sold with a 2p "Militia" definitive stamp (S.G. 101) affixed to convert them to 10½p and 11p air letters respectively.

SSA13

1977 (2 August). *Imprinted* 10p *and* ½p *stamps (designs similar to corresponding values in* 1974 *"Militia" definitives).*

SSA13	10½p blue (small format)	20	20

Reply Coupons

These coupons are priced unused only, since to be used they have to be given up at a post office.

Commonwealth Reply Coupons

1969 (1 October)–70.

SSR1	7d. black on red ("CHANNEL ISLANDS" 27½mm long)	30	—
SSR2	7d. black on red ("CHANNEL ISLANDS" 30½mm long) (16 March 1970) ..	30	—
SSR3	7d. black on red ("CHANNEL ISLANDS" 26mm long) (October 1970)	30	—

1971 (15 February). *SSR2 surcharged in decimal currency, in violet.*
SSR4   3p on 7d. black on red   40   —

1971 (May). *Inscribed with both forms of currency.*
SSR5   7d./3p black on red   40   —

1971 (1 July)—73.
SSR6   4p black on red (inscription ends
          "... 5c")   15   —
SSR7   4p black on red (inscription ends
          "... 1972") (August 1973)   35   —

1973. *Provisional Coupons.*
SSR8   6p on 4p black on red (SSR7 with
          manuscript surcharge) (10 September
          1973)   20   —
SSR9   6p on 7p black on red (SSR7 with hand-
          stamped surcharge in black) (1973)   20   —
SSR10   6p on 4p black on red (SSR7 with hand-
          stamped surcharge in violet (1973) ..   20   —

1974 (August).
SSR11   6p black on red   20   —

1975 (17 March). *Provisional Coupon.*
SSR12   7p on 6p black on red (SSR11
          surcharged)   20   —

1975 (July).
SSR13   7p black on red   30   —

Owing to the abolition of the concessionary rate to Commonwealth countries, Guernsey Commonwealth Reply Coupons were withdrawn from sale on 31 October 1975.

International Reply Coupons

1969 (1 October).
SSR14   1s. 3d. blue and red   40   —

1971 (15 February). *Provisional Coupon.*
SSR15   6p on 1s. 3d. blue and red (SSR14
          surcharged in violet)   .. .. ..   2·50   —

1971 (1 July)—74.
SSR15   10p blue and red (inscription ends
          "... l'étranger")   20   —
SSR16   10p blue and red (inscription ends
          "... Surface/Taxe") (1 November
          1972)   20   —
SSR17   10p blue and red (inscription ends
          "... surface") (25 February 1974) ..   20   —

1974 (24 June). *Provisional Coupon.*
SSR18   13p on 10p blue and red (SSR17
          surcharged in black)   85   —

1975 (2 January).
SSR19   13p blue and red   30   —

1976 (5 January). *Provisional Coupon.*
SSR20   20p on 13p blue and red (SSR19
surcharged)   40   —

1976.
SSR20   20p blue and red   40   —

1977 (15 June). *Provisional Coupon.*
SSR21   25p on 20p blue and red (SSR20
surcharged)   40   —

Registered Envelopes

The registered envelopes sold by the Guernsey Post Office do not bear imprinted stamps and cost only a few pence each. This explains the low "unused" prices; used prices are for covers with adhesive postage stamps affixed and cancelled.

Envelopes SSE4/9 were printed by McCorquodale & Co. Ltd.

The standard sizes used are G (156 × 95mm), H (203 × 120mm) and K (292 × 152mm).

1969 (1 October). *Inscribed* "REGISTERED/LETTER/RECOMMANDÉ".
SSE1   Size G   60   3·00
SSE2   Size H   80   3·00
SSE3   Size K . .   . .   1·00   3·00

1971 (15 February). *SSE3 with adhesive label bearing decimal compensation details and minimum fee 20p.*
SSE4   Size G   50   3·00

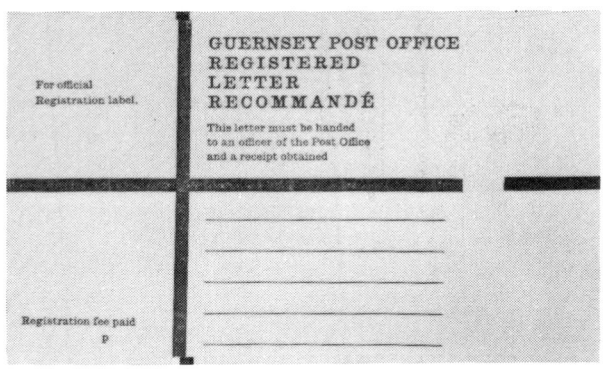

GUERNSEY POST OFFICE
REGISTERED
LETTER
RECOMMANDÉ

This letter must be handed
to an officer of the Post Office
and a receipt obtained

For official
Registration label.

Registration fee paid
p

SSE5

1971 (15 February)–73. *Inscribed* "GUERNSEY POST OFFICE/REGISTERED LETTER/ RECOMMANDÉ".

SSE5	Size G (1973)	35	2·00
SSE6	Size H	40	2·00
	a. Reprint with deep blue lines (1973) ..	40	2·00
SSE7	Size K	50	2·00

1974. *Change to white manila paper with blue lining. Inscribed as* SSE5/6.

SSE8	Size G (February 1974)	30	2·00
SSE9	Size H (June 1974)	30	2·00
SSE10	Size K (1974)	30	2·00

1975. *Envelopes now indicate minimum fee of 25p.*

SSE11	Size G	30	1·00
SSE12	Size H	30	1·00
SSE13	Size K	50	1·50

1975. SSE10/12 *with adhesive label on back indicating minimum fee of 45p.*

SSE14	Size G	20	1·00
SSE15	Size H	20	1·00
SSE16	Size K	20	1·00

1976 (May). SSE13/14 *with small adhesive label raising compensation on registered letters to other countries to £7.*

SSE17	Size G	15	1·00
SSE18	Size H	15	1·00

1976 (December). SSE17 *with additional label again altering rates of compensation.*

SSE19	Size G	15	1·00

1977 (May). *As* SSE18 *and* SSE17 *but text formerly on labels now printed directly on envelopes.*

SSE20	Size H	15	1·00
SSE21	Size K	15	1·00

Official Postal Stationery

This stationery is priced used only; prices for SSO4/7 are for "used on cover".

Envelope with Arms of Guernsey with "POSTAGE PAID" below in a box in black.

1969 (1 October).

SSO1	Four sizes	*each*	—	5

Philatelic Bureau Envelope with Guernsey map frank in blue.

1969 (1 October).

SSO2	One size	—	5

Registered Envelope with Guernsey map frank in blue.

1969 (1 October).

SSO3	One size	—	20

Adhesive Labels bearing franks as on SSO1/3.

1969 (1 October)–73.

SSO4	As frank on SSO1	—	5
SSO5	As frank on SSO2 (reading "Philatelic Bureau")	—	5
SSO6	As frank on SSO3 (reading "Guernsey Post Office")	—	25
SSO7	As SSO6 but with large sans serif lettering	—	20

B. JERSEY

JS 15 Elizabeth Castle

JS 16 La Hougue Bie (prehistoric tomb)

JS 17 Portelet Bay

JS 18 La Corbière Lighthouse

JS 19 Mont Orgueil Castle by Night

JS 20 Arms and Royal Mace

JS 21 Jersey Cow

JS 22 Chart of the English Channel

JS 23   Mont Orgueil Castle by Day

JS 25   Jersey Airport

JS 24   Queen Eliza-
beth II (after Cecil
Beaton)

JS 26   Legislative Chamber

JS 27   The Royal Court

JS 28   Queen Eliza-
beth II (after Cecil
Beaton)

(Designed V. Whiteley)
(Printed in photogravure by Harrison (½d. to 1s. 9d.) or Courvoisier (others))

1969 (1 Oct)–70. *Granite paper (2s. 6d. to £1). Multicoloured; frame colours given.* P 14 (½d. *to* 1s. 9d.) *or* 12 (*others*), *all comb.*

15	**JS 15**	½d. ochre (a)		30	35
		Sa. Thick paper (a)		1·50	2·00
16	**JS 16**	1d. brown (abc)		25	20
		Sb. Thick paper (a)		40	50
17	**JS 17**	2d. claret (a)		10	12
		Sa. Thinner paper (bc)		15	10
18	**JS 18**	3d. ultramarine (a)		10	15
		Sa. Thinner paper (d)		40	40
		Sb. orange omitted	90·00		
19	**JS 19**	4d. yellow-olive (a)		10	10
		V221. Blotch on castle wall ..	3·00		
		Sb. Thinner paper (c)		30	30
20	**JS 20**	5d. bistre (a)		20	12
		Sa. Thinner paper (c)		30	30
21	**JS 21**	6d. yellow-brown (ab)		50	75
		Sa. Thinner paper (e)		4·50	3·50
22	**JS 22**	9d. orange-brown (a)		1·00	1·25
		Sa. Thinner paper (d)		2·00	1·50
23	**JS 23**	1s. reddish lilac (a)		1·00	1·00
		Sa. Thinner paper (c)		2·00	1·50
24	**JS 22**	1s. 6d. myrtle-green (a)		1·50	1·75
		Sa. Thinner paper (d)		1·75	1·50
25	**JS 24**	1s. 9d. pale myrtle-green (a)		1·75	1·75
		Sa. Thinner paper (c)		9·00	8·00
26	**JS 25**	2s. 6d. black and pale mauve (a) ..		2·50	3·50
27	**JS 26**	5s. black and pale blue (a)		20·00	17·00
28	**JS 27**	10s. black & pale slate-blue (a) ..		35·00	28·00
		a. Error. Green border*	£2250		–
29	**JS 28**	£1 pale bistre (af)†		2·00	2·50

First Day Covers (Nos. 15/29) (3)	50·00
Presentation Packs (Nos. 15/19) (3)	60·00

* During the final printing of the 10s. a sheet was printed in the colours of the 50p, No. 56, i.e. green border instead of slate.

† Printing (f) is the decimal issue which can be positively distinguished from the inscriptions in the left sheet margin which read "Sheet value £25" at bottom and "Value per row £5" at top instead of "Sheet value £25 0s. 0d." and "Value per row £5 0s. 0d." respectively. It exists with more blue in the Queen's dress and less red in the drapery but this printing also includes intermediate shades close to printing (a).

No. 16Sb, the thick paper variety, comes from sheets used for Booklets B2 and B3.

The thinner paper varieties result from a deliberate change as the thicker paper did not adhere well; they may be further distinguished by the gum which is white instead of creamy.

Used copies of the 5d. are known with either the gold or the yellow omitted.

There are a number of shades in this issue which are in part due to the variation in the paper.

There was no postal need for the ½d. value as the ½d. coin had been withdrawn prior to its issue in anticipation of decimalisation.

Printings:

(a) 1.10.69	(b) 18.2.70	(c) 15.4.70	(d) 5.5.70
(e) 27. 5.70	(f) 3.73		

Variety

V221
4d. Black blotch on
castle wall (Pl. 1A, R.
4/2).

CYLINDER NUMBERS
(Blocks of four)

½d.	1A (×5)	..	1·75	9d.	1A (×6)	..	6·00
1d.	1A (×5)	..	1·50	1s.	1A (×5)	..	6·00
2d.	1A (×5)	..	60	1s. 6d.	1A (×6)	..	9·00
3d.	1A (×7)	..	60	1s. 9d.	1A (×6)	..	10·00
4d.	1A (×5)	..	60	2s. 6d. to £1 None		
5d.	1A (×6)	..	1·25			
6d.	1A (×6)	..	3·00			

BOOKLET PANES

A. From specially produced sheets of 48
The individual stamps are surrounded by blank margins and exist with three margins
when detached from the booklet or with four when complete.

Booklet pane with complete margins

Issued in Booklet B1:

Face value	Cat. No.		
1d.	16a. Booklet stamp with margins		
	(a)	50	60
	a.V258. Break in tree trunk	3·00	
4d.	19a. Booklet stamp with margins		
	(a)	50	50
	a.V222. Redrawn imprint	8·50	

Varieties

Normal

V222

V258
1d. Break in trunk of
tree over 2nd "E" of
"JERSEY" (Booklet
stamp).

4d. Imprint redrawn, the lettering being heavier and less even.
(Booklet stamp)

B. From normal sheets

The stamps used in the 7s. and 10s. booklets were taken from ordinary sheets of
stamps, the first and last vertical rows being utilised. Listings are for vertical pairs with
margin at left or right, showing stitch marks. These panes are priced in mint condition
only.

Issued in Booklets B2/3:

Face value	Cat. No.		
1d.	16Sba.	Booklet pane. No. 16Sb × 2	
		(a)	1·25
	16Sc.	Booklet pane. No. 16 × 2 (d)	70
4d.	19Sc.	Booklet pane. No. 19 × 2 (a)	35
	19Sba.	Booklet pane. No. 19Sb × 2	
		(d)	90
5d.	20Sb.	Booklet pane. No. 20 × 2 (a)	45
	20Sab.	Booklet pane. No. 20Sa × 2	
		(d)	90

Nos. 16Sc, 19Sba and 20Sab come from Booklets B2a/3a.

SET INFORMATION

Sheets: 60 (6 × 10) ½d. to 1s. 6d.; (10 × 6) 1s. 9d.; 25 (5 × 5) 2s. 6d. to £1.
Quantities sold:

½d.	999,439	5d.	4,886,016	1s. 9d.	306,674
1d.	1,050,124	6d.	550,766	2s. 6d.	244,894
2d.	726,837	9d.	954,649	5s.	206,629
3d.	635,019	1s.	577,086	10s.	179,981
4d.	7,148,849	1s. 6d.	419,872		

Sold out: 10.69 ½d.
Withdrawn: 14.2.72 (except ½d., sold out 10.69, and £1 withdrawn 31.8.77).

JS 29   First Day Cover

(Designed by R. G. Sellar)
(Printed in photogravure by Harrison)

1969 (1 Oct). Inauguration of Post Office. *Multicoloured; background colours given.* P 14 (C).

30	**JS 29**	4d. magenta	25	25
31		5d. new blue	50	50
32		1s. 6d. red-brown	3·50	4·00
33		1s. 9d. bright emerald	3·50	4·00

First Day Cover (Nos. 30/3)	8·50
Presentation Pack (Nos. 30/3)	10·00

CYLINDER NUMBERS
(Blocks of four)

4d.	1A (×4)	..	1·50	1s. 6d. 1A (×4)	..	21·00
5d.	1A (×4)	..	3·00	1s. 9d. 1A (×4)	..	21·00

Sheets: 60 (6 × 10).
Quantities sold: 4d. 1,483,686; 5d. 742,820; 1s. 6d. 272,155; 1s. 9d. 238,856.
Withdrawn: 1.10.70.

JS 30 "Lord Coutanche" (Sir James Gunn)

JS 31 "Sir Winston Churchill (D. van Praag)

JS 32 "Liberation" (Edmund Blampied)

JS 33 "S.S. *Vega*" (unknown artist)

(Designed (from paintings) by Rosalind Dease)
(Printed in photogravure by Courvoisier)

1970 (9 May). 25th Anniversary of Liberation. *Granite paper. P* 11½ (C).

34	**JS 30**	4d. multicoloured		20	20
35	**JS 31**	5d. multicoloured		30	25
36	**JS 32**	1s. 6d. multicoloured		3·25	3·00
37	**JS 33**	1s. 9d. multicoloured		3·25	3·00

First Day Cover (Nos. 34/7)	6·00
Presentation Pack (*pack printed in gold and blue-green*) (Nos. 34/7)	10·00
Presentation Pack (*pack printed in gold, red and blue-green on olive—as presented to Jersey school children*) (Nos. 34/7)	15·00

Sheets: 50 (10 × 5) 4d., 5d.; (5 × 10) 1s. 6d., 1s. 9d.
Quantities sold: 4d. 1,617,751; 5d. 1,296,678; 1s. 6d. 334,468; 1s. 9d. 319,893.
Withdrawn: 9.5.71.

JS 34   "A Tribute to Enid Blyton"

JS 35   "Rags to Riches"

JS 36   "Gourmet's Delight"

JS 37   "We're the Greatest"

(Designed by Jennifer Toombs)
(Printed in photogravure by Courvoisier)

1970 (28 July). "Battle of Flowers" Parade. *Granite paper. P* 11½ (C).

38	**JS 34**	4d. multicoloured	..	..	..	20	20
39	**JS 35**	5d. multicoloured	..	..	..	30	20
40	**JS 36**	1s. 6d. multicoloured	..	..	10·00	5·00
41	**JS 37**	1s. 9d. multicoloured	..	..	10·00	5·00

First Day Cover (Nos. 38/41)	10·00
Presentation Pack (Nos. 38/41)	25·00

Sheets: 50 (5 × 10).
Quantities sold: 4d. 1,905,109; 5d. 1,498,301; 1s. 6d. 262,072; 1s. 9d. 231,077.
Withdrawn: 27.7.71.

JS 38 Martello Tower, Archirondel

JS 39 Jersey Airport

(Designed by V. Whiteley)
(Printed in photogravure by Harrison (½ to 9p) or Courvoisier (others))

1970 (1 Oct)–74. Decimal Currency. *Designs as before, except for 6p, but inscribed with face values in decimal currency as in Type* **JS 39.** *Granite paper* (10, 20, 50p). *Multicoloured; frame colours given.* P 14 (½ to 9p) *or* 12 (*others*), *all comb.*

42	**JS 15**	½p ochre (*bhl*)	.. ..	8	8
		V302. Two spots over castle	..	75	
43	**JS 18**	1p ultramarine (*bo*)	.. .. ..	5	5
44	**JS 21**	1½p yellow-brown (*b*)	.. .. ..	5	5
45	**JS 19**	2p yellow-olive (*b*)	.. .. ..	5	5
46	**JS 20**	2½p bistre (*bl*)	.. ..	8	8
47	**JS 16**	3p brown (*bdi*)	.. ..	10	10
48	**JS 17**	3½p claret (*bi*)	.. ..	12	12
49	**JS 22**	4p orange-brown (*bgjnp*)	.. ..	12	12
49*a*	**JS 20**	4½p bistre (*k*)	.. .. ..	10	10
50	**JS 23**	5p reddish lilac (*blnp*)	.. .. ..	15	12
50*a*	**JS 21**	5½p magenta (*k*)	.. ..	12	12
51	**JS 38**	6p blue-green (*b*) ..	.. .. ..	15	15
52	**JS 22**	7½p myrtle-green (*b*)	.. .. ..	20	20
		V272. Missing lock of hair	..	50	
52*a*	**JS 19**	8p bright yellow (*k*)	.. .. ..	20	20
53	**JS 24**	9p pale myrtle-green (*b*)	.. ..	25	25
54	**JS 39**	10p black and pale mauve (*aei*)	..	30	30
55	**JS 26**	20p black and pale blue (*aei*) ..	..	50	50
56	**JS 27**	50p black and green (*am*)	.. ..	1·50	1·50

First Day Covers (Nos. 42/56) (3)	6·00
Presentation Packs (Nos. 29, 42/56)	
(*a*) Small format (4¼ × 5½ in.) (4)	6·00
(*b*) Large format (8½ × 4½ in.) (3)	4·00

The larger type of Presentation Pack, introduced during 1975, also has punched holes to enable it to be stored in a ring binder. Of the four packs in this series, that containing the 5p to 9p values was not produced in the larger size. It was replaced by a pack containing the 4½p to 9p values, which does exist in both sizes.

A number of different gums can be found on this issue. With the exception of the Courvoisier printings, which have gum arabic, all are of the PVA group with printings from 1974 having dextrin added.

Printings:

(*a*) 1.10.70	(*b*) 15. 2.71	(*c*) 15. 5.72 (booklets)	(*d*) 1. 8.72
(*e*) 15.11.72	(*f*) 1.12.72 (booklets)	(*g*) 1.10.73	(*h*) 3.12.73
(*i*) 1. 7.74	(*j*) 12. 8.74	(*k*) 31.10.74	(*l*) 1.11.74
(*m*) 28. 1.75	(*n*) 1. 4.75	(*o*) 21. 4.75	(*p*) 30.10.75

Varieties

V302
½p. Two coloured spots
over castle (Pl. 1A, R.
5/5).

V272
7½p. White flaw in
Queen's hair by ear
appearing as missing
lock (Pl. 1A, R. 2/4).

CYLINDER NUMBERS
(Blocks of four)

½p	1A (×5)	50	4½p 1A (×6)	60
1p	1A (×7)	25	5p 1A (×5)	90
	2A–1A (×6) (*n*)	25	2A–1A (×4) (*mo*)	90
1½p	1A (×6)	30	5½p 1A (×6)	75
2p	1A (×5)	35	6p 1A (×5)	90
2½p	1A (×6)	50	7½p 1A (×6)	1·25
3p	1A (×5)	60	8p 1A (×5)	1·25
	1A (×4)–2A (*i*)	60	9p 1A (×6)	1·50
3½p	1A (×5)	75	10p to 50p None	
4p	1A (×6)	75		
	2A–1A (×5) (*mo*)	75		

BOOKLET PANES
A. From specially produced sheets of 48

Sheets printed from these special booklet cylinders showed the stamps arranged in blocks of four, each block surrounded by perforated margins. When the stamps were separated into the individual booklet panes this resulted in two types, with margins at left and bottom, and with margins at left and top.

Type I. Margin at bottom

Type II. Margin at top

Issued in Booklets B4 (½, 2, 2½p), B10/11 (½, 2½, 3p), B18, B22 (3, 3½p), B21 (½, 3, 3½p):

Face value	Cat. No.				
½p	42a. Booklet stamp with margins				
	(Type I) (b)	..	.. ..	60	60
	Sab. Type II	..	.. ..	60	60
2p	45a. Booklet stamp with margins				
	(Type I) (b)	..	.. ..	50	50
	Sab. Type II	..	.. ..	50	50
2½p	46a. Booklet stamp with margins				
	(Type I) (b)	..	.. ..	60	60
	ab. Gold (mace) omitted		..	£200	
	ac. Gold (mace) ptd. double		..	£150	
	Sad. Type II	..	.. ..	60	60
3p	47a. Booklet stamp with margins				
	(Type I) (f)	..	.. ..	25	25
	Sab. Type II	..	.. ..	25	25
3½p	48a. Booklet stamp with margins				
	(Type I) (i)	..	.. ..	25	25
	Sab. Type II	..	.. ..	25	25

B. From normal sheets

Stamp booklets, other than those with single stamp panes were made up from normal sheet stock, utilising the first and last vertical rows or, in the case of Booklet B24, the first two and the last two vertical rows. Listings are for pairs or blocks (from B24) with margin at left or right, showing stitch marks. These panes are priced in mint condition only.

Vertical pairs. Issued in Booklets B5/6 (2, 2½p); B7, B12, B15 (2½p); B8, B13, B16 (3p); B9, B14, B17 (2½, 3p); B19/20 (3, 3½p); B23 (1, 4, 5p):

Face value	Cat. No.		
1p	43Sa. Booklet pane. No. 43 ×2 (n)	..	8
2p	45Sb. Booklet pane. No. 45 ×2 (b)	..	40
2½p	46Sb. Booklet pane. No. 46 ×2 (b)	..	40
3p	47Sb. Booklet pane. No. 47 ×2 (c)	..	40
3½p	48Sb. Booklet pane. No. 48 ×2 (i)	..	45
4p	49Sa. Booklet pane. No. 49 ×2 (n)	..	25
5p	50Sa. Booklet pane. No. 50 ×2 (n)	..	35

Blocks of Four. Issued in Booklet B24:

Face value	Cat. No.		
1p	43Sb. Booklet pane. No. 43 ×4 (*n*)	..	10
4p	49Sb. Booklet pane. No. 49 ×4 (*n*)	..	40
5p	50Sb. Booklet pane. No. 50 ×4 (*n*)	..	50

Sheets: 50 (5 × 10) $\frac{1}{2}$p to 8p; (10 × 5) 9p; 25 (5 × 5) 10p to 50p.
Withdrawn: 31.1.77 ($\frac{1}{2}$ to 9p); 31.8.77 (others).

JS 40   White-eared
Pheasant

JS 41   Thick-billed
Parrot

JS 42   Ursine Colo-
bus Monkey

JS 43   Ring-tailed
Lemur

(Designed by Jennifer Toombs)
(Printed in photogravure by Courvoisier)

1971 (12 Mar). Wildlife Preservation Trust (1st series). *Granite paper. P* $11\frac{1}{2}$ (C).

57	**JS 40**	2p multicoloured	..	..	..	..	60	20
58	**JS 41**	2$\frac{1}{2}$p multicoloured	..	..	..	..	60	25
59	**JS 42**	7$\frac{1}{2}$p multicoloured	..	..	..	.. 13·00	5·00
60	**JS 43**	9p multicoloured	..	..	..	.. 13·00	5·00

First Day Cover (Nos. 57/60)	..	..	..	..	10·00
Presentation Pack (Nos. 57/60)		..	..	..	30·00

Sheets: 50 (5 × 10) 2p, 9p; (10 × 5) others.
Quantities sold: 2p 1,025,544; 2$\frac{1}{2}$p 1,363,427; 7$\frac{1}{2}$p 233,147; 9p 220,710.
Withdrawn: 11.3.72.

JS 44 Royal British
Legion Badge

JS 45 Poppy Emblem
and Field

JS 46 Jack Counter
V.C. and Victoria
Cross

JS 47 Crossed Tri-
colour and Union Jack

(Designed by G. Drummond)
(Printed in lithography by Questa)

1971 (15 June). 50th Anniversary of Royal British Legion. *P* 14 (C).

61	**JS 44**	2p multicoloured	..	..	25	15
62	**JS 45**	2½p multicoloured	..	..	25	20
63	**JS 46**	7½p multicoloured	..	..	5·50	4·00
		V259. Spot over pocket	..	..	10·00	
64	**JS 47**	9p multicoloured	..	..	5·50	4·00
		V260. Green flaw	..	..	10·00	

First Day Cover (Nos. 61/4)	..	..	8·00
Presentation Pack (Nos. 61/4)	..	..	14·00

Varieties

V259
7½p Black spot over
soldier's right-hand
pocket (Pl. 1B, R. 9/4)

V260
9p Pale green spot
above intersection of
flag-poles (Pl. 1B, R.
2/5)

PLATE NUMBERS
(Blocks of four)

2p	1A (×4)	..	1·50	7½p 1A (×5)	..	33·00
	1B (×4) ..	..	1·50	1B (×5) ..	..	33·00
2½p	1A (×4)	..	1·50	9p 1A (×5)	..	33·00
	1B (×4) ..	..	1·50	1B (×5) ..	..	33·00

Sheets: 50 (5 × 10).
Imprint: Right-hand corner, bottom margin.
Quantities sold: 2p 1,381,873; 2½p 1,529,866; 7½p 239,477; 9p 226,407.
Withdrawn: 14.6.72.

JS 48 "Tante Eliza-
beth" (E. Blampied)

JS 49 "English Fleet
in the Channel" (P.
Monamy)

JS 50 "The Boyhood
of Raleigh" (Sir John
Millais)

JS 51 "The Blind
Beggar" (W. W.
Ouless)

(Designed and printed in photogravure by Courvoisier)

1971 (5 Oct). Paintings (1st series). *Granite paper.* P 11½ (C).

65	**JS 48**	2p multicoloured	.. ..	15	15
66	**JS 49**	2½p multicoloured	.. ..	20	20
67	**JS 50**	7½p multicoloured	.. ..	5·00	4·00
68	**JS 51**	9p multicoloured	.. ..	5·00	4·00

First Day Cover (Nos. 65/8)	8·00
Presentation Pack (Nos. 65/8)	14·00

Sheets: 50 (5 × 10) 2p, 9p; (10 × 5) others.
Quantities sold: 2p 1,243,198; 2½p 1,490,595; 7½p 264,532; 9p 251,770.
Withdrawn: 4.10.72.

JS 52 Jersey Fern

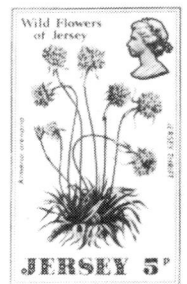

JS 53 Jersey Thrift

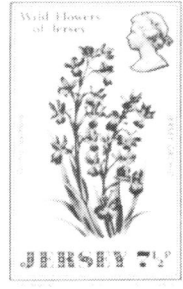

JS 54 Jersey Orchid

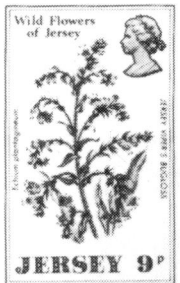

JS 55 Jersey Viper's
Bugloss

(Designed by G. Drummond)
(Printed in photogravure by Courvoisier)

1972 (18 Jan). Wild Flowers of Jersey. *Granite paper. P* 11½ (C).

69	**JS 52**	3p multicoloured	..	..	..	..	15	15
70	**JS 53**	5p multicoloured	..	..	..	..	1·00	1·00
71	**JS 54**	7½p multicoloured	..	..	..	..	5·00	4·50
72	**JS 55**	9p multicoloured	..	..	..	..	5·00	4·50

First Day Cover (Nos. 69/72)	9·00
Presentation Pack (Nos. 69/72)	13·00

Sheets: 50 (5 × 10).
Quantities sold: 3p 1,124,878; 5p 332,764; 7½p 202,404; 9p 196,998.
Withdrawn: 17.1.73.

JS 56   Cheetah

JS 57   Rothschild's
Mynah

JS 58   Spectacled Bear

JS 59   Tuatara Lizard

(Designed by Jennifer Toombs)
(Printed in photogravure by Courvoisier)

1972 (17 Mar). Wildlife Preservation Trust (2nd series). *Granite paper. P* 11½ (C).

73	**JS 56**	2½p multicoloured	..	..	..	15	15
74	**JS 57**	3p multicoloured	..	..	..	20	20
75	**JS 58**	7½p multicoloured	..	..	..	2·50	2·00
76	**JS 59**	9p multicoloured	..	..	..	2·50	2·00

First Day Cover (Nos. 73/6)	4·00
Presentation Pack (Nos. 73/6)	7·00

Sheets: 50 (10 × 5) 3p; (5 × 10) others.
Quantities sold: 2½p 1,223,916; 3p 1,631,752; 7½p 279,935; 9p 235,968.
Withdrawn: 16.3.73.

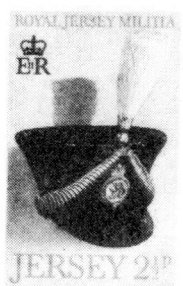

JS 60   Artillery Shako

JS 61   Shako (2nd
North Regiment

JS 62   Shako
(5th South-West Regi-
ment)

JS 63   Helmet (3rd
Jersey Light Infantry)

(Designed and printed in photogravure by Courvoisier)

1972 (27 June). Royal Jersey Militia. *Granite paper. P* $11\frac{1}{2}$ (C).

77	**JS 60**	$2\frac{1}{2}$p	multicoloured	..	..	..	..	15	15
78	**JS 61**	3p	multicoloured	..	..	..	..	20	20
79	**JS 62**	$7\frac{1}{2}$p	multicoloured	..	..	..	..	2·25	2·25
80	**JS 63**	9p	multicoloured	..	..	..	..	2·25	2·25

First Day Cover (Nos. 77/80)	..	..	..	..	5·00
Presentation Pack (Nos. 77/80)		..	..	..	8·00

Sheets: 50 (10 × 5).
Quantities sold: $2\frac{1}{2}$p 1,240,393; 3p 1,857,224; $7\frac{1}{2}$p 300,554; 9p 271,832.
Withdrawn: 26.6.73.

JS 64   Princess Anne

JS 65   Queen Elizabeth and Prince Philip

JS 66   Prince Charles

JS 67   Royal Family

(Designed by G. Drummond, from photographs by D. Groves)
(Printed in photogravure by Courvoisier)

1972 (1 Nov). Royal Silver Wedding. *Granite paper. P* 11½ (C).

81	**JS 64**	2½p multicoloured	.. ..	10	5
82	**JS 65**	3p multicoloured	.. ..	10	10
83	**JS 66**	7½p multicoloured	.. ..	60	65
84	**JS 67**	20p multicoloured	.. ..	60	75

First Day Cover (Nos. 81/4)	.. ..	2·00
Presentation Pack (Nos. 81/4)	.. ..	3·00

Sheets: 25 (5 × 5).
Quantities sold: 2½p 1,743,240; 3p 1,638,566; 7½p 424,029; 20p 418,824.
Sold out: by 23.1.73 (7½p, 20p); 16.5.73 (3p).
Withdrawn: 31.10.73 (2½p).

JS 68 Silver Wine
Cup and Christening
Cup

JS 69 Gold Torque

JS 70 Royal Seal of
Charles II

JS 71 Armorican
Bronze Coins

(Designed by G. Drummond)
(Printed in photogravure by Courvoisier)

1973 (23 Jan). Centenary of La Société Jersiaise. *Granite paper. P* 11½ (C).

85	**JS 68**	2½p multicoloured	.. ..	15	15
86	**JS 69**	3p multicoloured	.. ..	20	20
87	**JS 70**	7½p multicoloured	.. ..	1·00	1·00
88	**JS 71**	9p multicoloured	.. ..	1·00	1·00

First Day Cover (Nos. 85/8)	.. ..	2·00
Presentation Pack (Nos. 85/8)	.. ..	3·00

Sheets: 50 (5 × 10) 2½p, 9p; (10 × 5) others.
Quantities sold: 2½p 2,008,923; 3p 2,437,421; 7½p 363,543; 9p 327,917.
Withdrawn: 22.1.74 (7½p sold out by 31.10.73).

JS 72   Paris Balloon
Post, 1870

JS 73   "Astra" Sea-
plane, 1912

JS 74   Supermarine
"Sea Eagle", 1923

JS 75   De Havilland
"Express", 1935

(Designed and printed in photogravure by Courvoisier)

1973 (16 May). Aviation History. *Granite paper. P* 11½ (C).

89	**JS 72**	3p multicoloured	.. ..	15	15
90	**JS 73**	5p multicoloured	.. ..	20	20
91	**JS 74**	7½p multicoloured	.. ..	1·00	1·00
92	**JS 75**	9p multicoloured	.. ..	1·00	1·00

First Day Cover (Nos. 89/92)	.. ..	2·25
Presentation Pack (Nos. 89/92)	.. .. ..	2·50

Sheets: 50 (5 × 10).
Quantities sold: 3p 3,085,497; 5p 641,583; 7½p 368,069; 9p 356,379.
Withdrawn: 15.5.74 (7½p sold out by 31.10.73).

JS 76 "North Western"

JS 77 "Calvados"

JS 78 "Carteret"

JS 79 "Caesarea"

(Designed by G. Drummond)
(Printed in photogravure by Courvoisier)

1973 (6 Aug). Centenary of Jersey Eastern Railway. *Granite paper. P* 11½ (C).

93	**JS 76**	2½p multicoloured	..	.. .. ..	15	15
94	**JS 77**	3p multicoloured	..	.. .. ..	20	20
95	**JS 78**	7½p multicoloured	..	.. .. ..	85	85
96	**JS 79**	9p multicoloured	..	.. .. ..	85	85

First Day Cover (Nos. 93/6)	.. ..	1·75
Presentation Pack (Nos. 93/6) ..	.. .. ..	2·50

Sheets: 50 (5 × 10).
Quantities sold: 2½p 1,591,063; 3p 3,051,097; 7½p 396,919; 9p 365,310.
Withdrawn: 5.8.74 (7½p sold out by 31.10.73).

JS 80 Princess Anne
and Captain Mark
Phillips
(Designed and printed in photogravure by Courvoisier)

1973 (14 Nov). Royal Wedding. *Granite paper.* $P\ 11\frac{1}{2}$ (C).

97	**JS 80**	3p multicoloured	.. ..	8	8
98		20p multicoloured	.. ..	85	85

First Day Cover (Nos. 97/8)	.. ..	1·50
Presentation Pack (Nos. 97/8)	.. ..	1·50

Sheets: 25 (5 × 5).
Quantities sold: 3p 1,988,407; 20p 522,793.
Withdrawn: 30.11.74.

JS 81   Spider Crab

JS 82   Conger Eel

JS 83   Lobster

JS 84   Ormer

(Designed by Jennifer Toombs)
(Printed in photogravure by Courvoisier)

1973 (15 Nov). Marine Life. *Granite paper.* $P\ 11\frac{1}{2}$ (C).

99	**JS 81**	2½p multicoloured	.. ..	8	8
100	**JS 82**	3p multicoloured	.. ..	10	10
101	**JS 83**	7½p multicoloured	.. ..	35	45
102	**JS 84**	20p multicoloured	.. ..	35	45

First Day Cover (Nos. 99/102)	.. .. ..	1·50
Presentation Pack (Nos. 99/102)	.. .. ..	1·25

Sheets: 50 (5 × 10).
Quantities sold: 2½p 1,596,526; 3p 1,243,541; 7½p 501,541; 20p 517,440.
Withdrawn: 30.11.74 (7½p sold out by 28.2.74).

JS 85 Freesias

JS 86 Anemones

JS 87 Carnations and Gladioli

JS 88 Daffodils and Iris

(Designed by G. Drummond)
(Printed in photogravure by Courvoisier)

1974 (13 Feb). Spring Flowers. *Granite paper.* P $11\frac{1}{2}$ (C).

103	**JS 85**	3p multicoloured	..	..	..	8	8
104	**JS 86**	5½p multicoloured	..	..	..	12	12
105	**JS 87**	8p multicoloured	..	..	..	25	45
106	**JS 88**	10p multicoloured	..	..	..	25	45

First Day cover (Nos. 103/6)	..	1·00
Presentation Pack (Nos. 103/6)	..	1·00

Sheets: 50 (10 × 5).
Quantities sold: 3p 1,239,968; 5½p 590,376; 8p 475,665; 10p 507,542.
Withdrawn: 28.2.75.

JS 89 First U.K.
Pillar-box and Con-
temporary Cover

JS 90 Jersey Post-
men, 1862 and 1969

JS 91 Modern Pillar-
box and Cover

JS 92 Mail Trans-
port, 1874 and 1974

(Designed by G. Drummond)
(Printed in photogravure by Courvoisier)

1974 (7 June). Centenary of Universal Postal Union. *Granite paper. P* $11\frac{1}{2}$ (C).

107	**JS 89**	2½p multicoloured	5	5
108	**JS 90**	3p multicoloured	8	8
109	**JS 91**	5½p multicoloured	20	20
110	**JS 92**	20p multicoloured	80	80

First Day Cover (Nos. 107/10)	.. .. ..	1·00
Presentation Pack (Nos. 107/10)	.. .. ..	1·25

Sheets: 50 (5 × 10).
Quantities sold: 2½p 461,174; 3p 1,380,018; 5½p 421,674; 20p 386,348.
Withdrawn: 30.6.75.

JS 93 John Wesley

JS 94 Sir William Hillary (founder)

JS 95 Canon Wace (poet and historian)

JS 96 Sir Winston Churchill

(Designed, engraved and recess-printed by De La Rue)

1974 (31 July). Anniversaries. *P* 13 × 14 (C).

111	**JS 93**	3p	light cinnamon and black	5	8
112	**JS 94**	3½p	light azure and black	8	8
113	**JS 95**	8p	light mauve and deep ultramarine	20	20
114	**JS 96**	20p	pinkish stone and black	80	80

First Day Cover (Nos. 111/14)	.. .. ..	1·00
Presentation Pack (Nos. 111/14)	.. .. ..	1·25

Events: 3p Bicentenary of Methodism in Jersey; 3½p 150th anniversary of Royal National Lifeboat Institution; 8p 800th death anniversary; 20p Birth centenary.

PLATE NUMBERS
(Blocks of four)

3p 1A–1A	30	8p 1A–1A	1·25
1B–1B	30	1B–1B	1·25
3½p 1A–1A	50	2A–1A	1·25
1B–1B	50	2B–1B	1·25
2A–1A	50	20p 1A–1A	5·00
2B–1B	50	1B–1B	5·00

Sheets: 50 (10 × 5).
Imprint: Right-hand corner, bottom margin.
Quantities sold: 3p 908,852; 3½p 2,355,391; 8p 338,397; 20p 409,291.
Withdrawn: 31.7.75.

JS 97   Royal Yacht

JS 98   French Two-
decker

JS 99   Dutch Vessel

JS 100   Battle of Cap La Hague

(Designed (from paintings by Peter Monamy) and printed in photogravure by
Courvoisier)

1974 (22 Nov). Paintings (2nd series). *Granite paper. P* 11½ (C).

115	**JS 97**	3½p multicoloured	.. .. ..	8	8
116	**JS 98**	5½p multicoloured	.. .. ..	12	12
117	**JS 99**	8p multicoloured	.. .. ..	40	40
118	**JS 100**	25p multicoloured	.. .. ..	80	80

First Day Cover (Nos. 115/18)	.. .. ..	1·25
Presentation Pack (Nos. 115/18)	.. .. ..	1·40

Sheets: 50 (10 × 5) 8p; (5 × 10) others.
Quantities sold: 3½p 1,670,994; 5½p 448,137; 8p 416,296; 25p 415,991.
Withdrawn: 30.11.75.

JS 101   Potato Digger

JS 102   Cider Crusher

JS 103   Six-horse Plough

JS 104   Hay Cart

(Designed by G. Drummond)
(Printed in photogravure by Courvoisier)

1975 (25 Feb). 19th-Century Farming. *Granite paper. P* 11½ (C).

119	**JS 101**	3p multicoloured	.. .. ..	5	5
120	**JS 102**	3½p multicoloured	.. .. ..	8	8
121	**JS 103**	8p multicoloured	.. .. ..	20	20
122	**JS 104**	10p multicoloured	.. .. ..	30	30

First Day Cover (Nos. 119/22)	.. .. ..	70
Presentation Pack (Nos. 119/22)	.. .. ..	80

Sheets: 50 (5 × 10).
Quantities sold: 3p 588,185; 3½p 1,025,295; 8p 432,432; 10p 457,196.
Withdrawn: 28.2.76.

JS 105 H.M. Queen
Elizabeth, the Queen
Mother (photograph by
Cecil Beaton)

(Designed and printed in photogravure by Courvoisier)

1975 (30 May). Royal Visit. *Granite paper.* P 11½ (C).

123	**JS 105**	20p multicoloured	.. .. ..	45	45

First Day Cover (No. 123)	.. ..	65
Presentation Pack (No. 123)	.. ..	60

CYLINDER NUMBERS
(Blocks of four)

20p	A1–1–1–1–1	2·50
	B1–1–1–1–1	2·50

Sheets: 25 (5 × 5).
Quantity sold: 572,675.
Withdrawn: 31.5.76.

JS 106   Shell

JS 107   Parasol

JS 108   Deckchair

JS 109   Sandcastle
with Flags of Jersey
and the U.K.

(Designed (from holiday posters) by A. Games)
(Printed in photogravure by Courvoisier)

1975 (6 June). Jersey Tourism. *Granite paper. P* 11½ (C).

124	**JS 106**	5p	multicoloured	..	..	..	10	12
125	**JS 107**	8p	multicoloured	..	..	..	15	20
126	**JS 108**	10p	multicoloured	..	..	..	20	20
127	**JS 109**	12p	multicoloured	..	..	..	30	30

First Day Cover (Nos. 124/7)	75
Presentation Pack (Nos. 124/7)	90

CYLINDER NUMBERS
(Blocks of four)

5p	A1–1–1–1–1	 60	10p	A1–1–1–1–1 ..	.. 1·25
	B1–1–1–1–1	 60		B1–1–1–1–1 ..	.. 1·25
8p	A1–1–1–1–1	 90	12p	A1–1–1–1–1 ..	.. 1·75
	B1–1–1–1–1	 90		B1–1–1–1–1 ..	.. 1·75

MINIATURE SHEET

Illustration reduced, actual size 146 × 68 *mm.*

MS128   Containing Nos. 124/7   . .   . .   . .   1·00   80

First Day Cover (No. **MS**128) . .   . .   1·50

Sheets: 50 (10 × 5).
Quantities sold: 5p 1,377,519; 8p 368,521; 10p 467,278; 12p 389,574; **MS** 298,689.
Withdrawn: 30.6.76.

JS 110   Common Tern

JS 111   Storm Petrel

JS 112   Brent Geese

JS 113   Shag

(Designed by Jennifer Toombs)
(Printed in photogravure by Courvoisier)

1975 (28 July). Sea Birds. *Granite paper. P* $11\frac{1}{2}$ *(C).*

129	**JS 110**	4p multicoloured	..	.. ..	10	10
130	**JS 111**	5p multicoloured	..	.. ..	15	15
131	**JS 112**	8p multicoloured	..	.. ..	20	20
132	**JS 113**	25p multicoloured	..	.. ..	60	60

First Day Cover (Nos. 129/32)	.. .. ..	95
Presentation Pack (Nos. 129/32)	.. .. ..	1·25

Sheets: 50 (10 × 5).
Quantities sold: 4p 872,260; 5p 2,871,390; 8p 384,550; 25p 362,160.
Withdrawn: 31.7.76.

JS 114 Siskin "3-A"

JS 115 "Southampton"
Flying-boat

JS 116 Mk. 1 "Spitfire"

JS 117 Folland "Gnat"

(Designed by A. Theobald)
(Printed in photogravure by Courvoisier)

1975 (30 Oct). 50th Anniv. of Royal Air Force's Association, Jersey Branch. *Granite paper.* P 11½ (C).

133	**JS 114**	4p multicoloured	..	..	..	10	10
134	**JS 115**	5p multicoloured	..	..	..	12	12
135	**JS 116**	10p multicoloured	..	..	..	20	20
136	**JS 117**	25p multicoloured	..	..	..	60	60

First Day Cover (Nos. 133/6) ..	.. .. ..	1·00
Presentation Pack (Nos. 133/6)	.. .. ..	1·25

CYLINDER NUMBERS
(Blocks of four)

4p	A1–1–1–1–1	 50	10p	A1–1–1–1–1 ..	..1·25
	B1–1–1–1–1	 50		B1–1–1–1–1 ..	..1·25
5p	A1–1–1–1–1	 60	25p	A1–1–1–1–1 ..	..3·00
	B1–1–1–1–1	 60		B1–1–1–1–1 ..	..3·00

Sheets: 50 (5 × 10).
Quantities sold 4p 1,496,640; 5p 1,805,624; 10p 581,627; 25p 407,423.
Withdrawn: 30.10.76.

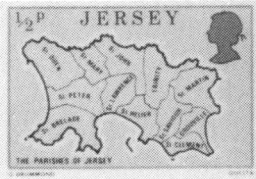

JS 118 Map of Jersey
Parishes

JS 119 Zoological
Park (Trinity)

JS 120 St. Mary's
Church (St. Mary)

JS 121 Seymour
Tower (Grouville)

JS 122 La Corbière
Lighthouse (St.
Brelade)

JS 123 St. Saviour's
Church (St. Saviour)

JS 124 Elizabeth
Castle (St. Helier)

JS 125 Gorey Har-
bour (St. Martin)

JS 126 Jersey Airport
(St. Peter)

JS 127 Grosnez
Castle (St. Ouen)

JS 128 Bonne Nuit
Harbour (St. John)

JS 129 Le Hocq
Tower (St. Clement)

JS 130 Morel Farm
(St. Lawrence)

JS 131 Parish Arms
and Island Scene

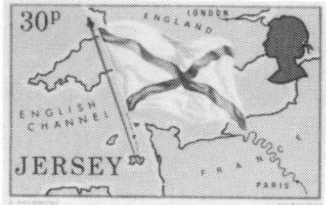

JS 132 Flag and Map

JS 133 Post Office
Headquarters and
Badge

JS 134 Parliament,
Royal Court and Jersey
Arms

JS 135 Government
House and Lieutenant-
Governor's Flag

JS 136 Queen Eliza-
beth II (photograph by
Alex Wilson)

(Designed by Courvoisier (£2) or G. Drummond (others))
(Printed in lithography by Questa (½p to 15p) or in photogravure by Courvoisier (others))

1976 (29 Jan)–78. Parish Arms, Views and Island Emblems. *Granite paper* (20p *to* £2). P
12 (20p *to* £2) *or* 14½ (*others*), *all comb.*

137	**JS 118**	½p multicoloured (*af*)	..	..	5	5
138	**JS 119**	1p multicoloured (*af*)	..	..	5	5
139	**JS 120**	5p multicoloured (*ad*)	..	..	8	10
140	**JS 121**	6p multicoloured (*ad*)	..	..	10	12
141	**JS 122**	7p multicoloured (*ad*)	..	..	12	15

142	**JS 123**	8p multicoloured (*ad*)	..	..	15	15
		SV2. Broken outline (*d*)	..	..	3·00	
143	**JS 124**	9p multicoloured (*a*)	..	..	15	20
144	**JS 125**	10p multicoloured (*af*)		..	20	20
145	**JS 126**	11p multicoloured (*a*)	..	..	20	25
146	**JS 127**	12p multicoloured (*a*)	..	..	20	25
147	**JS 128**	13p multicoloured (*a*)	..	..	25	25
148	**JS 129**	14p multicoloured (*a*)	..	..	25	25
149	**JS 130**	15p multicoloured (*a*)	..	..	25	30
150	**JS 131**	20p multicoloured (*c*)	..	..	35	40
151	**JS 132**	30p multicoloured (*c*)	..	..	55	65
152	**JS 133**	40p multicoloured (*c*)	..	..	70	80
153	**JS 134**	50p multicoloured (*c*)	..	..	85	95
154	**JS 135**	£1 multicoloured (*c*)	..	..	1·75	2·00
155	**JS 136**	£2 multicoloured (*d*)	..	..	3·50	3·75

First Day Covers (Nos. 137/55) (4) ..	.. ..	11·00
Presentation Packs (Nos. 137/55) (4)	.. ..	10·25

Printings: (*a*) 29.1.76; (*b*) 5.4.76 (booklets); (*c*) 20.8.76; (*d*) 16.11.77; (*e*) 28.2.78 (booklets); (*f*) 8.78.

Variety

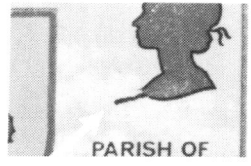

SV2
8p Black outline of Queen's head is broken and has black line extending from it (Pl. 1D × 4, ptg. (*d*) only, R. 2/1).

PLATE OR CYLINDER NUMBERS
(blocks of four)

½p	1A (×4)	..	.. ..	10	6p	1C (×4)	..	.. ..	60
	1B (×4)	..	.. ..	10		1D (×4)	..	.. ..	60
	1C (×4)	..	.. ..	10	7p	1A (×4)	..	.. ..	75
	1D (×4)	..	.. ..	10		1B (×4)	..	.. ..	75
1p	1A (×4)	..	.. ..	12		1C (×4)	..	.. ..	75
	1B (×4)	..	.. ..	12		1D (×4)	..	.. ..	75
	1C (×4)	..	.. ..	12	8p	1A (×4)	..	.. ..	90
	1D (×4)	..	.. ..	12		1B (×4)	..	.. ..	90
5p	1A (×4)	..	.. ..	50		1C (×4)	..	.. ..	90
	1B (×4)	..	.. ..	50		1D (×4)	..	.. ..	90
	1C (×4)	..	.. ..	50	9p	1A (×4)	..	.. ..	90
	1D (×4)	..	.. ..	50		1B (×4)	..	.. ..	90
6p	1A (×4)	..	.. ..	60		1C (×4)	..	.. ..	90
	1B (×4)	..	.. ..	60		1D (×4)	..	.. ..	90

10p	1A (×4)	1·25
	1B (×4)	1·25
	1C (×4)	1·25
	1D (×4)	1·25
	2A–1A–1A–2A ..	1·25
	2B–1B–1B–2B ..	1·25
	2C–1C–1C–2C ..	1·25
	2D–1D–1D–2D ..	1·25
11p	1A (×5)	1·25
	1B (×5)	1·25
	1C (×5)	1·25
	1D (×5)	1·25
12p	1A (×4)	1·25
	1B (×4)	1·25
	1C (×4)	1·25
	1D (×4)	1·25
	1A–1A–2A–2A ..	1·25
	1B–1B–2B–2B ..	1·25
	1C–1C–2C–2C ..	1·25
	1D–1D–2D–2D ..	1·25
13p	1A (×4)	1·50
	1B (×4)	1·50
	1C (×4)	1·50
	1D (×4) .. .. ..·	1·50
14p	1A (×4)	1·50
	1B (×4)	1·50
	1C (×4)	1·50
	1D (×4)	1·50
15p	1A (×4)	1·50

15p	1B (×4)	1·50
	1C (×4)	1·50
	1D (×4)	1·50
	1A–2A–1A–1A ..	1·50
	1B–2B–1B–1B ..	1·50
	1C–2C–1C–1C ..	1·50
	1D–2D–1D–1D ..	1·50
	1D–2D–2D–1D ..	1·50
	1A–3A–2A–1A ..	1·50
	1B–3B–2B–1B ..	1·50
	1C–3C–2C–1C ..	1·50
	1D–3D–2D–1D ..	1·50
20p	A1–1–1–1–1	2·00
	B1–1–1–1–1	2·00
	C1–1–1–1–1	2·00
	D1–1–1–1–1	2·00
30p	A1–1–1–1–1	3·25
	B1–1–1–1–1	3·25
40p	A1–1–1–1	4·25
	B1–1–1–1	4·25
50p	A1–1–1–1	5·00
	B1–1–1–1	5·00
£1	A1–1–1–1–1	10·00
	B1–1–1–1–1	10·00
£2	A1–1–1–1–1–1–1–1	20·00
	B1–1–1–1–1–1–1–1	20·00
	C1–1–1–1–1–1–1–1	20·00
	D1–1–1–1–1–1–1–1	20·00

BOOKLET PANES

These panes are all blocks of four stamps or, in the case of No. 138a, two stamps and two labels. Each pane is surrounded by perforated margins and the prices quoted are for panes with all margins intact. Prices are for mint panes only.

Booklet pane of two stamps with two *se-tenant* labels

Booklet pane of four

Issued in Booklets B25 (1p No. 138a, 5p, 7p), B26 (1p No. 138b, 5p, 7p), B27 (1p No. 138b, 6p), B28 (1p No. 138b, 8p).

Face value	Cat. No.			
1p	138a.	Booklet pane of 2 stamps plus two *se-senant* labels (*b*)	..	20
	138b.	Booklet pane of four (*b*)	..	20
5p	139a.	Booklet pane of four (*b*)	..	50
6p	140a.	Booklet pane of four (*e*)	..	40
7p	141a.	Booklet pane of four (*b*)	..	50
8p	142a.	Booklet pane of four (*e*)	..	60

SET INFORMATION

Sheets: 50 (5 × 10) $\frac{1}{2}$ to 15p; 25 (5 × 5) others.
Imprint: Right-hand corner, bottom margin ($\frac{1}{2}$ to 15p); central, bottom margin (others).

JS 141   Sir Walter Raleigh and Map of Virginia

JS 142   Sir George Carteret and Map of New Jersey

JS 143   Philippe Dauvergne and Long Island Landing

JS 144   John Copley and Sketch

(Designed by M. D. Orbell)
(Printed in photogravure by Courvoisier)

1976 (29 May). "Links with America". *Granite paper. P* 11½ (C).

160	**JS 141**	5p multicoloured	..	.. ..	10	12
161	**JS 142**	7p multicoloured	..	.. ..	15	15
162	**JS 143**	11p multicoloured	..	.. ..	25	25
163	**JS 144**	13p multicoloured	..	.. ..	25	30

First Day Cover (Nos. 160/3)	1·00
Presentation Pack (Nos. 160/3)	95

CYLINDER NUMBERS
(Blocks of four)

5p	A1–1–1–1–1	60	11p	A1–1–1–1–1	1·50
	B1–1–1–1–1	60		B1–1–1–1–1	1·50
7p	A1–1–1–1 ..	90	13p	A1–1–1–1 ..	1·50
	B1–1–1–1 ..	90		B1–1–1–1 ..	1·50

Sheets: 25 (5 × 5).
Quantities sold: 5p 980,029; 7p 1,352,629; 11p 582,706; 13p 435,561.
Withdrawn: 31.5.77.

JS 145   Dr. Grandin
and Map of China

JS 146   Sampan on
the Yangtze

JS 147   Overland Trek

JS 148   Dr. Grandin
at Work

(Designed by Jennifer Toombs)
(Printed in photogravure by Courvoisier)

1976 (25 Nov). Birth Centenary of Dr. Lilian Grandin (medical missionary). *Granite paper. P* 11½ (C).

164	**JS 145**	5p multicoloured	.. .. ..	10	10
165	**JS 146**	7p light yellow, yellow-brown and black	.. ..	15	15
166	**JS 147**	11p multicoloured	.. .. ..	25	25
167	**JS 148**	13p multicoloured	.. .. ..	30	30

First Day Cover (Nos. 164/7) ..	.. .. ..	1·00
Presentation Pack (Nos. 164/7)	.. .. ..	1·00

CYLINDER NUMBERS
(Blocks of four)

5p	A1–1–1–1	..	60	11p A1–1–1–1 ..	1·50
	B1–1–1–1	..	60	B1–1–1–1 ..	1·50
7p	A1–1–1	..	90	13p A1–1–1–1–1	1·75
	B1–1–1	..	90	B1–1–1–1–1	1·75

Sheets: 50 (5 × 10).

Quantities sold: 5p 757,843; 7p 1,043,198; 11p 384,436; 13p 354,096.

Withdrawn: 30.11.77.

JS 149 Coronation,
1953 (photograph by
Cecil Beaton)

JS 150 Visit to Jersey,
1957

JS 151 Queen Eliza-
beth II (photograph by
Peter Grugeon)

(Designed by G. Drummond)
(Printed in photogravure by Courvoisier)

1977 (7 Feb). Silver Jubilee. *Granite paper. P* 11½ (c).

168	**JS 149**	5p multicoloured	..	.. ..	10	12
169	**JS 150**	7p multicoloured	..	.. ..	15	15
170	**JS 151**	25p multicoloured	..	.. ..	60	65

First Day Cover (Nos. 168/70)	.. .. ..	90
Presentation Pack (Nos. 168/70)	.. .. ..	1·10

CYLINDER NUMBERS
(Blocks of four)

5p	A1–1–1–1–1	60	25p A1–1–1–1–1	3·50
	B1–1–1–1–1	60	B1–1–1–1–1	3·50
7p	A1–1–1–1–1	90		
	B1–1–1–1–1	90		

Sheets: 25 (5 × 5).
Imprint: Central, bottom margin.
Withdrawn: 6.2.78.

JS 152 Coins of 1871
and 1877

JS 153 One-twelfth
Shilling, 1949

JS 154 Silver Crown, 1966

JS 155 £2 Piece, 1972

(Designed by D. Henley)
(Printed in lithography by Questa)

1977 (25 Mar). Centenary of Currency Reform. *P* 14 (C).

171	**JS 152**	5p	multicoloured	.. .. ..	10	12
172	**JS 153**	7p	multicoloured	.. .. ..	15	15
173	**JS 154**	11p	multicoloured	.. .. ..	25	25
174	**JS 155**	13p	multicoloured	.. .. ..	30	35

First Day Cover (Nos. 171/4)	85
Presentation Pack (Nos. 171/4)	95

PLATE NUMBERS
(Blocks of four)

5p	1A (×5)	..	60	11p 1A (×5)	..	1·50
	1B (×5)	..	60	1B (×5)	..	1·50
7p	1A (×5)	..	90	13p 1A (×5)	..	1·75
	1B (×5)	..	90	1B (×5)	..	1·75
	1A–2A–1A–1A–1A		90			
	1B–2B–1B–1B–1B		90			

Sheets: 50 (5 × 10).
Imprint: Right-hand corner, bottom margin.
Withdrawn: 30.4.78.

JS 156   Sir William
Weston and *Santa
Anna*, 1530

JS 157   Sir William
Drogo and Ambulance,
1877

JS 158   Duke of
Connaught and
Ambulance, 1917

JS 159   Duke of
Gloucester and
Stretcher-team, 1977

(Designed by A. Theobald)
(Printed in lithography by Questa)

1977 (24 June). St. John Ambulance Centenary. *P* 14 × 13½ (C).

175	**JS 156**	5p multicoloured	..	.. ..	10	12
176	**JS 157**	7p multicoloured	..	.. ..	12	12
177	**JS 158**	11p multicoloured	..	.. ..	20	20
178	**JS 159**	13p multicoloured	..	.. ..	30	30

First Day Cover (Nos. 175/8) ..	.. .. ..	85
Presentation Pack (Nos. 175/8)	.. .. ..	85

PLATE NUMBERS
(Blocks of four)

5p	1A (×5)	.. ..	60	11p	1A (×6)	.. ..	1·25
	1B (×5)	.. ..	60		1B (×6)	.. ..	1·25
	1C (×5)	.. ..	60		1C (×6)	.. ..	1·25
7p	1A (×6)	.. ..	75	13p	1A (×5)	.. ..	1·75
	1B (×6)	.. ..	75		1B (×5)	.. ..	1·75
	1C (×6)	.. ..	75		1C (×5)	.. ..	1·75
					1B–2B–1B–1B–1B	1·75

Sheets: 40 (8 × 5).
Imprint: Bottom corner, right-hand margin.
Withdrawn: 30.6.78.

JS 160 Arrival of
Queen Victoria, 1846

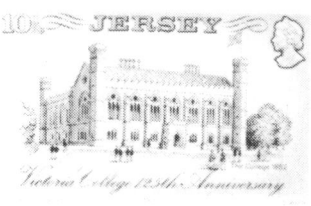

JS 161 Victoria
College, 1852

JS 162 Sir Galahad
Statue, 1924

JS 163 College Hall

(Designed by R. Granger Barrett)
(Printed in lithography by Questa)

1977 (29 Sept). 125th Anniversary of Victoria College. *P* 14½ (C).

179	**JS 160**	7p multicoloured	..	.. ..	15	15
180	**JS 161**	10½p multicoloured	..	.. ..	20	25
181	**JS 162**	11p multicoloured	..	.. ..	20	25
182	**JS 163**	13p multicoloured	..	.. ..	25	30

First Day Cover (Nos. 179/82)	.. .. ..	95
Presentation Pack (Nos. 179/82)	.. .. ..	1·00

PLATE NUMBERS
(Blocks of four)

7p	1A (×6)	90	11p	1A (×5)	1·25
	1B (×6)	90		1B (×5)	1·25
	1A–1A–2A–1A–1A–1A	90	13p	1A (×6)	1·50
	1B–1B–2B–1B–1B–1B	90		1B (×6)	1·50
10½p	1A (×5)	1·25			
	1B (×5)	1·25			

Sheets: 50 (5 × 10) 7p, 10½p; (10 × 5) others.
Imprint: Right-hand corner, bottom margin.
Withdrawn: 30.9.78.

JS 164   Harry Vardon
Statuette and Map
of Royal Jersey Course

JS 165   Harry Vardon's
Grip and Swing

JS 166   Harry Vardon's
Grip and Putt

JS 167   Trophies and
Book by Harry Vardon

(Designed by Jennifer Toombs)
(Printed in lithography by Questa)

1978 (28 Feb). Centenary of Royal Jersey Golf Club. *P* 14½ (C).

183	**JS 164**	6p multicoloured	.. .. ..	12	15
184	**JS 165**	8p multicoloured	.. .. ..	15	20
185	**JS 166**	11p multicoloured	.. .. ..	25	30
		SV3. Thread Flaw ..	.. ..	3·50	
186	**JS 167**	13p multicoloured	.. .. ..	30	30

First Day Cover (Nos. 183/6) ..	.. .. ..	1·00
Presentation Pack (Nos. 183/6)	.. .. ..	1·00

Variety

SV3
11p   Black   "thread"
joins   "11"   and   "p"
(R.10/1).

PLATE NUMBERS
(Blocks of four)

6p	1A (×5)	..	75	11p 1B (×4) ..	3·50
8p	1A (×4)	..	90	13p 2B–1B–1B–1B	1·75

Sheets: 50 (5 × 10).
Imprint: Right-hand corner, bottom margin.
Withdrawn: 28.2.79.

JS 168   Mont   Orgueil
Castle

JS 169   St. Aubin's
Fort

JS 170   Elizabeth
Castle

(Designed (from paintings by Thomas Phillips) and printed in photogravure by Courvoisier)

1978 (1 May). Europa. *Granite paper. P* $11\frac{1}{2}$ (C).

187	**JS 168**	6p	multicoloured	.. .. ..	12	15
188	**JS 169**	8p	multicoloured	.. .. ..	15	20
189	**JS 170**	10½p	multicoloured	.. .. ..	20	25

First Day Cover (Nos. 187/9)	65
Presentation Pack (Nos. 187/9)	70

CYLINDER NUMBERS
(Blocks of four)

6p	A1–1–1–1–1	75	10½p B1–1–1–1–1 ..	..1·75
	C1–1–1–1–1	75	D1–1–1–1–1..	..1·75
8p	B1–1–1–1–1	90		
	D1–1–1–1–1	90		

Sheets: 20 (5 × 4).
Imprint: Central, bottom margin.

JS 171 "Gaspe
Basin" (P. J. Ouless)

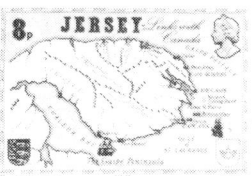

JS 172 Map of Gaspe
Peninsula

JS 173 Jersey Sailing
Ship *Century*

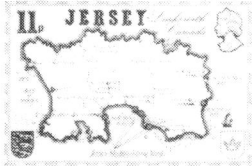

JS 174 Early Map of
Jersey

JS 175 St. Aubin's
Bay, Town and
Harbour

(Designed by R. Granger Barrett)
(Printed in lithography by Questa)

1978 (9 June). Links with Canada. *P* 14½ (C).

190	**JS 171**	6p multicoloured	..	..	..	12	15
191	**JS 172**	8p multicoloured	..	..	..	15	20
192	**JS 173**	10½p multicoloured	..	..	..	20	25
193	**JS 174**	11p multicoloured	..	..	..	25	25
194	**JS 175**	13p multicoloured	..	..	..	25	30

First Day Cover (Nos. 190/4)	..	..	..	1·25
Presentation Pack (Nos. 190/4)	..	..	..	1·00

PLATE NUMBERS
(Blocks of four)

6p 1A (×5)	..	75	11p 1C (×6)	..	1·50
8p 1C (×6)	..	90	13p 1C (×6)	..	1·50
10½p 1B (×6)	..	1·25			

Sheets: 50 (5 × 10).
Imprint: Right-hand corner, bottom margin.

JS 176 Queen
Elizabeth and Prince
Philip

JS 177 Hallmarks of
1953 and 1977

(Designed and printed in photogravure by Courvoisier)

1978 (26 June). 25th Anniversary of Coronation. *Granite paper. P* $11\frac{1}{2}$ (C).

195	**JS 176**	8p	silver, black and cerise	15	20
196	**JS 177**	25p	silver, black and new blue ..	50	60

First Day Cover (Nos. 195/6)	85
Presentation Pack (Nos. 195/6)	85

CYLINDER NUMBERS
(Blocks of four)

8p A1–1–1	90	25p A1–1–1	3·00
B1–1–1	90	B1–1–1	3·00

Sheets: 50 (10 × 5).

JS 178 Mail Cutter,
1778–1827

JS 179 *Flamer*,
1831–1837

JS 180 *Diana*, 1877–
1890

JS 181 *Ibex*, 1891–
1925

JS 182 *Caesarea*,
1960–1975

(Designed by Jersey P.O.)
(Printed in lithography by Harrison)

1978 (18 Oct). 200th Anniversary of First Government Mail Packet. *P* 14½ × 14 (C).

197	**JS 178**	6p	black, yellow-brown and yellow	12	15
198	**JS 179**	8p	black, green and pale green ..	15	20
199	**JS 180**	10½p	black, ultramarine and pale blue	20	25
200	**JS 181**	11p	black, purple and lilac	25	25
201	**JS 182**	13p	black, brown-red and pale brown-red	25	30

First Day Cover (Nos. 197/201)	1·25
Presentation Pack (Nos. 197/201)	1·00

PLATE NUMBERS
(Blocks of four)

6p	1A (×3)	..	75	11p 1B (×3)	..	1·50
8p	1A (×3)	..	90	13p 1B (×3)	..	1·50
10½p	1B (×3)	..	1·25		

Sheets: 50 (5 × 10)
Imprint: Right-hand corner, bottom margin.

POSTAGE DUE STAMPS

JSD 1

JSD 2   Map

(Designed by F. W. Guénier)
(Printed in lithography by Bradbury, Wilkinson and Co. Ltd.)

1969 (1 Oct). *P* 14 × 13½ (C).

D1	**JSD 1**	1d. bluish violet (*ab*)	.. .. ..	2·00	1·75
D2		2d. sepia (*ad*)	.. ..	1·75	1·75
D3		3d. magenta (*ad*)	.. ..	2·00	1·50
D4	**JSD 2**	1s. bright emerald (*acd*)	.. ..	7·50	5·00
D5		2s. 6d. olive-grey (*acd*)	.. .. ..	20·00	12·00
D6		5s. vermilion (*ad*) ..	.. .. ..	50·00	35·00

Printings: (*a*) 1.10.69; (*b*) 16.12.69; (*c*) 18.2.70; (*d*) 6.6.70.
Sheets: 120 (2 panes 6 × 10).
Imprint: Central, bottom margin.
Quantities sold: 1d. 98,535; 2d. 181,601; 3d. 155,832; 1s. 174,599; 2s. 6d. 205,962;
5s. 200,698.
Withdrawn and Invalidated: 14.2.72.

JSD 3   Map

(Designed by F. W. Guénier)
(Printed in lithography by Bradbury, Wilkinson)

1971 (15 Feb)–75. Decimal Currency. *P* 14 × 13½ (C).

D7	**JSD 3**	½p black (*a*)	5	5
		SV4. Extra serif on "2"	2·00	
D8		1p violet-blue (*a*)	5	5
D9		2p olive-grey (*a*)	5	8
D10		3p reddish purple (*a*)	8	10
D11		4p pale red (*a*)	10	12
D12		5p bright emerald (*a*)	10	12
D13		6p yellow-orange (*b*)	12	15
D14		7p bistre-yellow (*b*)	12	15
D15		8p lt. greenish blue (*c*)	20	25
D16		10p pale olive-grey (*a*)	25	30
D17		11p ochre (*c*)	25	30
D18		14p violet (*a*)	30	35
D19		25p myrtle-green (*b*)	55	65
D20		50p dull purple (*c*)	1·00	1·25

Presentation Pack (Nos. D7/20)	3·25

Printings: (*a*) 15.2.71; (*b*) 12.8.74; (*c*) 1.5.75.

Variety

SV4.
½p Extra serif on "2" of
"½" (R. 10/5).

PLATE NUMBERS
(Blocks of four)

½p 1*a*	2·00	7p 1*d*	75
1p 1*b*	15	8p 1*b*	1·25
2p 1*a*	30	10p 1*b*	1·50
3p 1*a*	50	11p 1*d*	1·50
4p 1*a*	60	14p 1*d*	1·75
5p 1*d*	60	25p 1*d*	3·75
6p 1*d*	75	50p 1*c*	6·00

Sheets: 50 (5 × 10).
Imprint: Central, bottom margin.
Withdrawn: 31.3.79.

JSD 4   Dovecote, Samares (St. Clement)

JSD 5   Handois Reservoir (St. Lawrence)

JSD 6   Sorel Point (St. John)

JSD 7   Pinnacle Rock (St. Ouen)

JSD 8   Quetivel Mill (St. Peter)

JSD 9   St. Catherine's Breakwater (St. Martin)

JSD 10   Harbour (St. Helier)

JSD 11   Highlands College (St. Saviour)

JSD 12   Beauport Bay (St. Brelade)

JSD 13   La Hougue Bie (Grouville)

JSD 14   Perry Farm (St. Mary)

JSD 15   Bouley Bay (Trinity)

(Designed by G. Drummond)
(Printed in lithography by Questa)

1978 (17 Jan). Parish Arms and Views. *P* 14 (C).

D21	**JSD 4**	1p dull green and black	5	5
D22	**JSD 5**	2p light orange and black	5	5
D23	**JSD 6**	3p chestnut and black	5	5
D24	**JSD 7**	4p Indian red and black	8	8
D25	**JSD 8**	5p dull blue and black	8	10
D26	**JSD 9**	10p brown-olive and black	20	20
D27	**JSD 10**	12p turquoise-blue and black ..	25	25
D28	**JSD 11**	14p red-orange and black	25	30
D29	**JSD 12**	15p bright magenta and black ..	25	30
D30	**JSD 13**	20p yellow-green and black ..	30	35
D31	**JSD 14**	50p deep brown and black	85	95
D32	**JSD 15**	£1 chalky blue and black	1·75	2·00

Presentation Pack (Nos. D21/32)	4·25

PLATE NUMBERS
(Blocks of four)

1p 1D–1D	..	..	12	12p 1C–1C	..	..	1·50
2p 1E–1E	..	..	25	14p 1A–1A	..	..	1·50
3p 1C–1C	..	..	35	15p 1B–1B	..	..	1·50
4p 1A–1A	..	..	50	20p 1F–1F	..	..	1·75
5p 1A–1A	..	..	50	50p 1D–1D	..	..	5·00
10p 1F–1F	..	..	1·25	£1 1F–1F	..	..	10·00

Sheets: 50 (10 × 5).
Imprint: Right-hand corner, bottom margin.

STAMP BOOKLETS

Prices given are for complete booklets. All booklets are stitched except for Nos. B25/8, which are stapled).

Type A. Map of Channel

Type B. Jersey Arms and Mace

Type C. Mont Orgueil Castle

1969 (1 Oct)–70.

2s. Booklet. Blue cover. Type A. *Panes of one.*

B1   Containing 4 × 1d. (No. 16a). 5 × 4d. (No. 19a) .. ..   4·00

7s. Booklet. Yellow cover. Type B. *Panes of two.*

B2   Containing 6 × 1d. (in No. 16Sba), 12 × 4d. (in No. 19Sc), 6 × 5d. (in No. 20Sb)   ..   8·00

B2*a*   Containing 6 × 1d. (in No. 16Sc), 12 × 4d. (in No. 19Sba), 6 × 5d. (No. 20Sab) (5.5.70)   .. .. 22·00

10s. Booklet. Pink cover. Type C. *Panes of two.*

B3   Containing 4 × 1d. (in No. 16Sba), 14 × 4d. (in No. 19Sc), 12 × 5d. (in No. 20Sb)   .. 14·00

B3*a*   Containing 4 × 1d. (in No. 16Sc), 14 × 4d. (in No. 19Sba), 12 × 5d. (in No. 20Sab) (5.5.70)   .. .. 20·00

The 7s. and 10s. booklets come with the panes either upright or inverted.

Type D. Martello Tower

Type E. The Royal Court

1971 (15 Feb). Decimal Currency.

    10*p Booklet. Blue cover. Type* D. *Panes of one.*

B4   Containing 2 × ½p (No. 42a), 2 × 2p (No.
45a), 2 × 2½p (No. 46a). *Margins at left
and bottom* .. ..   2·00

B4*a* Containing 2 × ½p (No. 42Sab), 2 × 2p (No.
45Sab), 2 × 2½p (No. 46Sad). *Margins at
left and top* .. ..   2·00

    35*p Booklet. Yellow cover. Type* E. *Panes of two.*

B5   Containing 10 × 2p (in No. 45Sb), 6 × 2½p
(in No. 46Sb) .. ..   4·00

    50*p Booklet. Pink cover as Type* E, *but showing
Elizabeth Castle. Panes of two.*

B6   Containing 10 × 2p (in No. 45Sb), 12 × 2½p
(in No. 46Sb) .. ..   5·00

The 35p and 50p booklets come with the panes either upright or inverted.

Owing to the postal information printed in the booklets being out of date, supplies of
Nos. B4/*a* dispensed from machines between 10 July and early September 1972 bore an
adhesive label on the front with the words "RATE TO UNITED KINGDOM LETTERS up to 4
ozs. and postcards 3p" in two lines. They were primarily to warn holiday-makers of the
new rate and were issued only through the machines. Of these about 52,000 were sold.

Quantities sold: B4/*a* 244,544; B5 20,875; B6 17,638.

1972 (15 May). *Covers as Type* E. *Panes of two.*

    20*p Booklet. Green cover, showing Jersey Cow.*

B7   Containing 8 × 2½p (in No. 46Sb) .. ..   12·00

    30*p Booklet. Yellow cover, showing Portelet Bay.*

B8   Containing 10 × 3p (in No. 47Sb) .. ..   20·00

    50*p Booklet. Pink cover, showing La Corbière Light-
house.*

B9   Containing 8 × 2½p (in No. 46Sb), 10 × 3p
(in No. 47Sb) .. ..   5·00

These booklets come with the panes either upright or inverted.

Quantities sold: B7 9,972; B8 9,956; B9 17,774.

1972 (1 Dec).

    10*p Booklet. Orange-yellow cover as Type* D, *but
showing Legislative Chamber. Panes of one.*

B10 Containing 3 × ½p (No. 42a), 2½p (No. 46a),
2 × 3p (No. 47a). *Margins at left and
bottom* .. ..   1·40

B10*a* Containing 3 × ½p (No. 42Sab), 2½p (No.
46Sad), 2 × 3p (No. 47Sab). *Margins at
left and top* .. ..   1·40

Quantity sold: 126,877.

1973 (1 June).

    10*p Booklet. Green cover as Type* D, *but showing
Mont Orgueil by night. Panes of one.*

B11 Contents as Booklet No. B10 .. .. ..   1·25

B11*a* Contents as Booklet No. B10*a* .. .. ..   1·25

Quantity sold: 109,129.

Type F. Jersey Wildlife Preservation Trust

1973 (10 Sept). *Covers as Type* F. *Panes of two.*
  20*p Booklet. Pale green cover. Type* F.
  B12   Containing 8 × 2½p (in No. 46Sb)   ..   .. 14·00
  30*p Booklet. Buff cover, showing Jersey Wild Flowers.*
  B13   Containing 10 × 3p (in No. 47Sb)   ..   ..   6·00
  50*p Booklet. Blue cover, showing "English Fleet in the Channel"* (*Peter Monamy*).
  B14   Containing 8 × 2½p (in No. 46Sb), 10 × 3p (in No. 47Sb)   ..   ..   5·00
These booklets come with the panes either upright or inverted.

Quantities sold: B12 8,790; B13 11,450; B14 14,145.

1974 (7 Jan). *Jersey Wildlife Preservation Trust. Covers as Type* F. *Panes of two.*
  20*p Booklet. Green cover, showing Spectacled Bear.*
  B15   Contents as Booklet No. B12   ..   ..   ..   5·00
  30*p Booklet. Yellow cover, showing White-eared Pheasant.*
  B16   Contents as Booklet No. B13   ..   ..   ..   4·50
  50*p Booklet. Pink cover, showing Thick-billed Parrot.*
  B17   Contents as Booklet No. B14   ..   ..   ..   4·00
These booklets come with the panes either upright or inverted.

Quantities sold: B15 14,283; B16 14,049; B17 15,976.

1974 (1 July).
  10*p Booklet. Orange cover as Type* D, *but showing Jersey Airport. Panes of one.*
  B18   Containing 3p (No. 47a), 2 × 3½p (No. 48a).
          Margins at left and bottom   ..   ..   ..   1·40
  B18*a* Containing 3p (No. 47Sab), 2 × 3½p (No. 48Sab). *Margins at left and top*   ..   ..   1·40

60*p Booklet. Pink cover as Type* F, *but showing Jersey Wildlife Preservation Trust—Ring-tailed Lemur. Panes of two.*

B19   Containing 6 × 3p (in No. 47Sb), 12 × 3½p
     (in No. 48Sb)   ..   ..   4·00

The 60p booklet comes with the panes either upright or inverted.

1974 (1 Oct).
     60*p Booklet. Green cover as Type* F, *but showing Jersey Wildlife Preservation Trust—Tuatara Lizard. Panes of two.*

B20   Contents as Booklet No. B19   ..   ..   ..   4·00

This booklet comes with the panes either upright or inverted.

Type G. Artillery Shako

1975 (25 Feb). *Royal Jersey Militia Headgear. Covers as Type* G. *Panes of one.*
     10*p Booklet. Grey cover. Type* G.

B21   Containing ½p (No. 42a), 2 × 3p (No. 47a),
     3½p (No. 48a). *Margins at left and bottom*   1·25

B21*a*   Containing ½p (No. 42Sab), 2 × 3p (No. 47Sab), 3½p (No. 48Sab). *Margins at left and top*   ..   ..   1·25

     20*p Booklet. Rose cover, showing Shako of* 2nd *North Regiment.*

B22   Containing 2 × 3p (No. 47a), 4 × 3½p (No. 48a). *Margins at left and bottom*   ..   ..   1·25

B22*a*   Containing 2 × 3p (No. 47Sab), 4 × 3½p (No. 48Sab). *Margins at left and top*   ..   1·25

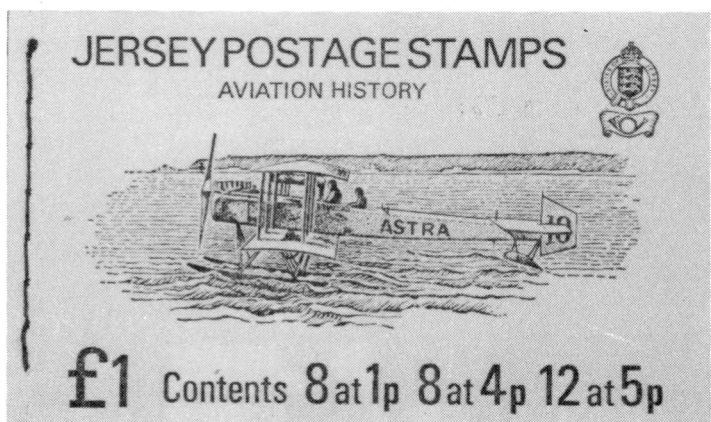

Type H. "Astra" Biplane

1975 (21 Apr). *Aviation History.*

    50*p Booklet. Pale blue cover as Type* F, *but showing Supermarine "Sea Eagle". Panes of two.*

    B23 Containing 6 × 1p (in No. 43Sa), 6 × 4p (in No. 49Sa), 4 × 5p (in No. 50Sa) .. .. 1·75

    £1 *Booklet. Yellow cover. Type* H. *Panes of four.*

    B24 Containing 8 × 1p (in No. 43Sb), 8 × 4p (in No. 49Sb), 12 × 5p (in No. 50Sb) .. .. 2·50

These booklets come with the panes either upright or inverted.

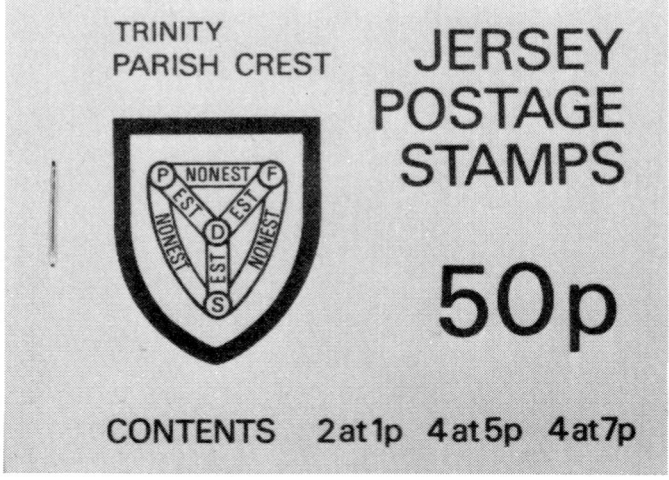

Type I. Trinity Parish Crest

1976 (5 Apr). *Parish Crests. Covers as Type* I. *Panes of four.*
    50*p Booklet. Green cover. Type* I.
    B25 Containing 2 × 1p (in No. 138a), 4 × 5p (in
          No. 139a), 4 × 7p (in No. 141a)   85
    £1 *Booklet. Magenta cover. showing St. Ouen*
    Parish Crest.
    B26 Containing 4 × 1p (in No. 138b), 8 × 5p (in
          No. 139a), 8 × 7p (in No. 141a) .. .. 1·75

1978 (28 Feb). *Parish Crests. Covers as Type* I. *Panes of four.*
    £1 *Booklet. Orange-red cover, showing Grouville*
    Parish Arms.
    B27 Containing 4 × 1p (in No. 138b), 16 × 6p (in
          No. 140a) .. .. 1·75
    £1 *Booklet. Pale blue cover, showing St. Saviour*
    Parish Arms.
    B28 Containing 4 × 1p (in No. 138b), 12 × 8p (in
          No. 142a) .. .. 1·75

STAMP SACHETS

These have folded card covers, sealed at foot, with individual stamps loose inside.

Type SA. Postal Administration
Emblem

1975 (1 Apr). *Red cover as Type* SA.
    SB1 20p sachet. Containing 2 × 1p (No. 43), 2 ×
          4p (No. 49), 2 × 5p (No. 50)   75

1976 (29 Jan). *Blue cover as Type* SA.
    SB2 20p sachet. Containing 3 × 1p (No. 138), 2 ×
          5p (No. 139), 7p (No. 141)   60

1976 (2 Nov). *Green cover as Type* SA.
    SB3 20p sachet. Contents as Sachet No. SB2 .. 35

1977 (29 Sept). *Brown cover as Type* SA.
    SB4 20p sachet. Contents as Sachet No. SB2 .. 35

1978 (May). *Violet cover as Type* SA.
    SB5 30p sachet. Containing 2 × 1p (No. 138), 2 ×
          6p (No. 140), 2 × 8p (No. 142)   55

POSTAL STATIONERY

Airletters

All the following basic airletters were photogravure-printed by McCorquodale & Co. Ltd.

SSA1

1969 (1 October). *Imprinted 9d. stamp showing map of Jersey (design as 1969 9d. definitive).*

SSA1	9d. blue	2·00	1·00

1971 (1 July). *Decimal Currency. Imprinted 5p stamp showing Mount Orgueil Castle (design similar to 1971 2p definitive).*

SSA2	5p blue	80	60

As from 10 September 1973, SSA2 was sold with a 1p adhesive attached to uprate it to 6p.

SSA3

1972 (1 December). *Imprinted 6½p stamp.*
  SSA3 6½p blue 80 60

  As from 10 September 1973, SSA3 was sold with a ½p adhesive attached to it to uprate it to 7p.

1973 (15 September). *Provisional Airletters.*
  SSA4 6p blue (5p airletter SSA2 with circular black handstamp "Official Postage Uprated 1p") 80 30
  SSA5 7p blue (6½p airletter SSA3 with circular black handstamp "Official Postage Uprated ½p") 70 50

1975 (1 April). *Provisional Airletters.*
  SSA6 8½p blue (5p airletter SSA2 with circular black handstamp "Official Postage Uprated 3½p") 50 30
  SSA7 9p blue (6½p airletter SSA3 with circular black handstamp "Official Postage Uprated 2½p") 50 25

  From 29 September 1975 SSA6 was sold with a 2p adhesive stamp attached to uprate it to 10½p, and SSA7 with a 2p adhesive attached to uprate it to 11p.

1975 (1 September). *Imprinted 8½p stamp showing La Corbière Lighthouse.*
  SSA8 8½p blue 60 80

1975 (30 October). *Provisional Airletters.*
  SSA9 10½p blue (8½p airletter SSA2 with circular black handstamp "Official Postage Uprated 2p") 60 30
  SSA10 11p blue (6½p airletter SSA3 with circular black handstamp "Official Postage Uprated 4½p") 20 20

1976. *Imprinted 10½p stamp showing Jersey Airport.*
  SSA11 10½p blue 20 20

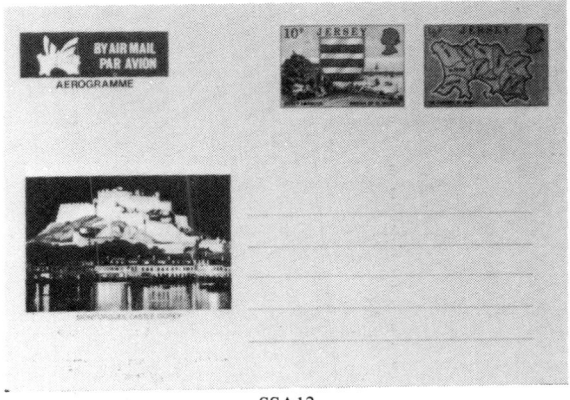

SSA12

1978. *Imprinted ½p and 10p stamps (designs as corresponding values in 1977 definitive series).*

      SSA12   10½p multicoloured (blue air letter)   ..   20   20

Reply Coupons

These coupons are priced unused only, since to be used they have to be given up at a post office.

Commonwealth Reply Coupons

1969 (1 October).
      SSR1   7d. black on red   40   —

1971 (15 February). *Dual Currency Issue.*
      SSR2   7d./3p black on red   40   —

1971 (1 July)–72.
      SSR3   4p black on red   30   —
                a. Revised inscription (excluding exchange in certain countries) (13 September 1972)   30   —
                b. Inscription ends "... Ceylon" .. 2·00   —

1973 (10 September). *Provisional Coupon. Surcharged in manuscript.*
      SSR4   6p on 4p black on red   15   —

1974 (28 January).
      SSR5   6p black on red   15   —

Commonwealth Reply Coupons were withdrawn from sale in Jersey when the concessionary rate to Commonwealth countries was abolished.

International Reply Coupons

1969 (1 October).
      SSR6   1s. 3d. blue and red   50   —

1971 (15 February). *Dual Currency Issue.*
      SSR7   1s. 3d./6p blue and red   50   —

1971 (1 July)–74.
      SSR8   10p blue and red (French text ends "... l'étranger")   30   —
                a. Revised text, ending "... surface" (28 January 1974)   30   —

1971 (12 September). *Provisional Coupon. SSR1 surcharged in manuscript.*
      SSR9   10p on 1s. 3d. blue and red   60   —

1974 (1 July). *Provisional Coupon. SSR8a surcharged in manuscript.*
      SSR10   13p on 10p blue and red   30   —

1975 (2 January). *Punctured "JE".*

SSR11	13p blue and red	30	—

1976 (2 January). *Provisional Coupon. SSR11 surcharged.*

SSR12	20p on 13p blue and red	30	—

1976.

SSR13	20p blue and red	30	—

1977 (13 June).

SSR14	25p blue and red	40	—

Registered Envelopes

Envelopes SSE1/6 were printed by McCorquodale & Co. Ltd.
The standard sizes used are G (156 × 95mm), H (203 × 120mm) and K (292 × 152mm).

1969 (1 October). *Embossed 3s. 5d. stamp in Tudor Rose design.*

SSE1	3s. 5d. blue (size G)	1·00	70
SSE2	3s. 5d. blue (size H)	1·00	70
SSE3	3s. 5d. blue (size K)	1·00	70

1971 (15 February). *Embossed $22\frac{1}{2}p$ stamp in Tudor Rose design.*

SSE4	$22\frac{1}{2}$p blue (size G)	80	60
SSE5	$22\frac{1}{2}$p blue (size H)	80	60
SSE6	$22\frac{1}{2}$p blue (size K)	80	60

1972 (3 January). *Provisional Envelopes. SSE4/6 each with circular violet handstamp "Official Postage Uprated $\frac{1}{2}p$".*

SSE7	23p blue (size G)	1·00	60
SSE8	23p blue (size H)	1·00	60
SSE9	23p blue (size K)	1·00	60

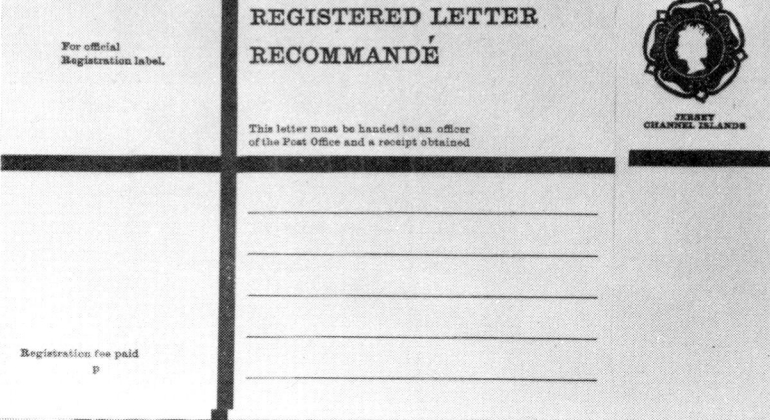

SSE10

1972 (27 July). *Embossed* 23p *stamp.*

SSE10	23p blue (size H)	.. ..	70	60
	a. British manila paper	.. ..	70	60
SSE11	23p blue (size K)	.. ..	70	60

1974 (1 July). *Provisional Envelopes.*

SSE12	28½p blue (Envelope SSE4 with circular black stamp "Postage and Registration Official Uprated 6p") (size G)	60	60
SSE13	28½p blue (Envelope SSE10 with circular black stamp "Postage and Registration Official Uprated 5½p") (size H)	60	60

1974 (12 August). *Cream manila paper with blue lining. Embossed* 28½p *stamp.*

SSE14	28½p blue (size H)	.. ..	50	50
SSE15	28½p blue (size K)	.. ..	50	50

1975 (25 February). *Cream manila paper with blue lining. Impressed circular design similar to SSE19 illustrated below.*

SSE16	28½p black (size H)	.. ..	50	70

1975 (1 April). *Provisional Envelopes.*

SSE17	40p blue (SSE4 with circular black stamp "Postage and Registration Official Uprated 17½p") (size G) ..	70	70
SSE18	40p blue (SSE15 with circular black stamp ("Postage and Registration Official Uprated 11½p") (size K) ..	70	70

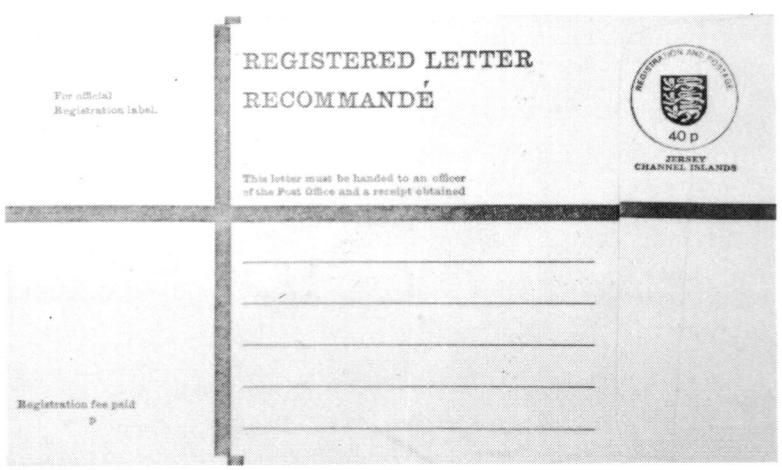

SSE19

1975 (1 April). *Impressed circular* 40p *stamp.*

SSE19	40p black (size H)	.. ..	70	60

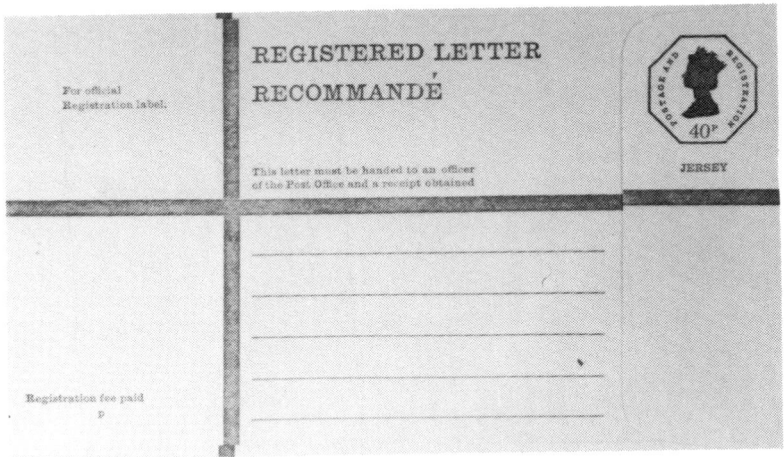

SSE20

1975 (1 July). *Cream manila paper with blue lining. Impressed* 40p *stamp.*

SSE20	40p blue (size H)	.. ..	60	60
SSE21	40p blue (size K)	.. ..	70	70

1975 (30 October). *Provisional Envelopes.*

SSE22	50p blue (SSE4 with circular black stamp "Postage and Registration Uprated Official 27½p") (size G) ..	70	75
SSE23	50p blue (SSE20 with circular black stamp "Postage and Registration Uprated Official 10p") (size H) ..	70	75
SSE24	50p blue (SSE21 with circular black stamp "Postage and Registration Uprated Official 10p") (size K) ..	75	80

1976 (29 January). *Cream manila paper with blue lining. Impressed circular* 52p *stamp (as* SSE19 *illustrated above).*

SSE25	52p black (size G)	.. ..	75	60
SSE26	52p black (size H)	.. ..	75	60
SSE27	52p black (size K)	.. ..	80	70

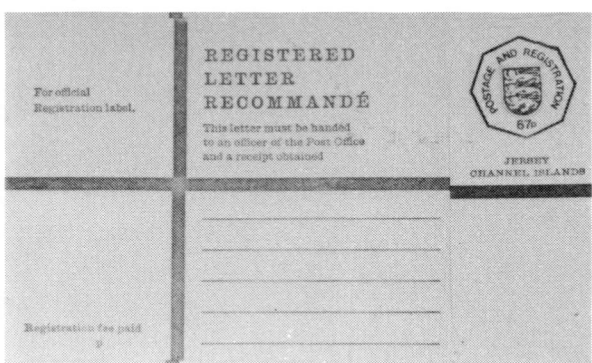

SSE28

1977 (13 June). *Cream manila paper with blue lining. Impressed 67p stamp.*

SSE28	67p	black (size G)	..	..	90	80
SSE29	67p	black (size H)	..	..	90	80
SSE30	67p	black (size K)	..	..	90	80

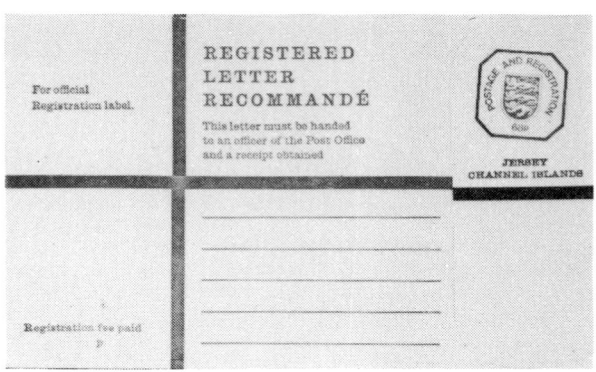

SSE31

1978 (17 January). *Cream manila paper with blue lining. Impressed 68p stamp.*

SSE31	68p	black (size G)	..	..	90	80
SSE32	68p	black (size H)	..	..	90	80
SSE33	68p	black (size K)	..	..	90	80

5. LOCAL DELIVERY SERVICES

Railway Companies

The Jersey Railways
    Two light railways functioned in Jersey: the Jersey Railway (later known as the Jersey Western Railway) and the Jersey Eastern Railway. For their respective routes see the map below.
    The Jersey Railway opened on 28 September 1870, with a standard gauge from St. Helier to St. Aubin. It later was extended to La Moye, and the existing section was re-laid to 3ft. 6in. gauge and opened on 5 August 1885. It was extended to Corbière in 1899. The main terminus was at the Weighbridge, St. Helier, and there were stations at West Park, First Tower, Millbrook, Bel Royal, Beaumont, La Haule, St. Aubin, Greenville, Pont Marquet, Don Bridge, Blanches Banques, La Moye and Corbière. Because of a fire on 19 October 1936 the railway closed and did not re-open.

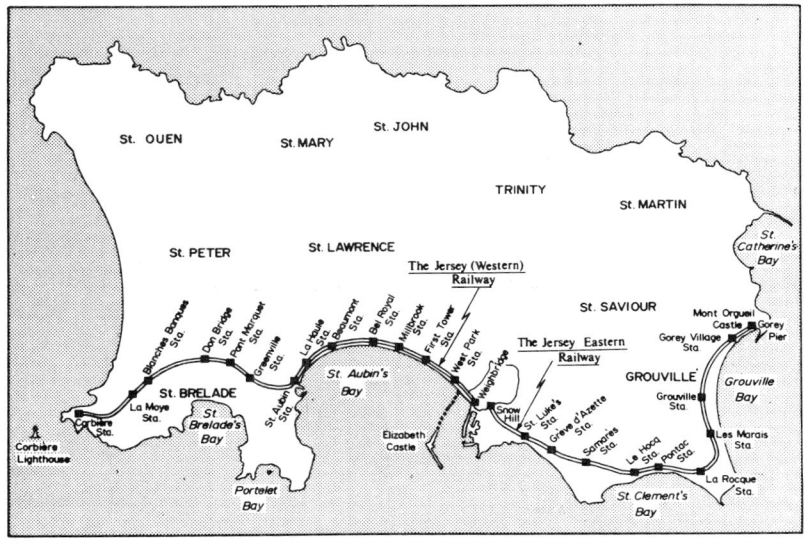

The Jersey Railways

    The Jersey Eastern Railway opened on 7 August 1873, with a 4ft. 8½in. gauge line from St. Helier to Grouville. It was extended to Gorey Village on 27 August 1873 and to Gorey Pier in 1891. The main terminus was at Snow Hill, St. Helier, and there were stations at St. Luke's, Grève d'Azette, Samarès, Le Hocq, Pontac, La Roque, Les Marais, Grouville, Gorey Village and Gorey Pier. The railway was closed on 21 June 1929.
    Each company had letter boxes fitted to the guard's vans of its trains. Members of the public could post their letters in these boxes. The letters were then taken to the termini at Weighbridge or Snow Hill from where they were collected by a postman after the last arrival each evening. Letters were not marked in any way by the railway companies,

neither did they bear any special cancellations. It is not known whether the railway companies received any payment from the Post Office for carrying the boxes, as all records of the service have unfortunately been destroyed.

Bags of mail from Gorey, Grouville, La Roque and Samarès were carried on the Jersey Eastern Railway's trains and collected at the St. Helier terminus by a postman with a hand-cart. At 11 a.m. each day the mail from St. Helier was carried to these sub-offices. A blue pennant was flown from a short mast on the train when mail was on board. No bags of mail were carried by the Jersey Western Railway.

Parcels were carried privately by the railway companies and gummed parcel labels or tickets were issued for prepayment. One used by the Jersey Railway (Type **JR1**) was issued in about 1910 for parcels left at the Town Station. Values of 3d., 6d., 8d. and 1s. are also believed to exist.

No labels have yet been recorded for the Jersey Eastern Railway, but they were undoubtedly issued.

Guernsey Electric Railway

Towards the end of the nineteenth century a number of British tramway companies issued stamps for the prepayment of fees for parcels carried by their services.

The first stamps issued were typeset, in the form of a square within double lines of type with blunt corners (Type **GR1**). At the top is "Guernsey Railway", at the bottom "Company, Ltd.", at the left "Parcel", and at the right "Ticket". The value (2d.) appears in the centre. On one stamp it is printed in green on yellow-buff and on the other in black on yellow. The stamps are perforated 11 at the top or on one side and are imperforate on the other three sides. They were issued between 1879 and 1892.

Four other typeset stamps are also known for this company. The first two are somewhat similar to the above design but have the value in a diamond in the centre with "GUERNSEY ELECTRIC RAILWAY COMPANY" set out in a diamond pattern with one word along each side (Type **GR2**). Values are 1d. black on pink, 1d. black on white, and 2d. black on blue; perforated 11 at top, imperforate on the other three sides. Their date of issue is believed to be about 1893.

In 1905 the Guernsey Electric Railway Company issued a large 1d. brown on green stamp (Type **GR3**), perforated 11 at the sides and imperforate at the top and bottom. It is inscribed "Parcel Ticket" and has a serial number in black at the bottom. For how long the stamp was used is not known but it is now very rare. It is illustrated and recorded in *Morley's Philatelic Journal* of November 1905, and is believed to have been issued in the autumn of that year. There was also a 2d. brown on orange in the same design but it has not yet been possible to find out when it was issued.

All these stamps were printed in rolls and not in sheets.

The Guernsey Steam Tramway had been opened on 6 May 1879. It ran due north from St. Peter Port to St. Sampson's Harbour two and a quarter miles away, and had six locomotives. There was a single-line track of 4ft 8½in. gauge with a loop at Salette Battery (half a mile from St. Peter Port) and stations at Vale Road and Channel Islands Road.

The tramway was electrified with an overhead wire in 1892 and then became the Guernsey Electric Railway. It then had eleven motor coaches (double-deck) and eight trailers (six open, one closed, and one double-deck). The tramway was closed on 9 June 1934, when the company introduced motor buses.

In October 1907 the Guernsey Post Office concluded an agreement with the Guernsey Railway Company whereby mails were conveyed by tram from St. Sampson's to St. Peter Port. The bags were padlocked in the driver's compartment by the sub-postmaster of St. Sampson's and the tram was met at St. Peter Port by a postman who held a key to the padlock. He conveyed the mail from the terminus to the Head Post Office on foot.

The same company also conveyed mails by omnibus from The Vale, Vale Road and L'Islet from the same date in 1907. The bags were secured in a similar fashion as on the trams, near the driver, by the respective sub-postmasters. These services continued until

June 1934, when the trams were withdrawn from service. The mail was then conveyed from St. Sampson's to St. Peter Port by omnibus and all the services continued until the Post Office provided its own transport in 1935.

Great Western Railway Company, Guernsey
Typeset labels were printed locally for use on parcels carried by the G.W.R. steamers to other Channel Islands and to England. They are of vertical format, rouletted at top and bottom and imperforate at the sides. They have "G.W.R. GUERNSEY" (or "G.W.R. JERSEY") in two lines at the top, "PREPAID PARCEL" reading upwards at the left, and "STAMP LABEL" reading upwards at the right. The value appears in large figures in the centre, with a box below it for the insertion of the number of packages. There have been seen 4d. and 11d. values printed in black on white. Others undoubtedly exist.

Southern Railway, Guernsey
Typeset labels were printed locally for the carriage of parcels on the company's steamers. An example seen is printed in black on white and has "SOUTHERN RLY." in a box at the top, with "GUERNSEY" in small capitals below it. In a separate horizontal panel across the centre there is the figure of value "6d.", with "PARCEL" reading upwards to the left of it, and "PAID" reading upwards at the right. In another horizontal panel below it there is a number and below that again is another panel divided into three sections, headed "No. of Pkgs.", "Weight" and "Rate". Other denominations undoubtedly exist.

Bus Services

Jersey Motor Transport Co.
From its foundation in 1923 until 1969 the Jersey Motor Transport Co. Ltd. carried parcels on its buses and issued parcel tickets for prepayment. These tickets were issued in rolls of 500. No details of the first ticket are now available, but there is a certain amount of information on the tickets and rates since 1945.

On 1 October 1945, 3d. black on red and 4d. black on blue tickets were issued and in May 1947, 4d. and 6d. tickets. On 4 October 1957 a 4d. black on blue parcel label was issued (Type **JB1**). It was printed in rolls of 500 by J. Williamson, Ticket printer, Ashton. The top half was stuck to the parcel and the bottom half was signed by the receiving clerk and handed to the sender.

On 16 May 1958 the rates were increased and a 6d. black on green label was issued. This was again printed in rolls of 500 by J. Williamson. It is also a double ticket with the receipt half at the bottom and is very similar to Type **JB1**. It exists with the printer's name at the bottom or at the right-hand side. The service was discontinued in 1969 and the last ticket was a 6d. black on blue.

The parcel rates were shown on the table below.

Year	Weight of Parcel				
	6lb.	12lb.	28lb.	56lb.	1cwt.
1945	3d.	4d.	6d.	1s.	1s. 6d.
1947	—	4d.	8d.	1s.	1s. 8d.
1958	—	6d.	1s.	1s. 6d.	2s.

Up to October 1960, parcels and newspapers were delivered to any address on a bus route. This meant up to thirty stops on some routes for delivery purposes and was very uneconomic. The service was therefore reorganised and parcels were then delivered only to agents (shops, etc.) close to the bus route. The list of agents was published in the timetable of the Jersey Motor Transport Co. Ltd. and comprised forty-eight names, of which at least six were post offices.

Guernsey Railway Co. Buses

Covers are known prior to the Second World War which were carried by the buses of the Guernsey Railway Co. Ltd. from St. Sampson's to St. Peter Port and then posted to London on arrival. They bear a 3d. bus ticket and postage stamps to the value of 1½d.; they were treated as railway letters.

Parcels are only carried on the Guernsey buses nowadays if they are collected at a bus stop. The charge is prepaid by means of a passenger ticket.

Shipping Companies

Mails between Guernsey and Sark were carried by vessels of Commodore Cruises Ltd. from about 1950 until 1969 (the name was changed to the Commodore Shipping Co. Ltd. in about 1954). This company also ran a parcel delivery service between the two islands, the parcels being left with one of the Sark stores for collection. Letters may also have been carried occasionally after the normal mail from Guernsey to Sark had closed (but this was quite unofficial and such covers were probably tied round with string and handed in as "parcels" to avoid infringement of the Post Office monopoly).

We list below those typeset labels which were issued between 1950 and 1961. The pictorial issues which have appeared for both Sark and Alderney from 1961 onwards, although widely used for the carriage of parcels, are omitted from this catalogue, along with other local carriage labels.

When the Commodore Shipping Co. lost the shipping contracts for Alderney and Sark in 1969, two new companies were established: the Alderney Shipping Co. Ltd. and the Isle of Sark Shipping Co. Ltd. Both issued parcel labels on 1 October 1969 and the original labels continued to be sold for their decimal equivalent until 1976 when the Sark labels were replaced by a violet handstamp denoting that the parcel fee had been paid.

CATALOGUE

JERSEY

JR1

Jersey Railways and Tramways Ltd.

1910. Parcel Stamp. *Typeset. Imperf.* × *perf.* 11. *Issued in rolls.*
JR1 **JR1**   1d. black on rose   ..   .. 15·00   15·00

JB1

Jersey Motor Transport Co. Ltd. Parcel Stamps

1945 (1 October). *Typeset by J. Williamson, Ashton. Issued in rolls of* 500.
JB1	**JB1**	3d. black on red	.. ..	2·00	1·00
JB2		4d. black on blue	.. ..	1·00	50

Unused prices are for double tickets; used for the top half only.

1958 (16 May)–65. *Typeset by J. Williamson, Ashton. Issued in rolls of* 500. *Design very similar to Type* **JB1.**
JB3	6d. black on green (printer's name at bottom)	75	50
JB4	6d. black on green (printer's name at side) (1961)	40	20
JB5	6d. black on blue (printer's name at side) (1965)	20	10

Unused prices are for double tickets; used for the top half only.

GUERNSEY

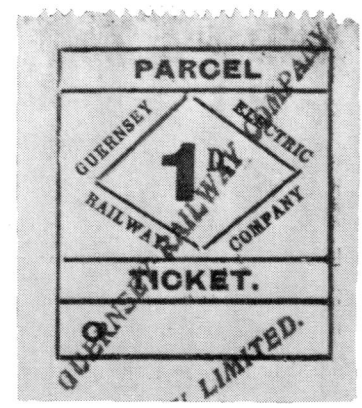

GR1   GR2

Guernsey Railway Co. Ltd. For carriage of parcels on the steam tramway between St. Peter Port and St. Sampson's.

1879–92. *Typeset. Perf.* 11 × imperf. Issued in rolls.

GR1	GR1	2d. green on yellow-buff	..	..	15·00	15·00
GR2		2d. black on yellow	..	..	..	15·00	15·00

Guernsey Electric Railway Co.

1893. *Typeset. Perf.* 11 × imperf. Issued in rolls.

GR3	GR2	1d. black on white	..	..	..	15·00	15·00
GR4		1d. black on pink	..	..	..	15·00	15·00
GR5		2d. black on blue	..	..	..	15·00	15·00

GR3

1905. *Typographed. Imperf.* × *perf.* 11. *Issued in rolls.*

GR6	**GR3**	1d. brown on green	..	..	.. 15·00	15·00
GR7		2d. brown on orange	..	..	.. 15·00	15·00

Great Western Railway, Guernsey

Date not known. *Typeset. Roul.* × *imperf. Issued in rolls.*

GR8	4d. green on white	..	..	.. — 5·00
GR9	11d. green on white	..	..	.. — 5·00
GR10	1d. black on white (slightly different type)	..	..	.. — 5·00
GR11	6d. black on white	..	..	.. — 5·00

Southern Railway, Guernsey

1909. *Typeset. Roul.* × *imperf. Issued in rolls.*

GR12	6d. black on white	..	.. ..	— 5·00

Commodore Shipping Company. For carriage of parcels from Guernsey to Sark.

1950. *Typeset label*, 68 × 33mm, *inscribed* "COMMODORE CRUISES Ltd./6d./parcel Receipt—Owner's Risk". *Imperf. on three sides, roul. at left-hand edge. Books of* 100.

CS1	6d. black on white	..	.. .. ..	5·00 5·00

1954. *Typeset labels inscribed* "COMMODORE SHIPPING CO., Ltd." *and value. Imperf. on three sides, roul. at left. Books of* 100.

CS2	6d. black on white (85 × 58mm)	..	1·00 1·00
CS3	9d. black on pink (72 × 43mm)	..	1·25 1·25
CS4	1s. black on yellow (85 × 57mm)	..	1·75 1·75
CS5	2s. 6d. black on pale green (65 × 39mm)		3·00 3·00
CS6	2s. 6d. black on deep green (different letters and figures)	.. ..	3·00 3·00

1958. *Typeset labels inscribed* "Commodore Shipping Co. Ltd." *and value. Imperf. on three sides, roul. at left-hand edge. Books of* 100.

CS7	7d. black on white (84 × 55mm)	..	1·00 1·00
CS8	10d. black on pink (85 × 59mm)	..	1·75 1·75
CS9	1s. 1d. black on yellow (84 × 55mm)		2·00 2·00
CS10	2s. 9d. on 2s. 6d. pale green (overprinted on CS5)	.. .. ..	3·00 3·00

1961 (1 April). *Typeset labels inscribed* "COMMODORE SHIPPING Co. Ltd." *and value. Imperf. on three sides, roul. at left-hand edge. Books of* 100. *Surcharged in manuscript on Nos.* CS7/10.

CS11	8d. on 7d. black on white	.. .. ..	1·00 1·00
CS12	1s. on 10d. black on pink	.. ..	1·75 1·75
CS13	1s. 3d. on 1s. 1d. black on yellow	..	2·00 2·00
CS14	3s. on 2s. 9d. black on green	.. ..	3·00 3·00

1961 (July). *Surcharges printed in lilac on Nos.* CS10 *and* CS9.

CS15	8d. on 2s. 9d. green	.. ..	4·00 4·00
CS16	1s. 3d. on 1s. 1d. yellow	.. .. ..	4·00 4·00

Alderney Shipping Company Ltd. For carriage of parcels between Guernsey and Alderney.

1969 (1 October). *Typeset labels, approx. size* 38 × 19*mm, inscribed* "ALDERNEY/ SHIPPING CO. LTD." *and value. Printed by Rex Printing Works, Guernsey, in sheets of* 33 (3 × 11). *Roul.*

A1	2s. 3d. black on blue	.. ..	20	20
A2	3s. black on green	.. ..	30	30

Isle of Sark Shipping Company Ltd. For carriage of parcels between Guernsey and Sark.

1969 (1 October). *Typeset labels, approx. size* 38 × 19*mm, inscribed* "ISLE OF SARK/SHIPPING CO. LTD." *and value. Printed by Rex Printing Works, Guernsey, in sheets of* 33 (3 × 11). *Roul.*

S1	1s. 6d. black on red	.. ..	15	15
S2	2s. black on yellow	.. ..	20	20
S3	2s. 6d. black on white	.. ..	25	25